THE WINES OF UMBRIA

A guide by Antal Kovács

Copyright © Antal Kovács 2013

The right of Antal Kovács to be identified as the author of this work has been asserted by him in accordance with the Copyright, Design and Patents Act 1988.

All rights Reserved

CONTENTS

Umbria	p	6
History	p	10
Grape varieties	p	15
Classification	p	23
Growing the grape	p	25
Making the wine	p	29
Areas of DOC and DOCG wines	p	36
The wine producers – an introduction	p	41
The wine producers – Orvieto	p	43
Argillae	p	45
Bigi	p	47
Cardeto	p	55
Carraia	p	74
Castello della Sala	p	80
Cirulli	p	89
Corini	p	95
Custodi	p	97
Falesco	p	101
Madonna del Latte	p	108
Monrubio	p	111
Mottura	p	115
Palazzone	p	118
Poggio de Lupo	p	124
Sassara	p.	128
Scambia	p	131
Velette	p	135
Vitalonga	p	138

The wine producers – Torgiano	p 142
Lungarotti	p 144
The wine producers – Montefalco	p 154
Adanti	p 156
Antano	p 159
Antonelli	p 162
Benincasa	p 168
Bocale	p 171
Caprai	p 173
Colleciocco	p 178
Colpetrone	p 181
Colsanto	p 184
Dionigi	p 187
Fongoli	p 195
Martinelli	p 199
Novelli	p 202
Rialto	p 210
Rocca di Fabbri	p 213
Romanelli	p 219
Ruggeri	p 223
Scacciadiavoli	p 225
Pardi	p 229
Perticaia	p 232
Tabarrini	p 235
The wine producers – Assisi	p 239
Sportoletti	p 240
Tili	p 243
Brognal - Antigniano	p 246
Brognal - Vignabaldo	p 252
The wine producers – Colli Perugini	p 259
Busti	p 260
Chiorri	p 262
Goretti	p 270
Sasso dei Lupip	p 279
Spina	p 283

The wine producers – Colli Martani   p 286
   Baldassari   p 288
   Custodia   p 291
   Di Filippo   p 296
   Peppucci   p 303
   San Rocco   p 305
   Sartori   p 309
   Trinci   p 314
   Todini   p 319
   Spoletoducale   p 323
   Tudernum   p 328
   Zàzzera   p 332

The wine producers – Lago di Corbara   p 334
   Castello di Corbara   p 336
   Salviano   p 343
   Barbi   p 347
   Barberani   p 350
   Vagile   p 355

The wine producers – Colli Amerini   p 358
   Le Crete   p 360
   Colli Amerini   p 364
   Montoro   p 374
   Palazzola   p 377
   Pizzogallo   p 379
   Poggette   p 380
   Ponteggia   p 383
   Castello delle Regine   p 388
   Ruffo   p 393
   Zanchi   p 394

The wine producers – Colli del Trasimeno	p 398
Bertaio	p 399
Carpine	p 402
Duca della Corgna	p 407
Fanini	p 413
Lamborghini	p 416
Mezzetti	p 419
Querciolana	p 421
Poggio	p 423
Pucciarella	p 426
The wine producers – Colli Altotiberini	p 429
Sant' Andrea	p 430
Blasi	p 436
Donini	p 439
Polidori	p 443
Author's note	p.446
References	p 447

UMBRIA

The unspoilt countryside of soft rolling hills, deep wooded valleys with crystal clear streams and lush upland plateaux is often called the green heart of Italy. The landscape is almost biblical and familiar. Subliminally, it is etched on to the Christian soul. It is easy to recognise the backdrop to medieval paintings depicting scenes from the bible and the life of saints. There is an air of culture about the place that people feel at ease with. Dotted around the undulating countryside, there are ancient hilltop towns and villages; some going back 3000 years. Each has its own character, unique in every way. The churches, palaces, museums and art galleries are crammed full of paintings, statues and architectural treasures, some dating back to the days of the Roman Empire and even before. Umbria is also known as *la terra santa*, the land of the saints. Montefalco is the birthplace of eight saints, which is some achievement for a small town with a population of just over 5000. Two of the best known saints are Umbrian: St Benedict of Norcia (AD 480-547), the patron saint of Europe, who is credited with saving Western civilisation during the Dark Ages; and St Francis of Assisi (AD 1182-1226), whose followers flock to the small hilltop town from every corner of the world.

With these abundant riches it could be easy to ignore the vineyards dotted all over the pastoral landscape, but the wines also deserve close attention. They are as diverse as the towns, and every wine cellar has its own hidden treasure, kept a close secret from the outside world. Dining out is an art anywhere in Italy, but more so in Umbria. The *Cittáslow* movement originated in Orvieto and there is not a single McDonalds or Kentucky Fried Chicken to be found in the city. In Umbria, food is taken seriously.

According to Pliny the Elder, the region was named after the mysterious tribe of the Umbrii, but he was probably wrong. Modern historians claim central Italy was originally populated by Lingurians, the pre-historic people of Liguria. Later, Acheans invaded Umbria and drove the Lingurians out. The Acheans were an ancient tribe of Greece, most likely to be Pliny's Umbrii. They settled in the region during the 6th Century BC.

672 BC is the legendary date of the foundation of Terni, the birthplace of San Valentino, who was the bishop of the town until his martyrdom in 273 AD. Incidentally, Terni is a steel town and one of the least romantic places in all Italy.

The Umbrii were, in turn, attacked by the Etruscans, who pushed them east of the river *Tevere* towards the uplands of *Monti Sibillini,* part of the Apennine range of mountains running along the spine of Italy. The Etruscans captured over 300 Umbrian towns. However, the Umbrii had not been eradicated in the conquered districts.

The origin of the Etruscans is still hotly debated, but most historians believe they came from Asia Minor around 700 and 500 BC. For some time the Umbrii and Etruscans co-existed in present day Umbria. When the Romans ousted the Etruscans they just integrated with the new rulers, like the Umbrii.

The Umbrian language existed without written characters, but the Eugubine Tablets found near the town of Gubbio record the sound of the language using Etruscan and Roman characters, which is a proof of sorts for the happy co-existence of the three different cultures. The seven bronze tablets were discovered in 1444 AD; they are the only extant record of the ancient Umbrian language found so far.

After the downfall of the Etruscans, in 308 BC, the Umbrii allied themselves with the Samnites in their war against Rome, but communications with *Samnium* were impeded by the Roman fortress of Narni, founded in 298 BC. At the subsequent battle of Sentium, south of Rome, the Umbrii offered little help and after the Roman victory, a period of integration followed

The Romans soon established a number of colonies, like *Spoletium* (Spoleto), and in 220 BC built the *via Flaminia,* which became the main thoroughfare for Roman development in Umbria. During Hannibal's invasion in the Second Punic War, the battle of Lake Trasimeno took place, but without involvement from the Umbrii. However, during the Roman Civil War between Octavian and Mark Antony, Perugia supported Antony, who duly lost. Octavian laid waste to the city.

Roman rule was almost universal in the region, however, in Pliny's time there were still some 49 independent communities, but Umbria was a much larger region at the time, extending as far as modern day Ravenna and included most of Marche.

As the Roman Empire collapsed, Ostrogoths and Byzantines struggled for supremacy in the region, but eventually, the Lombards triumphed. The barbarians from present day Germany ruled over the conquered territory for many centuries. They founded the Duchy of Spoleto, which covered most of the territory of modern day Umbria.

When Charlemagne conquered the Lombard kingdoms, some Umbrian territories were given to the Pope. At the same time, some city-states acquired a form of autonomy, the *comuni*, and fought each other constantly as part of the conflict between the Pope in Rome and the Holy Roman Empire of Austria; as well as between the Guelphs and the Ghibellines.

A long period of wars ended when Pope Paul III (1468-1549 AD) became the head of the Roman Catholic Church in 1534. He soon set out to conquer the region, then under the rule of the Baglioni family. He raised the tax on salt and thus provoked the Umbrians to revolt. When they rose against the extortionate tax he promptly dispatched the Papal army and laid siege to Perugia. His army won and captured the city, thus ending what was left of Umbria's independence.

After the French revolution and the following French conquest of Italy, Umbria became part of the extremely short-lived Roman Republic (1798-1799). Later, the region was under the rule of Napoleon's Empire (1809-1814). After Napoleon's defeat, Umbria became one of the Papal States again until 1860, when Garibaldi and his army liberated Umbria from the rule of Rome. After the *Risorgiomento* and the Piedmontese expansion, Umbria was incorporated in the Kingdom of Italy. The present day borders of Umbria were set in 1927.

Umbria is the only Italian region having neither coastline nor common border with other countries. It has a land area of 8,456 square kilometres and a population of 900, 000 (the density is half the national average). The capital is Perugia.

Umbria is bordered by Tuscany, Lazio and Marche. The eastern part is dominated by the Apennines, its highest point

Monte Vettore at 2,476 m. The river *Tevere* runs through the region mostly from north to south, with its lowest point at Attigliano, 96m. Its principal tributaries are the *Chiascio,* the *Topino* and the *Nera.*

Most Umbrians live in ancient hilltop towns and villages unchanged for centuries, overlooking the rich agricultural land, backed by distant snow capped mountains. It is a quiet, timeless place where the rest of the world's concerns do not seem to matter: an elegant and enchanting time warp.

Every settlement has a different character and history: Perugia, Assisi, Montefalco, Spoleto, Orvieto, Todi, Narni and Gubbio all have an interesting story to tell, but even the smallest hilltop village will have some historical monument worth exploring.

Umbria is divided into two administrative divisions: the Province of Perugia (population 660, 000) and the Province of Terni (population 230, 000).

Tourism and agriculture are the principal economic activities. Tobacco, olive oil and wine are the main products. Orvieto, Torgiano and Montefalco are noted for their outstanding wines, which draws an army of tourists to the vineyards. Another typical Umbrian product is the black truffle found in *Valnerina* (the valley of the river *Nera,* which flows from the *Monti Sibillini* to Terni and joins the *Tevere* south of Narni). The food industry processes pork meats (hams and salamis of Norcia), confectionery (chocolate of Perugia), pasta, lentils (Castelluccio) and a wide variety of wonderful cheeses. The other main industries are textiles, clothing, sportswear, iron and steel, chemicals and ornamental ceramics. Between 1970 and 1980 there was rapid expansion among small and medium sized firms providing the region with a new industrial base as an addition to the old established heavy industry centred on Terni. It is the only industrial part of Umbria, a very slight blot on an otherwise pastoral landscape.

HISTORY

Italy is the home to some of the oldest wine producing regions in the world. *Vitis viniferia* grew wild throughout Europe as well as central and eastern Asia, including the Holy Land. According to the Bible wine became a source of great embarrassment to Noah. "And Noah began to be an husbandman, and he planted a vineyard: And he drank of the wine, and was drunken; and he was uncovered within his tent." (Genesis 9:20-21).

Etruscans and Greek settlers produced wine in Italy long before the Romans planted their first vineyards in the second century BC. Images found on Etruscan cinerary urns and tomb paintings depict banquets from as early as 800 BC. Wine was imported from Greece then, but from 700 BC the Etruscans made an effort to become self-sufficient in wine production and towards the end of the century started exporting wine themselves. First, wine was used as an offering in Etruscan rituals, and then later it became a luxury item to the emerging ruling classes. However, drunkenness was frowned upon by the Etruscans, as well as the Greeks and Romans, and wine was drunk mixed with water. There were different types of ceramic vessels: the *amphora* contained wine, the *hydria*, water and the *krater* was the container where the wine and water were mixed together. The *kylix* was the cup used for drinking. Curiously, a bronze cheese grater was also part of a banquet service.

Between the third and second millennia BC wine was instrumental in spreading civilisation in the Aegean. Cycladic ships transported the nectar cargo all around the Mediterranean. Their adventures feature in the numerous episodes of Dionysian myths. The travels of Dionysus, the god of wine, encompass the islands and mainland of ancient Greece. He was celebrated in hundreds of different festivals. He is prominently displayed on vases and drinking cups with his retinue of Satyrs, Pans and Nymphs. The vintage festivals were occasions for joyful processions and general merriment. Dionysus was known as Bacchus to the Romans. Some of his celebrations degenerated into orgies and his worship was banned by the senate in 186 BC. Later, he was rehabilitated and his cult became a respectable religion and it was immensely popular. In Umbria small ceramic drinking jugs (*oinochoe*) were the gifts given to children on the second day of *Antesteria*, a festival in honour of Dionysus, as the god of the re-awakening of nature with the first spring flowers. During these festivities a drinking competition was held where the participants provided their own jugs. For the three-year olds, the gift of an *oinochoe*, was a token of confirmation of the god's protection as well as being a good luck charm.

As the Etruscans declined, Rome continued the production of wine. In the second century BC large-scale, slave-run vineyards sprang up throughout Italy. The planting of cereals was practically abandoned in favour of wine production and there was a serious shortage of wheat. Thus, in 92 AD, emperor Domitian ordered the destruction of a great number of vineyards in order to free up fertile land for food production. It forced the vineyards to move up the hills onto less fertile lands. During this period wine production outside the Italian peninsula was prohibited under Roman law. Gaul, and Provence in particular, supplied Rome with cereals, whilst Rome exported wine to the provinces, where it was greatly appreciated, so much so, that the practice of drinking it undiluted with water took hold.

What Greek and Etruscan wines tasted like is anybody's guess, but we have some historical evidence about Roman oenoligical practices from Lucius Junius Columella's book: "*De re rustica*". Since the Romans liked sweet things, they delayed the vintage as much as possible, sometimes as late as mid-November. In order to make stronger and sweeter wines; the must was also boiled to increase its sugar content before fermentation. These wines were referred to as *defrutum*. Another method was to add honey, producing a sickly sweet drink called *mulsum*. They also drank their wine hot, mixed with water, pepper, herbs and honey; they named this concoction *piperatum* or *conditum*.

After the collapse of the Roman Empire the cultivation of vineyards continued as before in spite of a series of barbarian invasions. There was nothing dark about the Dark Ages; life went on as before, but under a new set of rulers. Making wine changed little since Etruscan and Roman times, and in many ways, it continued right up to the eighteenth century. The grapes were crushed in large winepresses. The most commonly used in Umbria was the horizontal *Catone*, named after Cato, the Roman agronomist who lived around 100 BC. The one on display in the Torgiano Wine Museum was last used in 1973 AD. With the *Catone*, a horizontal beam applied pressure to a large wooden screw, assisted by the weight of a heavy stone attached to the end of the beam. The grapes were placed into a round wooden container below, with slats at the side, and the must was collected into rectangular stone wine tubs (*lacus*) through terracotta spouts. Fermentation took place inside terracotta pots (*olla*) and later in wooden barrels. A later model, a vertical winepress, *Plinio*, was named after Pliny the Elder who lived in the first century AD. In order to increase the sweetness and alcohol content of the wine, some of the must was placed in copper cauldrons and brought to the boil, then added to the rest of the must. Today, using the same method, *Vino cotto* (cooked wine) is produced in Le Marche and Abruzzo regions by winemakers for their own use, rather than commercially.

Agriculture in general was revived by the spread of newly established monasteries throughout Italy, instigated by Saint Benedict (480-547 AD). For three years he lived as a hermit in a cave on the ridge of *Monte Subasio*, performing a series of miracles. Later, he set up twelve religious houses of twelve men each, with their own patriarch. One day, he had a vision of a young student, Placidus, drowning in a lake. He ordered Maurus, a fellow monk to rescue the boy. As Placidus came from a wealthy family, his father thanked Saint Benedict by giving him the citadel on *Monte Cassino*. The monastery still stands there today, after it has been restored, having been almost destroyed during World War II.

The Benedictine Order spread throughout Europe and was responsible for the best known wine growing areas. Saying the Eucharist, the monks used red wine, representing the blood of our Lord, Jesus Christ; and they made sure that they produced only the best. They were mostly responsible for the characteristic Umbrian landscape: a mixture of olive trees and vineyards. During the Middle Ages vines were trained on the trunks of trees, before the use of trellises. Wine was also part of the monks' daily diet (mixed with water, naturally). *Vino Santo* or *Vinsanto* was offered to God during solemn religious ceremonies, and even today, Umbrians serve it at family celebrations. It is a sweet wine made from Moscato, Grechetto and Pecorino grapes. It is normally bottled during Easter Week, *Settimana Santa*, hence *Vino Santo*.

The good works of the monasteries were recognised by many donations of land, and the Benedictines found themselves with so many vineyards that it became common practice to rent them out. Between the tenth and fourteenth centuries there was an increase in the population. Accordingly, the amount of land under cultivation also grew larger. This lead to the development of sharecropping contracts, *mezzadria*, which lasted until 1860.

Wine production also increased. Monks in their monasteries needed wine for their religious services, medicines, meals and entertaining. Wine was also part of the daily diet of the general population and provided cheer for festive occasions, which were as numerous in the past as today. The intricate stone carvings of the *Fontana Maggiore* in Perugia, completed in 1278 AD, depict work in the vineyards month by month. *La Divina Villa*, written by the Perugian Corgnolo della Corgna, an agricultural treatise dealing with the annual wine growing cycle shows an uninterrupted continuity from the techniques used from Roman imperial times. Town councils throughout Umbria controlled all aspects of production, and the quality of wine was greatly improved. These edicts specified the period of harvest, traditionally in most areas not before 2nd October, the *festa di San Angelo*. Selling excess new wine, *alla frasca,* was also regulated: *frasca* was a leafy branch hung outside the wine cellars. Measuring jugs (*panate*) used in taverns were inspected and checked that they displayed the correct seals. Prices were controlled and fines imposed for profiteering. Heads of families were banned from frequenting taverns or staying there late at night. Games were also prohibited. Wine labels were introduced, but their function was mostly decorative and the sale of labelled bottles was restricted to a small social élite.

Wine had been an integral part of the Mediterranean diet and its use as a form of nourishment continued from imperial Rome through the Middle Ages, the Renaissance, and right up to our times. Most of the native Italian vines survived the Phylloxera epidemic during the nineteenth century in one form or another and nothing has been lost from the past. Suitable clones were found and selected; and today most European vines are grafted onto American rootstocks resistant to the Phylloxera insect. However, producing good wine was a hit and miss affair until modern science came to the aid of the winemaker. Today, every aspect of wine production is controlled: from the selection of the grape variety, to planting, nurturing, harvesting and making the finished product. The oenologists are free to experiment and they can make the wines they want. Their ideal is to reach the highest achievable quality possible for an affordable price. Each one squares this particular circle in a unique way.

GRAPE VARIETIES

The twenty wine growing regions in Italy correspond to the twenty political ones. They are diverse in geography, climate and regional dishes. The indigenous wines reflect this diversity. Some of the better known grape varieties are concentrated in Piedmont and Tuscany: the famous "Killer B's" are Barolo, Barbaresco and Brunello di Moltancino. They are all world famous, and in England some other varieties are also popular: Chianti, Soave, Frascati, Orvieto Classico, Lambrusco and Asti Spumante. However, Umbria is a little known region in England; Orvieto Classico and perhaps Sagrantino di Montefalco are the notable exceptions.

Italy's MIRAF (Ministry of Agriculture and Forestry) granted authorised status to 350 different grape varieties. There are a further 500 documented grapes, some of them only grown in Italy. The range is a lot narrower in Umbria; the most widely used varieties are as follows:

RED (ROSSO) Autochthonous or Native grapes.

Aleatico is believed to be a red mutation of the French *Muscat Blanc á Petits Grains*. It has been grown in Italy for so long, at least since the fourteenth century, that it is considered to be a native grape. It is popular in older vineyards and it has been re-discovered recently. It has unmistakable aromatic Muscat characteristics and it produces velvety, full-bodied sweet wines. It has a deep, ruby red colour; and an aroma of wild blackberries. *Aleatico* is frequently fortified and aged, with a changed bouquet of faded violets and roses; and earthy dried plum flavours.

Barbera probably originated around Monterferrato in Piedmont. There are mentions of a wine called *Barbero* going back to the thirteenth century. It is widely planted throughout Italy; it even beats *Sangiovese* for its popularity with wine producers. It is a typical workhorse of a wine and it takes a lot of care to make exciting wines from the grape. The wine is deep purple in colour with a shocking pink tint. It is high in acidity and it has a fruity bone-dry finish. There are some good DOC wines made from *barbera* in Piedmont, but in Umbria it is mostly used for blending with other grape varieties.

Canaiolo Nero is included in the composition of many DOC wines: such as *Rosso Orvietano* and *Lago di Corbara*. In its unblended form it gives a ruby red, full-bodied wine with notes of wild herbs and sour black cherry. In Tuscany, *Canaiolo Nero* was a key element in the blend that made *Chianti* famous; the berries were dried first and added after fermentation, a process called the *governo* system. However, *Canaiolo Nero* is a less often grown grape today as this practice has gone out of fashion.

Cesanese is a popular grape in Lazio and grown all over south and central Italy. It is also called *Bonvino Nero*, because it is easy to cultivate, but it has no outstanding features apart from being a good workhorse of a grape. In Umbria it is used as part of a blend.

Ciliegiolo is reputed to have arrived from Spain, brought in by the pilgrims returning from Saint James' shrine in Galicia. The pilgrims' way, *Chemin de St Jacques de Compostelle* was not only a conduit for architectural styles in churches, but also for viticulture. The famous Rioja vines originated from the Bordeaux region, taken there by pilgrims. *Ciliegiolo* is named after the Italian word for cherry. When produced on its own it makes a light, smooth and high alcohol content wine with the aroma and colour of ripe cherries. In its unblended form it makes good new wines (*vini novelli*), but *Ciliegiolo* is often blended with other grapes. It is used in the DOC *Torgiano Rosso*.

Colorino is a grape variety mainly grown in Tuscany, but it is also used for blending DOC red wines: *Rosso Orvietano* and *Lago di Corbara*. The grape gets its name from the dark red colour of its skin. It is rarely made into wine by itself; instead it is added to other grape varieties to deepen the colour of the wine and to increase its alcohol content.

Dolcetto comes from Piedmont. The name does not refer to its sweetness. The little sweet one is similar in sugar and acid levels to the other grapes in the region. It is easy to grow and produces early wines ideal for drinking in quantity. It competes against *Nebbiolo* and *Barbera*, all the same, it produces seven DOC wines in the north and it is the wine that most of Piedmont drinks.

Sangiovese is one of the most important red grapes. The name derives from *sanguis Jovis*, Jupiter's blood. *Sangiovese* originated in Tuscany (perhaps *Emilia-Romagna*) and it was probably known by the Etruscans, but it was not until the sixteenth century that it was described with precision. *Sangiovese* is divided into two families: *Sangiovese Grosso* and *Sangiovese Piccolo*. It produces vibrant, lighter-bodied red wines, like Chianti. In Umbria it is often blended with other grapes, but when it is made into wine by itself it is light and balanced with floral and fruity flavours. Its bouquet suggests leather, tobacco, truffles, figs, blackberry, raspberry, vanilla and cinnamon. When aged in barrels *Sangiovese* can have a hint of oak and even tar about it. It is a grape for all seasons. The original *Biondi-Santi Brunello di Montalcino* is a carefully selected clone of *Sangiovese*, and it happens to be one of the most expensive wines in Italy.

Montepulciano d'Abruzzo should not be confused with *Vino Nobile di Montepulciano*; a *Sangiovese* clone called *Prugnolo gentile* from the town of *Montepulciano* in Tuscany. *Montepulciano d'Abruzzo* probably originates from *Torre de Passeri* or *Conca Paglina*, both in the region of Abruzzo. The name is usually shortened to *Montepulciano* and it is Italy's most widely used native red grape after *Sangiovese*. It produces a fruity, dry wine: with soft tannins and notes of cherry and morello cherry. *Montepulciano* is widely planted around Orvieto and gives very good results, thanks to low yields and careful winemaking.

Sagrantino is an ancient vine, planted on roughly 250 hectares in the vicinity of Montefalco. Pliny the Elder described the *Itriola* grape, which some historians believe to be *Sagrantino*. Others claim the vines were imported from Asia Minor by followers of Saint Francis. The wines produced from it are blended with *Sangiovese* to produce *Rosso di Montefalco* or as a pure *Sagrantino*. It has a deep ruby colour with rustic fruit and heavy tannins and the wines can age for many years. It was traditionally partly dried in order to produce a sweet wine, *Sagrantino Passito*, but today a dry and more robust wine is also produced. It is considered to be one of the great wines of Italy, albeit, not so well known.

RED (ROSSO) Allochtonous or Foreign grapes.

Cabernet Sauvignon attains its full potential near Orvieto, because of good exposure, vine density and low yields. *Cabernet Sauvignon* is the typical Bordeaux grape, native to *Mèdoc* and *Graves*, but planted all around the world where winemakers attempt to produce a wine similar to claret. *Cabernet Sauvignon* has a soft, fruity flavour reminiscent of bilberry and blackcurrant with a peppery, sandalwood aftertaste. It has a high concentration of tannins and aromatic substances. Its robust structure makes it an ideal wine for ageing. In Umbria *Cabernet Sauvignon* is often blended with *Cabernet Franc*, *Merlot* and *Sangiovese*; as well as produced alone.

Cabernet Franc is low in tannins and has a lean structure, but at the same time, an aristocratic full-blooded flavour of raspberries and violets. It is usually bright red in colour. In France, *Cabernet Franc* is blended with *Merlot* for the great wines of *St Emilion*. It is also blended in Umbria and rarely produced alone.

Merlot is another Bordeaux red grape, where it is blended with *Cabernet,* and *Malbec*. It is widely planted in Umbria and mostly blended with *Cabernet Sauvignon, Sangiovese* and *Montepulciano*. The quality of *Merlot* is related to the yield and the terroir. When the yields are reduced the wine is deep ruby red and quite tannic, with notes of raspberry and blackcurrant; flavours range from spices, to roses and plum. *Merlot* is also used on its own, producing some excellent wines.

Pinot Nero originates from Burgundy (*Pinot Noir*), but it has been grown in Umbria for so long that it could be considered a native grape, especially as it was probably introduced to the Rhône Valley by Romans when they invaded Gaul. *Pinot Nero* needs a lot of attention during cultivation and vinification. It has a reputation for being an unpredictable grape, but it can produce outstanding wines, including white sparkling wines made in the champenoise method. The kind of wine produced from *Pinot Nero* has a wide range, depending on the terroir and vinification. When young, *Pinot Nero* has flavours of raspberry, strawberry, cherry, fruits of the forest and violet, but with ageing it develops spicy notes. Its colour can range from light red to dark ruby and *Pinot Nero* can have a high alcoholic content.

Gamay is the typical grape of Beaujolais, where it accounts for 98% of the vines planted. It is not found in many other parts of the world, however, it is widely planted in the *Colli del Trasimeno* surrounding *Lago Trasimeno*. It is used as part of a blend, or produced by itself. The *Trasimeno Gamay* has a dark, intense ruby red colour, a delicate and complex bouquet with notes of wild berries and fruits of the forest. It has a dry and elegant flavour with hints of cherry, plum and spices.

Syrah or **Shiraz** is the grape of *Hermitage* and *Côte Rôtie* wines of the *Rhône*. The grape originates from Asia Minor, from the town of Shiraz in the south east of today's Iran. Some experts believe the grapes were taken to Marseilles by the Phoenicians. According to others, Roman legionaries took the vine from Egypt to Gaul, via Syracuse in Sicily. *Syrah* is a relatively easy grape to grow, but it is more difficult to make a great wine from it. *Syrah* produces a dry, dark, dense and tannic wine. It has a fruity flavour of bilberry, blackcurrant and fruits of the forest. The wine is usually matured in French oak barrels.

WHITE (BIANCO) Autochthonous or Native grapes.

Drupeggio is a grape widely planted in the Orvieto district, where it is better known as *Canaiolo Bianco*. It is one of the many grapes used in the blend that makes white Orvieto wines. When vinified alone, it produces a greenish yellow wine with an intense and fresh bouquet and a soft flavour.

Garganega or ***Gargana*** is a variety of the *Soave* grape. It has been grown in the Veneto region for centuries. It is vigorous and produces large quantities of fruit, sold also as table grapes. The wine shows hints of almond typical of *Soave*. In Umbria it produces higher sugar levels than in its northern homeland and it is used for blending in the *Colli Amerini* Doc area.

Grechetto is an ancient grape imported from Greece as its name implies. It is the principal blend in Orvieto DOC wines (minimum 40%), but *Grechetto* is also produced on its own. It makes a high alcoholic content wine with good structure. It has a strong fruit flavour, yet it is dry and fresh on the palate.

Malvasia is yet another ancient grape used in the blend for Orvieto wines. Its name derives from *Monembasia*, an old Venetian fortress known in Italy as *Malvasia*. It is an old port with trading links with the Cyclades Islands. There are at least 17 different grape varieties in Italy called *Malvasia*. The one used in Umbria is *Malvasia Bianca del Chianti*. When vinified alone, *Malvasia* has a distinctive aromatic even musky perfume with sharp intense tones and a full and balanced flavour. Traditionally it has been used for rich and powerful dessert wines, but today *Malvasia* adds a spicy ingredient to a number of blends.

Procanico or ***Trebbiano Toscano*** is also used to make up the Orvieto blend. In Umbria it is called *Procanico* or sometimes *Rossetto*. It was the prevailing grape in Orvieto DOC, before *Grechetto* displaced it according to new regulations. When used by itself, *Procanico* gives a straw yellow wine (typical of Orvieto DOC), with a slight fragrance, medium bodied and slightly acid on the palate. It can also have a fruity and floral bouquet with the scent of dried flowers and white peaches.

Verdello gets its name from the greenish colour of its skin. It is believed to be related to the Portuguese *Verdelho* grown on the island of Madeira, however, it is considered to be a native grape of Umbria. *Verdello* is used for Orvieto Classico DOC. Used alone, it has no outstanding features, although it has a good structure, fresh fragrances and a fair acidity.

Vernaccia is grown around Orvieto in some of the older vineyards and it is one of the grapes making up the Orvieto DOC blend. The name is a derivation of the Latin *vernaculus*, meaning native to this place. In Tuscany, *Vernaccia di San Gimignano* is widely planted and it makes a dry, full-bodied wine with a slightly bitter flavour. Another variety is grown in Sardinia, *Vernaccia di Oristano*, where it produces a sherry type wine; but the only connection between the grape varieties is in the name.

Vermentino is also grown around Orvieto and it is considered to be a native grape, though it originates from Corsica, as well as Sardinia, where it is called *Vermentino di Gallura*. It was widely used in the past for the Orvieto blend, then it went out of fashion, but it is gaining popularity again. *Vermentino*, when vinified alone, produces a deep coloured, ripe fruit flavoured wine of real character.

WHITE (BIANCO) Allochtonous or Foreign grapes.

Chardonnay is a noble Burgundy grape and the most sought after varietal in the world. It is a most versatile grape and wine produced from it can vary from the flinty *Chablis* to the buttery *Meursaults* and New World wines bursting with fruit flavours as well as a high alcohol content. Some people associate it with apples, melon, and even pineapple. It is often matured in

French oak barrels to give it an aftertaste of smokiness. It is also one of the grapes used for the production of Champagne. *Chardonnay* is planted throughout Umbria to produce high quality wines; however, it is mostly blended with other grapes.

Sauvignon Blanc comes from the Bordeaux region. It produces dry, refreshingly zesty wines and combined with *Sémillion* it makes high quality dry white as in *Châteaux Haut-Brion* or sweet Sauternes. The grape produces aromatic wines with a smell reminiscent of unripe fruit or gooseberries and in some places it can be flinty or even smoky. It is mostly blended in Umbria and used for making late vintage "noble rot" wines around Orvieto.

Pinot Bianco otherwise known as *Pinot Blanc* is planted in some vineyards in Umbria, though it is more popular in the *Veneto*, *Friuli* and *Alto Adige* regions. Pinot Bianco makes an apple crisp wine with intense flavour, consistent structure, a straw yellow colour and good acidity.

Pinot Grigio or *Pinot Gris* is widely planted in the *Veneto*, *Friuli-Venezia Giulia* and *Alto Adige* regions, but it can also be found in Umbria in some vineyards. *Pinot Grigio* produces a dry, light bodied wine with a clean taste on the palate.

Viognier is an ancient grape that may have originated in Croatia, then taken by Roman legionaries to the *Condrieu* community in the Rhône Valley. It is grown in some vineyards in Umbria (Sugano) and it produces strong wines, high in alcoholic content, low acidity, floral and fruity aromas reminiscent of citrus fruits, peach and apricots and the fragrance of roses.

Riesling is one of the great grapes of Germany. It is planted all over the world and appreciated for its intense floral aromas of green apples, grapefruit, peach, honey and even rose blossom. *Riesling* produces wines of longevity and a good balance, with a crisp taste and reasonably high acidity. However, only a limited amount is grown in Umbria

CLASSIFICATION

The appellation system in Italy has four classes of wine.

1 *Vino da Tavola* (VDT) means that the wine is made in Italy, usually a basic wine for local consumption.
2 *Indicazione Geografica Tipica* (IGT) shows wine from a specific region. This classification was created in 1992 for wines considered to be of higher quality than ordinary table wines, but wines that did not conform to the strict wine laws for their region.
3 *Denominazione di Origine Controllata* (DOC). Controlled Place Name. The DOC system was introduced in 1963, seeking to establish a way of recognising quality wines and to protect their standing, nationally and internationally.
4 *Denominazione di Origine Controllata e Garantita* (DOCG). Controlled and Guaranteed Place Name. The main difference between DOC and DOCG wines is that the latter must pass a blind test for quality in addition to conforming to the strict legal requirements to be designated to the wine in question. In 1992 the laws relating to classification have been revised, and have made the system more transparent. The aim is to encourage winemakers to focus on quality and to maintain high standards. In 2006 there were 120 IGT, 311 DOC and 32 DOCG zones throughout Italy.

The requirements for both DOC and DOCG are as follows:
List of wines states the names of wines that can be produced in the specified name area (*bianco, rosso, rosato, novello, passito, vin santo, spumante* etc).
Varietal assortment specifies the grape varieties that must be used, and those that are optional. Also, their percentages are set. In case of wines referring to a single variety; this must represent at least 85% of the grapes.
Territorial boundaries are also set. The production zone is not confined to a specific administrative territory (municipality

or province etc.), but marked on the maps of the *Istituto Geografico Militare* (Military Geographical Institute), the Italian equivalent of the English ordinance survey maps. Within a denomination a number of different types of wines can co-exist. For example, some of the Orvieto DOC wines are produced in the Lazio region.

Vine density is strictly regulated by the number of vines allowed to be planted per hectare.

Unit production is specified, setting the maximum limits allowed for each type of wine.

Maximum sugar levels or alcoholic percentage are also set and controlled.

Physical/Chemical characteristics are tested on every batch of wines produced by a committee allocated to this task.

Register of vineyards is compulsory. All producers of IGT, DOC, and DOCG wines must be registered by the appropriate Chamber of Commerce.

In an ideal world the DOCG wines should be the most sought after and their prices would reflect this. Alas, in the real world this is not the case. Some IGT wines can fetch ten times the prices paid for DOCG. The classification system is designed to guarantee consistent quality and fair prices according to the law, which is strictly enforced. There is a predictable balance between price and quality. What makes an excellent wine is always a matter of taste, which involves personal choices. There is no accounting for taste, or lack of it. If a producer chooses to make wines that do not conform to the strict DOC and DOCG regulations, the best he can hope for is an IGT, even though the wine is excellent. There are vineyards making red wines in the *Orvieto Classico* (DOC) zone, which is strictly white, however good the finished product is, it only qualifies for an IGT label. I have sampled some of these wines and they were truly outstanding, thus my advice is, do not be put off by an IGT classification. There is a French equivalent to this quandary; some of the VDQS wines knock the socks off their AOC cousins – and cost less into the bargain. Neither classification nor price guarantees the best, as what is best depends on you. So, shop around.

GROWING THE GRAPE

The quality of grapes, and consequently the wine, depends on a combination of climate, soil, grape variety and the growing technique. The French use a single word to describe climate, sub-climate and the soil – *Terroir*. This shorthand for the geological location of a vineyard is used all around the world.

Umbria has the ideal climate for growing grapes: it is neither too hot, nor too cold – depending on the altitude of the vineyard. Anything over 600 metres is not suitable, and the fertile land of the valleys is used for growing cereals. This has been the case since the days of the Roman Empire, when cereals were at a premium. Fortunately for wine producers, vines thrive on relatively poor quality land on the hillsides.

Just as the landscape is diverse in Umbria, so is the soil: it ranges from volcanic tufa, to alluvial, fertile clay, and floodplains formed from sand and silt. With fertilisation all these lands are ideal for the growing of grapes. If irrigation is required, there is no shortage of water in Umbria (it is the green heart of Italy), and the weather is neither too wet, nor too dry. The sun shines all year, which is essential for producing quality grapes. Choosing the location for a vineyard is an art, but as grapes have been grown in the region for two thousands years, the best locations had been taken up since time immemorial.

Selecting the variety of grape is also important. The most suitable vines for any location are part of Umbrian folk memory: the farmers know what grows well where and their knowledge is passed on from generation to generation. Introducing new types of vines was always the mark of an adventurous winemaker and the experimentation with new varietals is an ongoing process.

Growing the grape is a year round activity and there is a natural rhythm to the vineyard cycle:

<u>Budburst</u>. In spring the dormant vines come alive and start sprouting new shoots. It is the beginning of the new growing

season and for the next four months the shoots will grow and need to be trained to produce a full, open canopy.

Flowering is closely followed by set, which is the beginning of the development of the berries. During this period the vine uses most of its energy growing new shoots, but the small berries also grow. By mid July the canopies are fully-grown and need to be trimmed. This is when the crop load is decided and excess fruit is thinned out.

Veraison is the next stage, when the colour of the grape berries changes. This takes place during September and it is the beginning of the ripening process. A further thinning out can be carried out at this stage, if needed. The individual bunches of grapes are closely inspected right up to harvest.

Leaf fall is after harvest, and when winter comes the vines remain dormant. They are then pruned to the required number of buds for the coming growing season.

Throughout the year, work for the winemaker never ceases; from the establishment of a new vineyard to the replacement of old vines. It takes around five years before wine can be produced from a newly planted vine and the life span of vines is between thirty and fifty years. Constant planning, making changes and renewal are essential for running a profitable business. Tastes change and new types of wines are demanded. Promoting the product has to respond to the needs of the market. As it takes years to alter course, a good wine producer needs to plan well ahead in order to compete successfully.

It all begins with the vine. The first step in establishing a vineyard is the small grafted vine plant: the *barbatella*. The grapevine root consists of two portions separated by the grafting point. The upper part is the European vine that provides the plant with the stem and the branches; the lower part is the rootstock, normally an American Phylloxera resistant plant. Most European vineyards were devastated during the epidemic that started in France in 1860 and spread throughout the continent like wildfire. Today, it is standard practice to use

Phylloxera resistant rootstock; thus every plant is hand crafted. Obviously, this is labour intensive, but necessary.

The density of a vineyard is also a consideration, particularly that for DOC and DOCG wines, this is specified by the regulations. In Umbria, the spacing of rows is usually 2 metres and the density of vines is between 4000 and 6000 per hectare.

There are three popular trellis systems for training vines:

<u>Spurred cordon</u> has a vertical trunk of about 60–90 cm with a permanent branch, or cordon. This is trained along a wire on one side of the vine. The cordon is never pruned away and bears a number of fruiting spurs set at an angle and the canes that originate from it are trained vertically to wires above. Cordons take up less space and crop earlier, which means more varieties of vines can fit into a small space. However, yields are lower per tree. This system is widely used in new vineyards in Umbria, because it allows mechanical operations and can also be used for high quality grapevines.

<u>Arched cane</u> has a vertical trunk with two fruiting canes (one-year-old branches), each with 6-10 buds: these canes are arched, rather than being tied horizontally. This method leads to better budburst in the centre of the canes and it is ideal for high quality grapevines, but not suitable for mechanical pruning.

<u>The Guyot</u> system gets is name from Dr Jules Guyot, a 19th century French scientist who devised it. It is a relatively simple design and easy to manage. The vine has a two-year old cane, which generates many more fruiting canes during the growing season. Shoots that emerge are trained upwards to wires above. This system can produce small yields of high quality grapes.

The day to day operation of managing a vineyard has a simple guideline: to achieve an optimum balance between vegetative growth and fruit production. In an ideal world all the vigour of the plant goes into the fruit. The work goes round all year, starting with winter pruning. It consists of selecting the buds to keep for the coming season, and maintaining the shape of the grapevine. Tilling the soil with harrows and hoeing machines is the best method of weed control.

Alternatively, letting grass grow between the rows gets rid of weeds, but the grass needs mowing and it also competes with the vines for water. This method is only suitable for vineyards where there is no shortage of water. This leads on to irrigation, which is necessary in some places, however; too much water can create just as many problems as lack of it. Fertilising with nitrogen, phosphorus and potassium is also required for the development and production of the vines. Pesticides are used in fighting pests: fungi, insects and mites. Some vineyards use biological methods for pest control and wines produced from these grapes are popular and, naturally, fetch a premium price. During the summer, further pruning is carried out in order to control the development of leaves; at the same time, excess suckers and sterile shoots are also removed. Some of the clusters of fruit are also thinned out, which improves the quality of the selected grapes. Harvesting (*vendemmia*) is the last stage, and it begins in August and goes on until October. Every variety of grape has an ideal time to be picked, and some of the dates for *vendemmia* are stipulated in the regulations for DOC and DOCG wines. In Umbria, harvesting is usually carried out by hand, but some mechanised systems are also used. The exact time of picking the grapes is as much an art as science, thus the grapes are constantly tested for levels of sugar and acidity.

MAKING THE WINE

The process of vinification starts with the grape. The fruit of the grapevine is a berry, which has a skin and an outer and inner flesh, which contains the seed. The berries are on stems that form the grape stalk or rasp. The aromatic substances, which give fragrance to the wine, and the polyphenols on which the colour depends, are in the skin, as well as the tannins. For white grapes they are flavonols and for red grapes, anthocyanins. Tannins are also present in the rasp and the pips. They give astringency, particularly to red wines, providing good balance and a full flavour. Tannins also determine the longevity of the wine.

The flesh contains the sugars and organic acids: tartaric, malic and citric. There are also vitamins, enzymes and nitrogen substances, indispensable for the life of the yeasts and bacteria, which are needed for fermentation.

Fermentation is the process by which the grape juice, must, is turned into wine by yeasts, which transfer glucose and fructose into ethyl alcohol (ethanol) and carbon dioxide. These yeasts are naturally present on the surface of ripe grapes; however, they are not enough to guarantee a perfect breakdown of the sugar contained in the must, because ethyl alcohol inhibits their activity. Selected yeasts are introduced into the must, which helps to achieve a precise enological result. The chemical process that turns must into wine also produces heat. If the temperature is too high, the effects on wine production will be negative; thus precise temperature control is essential for the production of quality wines.

In addition to alcohol, numerous other substances are also present in the wine, some were present in the grapes, and others acquired during fermentation. These substances, somewhere around 600, give a particular wine its characteristics: flavour, fragrance and tactile perception.

Flavour is given by the alcohol, the residual sugars, and the glycerine, that define sweetness and softness; and by the acids that add freshness and sharpness.

Fragrance comes from the aromas present in the grape, or acquired by the fermentation and ageing processes.

Tactile perception is connected to the presence of tannins that are responsible for a level of bitterness and astringency; or alcohol that gives a sensation of warmth.

Wine tasters often talk about a host of aromas, flavours, and bouquets found in wine. As with most things in life, it all seems to be a matter of taste and disagreements are not uncommon. Here is a list of the aromatic families most often referred to:

Floral. Acacia flower, hawthorn, rose, geranium, orange blossom, linden, verbena, violet, vine blossom, hyacinth, narcissus, jasmine, broom, heather, violets, etc.

Fruity. Apricot, pineapple, banana, cherry, strawberry, pear, blackcurrant, apple, raspberry, blackberry, quince, muscat grape, plum, lemon, citrus fruit, bitter almond, tropical fruit, etc.

Dried fruit. Dried figs, dried apricots, almond, hazelnut, walnut, prune, raisins, etc.

Vegetal. Green grass, hay, fern, mint, sage, tea, tobacco, olives, green pepper, mushrooms, truffles, musk, asparagus, oak wood, acacia wood, etc.

Spicy. Anise, caraway, cinnamon, clove, fennel, liquorice, nutmeg, bay leaf, thyme, vanilla, ginger, pepper, pine resin, incense, juniper berries, etc.

Food. Cocoa, coffee, chocolate, caramel, toasted bread, roast meat, game, cheese, yeast, butter, honey, cider, vinegar, etc.

Other. Soap, wax, disinfectant, nail polish, sulphur, etc.

Red wines can only be made from red grapes. Vinification begins with the removal of stalks from the grapes. The grape clusters are crushed, using a mechanical process to squeeze out the must. The resulting mixture of must and crushed grapes is then transferred to fermentation vats. In a couple of hours fermentation begins as the yeasts begin to convert the sugar into alcohol and carbon dioxide. A cap is formed, consisting of the skins of the grapes, which rise to the surface thanks to the action of carbon dioxide. During this stage, temperature is kept to 25-30 C° and this is when maceration takes place. Maceration is a process that allows for the exchange of substances between the solid parts (skins and seeds) and the liquid parts (must). These substances (anthocyanins and tannins) are essential as they provide the colour and structure of red wines. The period of maceration can be just a few days (for wines to be drunk when young) or a month (for wines intended for a long ageing process). Periodically, the floating cap on top is pushed down in order to draw out all the substances; the must from the bottom of the tub is also pumped over to the top for the same reason. At the end of maceration the free run juice is racked off; which is the first pressing (*vino fiore*). The residue, *marc* or *pomace* (skins, pips and pulp) are also pressed. Once the alcoholic fermentation is finished, the wine is treated to malolactic fermentation, which improves the flavour of the wine, makes it smoother, rounder and more complex. Depending on the type of wine to be produced, the young wine is kept in steel vats, or in *barriques*, or in larger wooden barrels. The *bordolese barrique* contains 225 litres, and it is used for the best quality wines. Barrels are much larger, containing several hectolitres of wine. In larger containers less of the wine's surface comes into contact with the wood and there is less interaction between wood and liquid. However, contact with wood enriches the wine with tannins and aromas; it also slows down oxygenation and thus stabilises the colour of the wine. The choice of wood for barrels can make a lot of difference to the finished product; each winemaker has his own preference, but French oak is used by most wineries. After the maturation period, the wine is bottled and further development is continued in an oxygen free environment. The ageing process in the bottle depends on the desired product, and it can be a couple of years for high quality wines.

New wines (*vini novelli*) are red wines made to be enjoyed while young; they are fruity and low on tannins. They are made by carbonic maceration. Whole clusters of red grapes are placed into hermetically closed vats, which creates an environment saturated with carbon dioxide. The vats are kept at 25-30 C°. In the absence of oxygen the grapes ferment in their own skins releasing a light fruity aroma to the wine. After a couple of days, the wine deposited at the bottom is pumped off, then the clusters of grapes are pressed separately. The two liquids obtained thus are mixed and placed in a new vat for alcoholic fermentation. The wine is normally ready to be bottled as early as November. In Umbria *Vini novelli* are nothing like *Beaujolais Nouveaux*.

Passito is a dessert wine made mostly from *Sagrantino* grapes. The individual grapes are placed on rush mats for a couple of months to intensify their sugar content. Fermentation is carried out on skins for a week, then alcoholic and malolactic fermentation follows in stainless steel tanks. The wine is aged in *barriques* for twelve months, then a further twelve months in stainless steel tanks. It is aged a further six months in bottles. The total ageing process has to be a minimum 30 months in order to qualify for DOCG status, but some wine producers keep the wine even longer. The minimum alcohol content is around 14.5%. Some winemakers also make *passito* wines from *Sangiovese* grapes.

White wines can be made from white or red grapes. Fermentation takes place without maceration. The grapes are crushed without tearing the skin tissues, pips and rasps. The juices are free running, but pressing is also used. These processes are carried out rapidly in order to minimise the time the must is in contact with the skins. At this stage, the must is cloudy, because of the solid particles contained within. They can be eliminated by a number of methods, chilling the must is the one most often used. Generally, fermentation for white wines takes place at much lower temperatures, 17-20 C°. The slower chemical process helps the aromatic substances to come through. At the end of the alcoholic fermentation the wine is decanted in order to separate the first pressing (*vino fiore*) from the residues: dead cells, coagulating substances and precipitated salts. After clarification and filtering the wine is ready to be bottled.

Vinification with cryomaceration is a similar process. The skins and crushed grapes remain in the vat at low temperatures for several hours prior to fermentation. This extracts the aromatic substances and allows them to pass into the must. The result is a high quality wine rich in primary aromas.

Vinification in barrique is carried out by placing the free running must directly into *barriques*. When the fermentation process is completed, the wine is left in contact with the sediment and lees, which are stirred up from the bottom periodically in a process called *batonage*. Malolactic fermentation follows in the *barrique*, which produces a smooth wine with a mature body.

Noble rot wines (*muffati*) are sweet wines produced with the help of a fungus, *botrytis cinerea*. Delaying the harvest, sometimes well into November, the grapes still on the vine undergo a process of dehydration, which increases their sugar content. *Botrytis cinerea* is a mould, which requires a special environment where fog and mist alternate with sunshine. The hills around Orvieto provide the ideal conditions with the humid autumn mists, followed by brilliant sunshine. However, the mould does not develop in a uniform fashion and, when harvesting, a number of passes are required before all the ideal bunches are picked. These late harvested grapes produce wines with golden colours, fruity and floral aromas, honey flavours and rich in alcohol content. *Muffato* is not unlike the world famous *Tokaji Asszú*, but the grape varieties used in Hungary are different. The climatic conditions on the hillsides of *Tokaj* are similar to that of Orvieto. In Umbria, there are only half a dozen wineries making *muffati* wines, and they produce less than 500 hectolitres per annum between them. The grape varieties used are *Sauvignon Blanc, Semillon, Riesling* and *Grechetto*. The must obtained is fermented for a long period (sometimes for years) and refined in *barriques*. The bottles usually contain 500ml.

Vino Santo or **Vinsanto** is a sweet white wine made in Umbria since the Middle Ages. First, it was used by monks in their services; today it is a wine for family celebrations. The grapes used are mostly *Trebbiano, Malvasia, Moscato, Grechetto* and *Pecorino* because of their high sugar content. After the grapes are picked, they are laid out on interwoven cane frames for three months to dry out and thus increase the sugar content. The fermentation and refinement takes place in special kegs (*caratelli*) for over three years. The wine has an intense aroma of dried fruit and honey. The flavour is sweet, full bodied and light; and the colour is usually golden, almost amber.

White *Passito* wines are also produced using similar methods as for *Sagrantino Passito*. In some vineyards the grapes are left on the vine for drying before harvesting. The grape varieties are *Malvasia, Grechetto* and *Moscato,* producing a sweet wine, with high alcoholic content. They are well matched with desserts.

Spumante is the sparkling wine of Italy, often produced using the classical French method Champenoise. The sparkling bubbles are made by the carbon dioxide left in the wine. Normally, this gas escapes during the fermentation process. Any number of grape varieties are used, though *Pinot Nero* is the most popular, as well as *Chardonnay*. There are a number of ways of keeping the carbon dioxide in the must and the subsequent wine. It is best to keep the fermentation and maturation process in the bottle, but this is labour intensive and, thus, costly. Alternatively, the hand picked grapes have a first slow fermentation in hermetically sealed stainless steel vats for two weeks at 15 C°, followed by a second fermentation in the bottle, which can last anything from three months onwards. However, each winemaker has his preferred way of producing his own distinctive *Spumante,* white or rosé.

Rosé wines (*vino rosato*) are made using the normal vinification process, but the maceration lasts only for a few hours when using red grapes. A mixture of red and white grapes can be used, but mixing red wine with white does not produce *vino rosato*. When using white grapes a certain amount of must pressed from red grapes is added until the desired colour is achieved, then the fermentation process follows as usual.

Grappa is a distilled spirit. Spirits can be made from anything from sugar cane to fruit, grains and even potatoes, and its production does not really belong to this guide about wines. However, most wine producers also make their own *grappa* and olive oil, hence, it deserves a mention. The large estates have always produced wine, *grappa* and olive oil, and this is the case today. In the distant past, grapevines were trained up the trunks of olive trees. It is a tradition. Olive groves and vineyards sit happily together in the Umbrian landscape.

The finest *grappas* are distilled from the finest wines, but not always. There are other factors to be taken into consideration. The origin of the fermented liquid is the most obvious, but some excellent *grappas* are made from indifferent wines. The degree and manner of distillation is equally important, like the skills of the distiller. Then, there is the maturation process: the casks, the humidity of the cellar they are kept in, and the length of time. Some of the best are forty years old before they are sold.

Grappa is just another word for brandy. The word is the anglicised form of the Dutch *Brandtjwyn* – meaning burnt wine. As the boiling point of alcohol is lower than that of water, the distillation process is a simple one: heat wine until the alcohol vapour escapes, and then collect it. Traditionally, spirits were distilled in pot stills made of copper. The flat bottom of the pot was heated and the vapours escaped through a long tapering neck attached to a spiral tube or condenser; the alembic *Charantais* system for making cognac. It is still used in Umbria, but today there are more modern and efficient ways of distilling, and each wine producer chooses the method best suited to his needs. A discontinuous distillation process is often used, powered by vapour stimulated copper elements. There is also a continuous method and some *grappas* are distilled twice. The period of maturation in casks, barriques or whatever, can be anything from a couple of months to thirty years. Take your choice.

AREAS OF DOC AND DOCG WINES

In the province of Perugia:

Assisi DOC. A number of vineyards in the low hill areas in the vicinity of Assisi, Perugia and Spello, ranging from 180 to 550 metres above sea level. The wines produced are *Bianco, Grechetto, Rosso, Rosato* and *Novello*. The main basis for red wine is the traditional *Sangiovese* grape, with some *Merlot* added.

Colli Altotiberini DOC. The hills by the banks of the upper Tiber including the districts of Citerna, Cittá di Castello, Gubbio, Monte Santa Maria Tiberina, Perugia, San Giustino and Umbertide. The wines produced are *Bianco* with *Trebbiano Toscano, Malvasia del Chianti* and an addition of three other white grapes from the local area. The wines are straw yellow in colour, with a dry aromatic bouquet and a minimum alcoholic content of 10.5%. *Rosso* and *Rosato* from *Sangiovese, Merlot, Trebbiano Toscano* and *Malvasia del Chianti* grapes. Other red vines from the area can also be used. The wines produced are intense ruby-red in colour, with a dry and rounded note, and a minimum alcoholic content of 11.5%.

Colli del Trasimeno or *Trasimeno* DOC. The hills surrounding Lake Trasimeno, including the districts of Perugia, Castiglione del Lago, Cittá della Pieve, Paciano, Panicale, Corciano, Magione, Passignano sul Trasimeno, and Tuoro sul Trasimeno. The red, white and rosé wines produced are *Bianco, Bianco Scelto, Cabernet Sauvignon, Gamay, Grechetto, Merlot, Rosato, Rosso, Rosso Scelto, Spumante Classico* and *Vino Santo* or *Vinsanto*. The main basis for red wine is *Sangiovese* grapes, but also used are *Gamay, Cabernet Sauvignon, Ciliegiolo* and *Merlot*. For white wines the basis is *Trebbiano* and *Grechetto* grapes, but also *Chardonnay, Pinot Bianco* and *Pinot Grigio*.

Colli Martani DOC. The zone including the towns of Perugia, Gualdo Catteneo, Giano dell'Umbria, Todi, Massa Martana, Monte Castello di Vibio, Montefalco, Castel Ritaldi, Spoleto, Bevagna, Cannara, Bettona, Deruta and Collazione. The main basis for red wines is *Sangiovese* grapes, but also *Canaiolo, Barbera, Montepulciano, Ciliegiolo* and *Merlot*. For white wines *Trebbiano, Grechetto, Malvasia bianca di Candia, Malvesia bianca del Chianti, Garganeca* and *Verdicchio*.

Colli Perugini DOC. The area in the *comuni* of Deruta, Marsciano, Fratta Todina, Monte Castello di Vibio, Piegaro and Perugia; plus San Venanzo in the province of Terni. The red, white, and rosé wines produced are *Bianco, Cabernet Sauvignon, Chardonnay, Grechetto, Merlot, Novello, Pinto Grigio, Rosato, Rosso, Sangiovese, Spumante, Trebbiano* and *Vino Santo* or *Vinsanto*. The main basis for red wines is *Sangiovese* grapes, but also *Canaiolo, Pinot Nero, Barbera, Montepulciano, Ciliegiolo* and *Merlot*. For white wines *Trebbiano, Grechetto* and *Malvasia*.

Montefalco DOC. The town of Montefalco itself and the surrounding hillsides; the districts of Gualdo Catteneo, Giano dell'Umbria, Castel Ritaldi and a part of Bevagna. The wines produced are *Montefalco Rosso* and *Montefalco Bianco*. The main basis for red wine is the *Sangiovese* and *Sagrantino* grapes. For white wine *Trebbiano* and *Grechetto* grapes.

Montefalco Sagrantino DOCG *Secco*. Made entirely from *Sagrantino* grapes. The wine displays an intense ruby-red colour. The taste is dry and harmonious with a delicate aroma reminiscent of oak. The minimum alcohol content is 13% and the wine has to be aged for at least 30 months.

Montefalco Sagrantino DOCG *Passito.* Made entirely from partially dried *Sagrantino* grapes. Similar in characteristics to the *secco*, but its minimum alcohol content is 14.5%. An ideal dessert wine.

Torgiano DOC. The district surrounding the town of Torgiano. The wines produced are *Bianco di Torgiano, Rosso di Torgiano, Rosato di Torgiano, Chardonnay di Torgiano, Pinot Grigio di Torgiano, Riesling Italico di Torgiano, Cabernet Sauvignon di Torgiano, Pinot Nero di Torgiano and Torgiano Spumante*. The red wines are made from *Sangiovese, Canaiolo, Trebbiano, Ciliegiolo* and *Montepulciano* grapes. The white wines from *Trebbiano, Grechetto, Malvasia* and *Verdello* grapes.

Torgiano Rosso Riserva DOCG. Has a higher alcoholic content than the *Rosso* DOC – minimum 12.5%. The wine is produced from the traditional *Sangiovese* and *Canaiolo* grapes blended with *Trebbiano Toscano, Ciliegiolo* and *Montepulciano* – maximum 10%. The wine has a transparent ruby colour; it is delicately dry with a rounded, good body. It has to be aged for at least 3 years.

In the province of Terni:

Colli Amerini DOC. The production area is situated in the hills overlooking the middle reaches of the rivers Tiber and Nera; and include the towns of Amelia, Narni, Calvi, Otricoli, Alviano, Lugano, Penna in Teverina, Giove and a part of Terni. The wines produced are *Bianco, Rosso, Rosato, Novello* and *Malvasia*. The red wines are made from *Sangiovese, Aleatico, Barbera, Sagrantino, Canaiolo, Merlot, Ciliegiolo, Cabernet Sauvignon, Syrah*, and *Montepulciano* grapes. The white wines from *Trebbiano, Riesling, Pinot Grigio, Grechetto, Malvasia, Verdello, Drupeggio, Garganega, Chardonnay* and *Moscato*.

Lago di Corbara DOC. The hills surrounding Lake Corbara, including the districts of Baschi, Corbara and Orvieto. The red wines have been granted DOC status in 1995; they are *Rosso, Cabernet Sauvignon, Merlot* and *Pinot Nero;* and they have to be made from at least 85% of the named variety. The additional grapes allowed are *Aleatico, Barbera, Cabernet Franc, Canaiolo, Cesanese, Ciliegiolo, Colorino, Dolcetto* and *Montepulciano*.

Orvieto DOC. The ancient white wine, known since antiquity and beloved by popes and princes around Europe, is still produced in all the 13 *comuni* in the province of Terni, plus 5 *comuni* in the province of Viterbo in Lazio. The production area includes Orvieto, Allerona, Alviano, Baschi, Castel Giorgio, Castel Viscardo, Ficulle, Guardea, Montecchio, Fabro, Montegabbione, Monteleone d'Orvieto, Porano, Castiglione in Teverina, Civitella d'Agliano, Graffignano, Lubriano and Bagnoregio. The wines produced are *Orvieto Bianco, Orvieto Classico* and *Orvieto Classico Superiore.* The grapes used are *Procanico or Trebbiano* (65%), *Verdello* (from 15% to 25%), *Grechetto, Drupeggio, Malvasia Toscana* (from 20% to 30%, but with no more than 20% of *Malvasia*). Not more than 110 quintals per hectare of grapes are allowed to be grown. The wines are dry (*secco*), medium dry, (*abboccato*), medium sweet (*amabile*) and sweet (*dolce*). Today dry wines are more popular, but in the past the sweeter varieties were preferred. There has been a general tendency all around the world for drinking dry wines. All Orvieto whites have a characteristic straw yellow colour with a soft, fruity bouquet, dry on the palate with a slightly bitter aftertaste. The denomination *Orvieto Classico* can only be used for grapes grown in the oldest vineyards around the tufa cliff of the city. In *Orvieto Classico Superiore* the yield is reduced from 110 quintals per hectare to 80. The alcoholic content should be at least 12%.

Late vintage types are restricted to DOC *Orvieto* and *Orvieto Classico*. Production of these wines is reduced to 70 quintals per hectare, and harvesting is not permitted before 1st October. The alcoholic content should be 13%. They are sweet dessert wines.

Muffato is also produced in the *Orvieto* DOC area, but only a handful of vineyards posses the climatic conditions required for *botrytis cinerea*, the mould that reduces the sugar content of the late picked grapes. The areas are limited for the production of this type of wine in Europe; examples are the Sauternes of Bordeaux, the Rhine Valley, and the Hungarian Tokay.

Orvieto is one of the best-known white wines around the world and, today, it alone represents 75% of Umbrian DOC wines. Each year over twenty million bottles are marketed in Italy and abroad.

Rosso Orvietano or *Orvietano Rosso* DOC. The production area includes Orvieto, Allerona, Alviano, Baschi, Castel Giorgio, Castel Viscardo, Ficulle, Guardea, Montecchio, Fabro, Montegabbione, Monteleone d'Orvieto, Porano and San Venzano. The wines produced always name the grape variety; thus *Rosso Ovietano Aleatico, Rosso Ovietano Cabernet, Rosso Ovietano Canaiolo, Rosso Ovietano Ciliegiolo, Rosso Ovietano Merlot, Rosso Ovietano Pinot Nero,* and Rosso *Ovietano Sangiovese*. Naturally, they all carry the characteristics of their grape, but all *Orvietano Rosso* wines age well and they are recommended to be kept for at least four years before consumption.

THE WINE PRODUCERS
An introduction

Vineyards in Umbria range from large estates, where wine is just one of many other agricultural products, to small family concerns with only a few hectares of vines planted, sometimes producing only a single type of wine. What they all have in common is a passion for winemaking and a desire to produce the best with an affordable price tag.

I spent four months visiting the wineries during 2011; I only include the places that I have seen. The technical details are taken from the producers' brochures. I have no preferences; my aim is simply to pass on the information.

Some of the wineries are easy to access (and to find); others are not. Some sell directly to the public, others have points of sale in the major towns, or sell only to the wine trade.

The people I met were friendly and hospitable. Their love for making wines was abundantly clear, and I strongly recommend visiting the wineries. Please telephone to make an appointment, as on some days there may be nobody there to meet you.

The first port of call for any serious wine lover should be the Regional Wine Cellar of Umbria. It is located in the former Convent of San Giovanni in Orvieto, once home to the Lateran canons (long before that it was a temple dedicated to Jupiter, and then later, a Roman theatre).

Il Palazzo del Gusto - L'Enoteca Regionale dell'Umbria
Via Ripa Serancia 1, 16 – 05018 Orvieto TR
Tel: 0763 341818 – 0763 393529
Fax: 0763 394 455
info@ilpalazzodelgusto.it
www.ilpalazzodelgusto.it

The *Enoteca* is a centre for locally produced food and wines. The labyrinth of underground caves has been completely restored, including a typical Etruscan cellar on three levels; the method of wine production of pre-Roman times. There are lots of books and leaflets and a permanent display of wine related activities. There are maps showing the *Strada dei Vini Etrusco-Romana* in the province of Terni, the wine road connecting the wine cellars in the region from Orvieto to Amelia and Terni. An association was formed in 2001 (to comply with law 38). Its principal aim is promoting Umbrian agricultural (viticulture in particular) products in Italy and abroad.

In the *Enoteca* a selection of the best quality Umbrian wines can also be tasted and purchased; more than 120 different bottles are on display with a touch screen system providing technical details. There are regular guided tours of wine and food tasting and seminars are arranged for larger groups. The *Enoteca* is an ideal place to experience a taste of Umbria.

The Wine Museum of Torgiano is another good place to visit, particularly for people based in Perugia or Assisi. Torgiano is only a short car journey from either place. The museum is run by *Fondazione Lungarotti;* opened in 1974. (There is more of the Lungarotti family in the later chapter on Torgiano wines). The museum provides a comprehensive history of wine making since Etruscan times to the present, with hundreds of artefacts exhibited inside the recently restored *Palazzo Graziani-Baglioni*, a noble summer residence dating from the seventeenth century. The collection is arranged in twenty rooms, showing different aspects of history, culture and commerce related to the art of winemaking. Naturally, the focus of attention is on Torgiano and Perugia, but a wider view of Umbria is not neglected. Also in Torgiano there is an Olive Oil Museum, and the *Cantine Giorgio Lungarotti* (of which there is a great deal more later).

THE WINE PRODUCERS
ORVIETO

Three quarters of the wines exported from Umbria are Orvieto Classico DOC. The starting point in history of winemaking also happens to be Orvieto, or the ancient *Velzna* (the Etruscan name for the town). When the Etruscans arrived in central Italy they found the bluff of tufa above the floodplains of the river *Paglia* the ideal location for a new settlement. Another name for *Velzna* was *Oinarea* (the city where wine flows); evidently, the production of wine began as early as the foundation of the town.

Tufa was the ideal material for digging caves, wells and a system of underground tunnels. Etruscan wine production was carried out on three levels: the grapes were crushed on the ground floor and the juice trickled down to a lower cave through terra cotta pipes. There, it fermented until it was drawn off from the vats and transferred to the deepest level, suited for ageing and conservation. In small oak barrels, the wine was kept in the caves at least for a year, sometimes longer. The low and constant temperature kept the wine in a state of continuous and very slow fermentation. This system has not changed right up to the twentieth century.

In 1931 Giorgio Garavini, the chief inspector of the Ministry of Agriculture and Forestry, stated that the typical Orvieto wine was the *abboccato* (medium dry, but probably sweet to most palates). According to Garavini, the wine had a pleasing sweetness, the aroma of fresh grapes, a golden yellow colour, and it was slightly sparkling with an alcoholic content of 11.5% and 12%. The Orvieto white was an unstable wine, and before it could be sold, the fermentation process had to be completed. This not only got rid of the carbon dioxide, but it also reduced the sugar content and, thus, it became a dry white wine with a higher alcoholic content. Stable or unstable, Orvieto white wine was sent to Rome since the Middle Ages.

During a period of constant political upheavals a number of popes took up residence in Orvieto. They sent regular supplies of the famous wine to their friends in Rome. Hence, Orvieto white was commonly known as popes' wine. With a number of visitors to the town who sampled the wine of old, its fame spread around the world and it was likened to a port or a sauterne.

Orvieto wine was also considered to be a magical elixir, a cure for all ailments. During the seventeenth century *Orvietan* or *Orvietano* was the name of the medicine widely sold around Europe by a host of unscrupulous profiteers. *Marchand d'Orviatan* (a merchant of Orvieto) was the French expression used to describe a charlatan or a quack. Genoramo Ferrante of Ficulle invented the formula, which was kept a secret. Initially there were 54 ingredients, most probably including honey and perhaps even opium. Later the number was reduced to 26, what they all were, is still a mystery today. Suffice to say that the *Orvietan* was dense, sweet and highly aromatic. Before he died, Genoramo Ferrante gave the secret recipe to his son, Gregorio, and his wife, Clarice Peranda. She later married an actor, Cristoforo Contugi, who marketed the medicine to the French aristocracy. In 1647 King Louis XIV was so impressed with the curative qualities of the elixir that he granted a patent for the exclusive marketing rights of *Orvietan* to the Contugi family. The magic potion was popular and widely marketed until the end of the eighteenth century.

Orvieto wine was appreciated by the Etruscans, who sent trading expeditions to northern Europe. When under Roman control, the wine was shipped to Rome via the port of *Palianum*, situated at the confluence of the rivers *Paglia* and *Tevere*. During the Middle Ages production continued, as it brought wealth to the city. Documents attest to the importance of this commercial activity dating back to 1295, which protected laws governing wine production. The Consuls appointed guardians, who controlled the vineyards, the production and the work on the farm throughout the year. The Colletta Statutes of 1334 set out punishments for those who passed off inferior wine as the genuine product. Measures of selling wine also had to carry the municipal seal. There were even laws to prevent drunkenness. Right up to present days every aspect of wine production has been strictly controlled by the Commune of Orvieto.

Argillae s.r.l. – Azienda Agricola

Voc. Pomarro, 45,
05011 Allerona TR
Tel: 0763 624604
Cell: 337 596358
Fax: 0763 629800

The Argillae estate covers an area of 258 hectares between the hills of Allerona and Ficulle, north-west of Orvieto. 70 hectares are dedicated to the growing of grapes. The vines are planted on clay and sand, *calanchi,* on the hillsides with excellent exposure and a microclimate conducive to the production of quality wines. The winery has installed the most modern, state-of-the-art equipment. Four types of wine are produced.

Orvieto DOC.

Grapes: Procanico, Grechetto, Malvasia di Candia, Chardonnay and Sauvignon Blanc.
Colour: straw yellow.
Fragrance: broad, floral scents of yellow flowers with a hint of citrus and tropical fruits.
Taste: it has a broad, complex, fruity and enduring taste with a refreshing finish.
Vinification: The grapes are pressed delicately and the resulting juice is racked and vinified at controlled temperature.
Qualification: dry white wine.
Food pairings: combines perfectly with pasta dishes made with vegetables, or fish, or white meats.
Serving temperature: 10-12 C°.

Grechetto Umbria IGT Bianco.

Grapes: Grechetto 100%.
Colour: dark straw yellow.
Fragrance and Taste: intense and direct with an almond and mineral flavour.

Vinification: The grapes are selected in the vineyard, submitted to a brief cold maceration. After pressing the juice is racked and vinified at controlled temperature, and fined on the lees.
Qualification: dry white wine.
Food pairings: best for regional cuisine; pasta, and second courses, and challenging fish and shellfish dishes.
Serving temperature: 12-14 C°.

Panata Umbria IGT Bianco.

Grapes: Chardonnay 100%.
Colour: dark straw yellow.
Fragrance and Taste: intense, citrus, fruity and tropical notes; complex structure and a gentle aftertaste.
Vinification: The grapes are selected in the vineyard, submitted to a brief cold maceration process in a closed press and pressed delicately. The must is vinified at controlled temperature in French oak barriques, both new and used. Fined on the lees.
Qualification: dry white wine.
Food pairings: white meats or fish in general.
Serving temperature: 10-12 C°.

Sinuoso Umbria IGT Rosso.

Grapes: Cabernet Sauvignon and Merlot.
Colour: dark, ruby red with a tinge of purple.
Fragrance: broad, enduring and intense with red berries (maraschino cherry and red currants).
Taste: dry, salty, warm, well structured; and with a long finish.
Vinification: 8-10 days maceration, with regular periodical pumping over of must on pomace. The alcoholic and malolactic fermentation in entirely carried out in stainless steel tanks. The wine is subsequently fined for several months and is periodically racked with the addition of oxygen. After bottling, it is submitted to a short bottle maturation process for a further 3-4 months before consumption.
Qualification: dry red wine.
Food pairings: regional dishes; especially game and venison.
Serving temperature: 16-18 C°.

Bigi Cantina

Loc: Ponte Giulio, 05018 Orvieto TR
Tel: 0763 315888 or 0763 316291
Fax: 0763 316376 or 0763 316226
bigi@giv.it
www.giv.it

The Luigi Bigi Winery (*La Casa Vinicola Luigi Bigi*) was established in 1880. For years Bigi has been considered to be one of the most prestigious producers of Orvieto Classico, thanks to the skilful work of its winemakers, its century's old experience and the avant-garde technology it adopted. Lately, the company has widened its range of classic white wines to include a selection of very interesting reds.

Orvieto Classico Secco DOC.

Grapes: 45% Trebbiano Toscano (Procanico), 20% Verdello, 15% Grechetto, 10% Malvasia Toscana; 10% Drupeggio.
Vineyard: selected hilly vineyards in the Classic DOC zone at 300 metres altitude facing south-west; the vines are trained by spurred cordon and Guyot systems on thin, clayey soil; the yield is 70 hectolitres per hectare.
Vinification: alcoholic fermentation and ageing in stainless steel.
Wine: pale yellow colour; fine bouquet with fresh fragrance of hawthorn blossom and traces of musk and almond; dry, full, soft but lively flavour with an attractively distinctive aftertaste of white peaches and almonds.
Alcohol: 12.50% vol.
Optimum keeping: 1-2 years in bottles stored horizontally in cool, dark conditions.
Food matches: hors d'oeuvres, fish, shellfish, eggs; young cheeses.
Serving temperature: 10-12 C°.

Orvieto Classico Amabile DOC.

Grapes: 50% Trebbiano Toscano (Procanico); 20% Verdello; 20% Malvasia Toscana, 5% Grechetto; 5% Drupeggio.
Vineyard: selected hilly vineyards in the Classic DOC zone at 300 metres altitude facing south-west; the vines are trained by the spurred cordon and Guyot systems on thin, clayey soil; the yield of wine is 70 hectolitres per hectare.
Vinification: the alcoholic fermentation in stainless steel tanks is stopped when there is still quite a lot of residual sugar left; ageing in stainless steel tanks.
Wine: clear, bright, golden yellow colour; strong bouquet of wild flowers, honey and musk with a hint of bitter almonds; sweet, soft but fresh and lively, with an aftertaste of ripe fruit.
Alcohol: 12% vol.
Optimum keeping: 1-2 years in bottles stored horizontally in cool, dark conditions.
Food matches: biscuits, fruit tarts, fresh fruit without too much acidity (strawberries, peaches, pears) and also shellfish and fish in sauce, spicy cheeses.
Serving temperature: 10 C°.

Vigneto Torricella Orvieto Classico Secco DOC.

Grapes: 40% Trebbiano Toscano, 20% Verdello, 20% Grechetto, 10% Malvasia Toscana, 10% Drupeggio.
Vineyard: 24 hectares in the locality of Torricella on the hills at 300 metres altitude. The vines are trained by the spurred cordon and Guyot systems on clayey soil well exposed to the south-west; 80 quintals of grapes per hectare, with a yield of 70% wine.
Vinification: picked in the second half of October, according to the ripening cycles of the different varieties. De-stemmed and vinified by the white wine method, with a gentle pressing. The young must is clarified by cold settling, then fermented at 15 to 16 C° for three weeks, with selected yeasts. The wine is aged in temperature controlled stainless steel tanks until the end of March, when it is cold, sterile bottled.
Wine: bright, straw colour; distinctive bouquet of broom flowers and lemon blossom, with softer hints of musk and exotic fruits;

dry very savoury, fresh and balanced flavour with a pleasant, lingering aftertaste of pears and bitter almonds.
Alcohol: 12.80% vol.
Optimum keeping: within 2 to 3 years of the vintage in bottles stored horizontally in cool, dark conditions.
Food matches: hors d'oeuvres, savoury first courses, fish and cold white meats.
Serving temperature: 12-14 C°.

Grechetto Umbria IGT (Grechetto dell'Umbria IGT).

Grapes: 100% Grechetto.
Vineyard: the most acclaimed parcels in the neighbourhood of Orvieto on hilly ground at 250 metres altitude; the vines trained by the spurred cordon and Guyot systems on clayey-stony soil; the yield of wine is 56 hectolitres per hectare.
Vinification: the alcoholic fermentation and ageing for 4-5 months in stainless steel tanks.
Wine: pale straw yellow; with a bouquet of white flowers (cherry and almond) and a hint of musk and dried apricots; velvety flavour, and a slightly bitter aftertaste of peach kernels.
Alcohol: 12.50% vol.
Optimum keeping: 2 years in bottles stored horizontally in cool, dark conditions.
Food matches: hors d'oeuvres, first courses, white meats, fish dishes, young cheeses.
Serving temperature: 12 C°.
Launch vintage: 1992.

Strozzavolpe Grechetto dell'Umbria IGT.

Grapes: 100% Grechetto.
Vineyard: selected parcels in the neighbourhood of Orvieto on hilly ground at 300 metres altitude facing south-west; the vines, planted with a density of 4.500 plants per hectare, are trained by the spurred cordon and Guyot systems on clayey-stony soil; the yield of wine is 56 hectolitres per hectare.
Vinification: the alcoholic fermentation and ageing 5 months in stainless steel tanks.

Wine: bright, pale yellow colour with golden tints; fine and elegant bouquet with a marked fragrance of exotic fruits and apricots; well-balanced, fresh, velvety flavour with a clean and pleasant, slightly bitter aftertaste of peach kernels.
Alcohol: 12.50% vol.
Optimum keeping: 1-2 years in bottles stored horizontally in cool, dark conditions.
Food matches: aperitif, hors d'oeuvres, first courses, fish, white meats, young cheeses.
Serving temperature: 11 C° as an aperitif, 13 C° with food.
Launch vintage: 2006

Sangiovese Umbria IGT.

Grapes: 100% Sangiovese.
Vineyard: selected vineyards in the hilly zone (from 200-400 metres altitude) in the neighbourhood of Orvieto, trained by the Guyot and spurred cordon systems on clayey soil; the yield of grapes is 80 quintals per hectare.
Vinification: the fully ripe grapes are harvested between the end of September and the beginning of October and are vinified by the red wine method with about ten days maceration and frequent pumping of the must over the cap. The fermentation takes place at 25-26 C° and the new wine rests in temperature regulated steel tanks until bottling.
Wine: ruby red; a bouquet of ripe grapes; hints of violets and black cherries; the flavour is full, clean and savoury, soft but firm and attractively fruity. It is a particularly well-balanced wine.
Alcohol: 12.80% vol.
Optimum keeping: within 2 years of the vintage in bottles stored horizontally in cool, dark conditions.
Food matches: savoury dishes, cured pork and white meats.
Serving temperature: 18 C°.

Sartiano Rosso dell'Umbria IGT.

Grapes: 80% Sangiovese, 15% Merlot, 5% Pinot Nero.
Vineyard: about fifteen years old in the Corbara zone at 300 metres altitude facing south-west, planted with a density of 4.500

plants per hectare on poor, pebbly soil, trained in the spurred cordon and Guyot systems and produces about 70 quintals per hectare, with a yield of 65% wine.

Vinification: the grapes, picked during September, are separately vinified by the red wine method, with a fermentation of about 10 days in contact with the skins at a temperature of 25-26 C° and frequent remontages. After racking and malolactic fermentation, the wine is put into French barriques where it stays for about 12 months; followed by several months of ageing in the bottle.

Wine: deep ruby red colour; a rich bouquet with marked notes of black fruits, black cherries, cinnamon and liquorice with a lingering, spicy aftertaste.

Alcohol: 13.50% vol.

Optimum keeping: 4-5 years in bottles stored horizontally in cool, dark conditions.

Food matches: roast or grilled meats, kid, mature cheeses.

Serving temperature: 16-18 C°.

Launch vintage: 2001.

Vipra Rossa Umbria IGT.

Grapes: 70% Merlot, 20% Sangiovese, 10% Montepulciano.

Vineyard: selected hilly vineyards in the Orvieto zone and neighbouring communes at 300 metres altitude facing south-west; the vines, planted with a density of 5.000 plants per hectare on poor, pebbly soil, are trained by the Guyot and spurred cordon systems; the yield of wine is 70 hectolitres per hectare.

Vinification: alcoholic and malolactic fermentation in stainless steel. Part of the wine is aged separately by variety, in French oak barriques for a minimum of 8 to a maximum of 12 months.

Wine: deep ruby red colour; rich bouquet with marked notes of blackberry and spicy aromas; balanced palate and good structure.

Alcohol: 13% vol.

Optimum keeping: 2-3 years in bottles stored horizontally in cool, dark conditions.

Food matches: roast or grilled meats, kid, mature cheeses.

Serving temperature: 16-18 C°.

Launch vintage: 2002

Vipra Rosa Montepulciano d'Abruzzo Cerasuolo DOC.

Grapes: 100% Montepulciano.
Vineyard: selected hilly vineyards in the DOC zone at 250 metres altitude; the vines, with a density of 2.500 plants per hectare; are trained by the Guyot system on sandy-clayey soil.
Vinification: by the white wine method with a short maceration of the skins in the must; the alcoholic fermentation and ageing in stainless steel tanks.
Wine: coral pink colour tending towards pale vermilion, fresh and fragrant bouquet, soft and balanced flavour, with fruity, cherry tones and floral hints of roses and violets.
Alcohol: 13% vol.
Optimum keeping: 1-2 years in bottles stored horizontally in cool, dark conditions.
Food matches: hors d'oeuvres, pasta, pizza, white meats and young cheeses.
Serving temperature: 12-14 C°.
Launch vintage: 2007.

Vipra Bianca Bianco dell'Umbria IGT.

Grapes: 60% Grechetto, 40% Chardonnay.
Vineyard: hills in the Orvieto zone and neighbouring communes at 300 metres, facing south-west, with a density of 4.500 plants per hectare. Trained by the Guyot and spurred cordon systems on thin, light soil. The yield is 56 hectolitres per hectare.
Vinification: the alcoholic fermentation in stainless steel tanks at 14-16 C° with selected yeasts for about 3 weeks; ageing for several months in stainless steel tanks.
Wine: bright, pale yellow colour with green tints; fine bouquet with hints of fresh almonds and acacia and citrus notes; rich, savoury, fresh, elegantly balanced flavour with a subtle softness.
Alcohol: 12.50% vol.
Optimum keeping: 1-2 years in bottles stored horizontally in cool, dark conditions.
Food matches: hors d'oeuvres, fish, white meats, young cheeses.
Serving temperature: 12 C°.
Launch vintage: 2006.

Vino Nobile di Montepulciano DOCG.

Probably Tuscany's most famous and expensive wine.
Grapes: 70% Prugnolo Gentile (Sangiovese Grosso), 20% Canaiolo Nero, 10% other varieties (Mammolo, Pulcinculo, Trebbiano, Malvasia).
Vineyard: selected vineyards on the hills of Montepulciano at 350-400 metres altitude; the vines are trained by the simple and double Guyot systems on soil of Pliocene origin, with clay and marl; the yield of wine is 52 hectolitres per hectare.
Vinification: maceration of the skins in the must for about 20 days; the alcoholic fermentation in stainless steel; ageing for two years in French oak casks and then for at least 6 months in bottle.
Wine: ruby red colour with bright garnet tints; intense and complex bouquet of exceptional finesse, with strong notes of dried plums, cloves and cinnamon and hints of violets and irises; dry, full, savoury and pleasantly tannic flavour, with a lingering aftertaste of plum preserve and toasted almonds.
Alcohol: 13% vol.
Optimum keeping: 7-8 years in bottles stored horizontally in cool, dark conditions.
Food matches: roast and grilled meats, kid and mature cheeses.
Serving temperature: 18-20 C°.

Est! Est!! Est!!! di Montefiascone DOC.

A wine from Lazio. In 1100 AD, the Bavarian bishop, Johann Defuk had to visit Italy to settle a controversy with Pope Pasquale II. He sent on ahead his steward, Martino, who had to indicate with the Latin word EST (is) the inns where one could drink the best wines. At Montefiascone, near Lake Bolsena, Martino wrote Est three times to emphasise the high quality of the local wine. The bishop enjoyed the wine so much that, at the end of the mission, he went back to Montefiascone and remained there until he died. Johann Defuk was buried in the temple of San Flaviano at Montefiascone; and, for a long time, it was the custom to pour a barrel of wine over his tomb. The annual production of Est! Est!! Est!! is 500.000 bottles.

Grapes: 65% Trebbiano Toscano (Procanico); 20% Malvasia Bianca Toscana; 15% Rossetto (Trebbiano Giallo).

Vineyard: vineyards in the DOC zone around Montefiascone, near Lake Bolsena, on hills of volcanic origin at between 250 and 350 metres altitude. The vines are trained by the Spalleria, Spurred Cordon and Palmetta systems on soils of loose or medium texture, without much structure, and with plenty of potassium and phosphoric carbon; the yield of grapes is 120 quintals per hectare, with an output of wine of 70%.

Vinification: the well-ripened grapes are harvested between the end of September and the beginning of October. After gentle pressing and a cold, natural clarification, the must ferments slowly at a controlled temperature (15-17 C°), with the addition of selected yeasts, which enhance the varietal aromas. The new wine rests in temperature regulated stainless steel tanks until March, when it is cold, sterile bottled.

Wine: bright, pale, yellow colour; generous distinctive bouquet, with a fresh fragrance of musk, hawthorn blossom and hints of ripe apples; dry soft, balanced flavour with elegant, lingering aftertaste of plums and bitter almonds.

Alcohol: 12% vol.

Optimum keeping: 1-2 years in bottles stored horizontally in cool, dark conditions.

Food matches: first courses, fish, egg based dishes.

Serving temperature: 10-12 C°

Cantina Cardeto.

Loc. Cardeto.
Fraz. Sferracavallo, 05010
Orvieto TR
Tel: 0763 341286 or 0763 343189
Fax: 0763 344123
www.cardeto.com
Point of sale:
Orvieto Scalo
Via A Constanzi, 51
Tel/Fax: 0763 300594

The wine growing and wine producing co-operative for the area of Orvieto (CO.VI.O) was founded in 1949 and initially it was located in Orvieto Scalo. The construction of the new wine co-operative of Cardeto started in 1990 and finished in 2004 with the building of the temperature controlled warehouse. In 2005 its name changed to Cantina Cardeto. The name derives from the area where cardoon (a type of globe artichoke) was grown in the past, which is the location of the new warehouse and offices.

The Cantina Cardeto has 1.200 hectares of vineyards. Almost all of them in the DOC Orvieto Classico and DOC Orvieto zones. Around 160 hectares are dedicated to the production of red grape varieties (Sangiovese, Merlot, Pinot, etc).

Cardeto uses a new low-pressure air press for the production of its wines, which extracts the juice from the grape leaving the skins intact. The technique of fermentation imitates ancient methods. Double stainless steel tanks are used with a gap between the layers, through which coolant liquid is circulated keeping a constant temperature of 14-16 C°. At this temperature the yeasts of the grapes pass on fragrances and aromas that would be killed off at a higher temperature (30/40 C° for example). The wine is stabilised with refrigeration and sterile filtering with a little addition of sulphur dioxide, followed by maturation in the bottle for two months. The co-operative has over 400 partners who have been producing wine for many generations. 700.000 bottles are sold with the Cardeto label each year. The wines are marketed in four separate lines. The names chosen for each line are as follows:

Linea Matile
Linea Torre del Moro
Linea Capitano del Popolo
Linea Araldica.

Linea Matile:

The name Matile is of medieval origin, or perhaps Etruscan. It is the way people of Orvieto describe a terrain consisting of sand from various sources, both volcanic and marine. The soil has a number of characteristics in common:
  Light, pale yellow straw colour
  An ability to reflect light, even moon light
  Compactness before ploughed
  Loose and porous after hoeing
  Poor water retention, but moist deep down

The white wines produced from grapes grown there have a fresh taste with mineral hints and an aroma of white peaches. The red wines are perhaps a little light in body, but excel in colour, with elegant fruity aromas and a hint of minerals.

Linea Matile Bianco IGT Umbria.

Grapes: Trebbiano 40%, Drupeggio 10%, Verdello 15%, and Chardonnay 15%.
Zone of production: Orvieto.
Size of vineyard: 10 Ha.
Altitude of vineyards: 300 meters above sea level.
Terrain: volcanic and sedimentary.
System of training: spurred cordon.
Density of vines: Traditionally 3.00x1.50 metres.
Production per Ha: 110 quintals.
Yield of wine: 77 hectolitre.
Medium age of vines: 20 years, newly planted vines 5 years.
Time of harvest: From the end of September until 10th October, with careful selection of the grapes.

Vinification: soft pressing of the whole grapes in a closed press and then the immediate separation of the skins, followed by cold settling for clearing the must.
Alcoholic fermentation: Controlled temperature (Maximum 15 C°), followed by filtered clarification.
Ageing: 60 days in bottles.
Alcohol: 12 % vol.
Acidity: 5.8 g/l.
pH: 3.49 g/l.
Dry extract: 21.8 g/l.
Colour: Pale straw.
Fragrance: Fine, characterised by rich notes of pears and honey.
Taste: Elegant fruit notes.
Food pairings: Aperitif, pasta, marinated fish; fish first courses.
Serving temperature: 10-12 C°.

Linea Matile Orvieto DOC.

Grapes: Trebbiano 60%, Drupeggio 10%, Verdello 15%, Malvasia 15%
Zone of production: Castiglione in Teverina, Allerona and Lubriano.
Size of vineyard: 50 Ha.
Altitude of vineyards: 320 meters above sea level.
Terrain: volcanic and sedimentary.
System of training: spurred cordon.
Density: Older 3.00x1.50 metres, newer 3.00x 1.00 metres.
Production per Ha: 110 quintals.
Yield of wine: 77 hectolitre.
Medium age of vines: 20-25 years.
Time of harvest: From the end of September until 10th October, with careful selection of the grapes.
Vinification: soft pressing of the whole grapes in a closed press and then the immediate separation of the skins, followed by cold settling for clearing the must.
Alcoholic fermentation: Controlled temperature (Max. 15 C°).
Ageing: 60 days in bottles.
Alcohol: 12.5% vol.
Acidity: 5.8 g/l.

pH: 3.49 g/l.
Dry extract: 21.8 g/l.
Colour: Pale straw.
Fragrance: Fine, rich notes of white fleshed fruit.
Taste: Elegant fruit notes.
Food pairings: Ideal aperitif, pasta, marinated fish dishes, and fish first courses.
Serving temperature: 10-12 C°.

<u>Linea Matile Pinot Grigio IGT Umbria.</u>

Grapes: Pinot Grigio 100%
Zone of production: Orvieto.
Size of vineyard: 10 Ha.
Altitude of vineyards: 300 meters above sea level.
Terrain: volcanic.
System of training: Guyot.
Density of vines: Traditionally 2.8 x 0.80 metres.
Production per Ha: 110 quintals.
Yield of wine: 77 hectolitre.
Medium age of vines: 5 years.
Time of harvest: From the end of August with careful selection of the grapes.
Vinification: soft pressing of the whole grapes in a closed press and then the immediate separation of the skins, followed by cold settling for clearing the must.
Alcoholic fermentation: Controlled temperature (Maximum 15 C°) followed by filtered clarification.
Ageing: 60 days in bottles.
Alcohol: 12% vol.
Acidity: 5.8 g/l.
pH: 3.49 g/l.
Dry extract: 21.8 g/l.
Colour: Pale straw.
Fragrance: Fine, characterised by rich notes of pears and honey.
Taste: Elegant fruit notes.
Food pairings: Ideal aperitif, marinated fish, and fish first courses.
Serving temperature: 10-12 C°.

Linea Matile Rosato IGT Umbria.

Grapes: Merlot, Sangiovese, Cabernet, and Ciliegiolo.
Zone of production: Orvieto.
Size of vineyard: 30 Ha.
Altitude of vineyards: 290-320 meters above sea level.
Terrain: volcanic, sedimentary and pebbly.
System of training: spurred cordon.
Density: Traditionally 3.00 x 1.50; new 3.00 x 1.00 metres.
Production per Ha: 120 quintals.
Yield of wine: 70 hectolitre.
Medium age of vines: 20 years, and new plantings 5 years.
Time of harvest: From 20th September until 10-15 October.
Vinification: Traditional maceration in contact with the skins for 24 hours, frequent remontages then separation of the must.
Alcoholic fermentation: Controlled temperature (Maximum 15 C°) using the varietal yeasts for obtaining unique aromas.
Ageing: 40-50 days in bottles.
Alcohol: 12% vol.
Acidity: 5.5 g/l.
pH: 3.5 g/l.
Dry extract: 23.9 g/l.
Colour: Deep pink.
Fragrance: Intense, aromatic, rich; red fruit and vegetable notes.
Taste: Dry, full and soft, elegant fruity notes with just the right amount of tannins.
Food pairings: Ideal for first courses with red meat; and fish based hors d'oeuvres.
Serving temperature: 10-12 C°.

Linea Matile Rosso IGT Umbria.

Grapes: Merlot, Sangiovese, Cabernet, and Ciliegiolo.
Zone of production: Umbria.
Size of vineyard: 10 Ha.
Altitude of vineyards: 290-320 meters above sea level.
Terrain: volcanic, sedimentary and pebbly.
System of training: spurred cordon.

Density: Traditionally 3.00 x 1.50; new 3.00 x 1.00 metres.
Production per Ha: 120 quintals.
Yield of wine: 70 hectolitre.
Medium age of vines: 20 years and new plantings 5 years.
Time of harvest: From 20th September until 10-15 October.
Vinification: Traditional maceration in contact with the skins for seven to eight days, frequent remontages and the subtraction of 10% of the must.
Alcoholic fermentation: Controlled temperature (Maximum 25 C°), using the varietal yeasts for obtaining unique aromas.
Alcohol: 12% vol.
Acidity: 5 g/l.
pH: 3.64 g/l.
Dry extract: 3.64 g/l.
Colour: Ruby red with violet tints.
Fragrance: Intense, aromatic, rich; with red fruit notes.
Taste: Dry, full and soft, elegant fruity notes with just the right amount of tannins.
Food pairings: First courses, roast and grilled meat.
Serving temperature: 14-16 C°.

Linea Matile Pinot Nero IGT Umbria.

Grapes: Pinot Nero 100%.
Zone of production: Orvieto.
Size of vineyard: 10 Ha.
Altitude of vineyards: 290-320 meters above sea level.
Terrain: volcanic and sedimentary.
System of training: Guyot.
Density: Traditionally 3.00 x 1.50; new 3.00 x 1.00 metres.
Production per Ha: 90 quintals.
Yield of wine: 60 hectolitre.
Time of harvest: From 15th September.
Vinification: Maceration in contact with the skins for ten days, frequent remontages and the subtraction of 20% of the must.
Alcoholic fermentation: Controlled temperature (Maximum 25 C°), with the addition of selected and original yeasts for obtaining unique aromas.
Annual production: 40.000 bottles.

Alcohol: 13.5% vol.
Acidity: 5 g/l.
pH: 3.64 g/l.
Dry extract: 3.64 g/l.
Colour: Bright, ruby red
Fragrance: Rich and fruity with notes of morello cherries, fruits of the forest and red currant.
Taste: Good body, full of tannins with excellent texture.
Food pairings: Perfect with furry and feathered game.
Serving temperature: 14-16 C°.

Linea Torre del Moro:

The tower was built in 1200 in the city centre. It is the tallest building (47-metre) and stands high above Orvieto's other hundred or so towers. It is almost perfectly oriented to the four cardinal points and overlooks all the rural parishes surrounding the city. During the XVI century it acquired the name *del Moro*, probably after Raffaele di Sante, who was known as *il Moro*. In 1866 the tower was restored and a mechanical clock, as well as two bells were installed. The smaller bell came from the church tower of St Andrea, the larger bell from the Palazzo del Popolo, where it had been since 1313, the year when Poncello Orsini, the "Captain of the People" had it cast. The bell bears his coat of arms, and the symbols of the twenty-five guilds and the seal of the city. Today it is possible to climb to the top of the tower and see the entire city of Orvieto from a high angle.

Linea Torre del Moro - Pierleone Orvieto Classico DOC.

Grapes: Procanico 50%, Malvasia 15%, Verdello 15%, Drupeggio 10%, and Grechetto.
Zone of production: Orvieto.
Size of vineyard: 50 Ha.
Altitude of vineyards: 320 meters above sea level.
Terrain: volcanic, sedimentary, sandy and clayey.
System of training: spurred cordon.
Density: Traditionally 3.00 x 1.50 metres; new 3.00 x 1.00.
Production per Ha: 110 quintals. Yield of wine: 77 hectolitre.

Medium age of vines: 20-25 years. New plantings 5 years.
Time of harvest: From 10th to 25th September.
Vinification: soft pressing of the whole grapes in a closed press and then the immediate separation of the skins, followed by cold settling for clearing the must.
Alcoholic fermentation: Controlled temperature (Maximum 18 C°) for 15 days in stainless steel vats, with the addition of selected and original yeasts. With racking subtract 10/15% of the must.
Ageing: 60 days in bottles.
Alcohol: 12% vol.
Acidity: 5.8 g/l.
pH: 3.42 g/l.
Dry extract: 20 g/l.
Colour: Pale straw yellow with light tints of green.
Fragrance: Intense and characterised by rich notes of fresh fruit.
Taste: Dry, full and fragrant, elegant and harmonious notes of white fruit, like peaches.
Food pairings: Ideal aperitif, noble fish dishes and white meat like turkey or chicken.
Serving temperature: 10-12 C°.

Linea Torre del Moro – Grechetto IGT Umbria.

Grapes: Grechetto 100%.
Zone of production: Orvieto.
Size of vineyard: 30 Ha.
Altitude of vineyards: 320 meters above sea level.
Terrain: volcanic and sedimentary.
System of training: spurred cordon.
Density of vines: Traditionally 3.00x1.50 metres.
Production per Ha: 90 quintals.
Yield of wine: 65/70 hectolitre per hectare.
Medium age of vines: 5 years.
Time of harvest: From 10th to 25th September.
Vinification: soft pressing of the whole grapes in a closed press and then the immediate separation of the skins, followed by cold settling for clearing the must.

Alcoholic fermentation: Only in barrels. Use of selected yeasts and aromatic varieties. 20% of the must is subtracted during racking for carbonic maceration.
Alcohol: 12 % vol.
Acidity: 5.8 g/l.
pH: 3.39 g/l.
Dry extract: 20 g/l.
Colour: Pale straw yellow with golden tints.
Nose: Large and fine, rich with notes of fresh fruit and complex hints of sandalwood.
Flavour: Dry, complex, smooth and elegant notes of ripe fruit and fine spices.
Food pairings: Soups, grilled vegetables and white meat.
Serving temperature: 14 C°.

Linea Torre del Moro – Rupestro IGT Umbria.

Grapes: Merlot 80% and Sangiovese 20%.
Zone of production: Orvieto.
Size of vineyard: 5 Ha.
Altitude of vineyards: 320 meters above sea level.
Terrain: volcanic and sedimentary.
System of training: spurred cordon.
Density: Traditionally 3.00 x 1.50; new 3.00 x 1.00 metres.
Production per Ha: 90 quintals.
Yield of wine: 60 hectolitre per hectare.
Medium age of vines: 20 years, 5 years for new vines.
Time of harvest: From 20th September to 15th October.
Vinification: Maceration in contact with the skins for 8 days, frequent remontages and the subtraction of 20% of the must.
Alcoholic fermentation: Controlled temperature (Maximum 25 C°), with the addition of selected aromatic yeasts.
Alcohol: 13% vol.
Acidity: 5.7 g/l.
pH: 3.42 g/l.
Dry extract: 30.10 g/l.
Colour: Bright, ruby red with purple tints.
Fragrance: Rich and aromatic with hint of cherries and red fruits.
Taste: Full bodied with extraordinary flavours and scent.

Food pairings: Pasta or red meat dishes: braised, roast or grilled.
Serving temperature: 14-16 C°.

Linea Torre del Moro – Novello IGT Umbria.

Grapes: Sangiovese, Ciliegiolo, and Merlot.
Zone of production: Umbria.
Size of vineyard: 10 Ha.
Altitude of vineyards: 290/320 meters above sea level.
Terrain: Sedimentary and stony.
System of training: spurred cordon.
Density: Traditionally 3.00 x 1.50; new 3.00 x 1.00 metres.
Production per Ha: 100 quintals.
Yield of wine: 70 hectolitre per hectare.
Medium age of vines: 15 years.
Time of harvest: From 10th September.
Vinification: Carbonic maceration of 50% gently pressed, 50% in contact with the skins for 7/8 days, frequent remontages and the subtraction of 10% of the must.
Alcoholic fermentation: Controlled temperature (Max. 25 C°), in stainless steel vats with the addition of selected aromatic yeasts.
Alcohol: 12% vol.
Acidity: 5 g/l.
pH: 5 g/l.
Dry extract: 36.70 g/l.
Colour: Ruby red with violet tints.
Bouquet: Intense and harmonious, rich with notes of red fruits.
Taste: Very full, very soft and elegant notes of red fruits.
Food pairings: Perfect with pasta or red meats, roasts, but also with pizza and appetisers.
Serving temperature: 14-16 C°.

Linea Torre del Moro – Orvieto Classico Amabile DOC.

Grapes: Trebbiano 60%, Malvasia 15%, Verdello 15%, and Drupeggio 10%.
Zone of production: Orvieto.
Size of vineyard: 10 Ha.
Altitude of vineyards: 320 meters above sea level.

Terrain: volcanic.
System of training: spurred cordon.
Density of vines: Traditionally 3.00x1.50 metres.
Production per Ha: 110 quintals.
Yield of wine: 77 hectolitre per hectare.
Medium age of vines: 20-25 years.
Time of harvest: From end of September to 10th October with careful selection of the grapes.
Vinification: soft pressing of the whole grapes in a closed press and then the immediate separation of the skins, followed by cold settling for clearing the must.
Alcoholic fermentation: At a controlled temperature, max 15 C° and stopping fermentation at the desired sugar content (30-40 g/l) by lowering the temperature, followed by filtered clarification.
Alcohol: 12 % vol.
Acidity: 5.75 g/l.
pH: 3.37 g/l.
Dry extract: 19.95 g/l.
Colour: Pale straw yellow with light green tints.
Bouquet: Intense, with rich notes of fresh fruit.
Taste: Pleasantly sweet, soft with elegant notes of fruit.
Food pairings: Ideal fish dishes.
Serving temperature: 10-12 C°.

Linea Capitano del Popolo.

In the beginning of the XIII century the medieval Commune of Orvieto was at its height of its economic power and political stability. The nascent middle classes were able to enter the political life and elect mayors of their choice. Orvieto elected a captain, who governed the city. The most famous captain was Ranieri Della Greca. He ordered demolition of a number of properties in order to form a new urban layout and to allow the building of the *Palazzo del Popolo*, the *Duomo*, the *Palazzo dei Sette* and the *Torre* (known at the time as *del Papa*, today known as the *Torre del Moro).*

Linea Capitano del Popolo – Spumante Brut.

Grapes: Trebbiano 50%, Verdello 15%, Chardonnay 15%, Pinot Nero 15% and other red grapes.
Zone of production: The hills around Orvieto.
Size of vineyard: 20 Ha.
Altitude of vineyards: 450 meters above sea level.
Terrain: volcanic and sedimentary.
System of training: spurred cordon.
Density of vines: Traditionally 3.00x1.50 metres.
Production per Ha: 100 quintals.
Yield of wine: 70 hectolitre per hectare.
Medium age of vines: 20 years.
Time of harvest: From late August with selection of the grapes.
Vinification: soft pressing of the whole grapes in a closed press and then the immediate separation of the skins, followed by cold settling for clearing the must.
Alcoholic fermentation: At a controlled temperature, max 15 C°, followed by filtered clarification.
Alcohol: 12 % vol.
Acidity: 6 g/l.
pH: 3.49 g/l.
Dry extract: 21.80 g/l.
Colour: Pale straw yellow.
Bouquet: Rich notes of dried white fruit.
Taste: Elegant and fruity.
Food pairings: Perfect with appetisers, marinated fish, seafood and pasta dishes.
Serving temperature: 10-12 C° in a glass flute.

Linea Capitano del Popolo – Colbadia IGT Umbria.

Grapes: Procanico 75%, and Sauvignon Blanc 25%.
Zone of production: Orvieto.
Size of vineyard: 20 Ha.
Altitude of vineyards: 320 meters above sea level.
Terrain: volcanic and sedimentary.
System of training: spurred cordon.
Density of vines: Traditionally 3.00x1.50 metres.

Production per Ha: 70 quintals.
Yield of wine: 49 hectolitre per hectare.
Medium age of vines: 5-7 years.
Time of harvest: From 5th to 15th September.
Vinification: soft pressing of the whole grapes in a closed press and then the immediate separation of the skins, followed by cold settling for clearing the must.
Alcoholic fermentation: At a controlled temperature, max 15 C° for an average of 15 days in stainless steel tanks with the addition of selected aromatic yeasts.
Alcohol: 13 % vol.
Acidity: 5.9 g/l.
pH: 3.34 g/l.
Dry extract: 20.80 g/l.
Colour: Intense straw yellow.
Nose: Elegant fruity aromas with great finesse and balance.
Taste: Full, very soft and elegant notes of red fruit.
Food pairings: Perfect with fish, vegetable pies, pasta with shellfish, and white meat.
Serving temperature: 12 C°.

Linea Capitano del Popolo – Alborato Rosé IGT Umbria.

Grapes: Pinot Nero, Merlot, Sangiovese, and Ciliegiolo.
Zone of production: Orvieto.
Size of vineyard: 20 Ha.
Altitude of vineyards: 290/320 meters above sea level.
Terrain: volcanic and sedimentary.
System of training: spurred cordon and Guyot.
Density of vines: Traditionally 3.00x1.50 metres, new vineyards 2.50 x 0.80 metres.
Production per Ha: 110 quintals.   Yield of wine: 70%.
Medium age of vines: 25 years, new vineyards 8 years.
Time of harvest: From 10th September.
Vinification: Flush with dry ice and soft pressing of the grapes.
Alcoholic fermentation: At a controlled temperature, max 15 C° with the addition of selected aromatic yeasts.
Ageing: 40–50 days in bottle.
Alcohol: 13 % vol.

Acidity: 5.6 g/l.
pH: 3.50 g/l.
Dry extract: 25.70 g/l.
Colour: Delicate pink.
Bouquet: Harmonious, with notes of strawberry and raspberry.
Taste: Fresh, soft and elegant notes of fruit.
Food pairings: Aperitif, first fish courses, and summer dishes.
Serving temperature: 10-12 C°.

Linea Capitano del Popolo – Alborato IGT Umbria.

Grapes: Merlot 70%, Cabernet Franc 30%.
Zone of production: Orvieto.
Size of vineyard: 10 Ha.
Altitude of vineyards: 320 meters above sea level.
Terrain: volcanic, sedimentary and stony.
System of training: spurred cordon.
Density of vines: Traditionally 3.00x1.50 metres, new vineyards 3.00x1.00 metres.
Production per Ha: 90 quintals.
Yield of wine: 60 hectolitre per hectare.
Medium age of vines: 20 years, new vineyards 5 years.
Time of harvest: From 20th September to 10-15th October.
Vinification: Traditional maceration on the skins for 7-8 days, with a lot of pumping over and 20% of the must is subtracted.
Alcoholic fermentation: At a controlled temperature, max 25 C° in stainless steel with the addition of selected aromatic yeasts.
Maturing: 90% steel tanks and 10% in French oak barrels
Ageing: 90 days in bottle.
Alcohol: 13 % vol.
Acidity: 5.3 g/l.
pH: 3.55 g/l.
Dry extract: 32.2 g/l.
Colour: Ruby red with violet tints.
Bouquet: Intense and harmonious, rich with notes of red fruit and hints of sweet spices.
Taste: Full bodied, smooth and elegant with hints of red fruit.
Food pairings: Pasta, and roast and grilled meats.
Serving temperature: 14-16 C°.

Linea Capitano del Popolo – Spumante Demi-Sec.

Grapes: Trebbiano 50%, Verdello 15%, Chardonnay 15%, and Ciliegiolo 15% and other red grapes.
Zone of production: The hills around Orvieto.
Size of vineyard: 20 Ha.
Altitude of vineyards: 450 meters above sea level.
Terrain: volcanic and sedimentary.
System of training: spurred cordon.
Density of vines: Traditionally 3.00x1.50 metres.
Production per Ha: 100 quintals.
Yield of wine: 70 hectolitre per hectare.
Medium age of vines: 20 years.
Time of harvest: From late August.
Vinification: soft pressing of the whole grapes in a closed press and then the immediate separation of the skins, followed by cold settling for clearing the must.
Alcoholic fermentation: At a controlled temperature, max 15 C°, fermentation is stopped by lowering the temperature when the desired sugar level is reached; followed by filtered clarification.
Ageing: 90 days in the bottle.
Alcohol: 12 % vol.
Acidity: 5.5 g/l.
pH: 3.49 g/l.
Dry extract: 21.80 g/l.
Colour: Pale straw yellow.
Bouquet: Rich notes of dried fruit, peaches, pears and honey.
Taste: Elegant and fruity.
Food pairings: Ideal after a meal to accompany desserts.
Serving temperature: 10-12 C° in a glass flute.

Linea Capitano del Popolo – L'Armida - Orvieto DOC Classico Superiore – Vendemmia Tardiva.

Grapes: Procanico 60%, Malvasia 15%, Verdello 15%, Drupeggio 5%, and Grechetto 5%.
Zone of production: Orvieto.

Size of vineyard: 5 hectares with suitable climatic conditions for the development of noble rot (botrytis cinerea).
Altitude of vineyards: 320 meters above sea level.
Terrain: volcanic and sedimentary.
Density of vines: Traditionally 3.00x1.50 metres.
Production per Ha: 60 quintals.
Yield of wine: 40 hectolitre per hectare.
Medium age of vines: 20-25 years.
Time of harvest: After 25th October into November, depending on the weather and the condition of the grapes, with careful selection of the grapes with noble rot.
Vinification: soft pressing of the whole grapes in a closed press and then the immediate separation of the skins, followed by cold settling for clearing the must.
Alcoholic fermentation: At a controlled temperature, max 18 C° in stainless steel vats, and stopping fermentation at the desired sugar content by lowering the temperature. A short period of maturation in small oak barrels.
Alcohol: 12 % vol.
Acidity: 5.55 g/l.
pH: 3.40 g/l.
Dry extract: 9.22 g/l.
Colour: Intense straw yellow.
Nose: Complex, rich with notes of ripe fruit and sweet spices.
Taste: Pleasantly sweet, soft with elegant notes of fruit.
Food pairings: Ideal for pastries and desserts.
Serving temperature: 12-14 C°.

Linea Araldica:

Heraldry aims to identify, recognise and catalogue certain persons, families, and groups of people and institutions by the use of graphic means. Heraldry developed in the Middle Ages throughout Europe as a coherent system of identification of individuals as well as clans. A shield could be passed on, expressing a degree of relationship. During jousting and individual combats, the knights could be recognised from afar. At the time of the Crusades the nobles, hidden behind armour, felt a need to be recognised amongst hundreds of other crusaders and, thus, the use of heraldry spread throughout Europe.

Linea Araldica – Febo Orvieto DOC Classico Superiore

Grapes: Procanico 55%, Verdello 15%, Chardonnay 15% and other allowable grapes 15%.
Zone of production: Orvieto.
Size of vineyard: 5 hectares.
Altitude of vineyards: 320 meters above sea level.
Terrain: mostly volcanic.
Training system: Guyot.
Density of vines: Traditionally 2.70x0.90 metres.
Production per Ha: 80 quintals.
Yield of wine: 55 hectolitre per hectare.
Medium age of vines: 20-25 years, new vineyards 5 years.
Time of harvest: From 15th September to 20th October.
Vinification: soft pressing of the whole grapes in a closed press and then the immediate separation of the skins, followed by cold settling for clearing the must.
Alcoholic fermentation: At a controlled temperature, max 18 C° for an average of 15 days in stainless steel vats with the addition of selected aromatic yeasts.
Alcohol: 13 % vol.
Acidity: 5.9 g/l.
pH: 3.34 g/l.
Dry extract: 21.2 g/l.
Colour: Intense straw yellow.
Nose: Rich and full with notes of white fruit and flowers.
Taste: Complex and delicate, with notes of pear and peach.
Food pairings: Ideal for terrines of fish, pasta with clams, vegetable pies and white meat.
Serving temperature: 12 C°.

Linea Araldica – Nero Della Greca IGT Umbria.

Grapes: Sangiovese 100%.
Zone of production: Orvieto.
Size of vineyard: 10 Ha.

Altitude of vineyards: 320 meters above sea level.
Terrain: volcanic and sedimentary.
System of training: spurred cordon.
Density of vines: Traditionally 3.00x1.50 metres, new vineyards 3.00x1.00 metres.
Production per Ha: 70 quintals.
Yield of wine: 50 hectolitre per hectare.
Medium age of vines: 20 years.
Time of harvest: From late September to early October.
Vinification: Traditional maceration on the skins for 15-18 days, with a lot of pumping over and 20/25% of the must is subtracted.
Alcoholic fermentation: At a controlled temperature, max 27 C° in stainless steel with the addition of selected aromatic yeasts.
Alcohol: 14 % vol.
Acidity: 5.9 g/l.
pH: 3.60 g/l.
Dry extract: 37.9 g/l.
Colour: Dark, ruby red.
Nose: Large and fine, with notes of red fruit, vegetable tones and sweet spices.
Taste: Full and elegant, with hints of ripe fruit and complex spices.
Food pairings: Braised, roast and grilled meats.
Serving temperature: 18 C°.

Linea Araldica –Arciato IGT Umbria.

Grapes: Merlot 55% and Cabernet 45%.
Zone of production: Orvieto.
Size of vineyard: 5 Ha.
Altitude of vineyards: 320 meters above sea level.
Terrain: volcanic and sedimentary.
System of training: spurred cordon.
Density of vines: Traditionally 3.00x1.50 metres, new vineyards 3.00x1.00 metres.
Production per Ha: 70 quintals.
Yield of wine: 49 hectolitre per hectare.
Medium age of vines: 5-6 years.

Time of harvest: From late September to early October with careful selection of the grapes.
Vinification: Traditional maceration on the skins for 12-15 days, with a lot of pumping over and 20% of the must is subtracted.
Alcoholic fermentation: At a controlled temperature, max 27 C° in stainless steel vats with the addition of selected aromatic yeasts.
Malolactic fermentation: In barrels.
Ageing: Twelve months in French oak barrels, 60% of it new.
Alcohol: 14 % vol.
Acidity: 5.9 g/l.
pH: 3.68 g/l.
Dry extract: 38.6 g/l.
Colour: Dark, ruby red.
Nose: Large and fine, with notes of red fruit and sweet spices.
Taste: Full and elegant, with hints of fruit and notes of spices, balsamic and cherry.
Food pairings: Ideal with braised, roast and grilled meats.
Serving temperature: 16-8 C°.

La Carraia

Loc. Tordimonte 56, 05018 Orvieto TR
Tel: 0763 304013
Fax: 0763 304048
www.lacarraia.it
info@lacarraia.it

The Gialetti and Cotarella families founded la Carraia in 1988. The winery made its debut with an Orvieto Classico DOC, the result of a meticulous selection of clones with low productivity and particularly interesting aromas. The traditional vines were flanked a few years later by an expressive and rotund Chardonnay. The result was Poggio Calvelli, a refined and fresh Orvieto Classico Superiore DOC, much appreciated for its quality/price ratio.

The focal point of the estate is the San Valentino vineyard where Merlot and Cabernet Sauvignon vines were cultivated, which was considered to be "heretical" in an area dominated by white wines. The Fobiano (1995) dispelled any sort of "heresy", as it was very similar to any outstanding Bordeaux red, matured for 12 months in French barriques. The success of Fobiano showed that excellent red wines could be produced around Orvieto, as they have been in the past.

During the sixteenth century, Sante Lancerio, in charge of supplying wine for the cellars of Pope Paul III, regularly bought locally produced red wines. His Holiness had a passion for a wine called "Sucano" produced in the hills near Orvieto (near the village of present day Sugano).

New plantings of Sangiovese and Montepulciano followed and the resulting wines proved equally successful. In 1997 Sangiovese was created, then later, Tizzonero followed; a blend of Sangiovese and Montepulciano. That led to the production of Giro di Vite in 2003; a pure Montepulciano wine.

Since 2006 new and challenging research began with regard to white wines. It resulted in "Le Basque", a Grechetto and Viognier blend. Ugolino di Biscaglia, the Carolingian officer who built his castle by the banks of the Tiber during the Middle

Ages, was also known as "Le Basque", and, thus, he gave the name to Baschi, a town that overlooks the vineyards.

A Chardonnay in purity (100%) followed in 2009.

La Carraia, which has made a name for itself on both national and international markets, maintains a special bond with the land and its rhythms. Today, Odoardo Gialetti and his sons Mauro and Marco make the rounds of the various vineyards overseeing the work to ensure quality is maintained.

Orvieto Classico DOC – La Carraia.

Grapes: Grechetto 40%, Malvasia 30%, and Procanico 30%.
Production area: Baschi.
Area of vineyard: 30 Ha.
Altitude: 330 metres above sea level.
Terrain: Volcanic.
Training system: spurred cordon.
Density of wines: 3.000 per Ha.
Production per Ha: 8.500 kg.
Yield in wine: 65%.
Average age of vines: 25 years.
Harvesting period: From September to October.
Vinification system: Cold maceration for 7 hours at 7 C°.
Alcoholic fermentation: In stainless steel tanks at 12/16 C°.
Malolactic fermentation: Not carried out.
Refining method: In bottles.
Alcohol: 12.5% vol.

Umbria Bianco IGT Chardonnay.

Grapes: Chardonnay 100%.
Production area: Baschi.
Area of vineyard: 5 Ha.
Altitude: 270-320 metres above sea level.
Terrain: Volcanic.
Training system: spurred cordon.
Density of wines: 4.500 per Ha.
Production per Ha: 7.500 kg.
Yield in wine: 60%.

Average age of vines: 8 years.
Harvesting period: August.
Vinification system: Cold maceration for 7 hours at 7 C°.
Alcoholic fermentation: In stainless steel tanks at 12/16 C°.
Malolactic fermentation: Not carried out.
Refining method: In bottles.
Alcohol: 13% vol.

Orvieto Classico Superiore DOC Poggio Calvelli.

Grapes: Grechetto 50%, Chardonnay 25%, and Procanico 25%.
Production area: Baschi.
Area of vineyard: 11 Ha.
Altitude: 350 metres above sea level.
Terrain: Volcanic.
Training system: spurred cordon.
Density of wines: 3.500 per Ha.
Production per Ha: 6.500 kg.
Yield in wine: 60%.
Average age of vines: 17 years.
Harvesting period: From August to October.
Vinification system: Cold maceration for 12 hours at 7 C°.
Alcoholic fermentation: In stainless steel tanks at 12/16 C°.
Malolactic fermentation: Not carried out.
Refining method: In bottles.
Alcohol: 13.5% vol.

Umbria Bianco IGT Le Basque.

Grapes: Grechetto 50%, and Viognier 50%.
Production area: Baschi.
Area of vineyard: 3 Ha.
Altitude: 300 metres above sea level.
Terrain: Calcareous and stony.
Training system: spurred cordon.
Density of wines: 3.800 per Ha.
Production per Ha: 6.500 kg.
Yield in wine: 60%.
Average age of vines: 11 years.

Harvesting period: September.
Vinification system: Cold maceration for 12 hours at 7 C°.
Alcoholic fermentation: In stainless steel tanks at 12/16 C°.
Malolactic fermentation: Not carried out.
Refining method: In bottles.
Alcohol: 13.5% vol.

Umbria Rosso IGT Sangiovese.

Grapes: Sangiovese 100%.
Production area: Baschi.
Area of vineyard: 46 Ha.
Altitude: 300 metres above sea level.
Terrain: Volcanic.
Training system: spurred cordon.
Density of wines: 4.000 per Ha.
Production per Ha: 7.500 kg.
Yield in wine: 65%.
Average age of vines: 20 years.
Harvesting period: From end of September to October.
Vinification system: skin contact for 16-20 days with several pressings carried out.
Refining method: In Nevers and Allier oak barriques for three months, and then in bottles.
Alcohol: 13% vol.

Umbria Rosso IGT Tizzonero.

Grapes: Sangiovese 50%, Montepulciano 50%.
Production area: Baschi.
Area of vineyard: 18 Ha.
Altitude: 350 metres above sea level.
Terrain: Volcanic with pebbles.
Training system: spurred cordon.
Density of wines: 5.000 per Ha.
Production per Ha: 6.200 kg.
Yield in wine: 60%.
Average age of vines: 11 years.
Harvesting period: From end of September to October.

Vinification system: skin contact for 18-20 days with several pressings carried out.
Refining method: In Nevers and Allier oak barriques for eight months, and then in bottles for six months.
Alcohol: 13.5% vol.

Umbria Rosso IGT Giro di Vite.

Grapes: Montepulciano 100%.
Production area: Baschi.
Area of vineyard: 6 Ha.
Altitude: 350 metres above sea level.
Terrain: Volcanic with pebbles.
Training system: spurred cordon.
Density of wines: 6.000 per Ha.
Production per Ha: 5.500 kg.
Yield in wine: 60%.
Average age of vines: 11 years.
Harvesting period: October.
Vinification system: skin contact for 20-24 days with several pressings carried out.
Refining method: In Allier oak barriques of the first and second passing for twelve months and then in bottles for six months.
Alcohol: 13% vol.

Umbria Rosso IGT Fobiano.

Grapes: Merlot 70%, Cabernet Sauvignon 30%.
Production area: Baschi.
Area of vineyard: 8 Ha.
Altitude: 350 metres above sea level.
Terrain: Volcanic with pebbles.
Training system: spurred cordon.
Density of wines: 5.000 per Ha.
Production per Ha: 6.200 kg.
Yield in wine: 60%.
Average age of vines: 17 years.
Harvesting period: Merlot from the end of August to the beginning of September; Cabernet Sauvignon end of September.

Vinification system: skin contact for 20-24 days with several pressings carried out.
Refining method: In Nevers oak barriques for eight months of the first and second passing for twelve months and then in bottles for six months.
Alcohol: 13.5% vol.

Castello della Sala

Azienda Agricola Castello della Sala
Marchesi Antinori S.r.l.
Localita: Sala 05016 Sala, Ficulle TR
Tel: 055 23595
Fax: 055 2359884
www.antinori.it
antinori@antinori.it

Castello della Sala stands on a rocky promontory at 534 metres high in the Umbrian Apennines, not far from the border with Tuscany and about 18 kilometres from Orvieto. The beautiful medieval fortress is surrounded by old Etruscan hill towns between the Paglia River and the peak of Mount Nibbio. The estate covers an area of 500 hectares, of which 160 are planted with vineyards at the altitude of 200-400 metres above sea level, on clayey soil of sedimentary and volcanic origin, rich in Pliocene fossils.

The vineyards were planted with a mixture of traditional grape varieties, mainly Procanico and Grechetto, which are still grown on the estate today. Procanico is a clone of Umbrian Trebbiano, grown around Orvieto since time immemorial. It differs greatly from the Tuscan Trebbiano grape in that the vine is less productive, the bunches are less compact, and the skin is yellow-pink instead of green. Grechetto is an Umbrian variety with thick, dark yellow skins, and is very acidic, low yielding and remarkably tannic: the wines made from this variety are mellow with a spicy, grassy aroma of freshly-mown hay, well-structured and stylish with good ageing potential.

The non-traditional varieties grown at the estate include several Chardonnay clones: 40 hectares at 230-340 meters altitude, 35 hectares of Sauvignon Blanc, 4.5 hectares of Pinot Nero planted in 1985, and a further 2.5 hectares on terraces in 1994, between 340-460 meters altitude.

The Antinori family has been making wine for over six hundred years; since Giovanni di Piero Antinori became part of the *Arte Fiorentina dei Vinnateri* in 1385. Throughout its history spanning 26 generations, the family had personally managed the business, making innovative, sometimes courageous choices with unwavering respect for tradition and the land.

Marchese Niccolo Antinori bought the estate in Umbria in 1940. He is the chairman of the company, today the business is managed by his son, Marchese Piero Antinori, a company director, assisted by his three daughters, Albiera, Allegra and Alessia, who are personally involved in the business.

The Castello della Sala property consisted of 29 farms, 483 hectares of fields and woods. Antinori improved the land, which also included 52 hectares of olive groves and extensive vineyards. He restored the castle, completely renovating some rooms, including the reception hall.

The castle was built in 1350 for Angelo Monaldeschi della Vipera, whose family had come to Italy with Charlemagne in the IX century. A family feud broke out during the XIV century over the control of Orvieto. The battles became so intense that Angelo and his three brothers each took a new name and created their own feudal clan. The eldest was called della Cervara, another del Cane and the third dell'Aquila; Angelo, who was probably the most warlike took the name della Vipera.

His grandson, Gentile, was the first to call himself della Sala. In 1437 he became the *capitano* of Orvieto and he was constantly at war with the della Cervaras. Later, he fought a twelve-year old battle for the rule of the whole region against the Venetian cardinal Pietro Barbo, who was to become Pope Paul II.

In 1480 the family called a truce, when Gentile's son, Pietro Antonio Monaldeschi della Vipera della Sala married his cousin Giovanna Monaldeschi della Cervara. Together they restored the castle, which became a symbol of this peace. The renaissance chapel below the castle gates may be a mark of their gratitude. The couple lived in the castle until 1518 when Pietro Antonio died and Giovanna gave the property to the *Opera del Duomo* in Orvieto, a charitable institute run by the Cathedral. The castle remained in their hands until the unification of Italy, when the state seized all church property. It had a series of owners, but little maintenance and restoration was carried out until 1940, when the Antinori family bought the estate. The rich and colourful history associated with the castle is reflected in some of the names given to the wines produced on the estate today.

San Giovanni della Sala. Orvieto DOC Classico Superiore.
Vintage: 2009.

Grapes: 50% Grechetto, 25% Procanico, and 25% Pinot Bianco, with Viognier and Riesling.

Climate and vintage: The springtime temperatures and the optimal availability of water caused all the varietals to develop well during the sprouting phase, which occurred slightly faster than average. This was followed by excellent conditions during flowering and fruit setting. The rains, which characterised the first part of summer, allowed the plants to maintain a good vegetative balance even during the hot month of August, thus, guaranteeing full veraison. The fluctuations between daytime and night temperatures, and the ready availability of water also permitted the grapes to ripen gradually, thereby creating healthy and full grapes. This is, surely, a memorable vintage. The climate remained stable throughout the harvest, allowing for the perfect moment to pick the varietals separately. Harvesting began during the last few days of August. The optimal fragrance of the grapes produced a wine with great balance and aromas, and with a solid structure and the right alcohol content.

Vinification: The vineyards have a low yield, 70 quintals per hectare. The grape bunches, which were picked at the moment of ripening when the sugar content was slightly higher than average, were quickly taken to the wine cellar and the different varietals were vinified separately. In order to obtain a good extract and aromas from the wine, part of the grapes were vinified using the technique of cold maceration (the must remained in contact with the skins for approximately six hours at a temperature of 10 C°). The wine was then kept in stainless steel tanks until it was blended and was subsequently bottled.

Alcohol content: 12% vol.

Taste and colour: straw yellow; a floral aroma, and endowed with warm notes reminiscent of ripe fruit. Sapid and smooth, with a hint of minerals; the wine has a long and rich finish.

Campogrande. Orvieto DOC Classico.
Vintage: 2009

Grapes: 40% Procanico, 40% Grechetto, 15% Verdello, and 5% Drupeggio and Malvasia.

Climate and vintage: Both the favourable spring temperatures and the availability of water allowed all of the grape varietals to sprout in the normal manner, even if slightly ahead of time, thus guaranteeing optimal conditions for fruit setting and flowering. The rains at the beginning of summer permitted the plants to maintain a good vegetative balance even during the month of August, giving a good start for ripening of the fruit. The fluctuations in temperatures between day and night allowed the grapes to ripen gradually, thereby permitting them to be harvested in a healthy state and with a potential for excellent quality. The weather remained stable throughout harvest time allowing the grapes to be picked in optimum conditions.

Vinification: The grapes were de-stemmed and gently pressed. The must was then cooled down to a temperature of 10 C° in order to encourage natural clarification. It was subsequently racked in the appropriate tanks where the alcoholic fermentation took place at a temperature not above 18 C°. The wine was then kept at a temperature of 10 C° until the moment of bottling. This procedure preserved the wine's aromas and freshness.

Alcohol content: 12% vol.

Taste and colour: Straw yellow, with tinges of lime green, and a hint of floral notes. It has full and fruity aromas reminiscent of pineapple and bananas. On the palate, the wine is full-bodied, luscious and soft.

Casasole. Orvieto DOC Classico Amabile.
Vintage: 2008. Casasole is a farmhouse on the estate.

Grapes: 60% Procanico, 20% Grechetto, 15% Verdello, and 5% Drupeggio and Malvasia.

Climate and vintage: The weather of 2008 was characterised by a rainy spring, which caused problems for flowering and fruit setting. Thanks to the summer being dry, but not too hot, the grapes were healthy with the right balance of acidity to sugar content at harvesting, which took place from the middle of September until the beginning of October. This produced a refined and elegant wine, perhaps better than the year before.

Vinification: The grapes were de-stemmed and soft pressed. The must was immediately cooled to a temperature of 10 C° in order to encourage natural clarification. The juice was then racked and transferred to temperature controlled stainless steel tanks where alcoholic fermentation began at 18 C°. When a certain quantity of residual sugar was still present in the wine, the alcoholic fermentation was arrested by suddenly lowering the temperature to 0 C°. The wine was then filtered and stored at a low temperature until bottling.

Alcohol content: 10.30% vol. + 2.3% vol.

Taste and colour: Straw yellow, with floral notes. The wine is nicely fruity and well balanced with a subtly sweetish finish.

Muffato della Sala. Umbria IGT.
Vintage: 2006.

Grapes: 60% Sauvignon Blanc, 40% Grechetto, and some Traminer and Riesling. Grown at 200-350 metres above sea level on clayey land rich in marine fossils.

Climate and vintage: The winter was quite cold, particularly the minimum temperatures, while the mild, well-balanced spring weather allowed good foliage development, if slightly delayed. After that, temperatures were close to the seasonal average, and flowering and fruit setting took place normally. The months of July and August were hot, and the grapes ripened gradually and evenly. Average rainfall allowed the wines to survive the summer without stress. During September and October occasional rain alternated with sunshine, which helped the onset of noble rot gradually and without compromising the health of the fruit. Harvesting began on 9th October with the Traminer, and continued with the Riesling and Sauvignon to conclude in the first ten days of November with the Grechetto.

Vinification: The grapes were picked by hand, returning to the same vineyard more than once, according to the onset of botrytis cinerea (noble rot). They were taken to the cellar for further selection on a belt, followed by soft crushing and de-stemming.

The must fermented for 18 days at a temperature of about 17 C°. The sweet wine obtained was placed in French oak barrique (Alliers and Tronçais), where it remained for about six months before blending and bottling.
Alcohol content: 12%.
Taste and colour: Golden yellow. Vibrant aromas and flavours with hints of candied fruit, honey and citrus fruit; excellent balance of acidity and sugar.

Conte della Vipera. Umbria IGT.
Vintage: 2008.

It takes its name from the first owners of Castello della Sala.
Grapes: Sauvignon Blanc with a small percentage of Chardonnay. Grown at an altitude of 250-350 metres above sea level, on soil rich in marine fossil sediments embedded in clay, which gives the grapes characteristic mineral elements.
Climate and vintage: The 2008 vintage is truly one to remember: the winter was rather mild, followed by a spring with heavy rain, which in turn, was followed by a summer of beautiful weather. This led to a very good harvest, starting at the end of August and ending at the beginning of October, according to the variety of grapes. The beautiful weather allowed for selecting the best and the most perfectly ripened grape bunches.
Vinification: The bunches were cooled on a refrigerated conveyor belt prior to pressing. Part of the Sauvignon Blanc underwent cold maceration for a few hours in special tanks to extract the full aromas from the skins. After a gentle pressing the must was kept at 10 C° for several hours in order to obtain natural clarification. It was then racked in stainless steel tanks at a controlled temperature, where the alcoholic fermentation took place not exceeding 16 C°. The wine was kept at a low temperature, approximately 10 C° in order to impede the malolactic fermentation and preserve the organoleptic characteristics in an unaltered state. The Sauvignon Blanc was then blended with the Chardonnay that had been aged in wood.
Alcohol content: 12% vol.
Taste: Intense aromas. Elegant, mineral, sapid and a very well structured white wine.

Bramito del Cervo. Umbria IGT.
Vintage: 2009.

Grapes: 100% Chardonnay. Grown at an altitude of 200-400 metres above sea level, on soil rich in marine fossil sediments embedded in clay.

Climate and vintage: The spring temperatures and frequent rain helped with the sprouting of the grapes. With good weather following, the conditions were excellent during flowering and fruit setting. The rains at the beginning of summer permitted the plants to maintain a good vegetative balance even during the month of August, giving a good start for ripening of the fruit. The fluctuations in temperatures between day and night allowed the grapes to ripen gradually, thereby permitting them to be harvested in a healthy state and with a potential for excellent quality. The weather remained stable throughout harvest time allowing the grapes to be picked in optimum conditions. The picking of the grapes started around the second half of August.

Vinification: The bunches of grapes were cooled down, pressed and placed in special tanks kept at 10 C°. After several hours of contact with the skins, the juice was transferred to French oak barrels (Alliers and Tronçais), where alcoholic fermentation and partial malolactic fermentation then took place. This was followed by five months of ageing in wood, after which the wine was bottled.

Alcohol content: 12.5% vol.

Taste and colour: Straw yellow colour with golden tinges. It has a fruity aroma with hints of vanilla and notes of toast. This wine is beautifully structured, elegant, with a slight taste of minerals.

Cervaro della Sala. Umbria IGT.
Vintage: 2008.

Grapes: 85 % Chardonnay and Grechetto 15%. Grown at an altitude of 200-400 metres above sea level, on soil from the Pliocene era, rich in marine fossil sediments embedded in clay. The vines are 15-20 years old.

Climate and vintage: The 2008 vintage is a memorable one: the winter was mild, followed by a spring with lots of rain, which in turn, was followed by a summer of beautiful weather. This led to a very good harvest, starting at the end of August and ending at the beginning of October. The best and the most perfectly ripened bunches were selected, promising a wine with wonderful balance, fragrance, good structure and high alcoholic content.

Vinification: The bunches were cooled on a refrigerated conveyor belt during crushing and de-stemming. The varietals were fermented separately: in order to enhance their aromatic properties the musts were left in contact with the skins for 8-12 hours at a temperature of about 10 C°. After this the musts were transferred to 225 litre new French barrique (Allier and Tronçais), where alcoholic fermentation took place over a period of 14 days. The wine remained in contact with the lees for approximately six months, during which time the malolactic fermentation took place. The wine was then blended and bottled. It was aged for another ten months before it was marketed.

Alcohol content: 13% vol.

Taste: Cervaro expresses an intense fragrance with aromatic notes of citrus, pears and acacia flowers, which blend with hints of vanilla to heighten the wine's complexity. It is full flavoured and well-structured, with sweet notes of butter and hazelnut and mineral elements.

Pinot Nero. Umbria IGT.
Vintage: 2007.

Grapes: Pinot Nero 100%. The 7 hectares of vines are 400 metres above sea level, grown on soil from the Pliocene era, rich in marine fossil sediments embedded in clay.

Climate and vintage: Winter temperatures were mild, rarely dropping below 0 C°. Thanks to sunny and calm weather during spring, vegetative growth was good and 15 days earlier than the year before. The months of July and August were hot but without excessive peaks in temperatures and the grapes ripened gradually. The absence of rain during the final stages of maturation produced concentrated and healthy grape bunches. Harvesting began during the first half of September.

Vinification: After de-stemming and partial pressing, the grapes were put into steel tanks. Maceration lasted for one week, during which time a lot of attention was focused on the maximum extraction of colour and tannins. Alcoholic fermentation took place at a temperature of 26 C° and finished in French barrique (Allier and Tronçais), and was followed by malolactic fermentation. The wine was left in barrique for eight months, and was then bottled and aged for an additional 15 months.
Alcohol content: 14.5% vol.
Taste: A burgundy style red wine with hints of cherry, raspberry and spices; well balanced and elegant.

Aziende Agricole Cirulli

Strada Provinciale della Sala
05016 Ficulle TR
Tel: 0763 624301
www.cirulliviticoltore.com

The winery has been established in 1861 by Valentino Cirulli's forefathers. The vineyards are situated near the border with Tuscany, in the hillsides of Ficulle, and cover 75 hectares at the altitude of 250-300 metres. The vineyards enjoy favourable exposure to the sun, facing south to south-west, with an ideal climate. The terrain ranges from calcareous-clayey soil with magnesium, perfect for red grapes, to soils of medium texture with a certain amount of fossils, ideal for growing white grapes.

Considerable investments have been made in research and innovative production technology in the vineyards and the wine cellars. For twenty years Cirulli has carried out studies to identify the best soils suited to the right clones. In addition to the local grapes, the principal international varieties are perfectly integrated in the vineyards. A rational choice of soil, a careful attention to the vineyard from pruning to harvesting and a low yield comply with the aim to improve quality.

The modern wine cellar is perfectly integrated in the surrounding countryside. The architectural design blends in with the green hills, and the reds, yellows and rusty colours of each season. An oasis of natural unspoilt greens, with vineyards and olive groves, creating a unique setting where time stands still. The key to the success of Cirulli wines is the territory, combined with advanced oenological techniques: from the vinification to the maturation process. Half the winery is constructed underground to ensure optimum temperatures for storing the wines in steel vats and in barrique. Careful attention to detail and rational farm management allows Cirulli to offer wines of great complexity and richness. Living on the land, watching the vines grow, and transforming the grapes to divine nectar is the life philosophy of the winemaker. The personality and identity of the Cirulli wines tell the story of the territory.

1861 San Valentino IGT Umbria.

Production area: The vineyards are situated at an altitude of 300-350 metres above sea level south of the municipality of Ficulle at the "Giubba" farm. Due to its particularly favourable exposure, this vineyard has always produced low yield of great quality.
Soil: Grey, medium clayey texture, with natural bone-meal.
Varieties: Merlot and Cabernet.
Training system: spurred cordon.
Planting density: 2.660 vines per Ha.
Vinification: Selected grapes are immediately cooled to 12-14 C°, followed by maceration in 8.000 litre barrels for 15-18 days. The malolactic fermentation is conducted in barrique where the wine ages for 12-18 months. The wine is released for sale only after an additional period of 8-10 months in the bottle.
Colour: Intense red with warm ruby reflections.
Nose: Red ripe fruit, prunes, mulberry followed by hints of balsamic, liquorice and chocolate.
Palate: Intense, warm and juicy; the tannins are velvety with hints of sweet vanilla and mint from the barrique.
Alcohol content: 14.5%.
Serving temperature: 18-20 C°.
Food match: First courses with game sauce, roast and braised meat, and strong cheeses.

Ritorto IGT Umbria.

Production area: The vineyards are situated at an altitude of 200-250 metres above sea level south of the municipality of Ficulle.
Soil: Grey, medium clayey texture with natural bone-meal.
Varieties: Grechetto and Chardonnay.
Training system: spurred cordon.
Planting density: 4.160 vines per Ha.
Vinification: The grapes are cooled to 4-5 C°, followed by a short cryomaceration. The juice is clarified through cold settling and then it ferments in new barrique for 6-8 months.

Colour: Straw yellow with vivid greenish highlights.
Nose: Intense fruit with bursts of citrus and flowers blended in sweet balsamic and spicy elements.
Palate: Velvety and powerful white wine, elegant balance of acidity, alcohol and hints of wooden balsamic notes.
Alcohol content: 14%.
Serving temperature: 12-14 C°.
Food match: Excellent with seafood, vegetables and pulses, freshwater fish, and cheese with fresh herbs.

Ginepreta IGT Umbria.

Production area: The vineyards are situated at 300 metres above sea level south of the municipality of Ficulle at Ginepreta.
Soil: Light grey colour typical of the Umbrian *calanchi* hills.
Varieties: Cabernet Sauvignon, Cabernet Franc and Merlot, picked and vinified separately.
Training system: spurred cordon.
Planting density: 4.160 vines per Ha.
Vinification: Selected grapes are cooled to 12-14 C°, the juice macerates in wooden barrels of 8.000 litres for 12-15 days. After the malolactic fermentation, the wine matures in 225-litres barrique for 12 months. Before being released for the market, the wine rests in the bottle for an additional six months.
Colour: Deep and intense ruby red.
Nose: Intensity, with notes of blackberry, red currant and cherry. Followed by hints of balsamic, spicy tobacco, and chocolate.
Palate: Broad, full-flavoured; yet austere, with notes of liquorice, spices and red fruit pulp.
Alcohol content: 14%.
Serving temperature: 18-20 C°.
Food match: First courses with truffle, braised meat or roast stuffed with chestnuts, game, and mature cheese.

Eliana IGT Umbria.

Production area: The vineyards are situated at an altitude of 250-300 metres above sea level south of the municipality of Ficulle.
Soil: Grey, medium texture with natural bone-meal.

Varieties: Grechetto and Chardonnay.
Training system: spurred cordon.
Planting density: 4.160 vines per Ha.
Vinification: The grapes are immediately cooled to 4-5 C°, followed by a short cryomaceration. The juice is clarified through cold settling for 24-36 hours. The wine ferments in new barrique for six months and matures in wood and steel vats.
Colour: Straw yellow with vivid greenish highlights.
Nose: Intense floral aroma with scents of citrus and white peach.
Palate: Sapid, elegant with good mineral content that evolves into a complex body with a long aromatic finish.
Alcohol content: 13%.
Serving temperature: 12-14 C°.
Food match: Antipasti, soups, seafood and young cheese.

Sediana IGT Umbria.

Production area: The vineyards are situated at 250 metres above sea level south of the municipality of Ficulle at Ginepreta.
Soil: Grey, clayey-calcareous with natural bone-meal.
Varieties: Cabernet Sauvignon, Cabernet Franc and Merlot, picked and vinified separately.
Training system: spurred cordon.
Planting density: 4.160 vines per Ha.
Vinification: Selected grapes are immediately cooled to 12-14 C°, followed by maceration for 8-10 days at 20-25 C°. The malolactic fermentation is performed in barrique. After 8-10 months' ageing the wines are blended and bottled. They are kept in the bottle for six months before release.
Colour: Deep ruby.
Nose: Ethereal, scents of mature forest fruits, violet and liquorice with herbaceous notes.
Palate: Warm and harmonious with firm tannins.
Alcohol content: 13.5%.
Serving temperature: 18-20 C°.
Food match: Ideal with red meat stuffed with chestnuts, game, and mature cheese.

Hédoné Bianco IGT Umbria.

Production area: The vineyards are situated at an altitude of 250-300 metres above sea level south of the municipality of Ficulle.
Soil: Grey, medium texture, calcareous with natural bone-meal.
Varieties: Trebbiano, Malvesia, Grechetto and Manzoni (Riesling and Pinot Bianco crossing).
Training system: spurred cordon.
Planting density: 4.160 vines per Ha.
Vinification: The grapes are immediately cooled to 10-12 C° and softly pressed; the juice is clarified through cold settling and ferments slowly for 15-18 days.
Colour: Bright yellow with greenish highlights.
Nose: Intense floral aroma with scents of citrus and white peach.
Palate: Ethereal, floral, fresh, with notes of peach and banana.
Alcohol content: 12.5%.
Serving temperature: 12 C°.
Food match: Aperitif, first courses, white meats and seafood.

Hédoné Rosso IGT Umbria.

Production area: The vineyards are situated at 250 metres above sea level south of the municipality of Ficulle.
Soil: Grey, clayey-calcareous with natural bone-meal.
Varieties: Sangiovese, Cabernet Sauvignon, Cabernet Franc and Merlot.
Training system: spurred cordon.
Planting density: 4.160 vines per Ha.
Vinification: The grapes are immediately cooled to 12-14 C°. The juice ferments at 24-25 C° for 10-12 days.
Colour: Lively red with violet reflections.
Nose: Fruity, with scents of prunes, cassis and sour cherry.
Palate: Fresh, velvety, but still firm with a soft finish.
Alcohol content: 12.5%.
Serving temperature: 16-18 C°.
Food match: White and red meat, fresh or slightly mature cheese.

Grappa 1861 San Valentino.

Production area: grapes from the Cirulli vineyards.
Soil: Grey, medium texture, clayey with natural bone-meal.
Varieties: Grechetto and Chardonnay.
The fermented marc is transported in 200 litre containers in order not to lose its aromatic substances.
Distillation method: the grappa is produced by discontinuous distillation. The marc preserves the characteristics of the wine and the grappa is further improved by ageing in wood.

Tenuta Corini

Vocabolo Casino 53, 05010,
Montegabbione TR
Tel/Fax: 0763 837535
www.tenutacorini.com
tenutacorini@yahoo.it

The Tenuta Corini is situated in an area of Umbria that is as beautiful as it is unknown, whose wine-growing potential is still entirely untapped. Montegabbione is the Corini family's town of origin, so returning after thirty years in Switzerland, the family decided to invest the fruits of their labour there. They built a new cellar, perfectly integrated with the surrounding landscape, and restored the adjacent villa to provide guest accommodation. Their aim is to make the area known for the production of great wines. The estate welcomes visitors and makes every effort to make them feel at home.

The previous vineyard in the same location had been abandoned for 35 years, before the Corini family bought the property in 1997. The vineyards were completely restocked and in the newly built wine cellars state-of-the-art equipment was installed. The first vintage was in 2001. The first harvest for Spumante from Pinot Nero was in progress at the time of my visit to the winery in 2010.

One of the driving forces behind the establishment of the new enterprise was Stefano Corini. Other members of the family and good friends assisted him. The hard work and enthusiasm shows in every aspect of the new winery: their aim is to produce great wines with distinctive features.

Castel di Fiori. Bianco IGT Umbria.

The wine takes the name from the castle on the hill. It is made entirely from Sauvignon Blanc grapes, one of the most famous grape varieties in the world, but never grown before in the neighbourhood of Montegabbione. The wine is matured in stainless steel tanks for seven months before it is bottled and marketed. It has a pale yellow colour with golden tints. It has a good body and an intense fruity scent, and fresh flavour. The ideal accompaniment for summer dishes or first courses.

Frabusco. Rosso IGT Umbria.

The name is an amalgam of names: FRA is the beginning of the mother's name – Frasconi. BU is the start of a good friend's name – Buser; and RINI is how the name Corini ends.
The grapes used are Sangiovese, Montepulciano and Merlot. Vinification is in stainless steel vats, followed by 12 months ageing in barrique, then in bottles. It has a concentrated ruby red colour; and a scent of fruits of the forest. It has a vigorous taste, deep and lush with plum and spice aromas. The palate is soft, full hearted with hints of sweet cherry and pleasing tannins in evidence. It is ideal with red meats and main courses.

Camerti. Pinot Nero IGT Umbria.

The wine has taken its name from the Camerti people who were the original inhabitants of the old region before the arrival of the Umbrii in central Italy. Tenuta Corini are responsible for introducing the Pinot Nero grape to the area, having recognised that both soil and climatic conditions were ideally suited for this variety of grape. The wine is made entirely from Pinot Nero grapes. Alcoholic fermentation is in stainless steel vats, followed by malolactic fermentation in barrique for 8 months. It is matured in the bottle for a further year. The wine has an elegant ruby red colour; a fragrance of forest fruits and liquorice. It is a well-balanced wine with long persistence.

Custodi

Azienda Agricola Custodi Gian Franco
Loc: Canale, Viale Venere, 05010,
Orvieto TR
Tel: 0763 29053
Fax: 0763 29305
www.cantinacustodi.com
info@cantinacustodi.com

The Custodi agricultural estate is situated on the hills of Orvieto in the locality of Canale. It covers an area of 70 hectares, carefully cultivated as olive groves, arable land and vineyards. Of the 37 hectares dedicated to the cultivation of vines, at least half produce DOC grapes used for the production of Orvieto Classico wine, the rest is used to produce Sangiovese and other highly prestigious non autochthonous vines such as: Chardonnay, Sauvignon Blanc, Merlot, Cabernet Sauvignon and Cabernet Franc, which all derive from a careful selection of clones. The philosophy of the estate is expressed in its attentive care of the vines, of the grapes and its vinification process in order to obtain a production of high quality wines in full respect of the land and its antique traditions.

Austero. Umbria IGT Merlot.

Grapes: 100% Merlot.
Soil: Volcanic soil speckled with tufa and clay.
Vineyard density: 3.00 x1.00 m.
Training system: spurred cordon.
Yield: 70-75 quintals per hectare – 45 hectolitre
Vinification: De-stalking, fermentation with skin contact for 12-15 days at the temperature between 25-28 C°. During the initial phase of fermentation numerous re-passing of must over the grape dregs are carried out every day, and the grape dregs are re-immersed. In the first four days of fermentation two *delestages* are carried out (the separation of part of the must for oxygenation).

Ageing process: Stainless steel for approximately 2-3 months, barrels 8-10 months, in bottle 2 months.
Bottling: December of the year following the harvest.
Annual production: About 5.000 bottles.
Colour: Strong ruby red with bright and dark purple tones.
Aroma: Full, with intense sensations of fruits and spices.
Taste: Full-bodied, strong, persistent and warm.
Alcoholic grade: 14% vol.
Ageing capacity: 4-5 years.
Serving suggestions: 18 C°.

Piancoleto. Umbria IGT Rosso.

Grapes: Sangiovese and Merlot.
Soil: Volcanic soil, sandy with clay banks.
Vineyard density: 3.00x1.00 m.
Training system: spurred cordon.
Yield: 90 quintals per hectare.
Vinification: De-stalking, followed by fermentation with skin contact at 25 C° for 5-6 days. During fermentation, five or six re-passing of the grape dregs are carried out to improve the extraction of the colour and the aroma of the wine.
Ageing process: Stainless steel for approximately 4-5 months, in bottle 2 months.
Bottling: February-March of the year following the harvest.
Annual production: About 15.000 bottles.
Colour: Ruby red with bright purple tones.
Aroma: Pleasant notes of mature red fruits, fresh, tonic.
Taste: Good -bodied, full, dry and persistent.
Alcoholic grade: 13.5% vol.
Ageing capacity: 2-3 years.
Serving suggestions: 16-19 C° in red wine glasses.

Belloro. Orvieto DOC Classico Secco.

Grapes: Procanico, Grechetto, Drupeggio, Verdello, Chardonnay.
Altitude about 300 metres above sea level.
Soil: loose volcanic soil.
Vineyard density: 3.00x1.00 m.

Training system: spurred cordon.
Yield: 100-110 quintals per hectare.
Vinification: Light crushing of the grapes after a precise harvest of the best bunches and immediately separated from the skins. Controlled fermentation at 15-16 C°, with added selected yeasts. Duration of the fermentation is about fifteen days.
Ageing process: Stainless steel for about 4 months, then in the bottle for 2 months.
Bottling: February-March of the year following the harvest.
Annual production: About 25.000 bottles.
Colour: Pale straw yellow.
Aroma: Fruity, flowery, pleasant and intense.
Taste: Harmonious, fruity and fresh.
Alcoholic grade: 12.5% vol.
Ageing capacity: 2 years.
Serving suggestions: 12 C°.

Pertusa. Orvieto DOC Classico Superiore. Vendemmia Tardiva.

Grapes: Procanico, Malvasia, Grechetto, Drupeggio, and Sauvignon Blanc.
Altitude: about 300 metres above sea level.
Soil: Mainly volcanic.
Vineyard: Selected for favourable exposure to encourage attacks by noble rot.
Vineyard density: 3.00x1.00 m.
Training: Runner system.
Yield: 60 quintals per hectare.
Picking period: After 25th October through to November, depending on weather conditions and the state of the grapes.
Vinification: Light pressing of the grapes. Immediate separation from the skins, followed by cold decanting of the must for clearing. Alcoholic fermentation at controlled temperature (maximum 18 C°) in stainless steel containers. The fermentation is arrested by cooling when the desired level of sugar is reached.
Maturation: in small oak casks.
Mean annual production: 3.000 bottles.
Colour: Intense straw yellow.

Taste: Broad and complex, rich with notes of mature fruit and pleasantly sweet spices.
Scent: sweet, soft and elegant with fruity notes.
Ageing capacity: 3-4 years.
Serving suggestions: 12-14 C°.

Falesco

Azienda Vinicola Falesco srl
Localita: San Pietro – 05020
Montecchio TR
Tel: 0744 9556
Fax: 0744 951219
www.falesco.it
info@falesco.it

The Falesco Winery was established in Montefiascone (Lazio, Viterbo province) in 1979. The owners are the brothers Riccardo and Renzo Cotarella, both respected oenologists in Lazio and Umbria. Retrieving historical vines was of paramount importance amongst their initial goals. This territory had been famous for centuries for its outstanding wines, and appreciated by the Roman aristocracy, yet, in recent years, it has almost sunk into oblivion. It took several years of painstaking research and selection before rediscovering old clones, which had been considered extinct; their matchless aroma and organoleptic values were almost lost with the planting of specialised vineyards in the 1960s.

Besides retrieving vines, Falesco identified the locations suitable for the growing of high quality grapes. The area occupied by the Poggio dei Gelsi vineyard, at 400 metres above sea level, with a south-west exposure looking towards Bolsena Lake was one of these. Here the rarest local varietals of white grapes survived, including the Roscetto.

At the same time Falesco built and equipped a modern cellar where the use of state-of-the-art technologies for the fermentation enabled them to enhance the aromas and taste of local selections. Ten years later, in 1989, Falesco started producing Est! Est!! Est!!!

Starting from vintage 1998, Falesco produced Ferantano, a red wine, which thoroughly expresses the potential and richness of the grapes.

Then another outstanding result was achieved with a red wine. This time the selected variety was a Merlot clone. Born with the

1993 vintage, Montiano has been acclaimed as one of the greatest and most innovative Italian red wines.

Furthermore, with the vintage of 2001, Falesco thought it would be worthwhile making the most of another variety in the Lake Bolsena area. Pomele came from the Aleatico grape variety, which is best known for its typical aroma, freshness and friendliness.

Recently Falesco has enriched its property with the acquisition of the Marciliano Estate of 260 hectares, which is situated on a hill south of Orvieto in the municipality of Montecchio. In these vineyards Merlot, Cabernet and Sangiovese grapes are grown for the production of Vitiano and Merlot dell'Umbria, but also Vermentino and Verdicchio to achieve the Vitiano Bianco. Marciliano is made with Cabernet Sauvignon grapes from the best vineyard in the estate.

In joint effort with Tuscia University in Viterbo, Falesco has planted an experimental vineyard in the same area with 32 different varietals ranging from Nero D'Avola to Primitivo, from Malbec to Tannat and again from Carmènere to Montepulciano and Teroldego. Falesco firmly believes in this territory and wants to experiment with more varieties in the Marciliano area.

The Falesco Winery is located in Umbria in the municipality of Montecchio, the area bordering on Lazio. Its vineyards straddle the border between Lazio and Umbria, from Lake Bolsena to the hills surrounding Orvieto. The climatic characteristics of this territory are similar. The soil is partly volcanic, partly sedimentary; both well suited to the growing of vines, as witnessed by centuries of wine production.

Quality in wine can be achieved only if one follows the whole production process, from selecting the ground, to the growing the grapes, then making the wine and bottling the finished product. Falesco's vineyards are planted on the best grounds in the area where the pedoclimatic conditions account for high quality grapes. The density of vines is increased in order to reduce the yield, yet keep the overall yield per hectare unchanged. Monitoring the changing of the seasons, the number of grapes is reduced through green harvesting. Vinification techniques are adapted to take into account and enhance the quality of the grapes achieved in the vineyard. The experience, competence and passion, both in the vineyard and in the winery, of the technical staff make an important contribution to producing wines rich in: structure, character, softness and elegance.

NB: I have omitted the wines of Lazio from the following list.

Grechetto IGT Umbria.

Grechetto is an autochthonous grape variety from Orvieto. Several years of selection has led to the identification of clones with small berries and a high sugar content in perfect balance with their acid components. The grapes are meaty and rich in extracts; they are the living proof that painstaking research for traditional vines pays good dividends.
Grapes: Grechetto 100%.
Production zone: Orvieto.
Size of vineyard: 5 hectares.
Altitude of vineyard: 200 metres above sea level.
Type of soil: Sedimentary, clayey.
Training system: spurred cordon.
Density of vines: 3.300 per hectare.
Production per hectare: 8.000 kg.
Yield of grapes into wine: 60%.
Average age of vines: 19 years.
Harvest time: Late September.
Vinification: cryomaceration with the skin for 10 hours at 7 C°.
Alcoholic fermentation: In stainless steel vats at a temperature of 13/15 C°.
Malolactic fermentation: not carried out.
Ageing: in bottles.
Alcoholic content: 13.10% vol.
Total acidity: 5.70 gr./lt.
Dry extract: 22.5 gr./lt.
pH: 3.1.
The wine: The wine has a bright straw yellow colour with greenish reflections. The scents are extremely elegant, with rich aromatic range, and a suggestion of small flowers. It is full in the mouth, with extremely pleasant flavours, a distinctive style

and a full body. It should be drunk at a temperature of 10 C° as an accompaniment to fish, meat *hors d'oeuvres* and delicate dishes with white meat.

Vitiano IGT Umbria. Bianca.

Grapes: Vermentino 50%, Verdicchio 50%.
Production zone: Montecchio, Orvieto.
Size of vineyard: 5 hectares.
Altitude of vineyard: 300 metres above sea level.
Type of soil: Sedimentary, rather clayey and calcareous.
Training system: spurred cordon.
Density of vines: 6.500 per hectare.
Production per hectare: 7.500 kg.
Yield of grapes into wine: 60%.
Average age of vines: 8 years.
Harvest time: September. The harvest takes place in two phases, on the basis of the different ripening time of the two varieties.
Vinification: Cold skin contact for 10 hours at 8 C°. 60% of the free-run must is pumped into stainless steel tanks to ferment at a temperature of 13/15 C° with indigenous yeasts as *pied de cuve*. After racking and fining, the wine is kept in stainless steel vats until February when it is bottled and aged.
Malolactic fermentation: not carried out.
Ageing: in bottles.
Alcoholic content: 13.30% vol.
Total acidity: 5.80 gr./lt.
Dry extract: 23.50 gr./lt.
pH: 3.20.
The wine: sapid, fresh, well balanced with an elegant softness, a good structure and lingering aromas.

Vitiano IGT Umbria Rosato

Grapes: Merlot 30%, Cabernet 30%, Sangiovese 30%, and Aleatico 10%.
Production zone: Montecchio, Orvieto.
Size of vineyard: 75 hectares.
Altitude of vineyard: 300 metres above sea level.

Type of soil: Sedimentary, rather clayey and calcareous.
Training system: spurred cordon.
Density of vines: 6.000 per hectare.
Production per hectare: 8.000 kg.
Yield of grapes into wine: 60%.
Average age of vines: 15 years.
Harvest time: Merlot early September, Cabernet and Sangiovese in the third week of September, and Aleatico in the middle of October.
Vinification: After pressing and blending, the grapes are put inside a stainless steel vat where the three different varieties ferment separately at a temperature of 13/15 C°. The cold maceration lasts for about 48 hours. Thus, the right colour and phenolic components are achieved.
Malolactic fermentation: not carried out.
Fining: in bottles.
Alcoholic content: 12.50% vol.
Total acidity: 6 gr./lt.
Dry extract: 26.50 gr./lt.
pH: 3.20.
The wine: bright rosé colour with purple glints, with elegant, scents of fresh fruit. Full bodied with lingering aromas, it is soft, balanced with a sapid finish.

Vitiano IGT Umbria Rosso.

Grapes: Merlot 33%, Cabernet 33%, and Sangiovese 34%.
Production zone: Montecchio, Orvieto.
Size of vineyard: 150 hectares.
Altitude of vineyard: 300 metres above sea level.
Type of soil: Sedimentary, rather clayey and calcareous.
Training system: spurred cordon.
Density: 6.000 per hectare.
Production per hectare: 8.000 kg.
Yield of grapes into wine: 65%.
Average age of vines: 16 years.
Harvest time: Merlot early September, Cabernet and Sangiovese in the third week of September. The production of grapes is limited to two kilograms per vine

Vinification: Maceration on the skins. Alcoholic fermentation in stainless steel for 16 days, and takes place at different times, depending on the varieties, and includes pumping over and hand pressing. The malolactic fermentation is in barrique, after blending the wines from the three different varieties.
Ageing: In Nevers barrique for 3 months, then in bottles.
Alcoholic content: 13.20% vol.
Total acidity: 5 gr./lt.
Dry extract: 31.50 gr./lt.
pH: 3.70.
The wine: Vitiano is a young, red wine and can be appreciated immediately after its sale. It has an intense ruby red colour with a fresh and tasty acidity. It is a versatile red, and adapts easily to any number of dishes; it should be drunk in wide crystal chalices where it can develop its bouquet at a temperature of 18-19 C°.

Pesano IGT Merlot Umbria.

Grapes: Merlot 100%.
Production zone: Montecchio, Orvieto.
Size of vineyard: 40 hectares.
Altitude of vineyard: 350 metres above sea level.
Type of soil: Sedimentary, rather clayey and calcareous.
Training system: spurred cordon.
Density: 6.000 per hectare.
Production per hectare: 7.000 kg.
Yield of grapes into wine: 60%.
Average age of vines: 10 years.
Harvest time: Early September.
Vinification: Maceration on the skins for 22 days, thus, the contact of the must with the skins is long and intense, and every day, hand pressing is performed.
Alcoholic fermentation: in stainless steel.
Malolactic fermentation: in barrique.
Ageing: In Nevers barrique for 6 months.
Alcoholic content: 13.20% vol.
Total acidity: 4.90 gr./lt.
Dry extract: 33.50 gr./lt.
pH: 3.70.

The wine: Deep, ruby red, with rich scents; soft and spicy; well balanced aromas, harmonious, with a long, lingering finish.

Marciliano IGT Umbria.

Grapes: Cabernet Sauvignon 70%, Cabernet Franc 30%.
Production zone: Montecchio, Orvieto.
Size of vineyard: 12 hectares.
Altitude of vineyard: 350 metres above sea level.
Type of soil: Sedimentary, rather clayey and calcareous.
Training system: spurred cordon.
Density: 7.000 per hectare.
Production per hectare: 4.000 kg.
Yield of grapes into wine: 50%.
Average age of vines: 10 years.
Harvest time: 20th September. Green harvesting reduces the production of grapes to 0.6/0.8 kilos per vine. The grapes are carefully selected and bunches are picked one by one.
Vinification: Maceration on the skins for 25 days with lots of hand pressings. Must extraction 20%.
Alcoholic fermentation: In stainless steel.
Malolactic fermentation: Totally carried out in the barrique.
Ageing: In Nevers and Tronçais barrique for 16 months.
Alcoholic content: 13.20% vol.
Total acidity: 4.50 gr./lt.
Dry extract: 38.50 gr./lt.
pH: 3.70.
The wine: deep ruby red; complex and warm bouquet, with hints of ripe blackberries, and it tastes spicy with assertive tannins.

Grappa di Vitiano

Grapes: Merlot 33%, Cabernet 33% and Sangiovese 34%.
Distillation period: Late November.
Method of distillation: Discontinuous system powered by vapour stimulated copper elements.
Ageing: In stainless steel tanks for 4/6 months.
Grappa: Colourless, limpid and transparent.
Alcoholic contents: 40% vol.

Madonna del Latte.

Azienda Vitivinicola Madonna del Latte
Localita: Sugano 11 – 05018 Orvieto TR
Tel/fax: 0763 217760
mazardo@libero.it

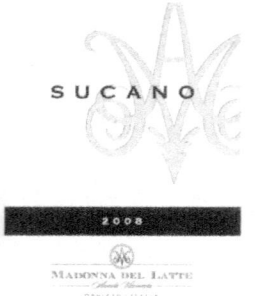

Manuela Zardo and Hellmuth Zwecker found the perfect location for their wine project in 2000 near the village of Sugano, tucked away in the hills overlooking Orvieto. They entrusted the agronomist, Federico Curtaz, to plant the vines in 2005 at 450 metres above sea level. The vines prospered on the volcanic soil with ideal exposure to the sun and the fresh mountain breezes.

Since July 2009, the oenologist, Dr Paolo Peira supervised the winemaking. He studied at the universities of Rome, Alba, and Bordeaux, where he now teaches. He is assisted by Leon Zwecker, who studied winemaking in Silberberg/Steiermark and in Krems. He gained further experience in South Tyrol, Friuli-Venezia Giulia, California and New Zealand.

The location of the vineyard has been the site for great red wines in times of the Papal States. Sante Lancerio, in charge of supplying wine for the cellars of the Vatican wrote a letter to Cardinal Guido Ascanio Sforza praising the divine drink favoured by His Holiness, who had a passion for a wine called "Castello Sucano" produced in the hills near Orvieto.

Today, Sucano is the name of the red wine produced by the Madonna del Latte estate. It is a manually produced niche product for epicures. This is guaranteed by the small amount produced annually – 10.000 to 15.000 bottles maximum.

In 2007 close to a hectare of Viognier vines were planted. It is a noble grape variety, from which the estate produces a white wine to accompany seafood, fish dishes, and Asian cuisine. The most famous Viognier comes from the Condrieu community in the Rhone Valley, but it has almost vanished. In 1970 there were just 14 hectares left. However, Viognier enjoyed a recent worldwide revival, and today, over 8.000 hectares are covered with this grape of great character.

Sucano IGT Umbria.

Grapes: Cabernet Franc 80%, Cabernet Sauvignon 20%.
Training system: head pruned (Albarello).
Age of vines: planted in 2005.
Altitude: 450 metres above sea level.
Alignment of slopes: south and south-east.
Density: 6.500 vines per hectare.
Yield: 8 tons per hectare.
Soil: Sandy, volcanic origin, with a high content of potassium and magnesium.
Harvest: mid-October, hand picked.
Vinification: De-stemming, and temperature controlled fermentation at 26-28 C°, maceration for approx. 10 days in stainless steel tanks. Then racking and controlled malolactic fermentation in French oak barrique, barrels and casks. Maturation in wood for approx. 12/14 months, then assembling in steel tanks before bottling, followed by maturation in the bottle for approx. 4/6 months.
Annual production: 10.000/15.000 bottles per annum.
The wine: intense and dark ruby red; the nose opens with hints of coffee and cocoa, backed by spicy notes of green pepper, sage and laurel. It has a complex palate with soft tannins, a fine acidity, and a long, lingering finish.
Serving temperature: 18 C°.
Food matches: Pasta dishes, savoury meat sauces, Parma ham, smoked sausages, wild boar, dove, pheasant, wild duck, all sorts of game, and mature cheeses.

Viognier IGT Umbria Viognier.

Grapes: Viognier 100%.
Training system: Guyot.
Age of vines: planted in 2007.
Altitude: 450 metres above sea level.
Alignment of slopes: south-east.
Density: 6.500 vines per hectare.
Yield: 7 tons per hectare.

Soil: Sandy, volcanic origin, with a high content of potassium and magnesium.
Harvest: Late September, hand picked.
Oenologist: Paolo Peira.
Vinification: pressing, settling for 12 hours at 10 C°, racking and addition of yeast cultures, temperature controlled fermentation at 17/18 C°, five months of maturation on dissolved yeasts, suppression of malolactic fermentation by cooling.
Bottling: in April, start of sale beginning of July.
Annual production: approx. 6.000 bottles per annum.
The wine: clear, straw yellow colour with a touch of green; with scents of citrus fruits, peach and apricots and the fragrance of roses. It is smooth on the palate, with a hint of pleasant bitterness in the finish.
Food matches: Seafood and fish dishes, spicy Asian cuisine.

Monrubio

Cantina Monrubio S.C.A.
Loc: Le Prese, 22, 05010
Monterubiaglio di Castel Viscardo TR
Tel: 0763 626064
Fax: 0763 626074
Cantina.monrubio@tiscali.it

Monrubio was established in 1957 in the municipal district of Castel Viscardo; a place with a legendary wine growing tradition going back to time immemorial. The area is protected by the surrounding high hills and suitably exposed to the south, with ideal soils for growing grapes of quality. The vineyards are located between the Orvieto DOC and Classico areas, and the winery has always tried to improve its viticultural heritage, selecting low-yield clones, which produce premium grapes and outstanding wines, both white and red.

Salaceto. Orvieto Classico DOC.

Grapes: Trebbiano, Malvasia, Verdello, Drupeggio, Grechetto and Chardonnay.
Altitude: about 250 metres above sea level.
Soil: Sedimentary and clayey.
Training system: spurred cordon.
Yield per hectare: 110 quintals.
Harvest time: September.
Vinification: Cold maceration on the skins for 10 hours at 10 C°, followed by alcoholic fermentation in stainless steel.
Alcohol: 12.50% vol.

Roio. Orvieto Classico DOC Amabile.

Grapes: Trebbiano, Malvasia, Verdello, Drupeggio, and Grechetto.
Altitude: about 300 metres above sea level.
Soil: Volcanic.

Training system: spurred cordon.
Yield per hectare: 110 quintals.
Harvest time: September to early October.
Vinification: alcoholic fermentation in stainless steel, at a controlled temperature of 15 C° maximum.
Alcohol: 11.50% vol. + 2% vol.

Soana. Orvieto Classico Superiore DOC.

Grapes: Trebbiano, Malvasia, Verdello, Drupeggio, Grechetto, and Sauvignon.
Altitude: about 200-250 metres above sea level.
Soil: Sedimentary and clayey.
Training system: spurred cordon.
Yield per hectare: 80 quintals.
Harvest time: September.
Alcoholic fermentation: In stainless steel.
Vinification: Cold maceration on the skins for 10 hours at 10 C°.
Alcohol: 12.50%.

Le Coste. Umbria IGT.

Grapes: Trebbiano, Malvasia, Verdello, Drupeggio, and Grechetto.
Altitude: about 100, 200, 300 metres above sea level.
Soil: Sedimentary, but mostly clayey.
Training system: spurred cordon.
Yield per hectare: 130 quintals.
Harvest time: September, early October.
Alcoholic fermentation: In stainless steel.
Vinification: Without skin contact.
Alcohol: 11.50%.

Le Coste Rosso. Umbria IGT.

Grapes: Sangiovese, Ciliegiolo, Montepulciano and Merlot.
Altitude: about 300 metres above sea level.
Soil: Sedimentary and clayey.
Training system: spurred cordon.

Yield per hectare: 110 quintals.
Harvest time: September.
Alcoholic fermentation: In stainless steel tanks for 30 days.
Vinification: With skin contact.
Alcohol: 12.50%.

Monrubio. Umbria IGT.

Grapes: Sangiovese, Ciliegiolo, Montepulciano and Merlot.
Altitude: about 200-250 metres above sea level.
Soil: Sedimentary and clayey.
Training system: spurred cordon.
Yield per hectare: 80 quintals.
Harvest time: September.
Alcoholic fermentation: In stainless steel.
Vinification: Cold maceration on the skins for 10 hours at 10 C°.
Alcohol: 12.50%.

Palaia. Umbria IGT.

Grapes: Merlot 34%, Pinot 33% and Cabernet Sauvignon 33%.
Altitude: about 300 metres above sea level.
Soil: Sedimentary and clayey.
Training system: spurred cordon.
Yield per hectare: 60 quintals.
Harvest time: September.
Alcoholic fermentation: In stainless steel.
Malolactic fermentation: In barrique.
Vinification: Maceration on the skins.
Ageing: In barrique for 12 months, then in bottles.
Alcohol: 13.50%.

Salceto Spumante Brut.

Grapes: Trebbiano, Grechetto and Chardonnay.
Altitude: about 200 metres above sea level.
Soil: Sedimentary, but mostly clayey and sandy.
Training system: spurred cordon.
Yield per hectare: 80 quintals.

Harvest time: Early September.
Alcoholic fermentation: In stainless steel for 15 days.
Vinification: Controlled temperature at maximum 15 C°.
Alcohol: 11.50%.

Salceto Spumante Demi-sec.

Grapes: Trebbiano, Grechetto and Chardonnay.
Altitude of the vineyards: About 200 metres above sea level.
Type of ground: Sedimentary, but mostly clayey and sandy.
Training system: Spurred Cordon.
Yield per hectare: 80 quintals.
Harvest time: Early September.
Alcoholic fermentation: In stainless steel for 15 days.
Vinification: Controlled temperature at maximum 15 C°.
Alcohol: 11.50%.

Grappa di Orvieto Classico.

Alcohol: 40% vol.
Taste: Transparent, crystal clear colour. Smooth scent with delicate flowery notes. Balanced and harmonious.
Serving temperature: 10-12 C°.
Recommended goblet: Small, tulip shaped crystal goblet.

Sergio Mottura

Loc: Poggio della Costa, 1
01020 - Civitella d'Agliano VT
Tel: 0761 914533
Fax: 0761 1810100
Vini@motturasergio.it

The vineyard is situated in the commune of Civitella d'Agliano in the province of Viterbo in the Lazio region. It is one of the five zones specified within the Orvieto DOC regulations. The variety of grapes grown in the vineyards are: Procanico, which produces sparse bunches, is resistant to rot, reddish-gold in colour, limited yield, but has a distinct personality. Verdello: has compact bunches, a dark green colour, high acidity and a delicate bouquet. Grechetto: the estate's favourite variety, of which three different clones have been selected, has rich, heady, lasting bouquets, together with full and persistent body. Drupeggio or Rupeccio: has a flowery bouquet and velvet smooth body.

The winery also produces Lazio red IGT wines, using different varieties, including: Merlot, Montepulciano d'Abruzzo and Pinot Nero. The other wines marketed are: Latour a Civitella, Poggio della Costa, Nenfro, Magone, Civitella Rosso, and Spumante Brut Millesimé.

The Mottura vineyards are worked in the traditional manner, using only natural fertilisers, and the grapes are picked by hand. For vinification, the estate employs the most up-to-date technology to the exclusion of all chemical additives. The harvest is gently crushed in horizontal presses. The must is immediately cooled to hasten the sedimentation of all foreign matter (soil, skins, seeds, etc) and fermentation occurs "in bianco" that is after the skins have been removed from the pure, clear juice. During fermentation the temperature is maintained at between 18 and 20 C°, the optimum to preserve and encourage the development of the natural flavours of the must. The wine is then left to rest for several months on its lees and the winter climate helps it to clarify. The wines are all bottled on the estate, and laid down to age for several years in the cool underground tufa caves that serve as the Sergio Mottura wine cellars.

Orvieto Secco DOC – Orvieto dry DOC.

Grapes: Procanico 50%, Verdello 25%, and Grechetto 25%.
Vineyard: lower slopes of the hills on the right-bank of the Tiber.
Vinification: Soft pressing, preventive static purification of the must by lowering the temperature. Fermentation at a controlled temperature, separately, according to the grape variety.
Maturation: in stainless steel containers.
Bottling: in January following the harvest.
Refining: in the bottle for two months.
Longevity: Best drunk within two years of harvesting.
Colour: Clear pale yellow with natural gold highlights.
Aroma: Fruity, fragrant, with hints of wild mint and herbs.
Flavour: Dry, but with a slightly bitter aftertaste.
Serving temperature: 8 C°.
Food matches: aperitif, or local dishes, lasagne, spaghetti with vegetable sauces, asparagus crêpes, country style chicken or rabbit, stewed cod and other fish dishes, and fresh cheeses.
Alcohol content: 13% vol.
Acidity: 5.60 g/l.

Orvieto Amabile DOC – Orvieto secco DOC.

Grapes: Procanico 45%, Verdello 25%, Grechetto 20% and Rupeccio 10%.
Vineyard: lower slopes of the hills on the right-bank of the Tiber.
Vinification: Soft pressing, preventive static purification of the must by lowering the temperature.
Maturation: in stainless steel containers.
Refining: in the bottle for two months.
Longevity: Best drunk within two years of harvesting.
Colour: Clear pale yellow with natural gold highlights.
Aroma: Fruity, fragrant, with hints of wild mint
Flavour: Dry, but with a slightly bitter aftertaste.

Serving temperature: 8/10 C°.
Food matches: aperitif or local dishes, lasagne, spaghetti with vegetable sauces, asparagus crêpes, country style chicken or rabbit, stewed cod and other fish dishes, and fresh cheeses.

Vigna Tragugnano DOC – Orvieto dry DOC.

Grapes: Procanico 40%, Verdello 30%, and Grechetto 30%.
Vineyard: Tragugnano, extends to 13 hectares, facing south at an altitude of about 160/180 meters.
Soil: Clayey of medium consistency.
Vinification: Soft pressing, preventive static purification of the must by lowering the temperature; deliberately slow fermentation of the clean must under a controlled temperature.
Maturation: In stainless steel vats, on fine lees, until the end of March.
Refining: In the bottle for two months.
Longevity: a complex wine; it greatly benefits from several years of ageing.
Colour: Clear pale yellow with natural gold highlights.
Aroma: Initially sweet, warm fragrance of wild mustard flower and vanilla; with maturity it reveals stronger scents, such as mint, sage, thyme and certain resins.
Flavour: Dry, but rounded, mellow, complex and persistent.
Serving temperature: 8/10 C°.
Food matches: aperitif, regional dishes, like croutons of tomato and basil, fresh pecorino and mozzarella cheeses.
Alcohol content: 13.5 % vol.
Acidity: 5.90 g/l.
Dry extract: 18.91 g/l.

Palazzone

Loc: Rocca Ripesena 68,
05019 - Orvieto TR
Tel: 0763 344921
Fax: 0763 394833
www.locandapalazzone.com
www.palzzone.com
info@palzzone.com

In 1969 the Dubini family bought the property "Il Palazzone". It was originally built by Cardinal Teodorio, at the bidding of Pope Boniface VIII, as a hostel for pilgrims on their way to Rome to celebrate the Jubilee of 1300 AD.

The hilly portion of the land adjacent to Rocca Ripesena has a superb view of Orvieto, which dominates the green valleys below. The land is made up of sedimentary soil and clay, ideal for growing vines. Consequently, Angelo Dubini decided to plant 25 hectares of the estate with a number of varieties of vines that he expected would make wines of great complexity and character.

In 1982 his two sons, Giovanni and Lodovico, made the first vintage from these grapes. Their 1988 vintage was sufficient to justify the construction of a winery to process all their own grapes, and also to market Palazzone wine, which is generally regarded as one of the most significant labels in Umbria.

Terre Vineate. Orvieto Classico DOC Superiore.

The name was found in medieval land registries; Terre Vineate describes a piece of land with vines.
First year of production: 1984.
Grapes: Procanico 50%, Grechetto 20%, Verdello, Drupeggio and Malvasia 30%.
Soil: sedimentary clay.
Exposure: to the east.
Altitude: 210 to 340 metres above sea level.

Yield per hectare: 80 quintals (8 tonnes) of grapes, which produce 45 hectolitres of wine.
Vinification: Soft pressing of whole hand picked bunches, followed by fermentation at a constant temperature of 20 C° in stainless steel vats for 20 days.
Bottling: In March after the harvest.
Sale: starting from April after the harvest.
Production: 45 000 bottles (750 ml Bordeaux style).
Taste: Deep, straw yellow in colour; with an elegant, vivid bouquet and the scent of hazelnut. The impact on the palate is intense, yet refreshingly dry, and the finish is the perfect balance between the perfume of fruits and a touch of bitterness.
Serving suggestion: Pasta dishes, fish, and meat in rich sauces.

Campo del Guardiano. Orvieto Classico DOC Superiore.

Local people call this part of the estate the "Warden's Field", and the name was retained for the wine produced from there.
First year of production: 1989.
Grapes: Procanico 50%, Grechetto 25%, Verdello, Drupeggio and Malvasia 25%.
Vineyard: Campo del Guardiano.
Soil: Sedimentary clay.
Exposure: east to north-east.
Altitude: 260 metres above sea level.
Yield per hectare: 80 quintals (8 tonnes) of grapes, which produce 40 hectolitres of wine.
Harvest: Early October.
Vinification: Soft pressing of un-stemmed grapes, followed by fermentation at a constant temperature of 20 C° in stainless steel vats for 20 days.
Bottling: In April after the harvest.
Ageing: 16-18 months in bottles, laid down horizontally on shelves in a tufa cave at a constant temperature of 14 C°.
Sale: 22-24 months after the harvest.
Production: 7 000 bottles (750 ml Bordeaux style).
Taste: deep straw yellow in colour with a soft green hue. It is a wine of remarkable depth and a continuous bouquet. It is soft on the palate with a silky finish and lasting fruity flavours.

Food matches: complex dishes – it has the body to complement creative food and it is particularly good with mussels, clams, scampi and octopus.

L'Ultima Spiaggia. Umbria IGT Bianco.

The name means "Last Chance". It was given to an experiment with a "non-indigenous" grape variety, Viognier. In 1991 the vines were planted double the traditional density and trained in the Guyot trellis system. The experiment was successful and timely, as recently Viognier has become a much talked-about grape variety amongst the cognoscenti.
First year of production: 1994.
Grapes: Viognier 100%.
Terrain: Sedimentary clay.
Exposure: east to north-east.
Altitude: 220 metres above sea level.
Yield per hectare: 60 quintals (6 tonnes) of grapes; somewhere around 1.5 to 2 kg per vine.
Harvest: At the end of August.
Vinification: Soft pressing of whole bunches. The fermentation takes place in barrique for 20 days.
Ageing: 6-9 months in barrique.
Bottling: in June after the harvest.
Refining: in bottles for 2 months.
Production: 5 000 bottles (750 ml Bordeaux style).
Taste: warm, golden straw in colour. In the nose, the floral tones are countered by the oak, in which the wine has been fermented. There is a sense of the fruit bursting forth from this constraint. On the palate, the wine is soft and lingering.
Food matches: a wine for summer dishes, and robust vegetable soups, like minestrone. Excellent with sea fish and crustaceans cooked with simplicity.

Grechetto. Umbria IGT Bianco.

First year of production: 1997.
Grapes: Grechetto 100%.
Soil: Sedimentary clay.

Exposure: Northeast.
Altitude: s 240 metres above sea level.
Yield per hectare: 90 quintals (9 tonnes) of grapes, which produce 50 hectolitres of wine.
Vinification: Soft pressing of un-stemmed grapes, followed by fermentation at a constant temperature of 20 C° in stainless steel vats for 20 days.
Bottling: In March after the harvest.
Sale: Starting from May after the harvest.
Production: 6 000 bottles (750 ml Bordeaux style).
Taste: It is a light bodied wine with a delicate straw-yellow colour. It has a fresh, inviting nose, full of flavour and finishes with a fruity fragrance and a slight touch of tannins.
Food matches: This is a wine that perfectly complements simple dishes of fresh sea fish and crustaceans.

Muffa Nobile. Umbria IGT Bianco.

Orvieto is one of the rare Italian locations suitable for producing this type of sweet wine. The vines are planted in a hollow, where morning mists gather and encourage the formation of a fungus called Botrytis Cinera (Noble Rot). The fungus causes no harm; it only uses up some of the water inside the grape berries, and, thus, concentrates the sugar content of the fruit.
First year of production: 1994.
Grapes: Sauvignon Blanc 100%.
Soil: Sedimentary clay.
Exposure: North to north-west.
Altitude: 220 metres above sea level.
Yield per hectare: 12 hectolitres (1 200 litres) of wine.
Harvest: End of October until 15th November. The grapes are picked at a number of different times, selecting only the bunches affected by Botrytis Cinerea.
Vinification: Soft pressing of un-stemmed grapes, followed by fermentation in barrique for 30 to 35 days.
Bottling: In April after the harvest.
Ageing: In bottles for 8 months.
Production: 4 000 bottles (375 ml Bordeaux style).

The wine: warm, golden in colour. It has the aroma of candied fruit and the mysterious touch of noble rot. The taste is rich, sweet, long and silky with hints of apricots and honey.
Food matches: Muffa Nobile is ideal for finishing meals with game dishes and strong cheeses as well as chocolates.

Rubbio. Umbria IGT Rosso.

The name of this wine comes from a medieval measure used in the surveying of land.
First year of production: 1988.
Grapes: Sangiovese 60%, Cabernet Sauvignon 20%, and Merlot 20%.
Soil: Sedimentary clay.
Exposure: East.
Altitude: 220 metres above sea level.
Yield per hectare: 70 quintals (7 tonnes) of grapes.
Vinification: Whole bunches of grapes with the skins left on; maceration in stainless steel vats for 10 days with frequent manual plunging down the cap. Both the alcoholic and malolactic fermentation takes place partly in stainless steel tanks and partly in barrique.
Ageing: 6-8 months; 50% in small barrique, 30% in larger vats, and 20% in stainless steel.
Bottling: April after the harvest.
Refining: In the bottle for 2 months.
Sale: Starting from June after the harvest.
Production: 10 000 bottles (750 ml Bordeaux style).
The wine: deep ruby red colour; acidity and tannins are nicely balanced with a full body from the fruit.
Food matches: Meat dishes – porchetta, casseroles of rabbit or hare, and vegetable dishes cooked in olive oil with herbs.

Armaleo. Umbria IGT Rosso.

In 1986 the estate began an experiment with Cabernet Sauvignon and Cabernet Franc and planted a vineyard; double the traditional density, also using an old Etruscan system of training the vines in order to maximise the sun and light available to the grapes.

First year of production: 1992.
Grapes: Cabernet Sauvignon 95% and Cabernet Franc 5%.
Soil: Sedimentary clay.
Exposure: East to north-east.
Altitude: 260 metres above sea level.
Yield per hectare: 60 quintals (6 tonnes); 1.5/2 kg per vine.
Vinification: Fermentation with the skins for 10 days. Both alcoholic and malolactic fermentation in stainless steel tanks.
Ageing: In barrique for 12-14 months.
Refining: In the bottle for 6-8 months.
Sale: 20-22 months after the harvest.
Production: 3 000 bottles (750 ml Bordeaux style).
The wine: ruby red in colour; hints of mineral traces, with aromas of rosemary and dark fruits. It has a long, rich finish.
Food matches: lamb, goat, and pork, as well as all kinds of game, and fully matured goat's cheese.

<u>Piviere san Donato. Umbria IGT Rosso.</u>

The wine is named after the medieval district in which the Palazzone estate is situated.
First year of production: 2001.
Grapes: Sangiovese 90% and Cabernet Sauvignon 10%.
Soil: Sedimentary clay.
Exposure: East to north-east.
Altitude: 290 metres above sea level.
Yield per hectare: 5.5 quintals (5.5 tonnes); 1.2 Kg per vine.
Vinification: Whole bunch fermentation for 14 days. Alcoholic and malolactic fermentation in stainless steel tanks.
Ageing: In barrique for 12 months.
Refining: In the bottle for 8 months.
Sale: 20-22 months after the harvest.
Production: 3 000 bottles (750 ml Bordeaux style).
The wine: ruby red in colour with tints of purple. The nose is intense with the perfume of red fruits. The flavour is long and concentrated with tannins from the oak barrel maturation.
Food matches: Umbrian traditional dishes, like home made pasta with rich sauces, roast game, grilled meats and roast poultry.

Tenuta Poggio del Lupo.

Vocabolo Buzzaghetto, 100
05011 Allerona TR
Tel: 0763 628350
Fax: 0763 628005
www.tenutapoggiodellupo.it
info@tenutapoggiodellupo.it

Facing south-east towards the Duomo of Orvieto, the Poggio del Lupo farm extends into the Allerona district, North of the Paglia River, on the Lupo hill at an altitude of 315 meters above sea level. It took its name in the Middle Ages from the place where wolves usually gathered at night; Poggio del Lupo means Wolf Knoll. The farm covers 116 hectares, more than 40 of which are dedicated to a specialist vineyard for the production of high quality wines.

In 2002 the Polato family set out on a great adventure by purchasing the Poggio del Lupo farm. They embarked on a long journey with enthusiasm, tenacity and a spirit of sacrifice in their search for excellence and quality. Their motto was: "The personal interpretation of the traditional local white wines, along with the introduction of innovative red wines, increasingly enhancing the use of native vines in all of them."

The incessant search for excellence starts with the selection of the grape variety to suit the terroir. Nurturing the fruit with expertise is the next stage. When the grapes reach optimum maturation and the desired levels of: sugars, acids and tannins; the selected bunches are hand picked and taken to the cellar. The process of transferring them into top quality wines is carried out with great attention to detail with all the help that modern technology offers. The work in the wine cellars is carried out with the technical collaboration of Riccardo Cotarella.

Novilunio. Orvieto DOC.

Production area: The vineyards are located in the extreme north-west zone of the Orvieto DOC area.
Grapes: Trebbiano 40%, Grechetto 20%, Verdello 20%, Drupeggio 10%, and Malvasia 10%.
Soil: mostly composed of big blocks of calcareous clay (*marne*) with sediments and fossils of marine origin.
Exposure: South to south-west, well exposed to sunlight.
Altitude: 300 metres above sea level.
Training: spurred cordon
Density: 4 000 plants per hectare.
Yield per hectare: 90 quintals of grapes, 60 hectolitres of wine.
Vinification: Soft pressing of the hand picked grapes, followed by cold settling for clearing the must. Fermentation is carried out under controlled temperature, followed by filtered clarification and sterilised cold bottling.
The wine: Straw yellow with green tints; a delicate perfume with flowery notes, and a dry and lively flavour.
Food matches: fish dishes, boiled meat and fresh cheeses.
Alcohol: 12% vol.
Serving temperature: 10 C° in Bordeaux glass.

Màrneo. Umbria IGT.

Production area: The vineyards are located in the extreme north-west zone of the Orvieto DOC area.
Grapes: Grechetto 40%, Chardonnay 30%, and Sauvignon Blanc 30%.
Soil: mostly composed of big blocks of calcareous clay (*marne*) with sediments and fossils of marine origin.
Exposure: South to south-west, well exposed to sunlight.
Altitude: 310 metres above sea level.
Training: spurred cordon.
Density: 4 500 plants per hectare.
Yield per hectare: 80 quintals of grapes, 55 hectolitres of wine.
Vinification: Soft pressing of the hand picked grapes, followed by cold settling for clearing the must. Fermentation is carried out under controlled temperature with the addition of selected

enzymes and yeasts; followed by static settling and filtered clarification, then sterilised cold bottling.
Colour: Straw yellow.
Perfume: deeply flowery and persistent.
Flavour: dry and mineral.
Food matches: fish dishes, white grilled meat, and cheeses.
Alcohol: 12.5% vol.
Serving temperature: 10 C° in Bordeaux Medium glass.

Lupiano. Orvietano Rosso DOC.

Production area: The vineyards are located in the extreme north-west zone of the Orvietano Rosso DOC area.
Grapes: Merlot 40%, Cabernet Sauvignon 40%, and Ciliegiolo 20%.
Soil: mostly composed of big blocks of calcareous clay (*marne*) with sediments and fossils of marine origin.
Exposure: South to south-west, well exposed to sunlight.
Altitude: 310 metres above sea level.
Training: spurred cordon.
Density: 4 500 plants per hectare.
Yield per hectare: 80 quintals of grapes, 55 hectolitres of wine.
Vinification: the grapes are selected and harvested before being pressed. Then alcoholic fermentation and maceration (pumping the must over the cap frequently) takes place over 12 to 14 days in stainless steel tanks at a controlled temperature. The must is then racked off and malolactic fermentation takes place in French oak barrique (228 litres) where the wine rests for about three months. Refining and ageing is in bottles.
Colour: Ruby with purple tints.
Perfume: Elegant with fruity notes.
Flavour: Dry and quite tannic.
Food matches: A good complement to grilled meat and medium matured cheeses.
Alcohol: 13% vol.
Serving temperature: 18 C° in *Ballon* glass.

Silentis. Umbria IGT.

Production area: The vineyards are located in the extreme north-west zone of the Orvietano Rosso DOC area.
Grapes: Montepulciano 100%.
Soil: mostly composed of big blocks of calcareous clay (*marne*) with sediments and fossils of marine origin.
Exposure: South to south-west, well exposed to sunlight.
Altitude: 330 metres above sea level.
Training: spurred cordon.
Density: 5 500 plants per hectare.
Yield per hectare: 60 quintals of grapes, 45 hectolitres of wine.
Vinification: Following a final thinning out to obtain a low yield, the grapes are selected and harvested by hand. After soft pressing the alcoholic fermentation and maceration (pumping the must over the cap frequently) takes place over 22 to 24 days in stainless steel tanks at a controlled temperature. The must is then racked off and malolactic fermentation takes place in French oak barrique (228 litres) where the wine rests for about 12 months.
Refining and ageing is in bottles.
Colour: Deep ruby.
Perfume: Rich with notes of mellow fruit.
Flavour: Full bodied and tannic.
Food matches: all kinds of meat and mature cheeses.
Alcohol: 13% vol.
Serving temperature: 18 C° in *Ballon* Magnum glass.

SassarA

Azienda Agricola Luciano SassarA
Loc: Pian del Vantaggio, 43
05019 Orvieto TR
Tel: 0763 215119
Fax: 0763 215119
e-mail:sassaravini@libero.it

Roberto Sassara and his son, Luciano, founded the company in 1979. They bought a farm near Orvieto with eighteen hectares of land, of which eight were dedicated to the production of Orvieto Classico wine. Twenty-three years later the vineyards expanded and now cover a total of 111 hectares in three different locations. Ficulle: 15 hectares growing grapes for the production of the Sant 'Egidio Orvieto DOC wine. Castiglione in Teverina (Lazio): 21.50 hectares growing grapes for the production of Orvieto DOC wine. Orvieto: 16 hectares are growing grapes for the production of Orvieto DOC wine; and 12 hectares for the production of red Umbria IGT wines: with Merlot, Cabernet, and Sangiovese grapes.

The Sassara family's residence is above the wine cellar. The grapes from the other vineyards are taken there for vinification. The cellar is furnished with modern equipment, including 8 000 hectolitre stainless steel tanks, facilities for soft pressing, must filtering and temperature controlled vats, where fermentation takes place. Roberto and Luciano Sassara manage the company with the collaboration of Riccardo Cotarella.

Sant 'Egidio. Orvieto DOC.

Grapes: Trebbiano, Malvasia Toscana, Verdello, Drupeggio, and Grechetto.
The vineyards are cultivated in the traditional manner, using only natural fertilisers and methods of weed control.
Vinification: the wine is produced following the rules of modern technology: soft pressing, must filtering, temperature controlled fermentation with the addition of selected yeasts.

Colour: pale straw yellow with greenish tints.
Bouquet: intense, persistent, with a clean almond taste.
Taste: Dry and velvety, with a slightly bitter aftertaste.
Alcohol: 12% vol.
Serving temperature: 10-12 C°.
Food matches: aperitif, soups, fish, risotto, and white meat.

La Pieve. Orvieto Classico DOC.

Grapes: Trebbiano, Malvasia Toscana, Verdello, Drupeggio, and Grechetto.
Only natural fertilisers and methods of weed control are used.
Vinification: soft pressing, must filtering, temperature controlled fermentation with the addition of selected yeasts.
Colour: pale straw yellow with greenish tints.
Bouquet: intense, persistent, with a clean almond taste.
Taste: Dry and velvety, with a slightly bitter aftertaste.
Alcohol: 12% vol.
Serving temperature: 10-12 C°.
Food matches: aperitif, soups, fish, risotto, and white meat.

Poggio del Ciculo. Orvieto Classico DOC.

Grapes: Grechetto 40%, Trebbiano, Malvasia Toscana, Verdello, and Drupeggio.
Only natural fertilisers and methods of weed control are used. The vines are grown on a hillside facing South on the Orvieto estate. The grapes are carefully selected and hand picked when they are at their best state of ripeness.
Vinification: soft pressing, must filtering, temperature controlled fermentation with the addition of selected yeasts.
Colour: pale straw yellow with greenish tints.
Bouquet: intense, persistent, with a clean almond taste.
Taste: Dry and velvety, with a slightly bitter aftertaste.
Alcohol: 13% vol.
Serving temperature: 10-12 C°.
Food matches: aperitif, soups, and fish.

Vantaggio. Umbria IGT Rosso

Grapes: Merlot 100%.
The vines are grown on the Orvieto estate, on a hill called Vantaggio. They have been planted with low yield and high density in mind. The grapes are selected and picked by hand.
Vinification: Fermentation with the skins for a long period in order to give an intense colour to the wine.
Colour: shining garnet red.
Bouquet: persistent, with a spicy perfume.
Taste: soft and velvety.
Alcohol: 12.5% vol.
Serving temperature: 20-21 C°.
Food matches: game, red meats, and mature cheeses.

Cantine Scambia

Tenuta Antica Selva di Meana
05011 Allerona TR
Tel: 0763 624157
Fax: 0763 624285
www.viniscambia.it
info@viniscambia.it
e-mail: cantinescambia@tiscali.it

Scambia, also known as the Antica Selva di Meana Estate (Old Woods of Meana) is six miles north of Orvieto, near Allerona. The estate extends over 600 acres of rolling hills that gently descend towards the left bank of the river Paglia, at an altitude from 50 to 250 metres above sea level. They date back to the Etruscans, then followed by the Romans. In the Middle Ages the Meana was a part of the Papal States during a period of social progress, when demand for wine increased. Apart from meeting the needs of Rome, the emerging middle classes in Orvieto also had to be satisfied. According to the land register of 1365, the highest number of vineyards was in Allerona.

The Scambia family took over the estate in 1977, when Dr. Antonio Scambia recognised the wine growing potential of the area. He made good use of the existing grapevines, and added new varietals. Exposure to sunlight, a gentle microclimate, and a soil of Pliocene sands, rich in minerals and fossils have provided the conditions for producing excellent wines. To ensure the highest quality, grape production is limited to between 50 and 80 quintals per hectare. The vines are cultivated without the use of herbicides. Fungicide treatments are carried out with great care and pesticides are absolutely banned. Harvest time is decided by the variety of the grape and its ripeness. There are three cellars, with a capacity of 6 000 hectolitres of wine. One is modern and equipped with the most advanced technology; the other two are more traditional, with large old Slovenian oak barrels, where the best wines are aged.

Gualdo di Meana. Orvieto Classico DOC

Vintage: 2009. Made from selected grapes of Grechetto, Procanico, Pinot Bianco and others specified in the designed Classico zone. Very clean, crisp and lively, offering quince, green apple, lime, and mineral notes with fresh acidity and a pleasant, long cleansing finish with a touch of bitter almonds.
Alcohol: 12.5% vol.

Rivarcale. Allerona IGT.

Vintage: 2008. Pretty, crispy and classy in style, this white wine is made from Pinot Nero grapes, off the skins. It has a remarkable balance, purity and pleasantly firm acidity. Fruity and delicate with apple and lemon on an effervescent palate and a long aftertaste. Refreshing, to enjoy as an aperitif or with a first course.
Alcohol: 11.5% vol.

Pinot Bianco. Allerona IGT.

Vintage: 2008/2009. Made from 100% Pinot Blanc grapes. Smooth and rich, bright golden colour with subtle aromas of ripe apple, pineapple and spices. Floral and mineral notes emerge when the wine opens. Impressive texture, balanced by ripe acidity that supports a long clear finish.
Alcohol: 12.5% vol.

Fontanile. Bianco Umbria IGT.

Vintage: 2008. Grechetto and Vermentino grapes. Fresh and easy with lovely fruity perfumes and an intense character of lemon peel with mineral hints. Medium bodied with good acidity and a long and flavourful finish.
Alcohol: 12.5% vol.

Don Tallaro – Novello. Allerona IGT/

Vintage: 2009. Obtained in 100% carbonic maceration method from Montepulciano, Malvasia and Ciliegiolo grapes. It displays a deep purple colour and it is fruity with hints of black cherries, plums and a nice balance of firm tannins. Its concentration and structure are bigger and deeper than usual. It is a wine with a clean and fruity finish. It can easily last for more than 2-4 years.
Alcohol: 12% vol.

Ripuglie. Rosso Umbria IGT.

Vintage: 2009. Ciliegiolo grapes. Light red in colour; well balanced with minerals that provide a silky feel. Full bodied with lovely fruit flavours and fine tannins. Lots of great acidity, makes it fresh and zesty. Long pleasant finish.
Alcohol: 12.5% vol.

Crognitello. Rosso Umbria IGT

Vintage: 2008. Sangiovese and Canaiolo grapes. A red wine that emphasises finesse and power. Bright and fruity with touches of spices. Balanced, with smooth tannins. Well made and pleasant from start to finish.
Alcohol: 13% vol.

Runico. Rosso Orvietano DOC.

Vintage: 2006. A pretty, refined and easy red from Sangiovese, Montepulciano, and Ciliegiolo grapes. Ruby in colour, it has cherry and crisp lemon notes with a hint of pepper. It is medium bodied with zesty, fresh acidity, light tannins and a long finish.
Alcohol: 13% vol.

Grabovio. Allerona IGT.

Vintage: 2005. 100% Sagrantino grapes. Deep ruby colour. Attractive, rich and warm with complex aromas of blackberry, ripe peach and vanilla. Full bodied with round and soft tannins

and firm acidity. The long concentrated fruity finish has a hint of currants and toast.
Alcohol: 14% vol.

Grottone. Allerona IGT.

Vintage: 2001. Made from 100% Montepulciano; aged in big oak casks. It is round, rich and balanced with blackberry, tobacco, chocolate and a hint of spicy notes. Full-bodied, velvety tannins and a long succulent finish.
Alcohol: 13% vol.

Tenuta Le Velette

Loc: Le Velette, 23
05018 Orvieto TR
Tel: 0763 29090
Fax: 0763 29114
www.levelette.it
tenuta.le.velette@libero.it

Le Velette lies in the centre of the production zone of Orvieto Classico on a plateau that faces the cliffs of the city of Orvieto. Their cellars were hand-carved into the tufa rock during the Etruscan period. The estate was the property of the Count Negroni until the 1800s. It was purchased in the latter half of the nineteenth century by the Felici family, from which the current owners are descended. The estate guards its ancient traditions, which they combine with the best of modern technology to produce wines of quality. The wines are estate-bottled and also made exclusively from their own grapes.

Lunato. Orvieto DOC Classico Superiore.

Grapes: Trebbiano 40%, Verdello 20%, Malvasia 5%,
Grechetto 30%, and Drupeggio 5%.
Soil: volcanic.
Age of vineyards: 18-30 years old.
The wine: intense straw yellow in colour enriched with golden reflections. Complex bouquet, with hints of candied fruits, and vanilla. It is a soft and rounded wine, while remaining dry. It has a long and persistently aromatic finish.

Berganorio. Orvieto DOC Classico Secco.

Grapes: Trebbiano 40%, Verdello 20%, Malvasia 5%,
Grechetto 30%, and Drupeggio 5%.
Soil: volcanic.

Age of vineyards: 6-30 years old.
The wine: straw coloured with greenish reflections, a fruity bouquet, harmonious with good complexity. It has a full flavour, pleasingly fresh and an aftertaste of bitter almonds.

Rasenna. Orvieto DOC Classico Amabile.

Grapes: Trebbiano 40%, Verdello 20%, Malvasia 5%, Grechetto 25%, Drupeggio 5%, and Sauvignon 5%.
Soil: volcanic.
Age of vineyards: 6-30 years old.
The wine: straw coloured with golden reflections, a bouquet of ripe fruits, rich in flavour due to the vinification of late vintage grapes. It is slightly sweet with a slight hint of wood.

Traluce. Umbria IGT.

Grapes: Sauvignon Blanc 100%.
Soil: volcanic.
Age of vineyards: 4-8 years old.
The wine: straw coloured with greenish reflections; an intense bouquet and elegant structure. Pleasingly aromatic, it is an outstanding example of the potential of Sauvignon varietal introduced in this area.

Sole Uve. Umbria IGT Grechetto.

Grapes: Grechetto 100%.
Soil: volcanic hills at an altitude of 300 metres above sea level.
Age of vineyards: 4-8 years old.
Harvest: mid September.
Vinification: fermentation in barrique.
Refining: in barrique for six months with *batonage* (the wine is left in contact with the sediment and lees, and frequently stirred up from the bottom).
Alcohol: 13.5% vol.

Rosso di Spicca. Rosso Orvietano DOC.

Grapes: Sangiovese 85% and Canaiolo 15%.
Soil: volcanic.
Age of vineyards: 5-30 years old.
The wine: ruby red colour with good intensity, persistent scent with a harmonious bouquet. One can taste the brief ageing in wood in full, round flavour and the pleasing tannins.

Calanco. Umbria IGT.

Grapes: Sangiovese 65% and Cabernet Sauvignon 35%.
Soil: volcanic.
Age of vineyards: 5-30 years old.
The wine: ruby red colour with violet reflections and a bouquet of ripe red berries and undertones of vanilla. The taste is intense, with a slight hint of paprika. It has well-structured tannins and a harmonious powerful body. The ageing in barrique gives it delicate vanilla tones.

Gaudio. Umbria IGT.

Grapes: Merlot 100%.
Soil: volcanic.
Age of vineyards: 8-15 years old.
The wine: deep ruby red colour with violet reflections and a full complex bouquet with hints of cocoa, tobacco and a touch of leather; a good balance between acidity and soft tannins.

Accordo. Umbria IGT.

Grapes: Sangiovese 100%.
Soil: South-west facing, and of volcanic origin.
Age of vineyards: 8-30 years old.
The wine: ruby red in colour with glints of light purple. Rich varied perfume, intensely fruity, with a hint of toasted hazelnut.

Tenuta Vitalonga

Agricola Maravalle
Loc: Montiano
05016 Ficulle TR
Tel: 0763 836722
Fax: 0763 836649
www.vitalonga.it
info@vitalonga.it

TERRA DI CONFINE

2005

UMBRIA

Gian Luigi and Pier Francesco Maravalle chose to produce only red wines in an area best known for its classic whites. They succeeded beyond expectations. Terra di Confine and Elcione have won prizes around the world that puts them amongst the top wine producers in Umbria. The Maravalle family has owned Vitalonga hill for over half a century. There have been about 60 harvests overseen by three generations.

The estate is located on the hills facing Orvieto in the south, just a few kilometres from the border with Tuscany and Lazio. "It is on a slope blessed for the production of great wines", according to Riccardo Cotarella, a friend of the family and wine maker of world renown who helped with the new enterprise.

The estate covers ninety hectares, twenty of them dedicated to vineyards, and there are also 1 500 olive trees planted on the hillsides. The altitude varies from 350 to 450 metres above sea level. The vineyards thrive in a chalky-clayey soil, Pliocene fossil rich land with sediments of marine origin. The hill enjoys good exposure to the sun, and the climate is ideal for the cultivation of grapes. The summers are warm with fresh nights and mostly dry; winters are mild, only with sporadic snow. There is always a gentle breeze blowing, inhibiting moulds and parasites, which makes for healthy plants. The principal grape varieties are Montepulciano, Sangiovese, Cabernet Sauvignon and Cabernet Franc. On average 5 400 vines are planted per hectare, trained in the spurred cordon system, with a plant spacing of 2.20 x 0.80 metres. A modern drip irrigation system is used when needed.

The cellar retains all the features of traditional rural architecture while it has been completely redesigned and installed with modern state-of-the-art equipment. There are sorting tables for grape selection during the harvest, temperature controlled stainless steel vats used for fermentation and a barrique storage cellar for ageing the wine. Only selected French oak barrels are used, which are replaced after 36 months. Ageing in the bottle takes place partially underground in a dry atmosphere kept at a constant temperature.

Terra di Confine. Umbria IGT.

The power of Montepulciano meets the soft charm of Merlot revealing notes of intensity. Terra di Confine is a complex and structured red wine, suitable for keeping.
Grapes: Montepulciano 80% and Merlot 20%.
Density of vines: 5 4000 per hectare.
Production per hectare: 40 quintals.
Yield of grapes into wine: 50%.
Harvest time: For Merlot, the first ten days in September. For Montepulciano, the first ten days in October.
Vinification: Maceration on the skins for 25 days with lots of hand pressing and the extraction of 20% of the must.
Alcoholic fermentation: in stainless steel tanks.
Malolactic fermentation: in oak barrels.
Ageing: 12 months in French oak barrels or barrique (Allier, Nevers and Tronçais).
Alcohol content: 13.5% vol.
Acidity: 5.50 g/l.
Dry extract: 31.06 g/l.
pH: 3.70 g/l.
Oenologist: Riccardo Cotarella.
Colour: intense deep ruby red.
Fragrance: red fruits with light touches of spices and liquorice.
Palate: complex and well rounded, great structure, soft and elegant, well balanced tannins, and a softly persistent finish.
Serving temperature: 18 C° served in a wide *ballon* glass.
Food matches: meat dishes, game, and mature cheeses.

Elcione. Umbria IGT.

Merlot and Cabernet show their Umbrian soul to the full. It is an international taste made of elegance and balance, a pleasant and versatile red wine.
Grapes: Merlot 50% and Cabernet 50%.
Altitude: 350 metres above sea level.
Soil: Chalky-clayey, rich in Pliocene fossils.
Density of vines: 5 4000 per hectare.
Production per hectare: 50 quintals.
Yield of grapes into wine: 70%.
Harvest time: For Merlot, the first ten days in September. For Cabernet the last ten days in September.
Vinification: Maceration on the skins for 15 days with lots of hand pressing and the extraction of 15% of the must.
Alcoholic fermentation: in stainless steel tanks.
Malolactic fermentation: in oak barrels.
Ageing: 6 months in French oak barrels or barrique (Allier, Nevers and Tronçais).
Alcohol content: 13.5% vol.
Acidity: 5.45 g/l.
Dry extract: 31.13 g/l.
pH: 3.62 g/l.
Oenologist: Riccardo Cotarella.
Colour: ruby red.
Fragrance: red fruits with touches of spices and herbs.
Palate: fruity with traces of vanilla and spices and a softly persistent finish.
Serving temperature: 18 C° served in a wide *ballon* glass.
Food matches: first courses, meat dishes, salamis made in the Italian tradition, and medium mature cheeses.

Nautica Rosé. Umbria IGT.

Vitalonga rosé has been born thinking about the sea; a very special rosé, rich with enticing aromas and secrets to discover, like the distant horizon of the sea calling.
Grapes: Merlot 50% and Cabernet 50%.
Altitude: 350 metres above sea level.

Soil: Chalky-clayey, rich in Pliocene fossils.
Density of vines: 5 4000 per hectare.
Production per hectare: 50 quintals.
Yield of grapes into wine: 70%.
Harvest time: For Merlot, the last ten days in August. For Cabernet the second half of September.
Vinification: Cold maceration on the skins for 48 hours.
Alcoholic fermentation: in stainless steel tanks at a controlled temperature of 14 C°.
Malolactic fermentation: Not carried out.
Alcohol content: 12.5% vol.
Acidity: 5.90 g/l.
Dry extract: 22.62 g/l.
pH: 3.19 g/l.
Oenologist: Riccardo Cotarella.
Colour: brilliant and deep pink.
Fragrance: intense red fruits with touches of rose petals.
Taste: elegant, persistent and unusually full-bodied with a balanced and smooth finish.
Serving temperature: 12-14 C° served in a tulip glass.
Food matches: Traditional Italian dishes, appetisers, pasta, rice, fish, meat and mild cheeses.

THE WINE PRODUCERS
TORGIANO

In 1968 the production area of Torgiano was the first one to be awarded the DOC status in Umbria. It was also the first to obtain a DOCG in 1990, mostly due to the efforts of Giorgio Lungarotti. His name stands out amongst the new generation of Italian wine producers. In the late 1950s Lungarotti set out on a mission to re-launch Umbria's viticulture. He had a vision for the future. His family was already renowned for its small production of wines that were greatly appreciated in the area; but Lungarotti was not content with that, and he revolutionised every aspect of wine production. His guiding light was his love for the land and its traditions, at the same time he fully embraced new technology. His project of modernisation constantly evolved with new developments in viticulture, and he managed to maintain an Umbrian dimension. He was awarded the title of *Cavaliere del Lavoro* as recognition for putting Umbria on the world wine map.

Today, every member of the family plays a part in Giorgio's project, the process of evolution continues with the help of his wife, Maria Grazia, and his two daughters, Teresa and Chiara. The family business keeps on extending and not just in producing wines, but in preserving the Umbrian cultural heritage. The Wine Museum was created in 1974 and the Olive and Oil Museum in 2000. Cultural heritage and the love of wine are the key concepts in everything. The Lungarotti Foundation (*Fondazione Lungarotti*) has been set up to run both the museums, as well as promoting Italian wine production by organising scientific and cultural events: such as conferences, seminars and exhibitions, not only related to viticulture, but the wider artistic heritage of Umbria.

Visitors to Torgiano are well catered for by the Lungarotti hospitality. A five star hotel, a vino-therapy spa, an agriturismo hostel, tours of the vineyards, wine cellars and wine tasting sessions are all organised by the family. Today, the Lungarotti name is almost synonymous with Torgiano.

Torgiano is a fortified medieval town built on the site of an old Roman *castrum* (castle). Its name derives from the ancient tower, Tower of Janus (*Torre di Giano)*, which was dedicated to the two faced Roman god Janus, the god of all doorways and public gates. The tower still stands today, although no road passes through its gates. The highway running along the Tevere Valley (E45) bypasses the town by some kilometres to the west. The historical town centre, within the fortified walls, consists of but a handful of streets, however, it has a number of beautiful buildings dating back to the Middle Ages.

Both the Wine Museum and the Olive and Oil Museum are located in the centre of the town, which has a population of around 5 000. Torgiano may be a quiet backwater today, but once it was a thriving centre for agriculture and industry: wine production, textiles and ceramics in particular.

Torgiano is situated on a 200-metre hilltop overlooking two valleys at the confluence of the Chiascio and Tevere rivers, perched above a typical Umbrian countryside of rolling hills, vineyards and olive groves. It is a ten-minute drive from Perugia, or twenty minutes from Assisi and Todi. Montefalco is even closer, just over the next hill towards the South. The main business of both present day Torgiano and Montefalco is tourism and wine production. The vineyards and DOC zones tend to overlap. Lungarotti has vineyards and cellars in both places.

Cantine Giorgio Lungarotti SRL

Via Giorgio Lungarotti, 16
06089 Torgiano PG
Tel: 075 988661
Fax: 075 9886650
www.lungarotti.it

In Torgiano the productive lands were consolidated in order to unify the vineyards; of which Lungarotti owns 250 hectares, plus some other vineyards on lease. The lower slopes are planted with white grapes, while the hillsides are reserved for the reds. The vineyards continue along a ridge running from Torgiano to Brufa, the most prized area for vine cultivation.

The Lungarotti method of viticulture is eco-friendly, using the experience gained over many years, and include organic fertilisers and mechanical weed control. Short winter pruning and green pruning during the growing season improves the quality of the grapes, with ideal levels of sugar and polyphenol concentrations for the red grapes and good acidity for the whites.

The winery is just outside the town walls. In the cellars the technology is ultramodern, yet the procedures are ancient: a measured use of wood ageing in French oak barrique is combined with careful temperature control. In addition, the ancient ageing cellars greatly increase the quality of the wines.

In Montefalco the vineyards surround the winery at Turrita, at an altitude of almost 400 metres above sea level, where Lungarotti planted 20 hectares with Sagrantino, Sangiovese and Merlot vines. The underground cellar was built in an innovative way: the grapes arrive at ground floor level and are sent to the fermentation tanks below by the force of gravity. The underground cellars provide constant temperatures all year round, thus, saving energy. Wine production is limited to a few classic quality wines using mostly Sagrantino grapes, a varietal that makes Montefalco world famous.

Torre di Giano. Bianco di Torgiano DOC.

It is one of the first Italian DOC wines (1968).
Grapes: Trebbiano 70%, and Grechetto 30%.
Training: double Guyot pruning system.
Harvest: September.
Vinification: From free run juice, cryomaceration and further fermentation takes place in stainless steel; the wine is kept on the lees until bottling. Best consumed fresh, 1-2 years old.
The wine: straw coloured with greenish reflections, fruity with long-lasting, intense bouquet, with hints of citrus fruit, orange blossoms and fresh fruit salad; dry and with good structure, it is fragrant with delicate acidity and a long finish.
Serving temperature: 10-12 C°.
Food matches: Aperitif, pastas, risotto, white meats, fish, seafood, onion soup, and soft cheeses.

Torre di Giano Vigna Il Pino. Bianco di Torgiano DOC.

A special selection of Torre di Giano, it was one of the first Italian white wines to be aged in wood, as early as the 1970s, many years before the more recent trends.
Grapes: Trebbiano 70%, and Grechetto 30% from the Il Pino hillside vineyard.
Training: double Guyot pruning system.
Harvest: September, picked by hand in small crates.
Vinification: After cryomaceration, 30% is fermented on the fine lees in barrique for 3 months; the remaining 70% in stainless steel. The blend is then matured in wooden casks until the following spring. It is a wine with long ageing potential.
The wine: good structure, balanced and elegant. Straw yellow in colour with good intensity; the bouquet has floral scents and notes of linden, thyme, and acacia flowers, delicate hints of coconut, vanilla and white chocolate; sapid and fragrant flavour with a long finish as well as balanced, refreshing acidity.
Serving temperature: 12-14 C°.
Food matches: Dishes of haute cuisine, particularly with fish and seafood, pastas and soups, creamy risotto with truffles, vegetables and white meat flans.

Rubesco. Rosso di Torgiano DOC.

A DOC wine since 1968; Lungarotti's most popular wine, sold all around the world. Rubesco is a proprietary brand
Grapes: Sangiovese 70%, and Canaiolo 30%
Training: spurred cordon.
Harvest: September and October.
Vinification: Fermented in stainless steel with 15 days of skin maceration; aged for one year in casks and one in bottle. It is suitable for average ageing of 10-15 years.
The wine: a balanced body and a fine ruby colour. Its aromas are spicy, peppery, with hints of tobacco and violet. It has harmonious tannins with a long lasting fruity finish.
Serving temperature: 16 C°.
Food matches: pastas and risotto, barbecues, and roasted meat and cheeses. Also well suited for preparing sauces.

Rubesco Riserva Vigna Monticchio.
Torgiano Rosso Riserva DOCG.

A DOCG wine since 1990, with retroactive recognition to the 1983 vintage; it is a great classic.
Grapes: Sangiovese 70%, and Canaiolo 30% from the vineyard of Monticchio.
Training: double spurred cordon.
Harvest: October.
Vinification: Fermented in stainless steel with 15-20 days of skin maceration; barrique aged for one year and bottle aged for several years. Suitable for ageing of 30-35 years.
The wine: elegant, solid structure, a deep ruby colour and a complex aroma recalling maraschino cherries and blackberries, and notes of violet. It has soft tannins with a long finish.
Serving temperature: 16-18 C° in a large stem glass.
Food matches: roasted and braised red meats and mature cheeses.

Aurente. Umbria Chardonnay IGT.

Grapes: Chardonnay 90%, and Grechetto 10%
Training: double Guyot and double spurred cordon.
Harvest: August-September, hand picked in small crates.
Vinification: After cryomaceration in stainless steel it is completely fermented in barrique, where it remains for six months on the lees, with periodical batonage. It then remains for eight months in the bottle. It has long ageing potential.
The wine: intense straw yellow in colour with golden reflections. It has scents of orange blossom, banana, peach, pineapple, and light notes of oak, and vanilla; a flavour of fresh fruit and sapid, delicate citrus acidity and a long finish
Serving temperature: 12-14 C° in large stem glasses.
Food matches: truffle risotto, fish with sauce, or roasted white meats, lamb fricassee, and mature cheeses.

San Giorgio. Umbria Rosso IGT.

It bears the signature of Giorgio Lungarotti. It was an unusual blend for its time, and created the first "Superumbrian" in 1977. On the label, Saint George and the dragon is a detail from the famous painting by Raffaello, which is on display in the Louvre. On the national feast day of Saint George on 23rd April, it is a custom to light bonfires in the vineyards around Torgiano.
Grapes: Cabernet Sauvignon 50%, Sangiovese 40%, and Canaiolo 10%.
Training: double spurred cordon
Harvest: September and October, hand picked in small crates.
Vinification: Fermented in stainless steel with 15-20 days of skin maceration; followed by 12 months in barrique, and over 3 years in the bottle. It has a very long ageing potential.
The wine: solid structure and an intense ruby red colour with garnet reflections. The aroma releases notes of blackcurrant and bilberry and plum jam, light oak with a background of cinnamon, cocoa and balsamic notes. Concentrated flavour with mature tannins with a long lasting finish.
Serving temperature: 16-18 C° in large stem glasses.
Food pairings: roasted red meats, game, and sharp cheeses.

Lungarotti Brut.

VSQ (Vino Spumante di Qualitá) Classical Method, Vintage.
Making sparkling wines in Umbria began in the early 1980s; the soils and the micro climates are very good for the production of grapes with good acidity. Careful vinification makes for much sought after spumante wines.
Grapes: Chardonnay 50%, and Pinot Nero 50%.
Training: spurred cordon.
Harvest: August and the beginning of September.
Vinification: Classical Method: 36 months bottle fermentation and shaking by hand on *pupitres* for 40-45 days; the bottle then rests one month in the neck down position before *dégorgement* (removal of the cork with the sediment), and a further three months before release to the market.
The wine: golden in colour, clear and brilliant. It has fine and persistent *perlage* (bubbles), and a bouquet recalling almonds, hazelnuts and a hint of bread crust. It has a floral note on the finish; dry, fruity with a touch of citrus; fresh and clean acidity.
Serving temperature: 8-10 C° in champagne flute.
Food matches: aperitif, it is also great for the rest of the meal.

Torveto. Umbria Bianco IGT.

The marble column on the label is by Beverly Pepper, an American artist who has adopted Umbria as her home. It was sculpted as a symbol of her friendship for Maria Grazia, Chiara, and Teresa.
Grapes: Chardonnay 50% and Vermentino 50%.
Training: double Guyot.
Harvest: August and September.
Vinification: free running juice; a short cryomaceration, then fermentation in stainless steel and aged for two months in barrique. Kept on the fine lees until bottling.
The wine: straw yellow in colour with green reflections. The aroma is delicate and continues to evolve well in the glass, releasing notes of peach, apricot and citrus fruit on the finish.

With a dry flavour and good acidity, it has a remarkable fragrance and long, refreshing finish.
Serving temperature: 12-14 C° in large stem glasses.
Food matches: Starter dishes including cheese or black truffles, baked fish, meat casseroles and soft cheeses.

Toralco. Umbria Rosso IGT.

The marble column on the label is by Beverly Pepper, an American artist who has adopted Umbria as her home. It was sculpted as a symbol of her friendship for Maria Grazia, Chiara, and Teresa.
Grapes: Cabernet Sauvignon 50%, Merlot 30%, and Sagrantino.
Training: double spurred cordon.
Harvest: Merlot in September, Cabernet and Sagrantino in October.
Vinification: Fermented in stainless steel with 20 days of skin maceration; barrique aged for 10 months and bottle aged until release on the market at about 18 months from the harvest.
The wine: deep ruby red with vibrant violet reflections. A complex bouquet, with delicate light notes of oak, vanilla, chocolate and sweet spices, finishing with balsamic and blackberry notes; good acidity and a long, lingering finish with delicate hints of minerals.
Serving temperature: 12-14 C° in large stem glasses.
Food matches: roasted red meat, game, venison, and sharp cheeses. Also risotto with Toralco and Gorgonzola cheese.

Giubilante. Umbria Rosso IGT.

The oil painting named Giubilante is shown on the label; it is by Piero Dorazio (1988).
Grapes: Syrah, Sangiovese and Merlot in equal parts.
Training: spurred cordon.
Harvest: Merlot is harvested in September, the rest in October.
Vinification: Fermented in stainless steel with 15-20 days of skin maceration. Ageing eight months in barrique followed by a little more than a year in the bottle.

The wine: intense ruby red colour and brilliant violet touches; vibrant aromas of liquorice, pine resin and sweet tobacco with finishing notes of jam and maraschino cherries. It has an elegant, full flavour palate, recalling berries and balsamic touches, balanced with soft tannins and a delicate final finish.
Serving temperature: 16 C°.
Food matches: Extremely versatile wine, because of its soft tannins, suitable for an evening of creative cooking.

Rosso di Montefalco. Montefalco Rosso DOC.

On the label there is a view of the Montefalco winery, with a falcon in the foreground. The great passion of Emperor Frederick II of Swabia was hunting with falcons in the countryside surrounding Montefalco.
Grapes: Sangiovese 70%, Merlot 20%, and Sagrantino 10%.
Training: double spurred cordon.
Harvest: Sagrantino is harvested in October, the others are in September.
Vinification: Fermented in stainless steel with skin maceration for 25 days; then aged in barrique for twelve months and in the bottle for six months, before release to the market, according to legislation, at eighteen months from the harvest.
The wine: full-bodied, ruby red colour with violet reflections; intense bouquet with notes of cocoa, green spices, cloves, cinnamon, wild berries and plum jam. The flavour is dense, with soft tannins, balanced acidity and moderately austere finish.
Serving temperature: 16 C° in large stem glasses.
Food matches: roasted red meats, game, and mature cheeses.

Sagrantino. Montefalco Sagrantino DOCG.

Sagrantino is one of Umbria's most ancient native grapes: it is a wild beast and be understood and tamed by the best vine growing practices. On the label there is a view of the Montefalco winery.
Grapes: Sagrantino 100%.
Training: double spurred cordon.
Harvest: mid-October.

Vinification: Fermented in stainless steel with skin maceration for 28 days; then followed by twelve months in barrique and a further twenty months in the bottle, before being released to the market, according to legislation, at thirty-three months from the harvest. The wine: intense purple red, with great richness and a very long ageing potential. It has a complex bouquet of red fruit, maraschino cherries, blackcurrants and raspberry with delicate touches of sweet tobacco, cocoa and herbs. The structure is dense yet well balanced with rich tannins; fruity and supported by fresh acidity.
Serving temperature: 16-18 C° in large stem glasses.
Food matches: roasted red meats, game, and mature cheeses.

Sagrantino Passito. Montefalco Sagrantino Passito DOCG.

Sagrantino is one of Umbria's most ancient grapes; traditionally the wine produced from it was always a passito.
Grapes: Sagrantino 100%
Training: double spurred cordon.
Harvest: mid-October, then left to dry for two months on ventilated grates in order to avoid any risk of mould. Consequently, the sugars in the grapes are concentrated, which makes for a sweeter wine with a much higher alcoholic content.
Vinification: Fermented in stainless steel with skin maceration for 20 days; then followed by twelve months in barrique and a further eighteen months in the bottle.
The wine: a dessert wine with an intense ruby colour. It has rich aromas and hints of jam, prunes, bilberry and cloves. It is complex, with a soft sweetness and a tantalising finish of dark chocolate and spices. It has a long ageing potential.
Serving temperature: 14 C°.
Food matches: Excellent with fruit pies with berries, and pastries, as well as with mature cheeses.

Brezza. Umbria Bianco IGT.

The label shows an ancient compass rose taken from a captain's logbook; a reference to the sea for a wine with a refreshing taste.
Grapes: Chardonnay, Pinot Grigio and Grechetto in equal parts.

Training: double Guyot.
Harvest: at the end of August and the beginning of September.
Vinification: Cryomaceration in stainless steel.
The wine: straw yellow in colour, with greenish reflections. It is fragrant and recalls white fruits with floral notes; lively and slightly acidic, it has a soft, fruity finish that is lingering and refreshing. It is ready to drink in November, months before other white wines.
Serving temperature: 8-10 C° in large stem glasses.
Food matches: Aperitif, starter dishes, cured meats, soups, meat and vegetable flans, white meats, fresh water and sea fish. As it is not completely dry, it also goes well with fruit pies. Best drunk young, excellent in all seasons and particularly in summer.

Castel Grifone. Umbria Rosato IGT.

The label shows Castel Grifone, a medieval hilltop castle at Brufa. It overlooks Perugia, Assisi, and Torgiano.
Grapes: Sangiovese 70% and Canaiolo 30%.
Training: spurred cordon.
Harvest: in September.
Vinification: a brief maceration, then separation from the skins, and fermentation in stainless steel at controlled temperatures.
The wine: Fresh and vibrant, pale salmon pink in colour, its floral bouquet recalls roses and star anise. It is freshly acidic, with mineral hints; sapid with a soft aftertaste.
Serving temperature: 12 C°.
Food matches: Aperitif, cured meats, antipasti, soups, vegetable or meat casseroles, white meats, fresh water or sea fish, egg and omelettes. Preferably drunk fresh, but excellent all year round, particularly in summer.

Dulcis.

The label shows an engraved wafer iron from the sixteenth century, which is on display in the Lungarotti Foundation's Wine Museum.
Grapes: Trebbiano and other traditional white varietals.
Harvest: in September-October.

Vinification: the must undergoes the process for fortified wines; its two-year ageing in small oak casks provides it with an added dimension. Given the oxidation reached during the ageing process, the wine can be kept for many years in the bottle.
The wine: a sweet wine ennobled by a long wood ageing. Brilliant topaz colour, it recalls orange blossoms with a delicate aroma of almonds and candied fruit; soft, warm and delicately alcoholic, with an aftertaste hinting at apricots and figs.
Serving temperature: Fresh or refrigerated.
Food matches: Desserts, fruit pies; but it also goes well with foie gras, and soft cheeses like Gorgonzola and Roquefort.

Grappa Rubesco.

The label shows a bas-relief depicting a harvest detail from the Fontana Maggiore of Perugia.
Grapes: the marc of Sangiovese 70% and Canaiolo 30%.
Harvest: in September-October and de-stemmed before fermentation.
Distillation: Produced with still dripping marc, using the discontinuous method, with the elimination of the head and tail, in order to keep only the best part of the distillation.
Serving temperature: 12 C° in a glass for grappa.
Food matches: A classic end-of-the-meal drink after coffee, it is also good poured on strawberries or ice cream.

Grappa Riserva di Sagrantino.

The label shows a view of the Montefalco winery.
Grapes: Sagrantino marc of grapes harvested in October and de-stemmed before fermentation.
Distillation: Produced with still dripping marc, using the discontinuous method, with the elimination of the head and tail, in order to keep only the best part of the distillation. The grappa is aged in wood for 18 months, which gives it roundness.
Serving temperature: 16-18 C° in tulip shaped stem glass or brandy snifter.
Food matches: It should be enjoyed in tranquillity to appreciate its aroma and flavour.

THE WINE PRODUCERS
MONTEFALCO

The red wines of Montefalco are just as legendary as Orvieto whites and their fame goes back to Roman times. Pliny the Elder, who lived in the first century AD, described the *Itriola* grape in his Natural History. Most probably it was Sagrantino. It is not an easy vine to cultivate, but that had not stopped the people of Montefalco for the past couple of thousand years. The wine has a deep ruby colour with heavy tannins. The grapes were traditionally dried in order to produce Sagrantino Passito, a sweet wine for meditation, as the Italians refer to it. Sagrantino is considered to be one of the great grape varieties of Italy, albeit, not so well known as it is not grown anywhere else in Europe.

Sagrantino had been cultivated throughout the Middle Ages; the vineyards of Montefalco are mentioned in documents written in 1088 AD. During the fourteenth century the Commune of Montefalco drafted statutes regulating the vine growers. In 1540 the date of the harvest was set. In 1622 Cardinal Boncompagni revised the regulations and decreed harsher sanctions: the penalty for cutting the vines was nothing less than hanging.

Producing wine was a serious business then, just like it is today and as the good news about Sagrantino spreads, new wine producers move into the area. Lungarotti is just one of many leading wine makers who are better known in other wine growing regions, from Tuscany to Piedmont. The fame of Sagrantino is bound to spread even further.

The history of Montefalco goes back a long way. In the days of the Roman Empire there was a settlement on the top of the mount, Mons Faliscus, which was destroyed during the civil wars of first century BC. The town built in its place was known as Coccorone until the armies of Emperor Federico II of Swabia destroyed it in 1249. The prosperous and thriving medieval town he built in its place is today's Montefalco.

Montefalco translates as Falcon's Mount, appropriately named, as the Emperor was a keen falconer and wrote a book on the art of hunting with birds of prey.

The fortress towering above the town was constructed on the orders of Pope Giovanni XXII in 1329. Then, the Trinci family of Foligno, who became the new rulers, demolished the fortress. During the fourteenth century, when the popes defected to Avignon, due to never ending civil wars, Spoleto's papal governors took refuge in Montefalco.

Later, the town became part of the Papal States, and given the status of a city by Pope Pio IX in 1848. There is evidence of ecclesiastical presence everywhere one looks. The city is also the birthplace of eight saints, which is no mean achievement for Umbria, which is not only the green heart of Italy, but also the land of the saints – *la terra dei santi*.

The city is perched on top of a solitary hill in the mountain range flanking the Vale of Spoleto. It enjoys magnificent and wide-open views in every direction of the compass. It is dubbed *la ringheria dell'Umbria* - the balcony of Umbria. With a population of just over 5 000, it could hardly be called a *città* - but as it has a cathedral, it qualifies. There are also some magnificent old churches and art galleries in its historical centre. The richness of the city's churches is out of proportion considering the size of the place. Its sloping cobbled lanes are lined with tall and intricately decorated buildings that evoke another time, another civilisation. Unusually for a medieval city, it is bright and light; and extremely close to the sky.

Today, it is a quiet backwater. Inside its walls, it is completely untouched by modern development. Montefalco is a clean, quiet, civilised place with a high quality of life. Mercifully, it is hardly visited by tourists for a place with so many attractions. The vineyards and wine cellars are located in the surrounding countryside, some at a long distance from the city, dotted around an almost biblical landscape. Here time seems to stand still.

Azienda Agricola Adanti

06031, Arquata di Bevagna, PG
Tel: 0742 360295
Fax: 0742 361270
www.cantineadanti.com
info@cantineadanticom

The Adanti Farm is spread over 50 hectares; 30 are vineyards and 20 olive groves, within the municipality of Bevagna. The vineyards are situated in the hilly areas of Arquata, Colcimino, Torre del Colle, famous for its high quality wines. The vineyards extend over both the Montefalco and Colli Martani DOC zones. The vines are selected autochthonous grape varieties, such as Sagrantino, Sangiovese and Grechetto; as well as allochtonous grapes, namely Barbera, Cabernet, Chardonnay and Merlot.

The wine cellars are housed in a restructured convent, once belonging to an order of Philippine monks, originally built on ruins dating back to the Roman period. They are equipped with the best modern technology can offer. Adanti respects the territory and its ancient traditions, but it has also adapted modern methods of production in order to produce high quality wines.

Arquata Montefalco Bianco DOC.

Grapes: Grechetto, Trebbiano, and Chardonnay.
Vinification: fermentation off skins at controlled temperatures.
Refining: stainless steel vats and in the bottle.
Colour: green with gold tints.
Taste: vigorous, firm-bodied, with a delicate structure.
Bouquet: intense, lingering, delicate, fruity and floral.

Arquata Grechetto Colli Martani DOC.

Grapes: Grechetto 100%.
Vinification: fermentation off skins at controlled temperatures.
Refining: stainless steel vats and in the bottle.

Colour: straw coloured with green tints.
Taste: delicate, refined and lingering, smooth and full.
Bouquet: fruity, reminiscent of apple and rose.

Nispero Rosso dell'Umbria IGT.

Grapes: Sangiovese and Merlot.
Vinification: traditional fermentation on skins.
Refining: in oak barrels, then in bottle for one year.
Colour: ruby red with purple reflections.
Taste: intense, ample and persistent.
Bouquet: fruity.

Arquata Montefalco Rosso DOC.

Grapes: Sangiovese, Sagrantino, Merlot and Barbera.
Vinification: traditional fermentation on skins.
Refining: in oak barrels, then in the bottle for one year.
Colour: intense garnet.
Taste: intense, lingering, smooth and mouth filling.
Bouquet: fruits of the forest.

Arquata Rosso dell'Umbria IGT.

Grapes: Barbera, Cabernet Sauvignon and Merlot.
Vinification: traditional fermentation on skins.
Refining: in oak barrels, then in the bottle for three years.
Colour: intense ruby red with garnet tints.
Taste: harmonious and velvety, with a taste of blackberries.
Bouquet: lingering, reminiscent of blackberries and vanilla.

Arquata Montefalco Sagrantino DOCG.

Grapes: Sagrantino 100%.
Vinification: traditional fermentation on skins.
Refining: in oak barrels, then in the bottle for three years.
Colour: deep ruby red with garnet tints.
Taste: intense, fairly tannic, mouth filling.
Bouquet: intense, reminiscent of blackberries.

Arquata Montefalco Sagrantino Passito DOCG.

Grapes: Sagrantino 100%, after natural drying for approximately three months.
Vinification: traditional fermentation on skins.
Refining: in oak barrels, then in the bottle for three years.
Taste: rich and slightly dry, refined, and harmoniously semi-sweet.
Bouquet: blackberry jam, morello cherries with a hint of vanilla.

Arquata Grappa di Sagrantino.

A young grappa obtained from grape stalks. It is distilled by traditional methods, in a discontinuous plant (made entirely of copper) with small steam boilers.

Milziade Antano Fattoria Colleallodole

Voc. Colle Allodole, 3
Bevagna PG
Tel: 0742 360371
Fax: 39 361897
Cell: 39 4520251
www.fattoriacolleallodole.it
info@fattoriacolleallodole.com

The vineyards are on the border of the Montefalco and Colli Martani DOC zones. The farm (*fattoria*) is spread over thirty hectares; five and a half hectares growing vine. It was created in the 1970s when Milziade Antano first planted his vines on the hills outside Montefalco. For years Antano's family had earned a living in the sharecropping system, in which the grapes were sold to the local co-operative. But Milziade recognised the potential of the region, and after a short period of time spent abroad studying wine production, he returned home and planted his own vines. His methods, though considered modern by today's standard, were revolutionary during the 1970s. Tight density planting, south facing vines and a double Guyot training system, all played a role in creating healthy and robust grapes. Milziade was insistent on low yields and aggressive green harvesting. He treated the soil with respect, and had not used chemicals and pesticides.

During the 1990s Milziade's son, Francesco, took over the running of the business. He followed in his father's footsteps. He is quoted saying: "The wine producer has to create a product of which he is proud." The *fattoria* adheres to the rules of the old school in winemaking. A desire for quality is Francesco's driving force. His wines speak out about the quality of the land, and the passion of the people who till and harvest its fruits.

Sagrantino. Sagrantino di Montefalco DOCG.

Grapes: Sagrantino 100%.
Vinification: traditional for reds.
Refining and ageing: in oak and in the bottle.
Colour: ruby with violet reflections.
Taste: harmonious, full-bodied with rich tannins.
Fragrance: fruity with hints of jam.

Sagrantino Colleallodole. Sagrantino di Montefalco DOCG.

Grapes: Sagrantino 100%.
Vinification: traditional for reds.
Refining and ageing: in oak and in the bottle.
Colour: ruby with garnet reflections.
Taste: dry, robust, with persistent and refined tannins.
Fragrance: characteristic taste of oak.

Sagrantino Passito. Sagrantino di Montefalco DOCG Passito.

Grapes: Sagrantino 100%.
Vinification: traditional for reds.
Refining and ageing: in oak and in the bottle.
Colour: intense ruby.
Taste: sweet, hints of blackcurrant and redcurrant jam, aromatic herbs steeped in alcohol, liquorice, coffee and sweet spices.
Fragrance: intense and velvety.

Rosso di Montefalco. Montefalco Rosso DOC.

Grapes: Sangiovese, Sagrantino, and Merlot.
Vinification: traditional for reds.
Refining and ageing: in oak and in the bottle.
Colour: dense ruby.
Taste: dry, harmonious, with refined tannins.
Fragrance: fresh and delicate, with floral hints of red fruits.

Rosso Riserva. Montefalco Rosso DOC Riserva.

Grapes: Sangiovese, Merlot, Sagrantino, and Cabernet.
Vinification: traditional for reds.
Refining and ageing: in oak and in the bottle.
Colour: dark ruby.
Taste: full, concentrated and elegant, with a harmonious and persistent taste of jam.
Fragrance: intense and rich, with hints of fruit.

Grechetto. Grechetto Colli Martani DOC.

Grapes: Grechetto 100%.
Vinification: traditional for whites.
Refining and ageing: in stainless steel.
Colour: straw yellow.
Taste: warm and soft, with a delicate flavour.
Fragrance: delicate notes of pears, peaches, and cedar bark.

Azienda Agricola Antonelli San Marco s.s.

Località San Marco, 59
06036 Montefalco PG
Tel: 0742 379158
Fax: 0742 371063
www.antonellisanmarco.it
info@antonellisanmarco.it

The estate's origins are embedded deep in local history. Some medieval documents mention San Marco de Corticellis as a Longobard cohort situated in one of the most suitable areas for wine and oil production. The estate belonged to the Bishop of Spoleto from the 13th to the 19th centuries. The boundaries of the estate are still the same as those described in the 13th century document kept in the Bishop's Archive in Spoleto.

In 1881 Francesco Antonelli, a lawyer from Spoleto, bought the property and began extensive modifications, including the planting of specialised vineyards; a report, dated 1899, mentions the planting of five thousand vines per hectare. Antonelli was also concerned for his tenant farmers' welfare: "their health, the ease with which they can resolve their domestic needs makes them more efficient in their labour and causes them to care for the property". In 1979 the estate began to bottle and market its own wines; until then they were mostly sold in bulk.

The estate extends over 170 hectares in the Montefalco DOCG zone, of which 40 hectares are dedicated to vineyards. The average altitude is 350 metres above sea level. The Pleistocene hills are formed from alluvial clayey soil; rich in limestone, marl, sand, and fossils. The vineyards are mostly exposed to the south and west.

The cellars are situated at the heart of the estate, below the manor house. They have been enlarged to accommodate a system using the force of gravity during vinification, which eliminates the need for pumps and saves energy. The wines are made exclusively from grapes grown on the estate, allowing the winemaker to keep close control of the production. The estate also runs a cookery school, *Cucina in Cantina*, equipped with a state-of-the-art De Manicor professional kitchen.

Montefalco Rosso DOC.

Grapes: Sangiovese 70%, Sagrantino 15%, and Merlot 15%.
First vintage: 1979.
Yield per hectare: 55 hectolitre or 2 kg per plant.
Harvest: Sangiovese is hand picked in the last week of September.
Vinification: each varietal is vinified separately. Maceration and fermentation is in contact with the skins for 14 days at 25 C°. After malolactic fermentation the wine clarifies spontaneously, without need for filtration.
Ageing: the three component varietals are blended, then aged in 25 hectolitre oak barrels for 3 months.
Bottle ageing for 6 months.
The wine: ruby red in colour with purple tints. It has a bouquet of wild berries, cherries, and plums; warm and well balanced.
Serving temperature: 16 C°.
Food matches: first courses like risotto, tagliatelle, ravioli, roast and grilled meats, and poultry, and mature hard cheeses.

Montefalco Rosso DOC Riserva.

Grapes: Sangiovese 70%, (selected from the oldest vines), Sagrantino 15%, Cabernet Sauvignon 10%, and Merlot 5%.
First vintage: 1998.
Yield per hectare: 50 hectolitre or 1.6 kg per plant.
Harvest: Sangiovese is hand picked in the last week of September. They undergo a final selection in the cellar.
Vinification: each varietal is vinified separately. Fermentation is in contact with the skins for 15-20 days at 25 C°.
After malolactic fermentation the wine clarifies spontaneously without need for filtration.
Ageing: the four component varietals are blended, then aged in lightly toasted 500 litre barrels for 6 months, then larger 25

hectolitre barrels for 12 months. Clarification occurs in cement vats for 3 months.
Bottle ageing for 12 months.
The wine: intense ruby red in colour. The bouquet presents delicate notes of plums, cherries, and spice. The taste is elegant with ripe red fruits and balanced final tannins.
Serving temperature: 18 C°.
Food matches: roast and grilled meats, and mature cheeses.

Chiusa di Pannone. Sagrantino di Montefalco DOCG.

Grapes: Sagrantino 100%.
First vintage: 2003.
Vineyard: Chiusa di Pannone (2.70 hectares) at 400 metres above sea level, with a southern exposure.
Year planted: 1995.
Planting density: 2.50 x 0.80 metres/5000 vines per hectare.
Soil: Pleistocene origin, calcareous clay, with riverbed gravel.
Yield per hectare: 30 hectolitre or 1 kg per plant.
Harvest: the second or the third week of October, the grapes are handpicked into crates of 15 kg.
Vinification: Fermentation in contact with the skins for 20 days at a maximum 28 C°; then malolactic fermentation in the wood.
Ageing: in lightly toasted 500 litre barrels for 6 months, then in 25 hectolitre barrels for 15 months, followed by assembling and clarifying in cement vats for 3 months. Final ageing in the bottle for 2 years. The wine is not stabilised or filtered.
Serving temperature: 18 C°.

Sagrantino di Montefalco DOCG.

Grapes: Sagrantino 100%.
First vintage: 1981.
Yield per hectare: 40 hectolitre or 1.4 kg per plant.
Harvest: the grapes are handpicked in the second week of October, then there is a final selection in the cellar.
Vinification: Fermentation is in contact with the skins for 15-20 days at 25 C°. Then malolactic fermentation takes place, and the wine clarifies spontaneously without need for filtration.

Ageing: in lightly toasted 500 litre oak barrels for 6 months, then in larger 25 hectolitre oak barrels for 12 months, followed by assembling and clarifying in cement vats for 3 months. Final ageing in the bottle for 12 months.
Serving temperature: 18 C°.
Food matches: grilled and roast meats, stewed beef and lamb, game, wild boar, guinea fowl, pigeon, and mature hard cheeses.

Sagrantino di Montefalco DOCG Passito.

The name Sagrantino derives from the Latin "Sacer", a holy wine destined for consumption during the Christian festivals. The Passito, a sweet dessert wine, is the traditional version of Sagrantino in Montefalco.
Grapes: Sagrantino 100%.
First vintage: 1979.
Yield per hectare: 20 hectolitre or 1.4 kg fresh grapes per plant.
Harvest: the grapes are handpicked in the second week of October, and placed in single layers in crates. Bunches that have received the most amount of sun are selected. The grapes are dried naturally on cane trellises for 75 to 90 days.
Vinification: Maceration and fermentation are carried out in contact with the skins for 8 days at 25 C°. Then malolactic fermentation takes place; the wine clarifies spontaneously without need for filtration.
Ageing: in 10 hectolitre oak barrels for 15 months. Final ageing in the bottle for 12 months.
The wine: rich ruby in colour, with garnet tints. It resonates with blackberry, blackcurrant and raspberry jam, and spices. It has a good balance of sweetness and the freshness of red fruit.
Serving temperature: 14 C°.
Food matches: red fruit tarts, sweet biscuits (*tozzetti*), *giandula* chocolate, and mature cheeses.

Baiocco. Umbria Rosso IGT.

Umbria was once part of the Papal States. Baiocco was a type of coin in the currency used at the time.
Grapes: Sangiovese 90%, and Merlot 10%.

Yield per hectare: 60 hectolitre or 2.2 kg per plant.
Harvest: grapes are handpicked in the third week of September.
Vinification: fermentation is in contact with the skins for 8 days at 25 C°, followed by malolactic fermentation.
Ageing: stainless steel vats for 5 months, then in the bottle for at least 3 months.
The wine: ruby red in colour; an array of fruit and flowers on the nose, and notes of cherries, and red berries. It is lively and balanced, with a fresh finish.
Serving temperature: 16 C°.
Food matches: starters, light first courses, white meats (veal, chicken, and pork) and fresh cheeses.

Contrario. Umbria Rosso IGT.

A new interpretation of the Sagrantino grape, vinified in such a way that it produces young, fresh, and instantly drinkable wine.
Grapes: Sagrantino 100%.
First vintage: 2008.
Yield per hectare: 50 hectolitre or 1.6 kg per plant.
Harvest: last week of September, the grapes are handpicked into small crates and undergo a final selection.
Vinification: Fermentation is in contact with the skins for 10-15 days at 25 C°, followed by malolactic fermentation; the wine clarifies spontaneously without need for filtration.
Ageing: stainless steel vats for 12 months, then assembling and clarifying in cement vats for 3 months, then in the bottle for at least 4 months.
The wine: dense ruby red in colour. A rich and intense nose, featuring fruits with marked notes of cherry, wild berries and citrus fruits; fresh on the palate; very pleasant and fruity finish.
Serving temperature: 16-18 C°.
Food matches: first courses, soups, poultry and red meat.

Grechetto dei Colli Martani DCO.

Grechetto is used as a component in blends in Orvieto, but in the Todi area, known as Colli Martani, it is used 100%. Some of the Montefalco vineyards are in this geographical area.

Grapes: Grechetto 100%.
Yield per hectare: 60 hectolitre or 2 kg per plant.
Harvest: handpicked in the third week of September.
Vinification: Fermentation is at 18 C°. The wine is kept in contact with the yeasts for 90 days after fermentation has been completed.
Ageing: in stainless steel, then in the bottle for 3 months.
The wine: deep straw yellow in colour with green hues. Fresh, fruity, floral bouquet with notes of peach, almonds and hawthorn blossom. It has good balance and pleasant alcoholic backbone.
Serving temperature: 12 C°.
Food matches: Seafood starters and first courses. Soups with pulses and cereals, savoury pies, grilled fish and white meats, fresh cheeses and spicy salamis.

Trebbiano Spoletino. Umbria Bianco IGT.

Grapes: Trebbiano Spoletino 100%; the vines are grown according to the ancient training system between maple trees. The vineyard is situated on a hill, at the altitude of 350 metres above sea level with western exposure.
First vintage: 2007.
Harvest: handpicked in mid October, into small crates.
Vinification: skin contact maceration, soft pressing, static cold clarification; fermentation in 25 hectolitre oak barrels at 20 C°.
Ageing: in 25 hectolitre barrels for 9 months; then in the bottle for 3 months.
The wine: intense straw yellow colour, with gold and green tints; fruity and floral, with aromas of almonds and hawthorn blossom, tropical fruit and cedar, with a spicy finish. It is dry, warm and soft on the palate, with a full acidic structure.
Serving temperature: 14 C°.
Food matches: cold cuts, such as prosciuto ham or culatello, terrines and *carpaccio*. Also first course fish dishes, *spaghetti alla carbonara*, and saffron risotto, or with main dishes such as rich fish stews, and English style rare roast beef. Excellent with aged semi hard cheeses.

Benincasa Vini Montefalco

Via Capro, 23 – 06031 Bevagna PG
Tel & Fax: 0742 361307
www.aziendabenincasa.com
info@aziendabenincasa.com

The company was established by Domenico Benincasa. At the beginning of the 1970s he created the first single varietal vineyard using Sagrantino grapes exclusively. He started with the few remaining vines left from an old fashioned farm of mixed agricultural crops. In 2000 the company was handed over to a third generation of the Benincasa family: Marco and Roberto Alimenti, the grandsons of the founder.

The Benincasa farm is spread over 45 hectares of land between the towns of Bevagna and Gualdo Cattaneo. Amongst the olive groves and arable land, 10 hectares are planted with vines on gentle, sunny hills in the middle of the Montefalco production area.

Sagrantino di Montefalco DOCG.

Grapes: Sagrantino 100%.
Soil: clay, rich in limestone, marl, sand, and fossils.
Yield per hectare: 50 quintals.
Yield of grapes into wine: 55%.
Vinification: macerated on the skins with pre-fermentative cold maceration for 3 days, and further 12 days of maceration at a controlled temperature.
Refinement: in barrique for 12 months, before being bottled.
Ageing: in barrique for 12 months.
The wine: intense ruby red in colour, with the distinct taste of blackberries. It is full-bodied and well-structured, with a dry flavour and powerful tannins that develop further in the bottle. It is an ideal wine for laying down for several years.
Food matches: red meats, game, and mature cheeses.

Rosso di Montefalco. Montefalco Rosso DOC.

Grapes: Sangiovese 70%, Sagrantino 15% and Merlot 15%.
Soil: clay, rich in limestone, marl, sand, and fossils.
Yield per hectare: 80 quintals.
Yield of grapes into wine: 70%.
Harvest: during the last week of September.
Vinification: The grapes are handpicked and immediately taken to the cellars where they are macerated for 15 days, and then produced in the traditional method for red wines.
Refinement: in barrique.
Ageing: in barrique for 12 months, before being bottled.
The wine: ruby red in colour, with a good body and structure, sharp red fruit tones and well-balanced tannins. It is a suitable wine for laying down.
Food matches: roast white meats, pork, and cured hams and salamis, as well as semi mature cheeses.

Vincastro. Vino Rosso dell'Umbria IGT.

Grapes: Sangiovese 80%, and Merlot 20%.
Soil: clay, rich in limestone, marl, sand, and fossils.
Yield per hectare: 80 quintals.
Yield of grapes into wine: 75%.
Vinification: The grapes are handpicked, then macerated on the skins for 15 days, with frequent punching down and pumping over; followed by pressing, using a pneumatic press.
Refinement: in stainless steel vats.
Ageing: in reinforced cement barrels before bottling. The wine is usually marketed 12 months after the harvest.
The wine: ruby red in colour, with a medium body and structure, and the scent of freshly cut grass; fresh with a fruity finish.
Food matches: first courses, white meats, salamis, fresh and medium mature cheeses.

Vigna la Fornace. Vino Rosso dell'Umbria IGT.

Grapes: Barbera 40%, Merlot 40% and Sagrantino 20%.
Soil: clay, rich in limestone, marl, sand, and fossils.

Yield per hectare: 70 quintals.
Yield of grapes into wine: 75%.
Vinification: The grapes are handpicked and selected, then macerated on the skins for 16-18 days, followed by malolactic fermentation in barrique.
Refinement: in barrique.
Ageing: in barrique. The wine is bottled and sold 24 months after the harvest.
The wine: ruby red in colour, full-bodied, with a dry taste and spicy fragrance, and a fruity finish. The Barbera grapes were widely used in Umbria until the 1970s.
Food matches: grilled and roast beef, and mature cheeses.

Poggio dell'Annunziata. Grechetto dell'Umbria IGT.

Grapes: Grechetto 100%.
Soil: clay, rich in limestone, marl, sand, and fossils. The vineyard is 430 metres above sea level.
Yield per hectare: 80 quintals.
Yield of grapes into wine: 75%.
Harvest: during the first week of September.
Vinification: Maceration is carried out on the skins, then the must is transferred to oak barrels where periodical "batonage" is carried out (the wine is left in contact with the sediment and lees and frequently stirred up from the bottom).
Refinement: in barrique.
Ageing: in barrique for 6 months.
The wine: deep straw yellow in colour, with a soft green hue; a medium body and structure, with a delicate scent of freshly cut grass: fresh on the palate with a fruity finish.
Food matches: first courses, white meats, soups, salamis, fresh and medium mature cheeses.

Azienda Agricola Bocale di Valentini

Via Fratta Alzatura
06036 Montefalco PG
Tel: 0742 399233
Fax: 0742 510015
www.bocale.it
info@bocale.it

Having settled in Montefalco during the 1920s, the Valentini family is dedicated to producing wines on their hillside farm in Alzatura. The vineyards are situated in the zone of Madonna della Stella, six kilometres from the town of Montefalco.

Bocale is a nickname given to members of the family working in the vineyards; *bocale* (or often written *vocale*), is a local dialect word for a wineglass, jug or a straw covered bottle for wine or olive oil. The winery was founded in 2002. It is very much a family business, as the farm is spread out over just five hectares, four of which are vineyards; 2 of Sagrantino, and 2 of Sangiovese and Merlot (the remaining hectare is set aside for olive groves). The modern cellars are situated in the middle of the vineyards. The annual production is about 10 000 bottles of Montefalco Sagrantino, and 20 000 of Montefalco Rosso.

Montefalco Sagrantino DOCG.

Grapes: Sagrantino 100%.
Harvest: handpicked during the first ten days of October.
Fermentation: crushed for at least 25 days, using only the natural yeasts. The wine is not treated to any form of stabilising or filtration. Possible sediments should be considered as a form of guarantee for a genuine product.
Maturation: in barrique for 14 months; in the bottle for 9 months.
Ageing: It is a wine that can be kept for 7-10 years.
Production: 6 000 bottles in 2009.

The wine: intense ruby red in colour, with purple tints; with the aromas of blackberries, blackcurrants, spices and vanilla. It has a good structure, with smooth tannins, and a long finish.
Serving temperature: 18-20 C°.
Food matches: rich first courses, red meat, and mature cheeses.
Alcoholic content: 14.5% vol.

Montefalco Rosso DOC.

Grapes: Sangiovese, Sagrantino and Merlot.
Harvest: handpicked during the last week of September to the first week of October.
Fermentation: using only natural yeasts. The wine is not treated to any form of stabilising or filtration. Possible sediments should be considered as a form of guarantee for a genuine product.
Maturation: in barrique for 6 months; in the bottle for 3 months.
Ageing: It is a wine that can be kept for 5-6 years.
Production: 9 000 bottles in 2007.
The wine: intense ruby red in colour with purple tints, with the aromas of violets, ripe cherries and subtle spices. It is a well-structured wine, with sweet tannins, and a persistent finish.
Serving temperature: 18 C°.
Food matches: rich first courses, red and white meat, cold cuts of meat, and mature cheeses.
Alcoholic content: 14 % vol.

Arnaldo Caprai – Società Agricola s.r.l.

Località Torre
06036 Montefalco PR
Tel: 0742 378802
Fax: 0742 378422
www.arnalcocaprai.it
info@arnaldocaprai.it

Arnaldo Caprai is one of the leaders in the production of top quality Sagrantino di Montefalco. Tradition, innovation and territory are the key words in the company's philosophy. Back in 1968, Marco Caprai identified the opportunities that could come from such a long tradition, especially when combined with a modern and innovative approach to the cultivation of vines and to wine production.

The company estate extends for about 150 hectares, 136 of which are currently in production. The vineyards are located in the area of Montefalco, Gualdo Cattaneo and Bevagna, which is the production zone of the DOC Montefalco, Grechetto dei Colli Martani, and also the DOCG Sagrantino di Montefalco. To obtain top quality grapes different types of experimental training systems are used, combined with natural and artificial grassing, and a rational approach to plant protection, which includes the reduced use of nitrogen fertilisers.

The cellars are equipped with stainless steel tanks of 13 500-hectolitre capacity. The company owns Slovenian barrels, adding up to 1 100-hectolitre capacity, in addition to small oak barrels from Allier, Tronçais, Nevers and Vosges. The cellars are air conditioned to control the slight temperature and humidity variations needed for an optimal ageing process. The company's yearly output totals 650 000 bottles of wine, with the final objective to reach a million bottles in the next few years.

25 Anni. Sagrantino di Montefalco DOCG.

It is the result of in-depth research, and careful clonal selection of the best Sagrantino grapes. A jubilee wine produced for the first time in 1993 to celebrate the 25th anniversary of the winery.
Grapes: 100% Sagrantino.
Yield per hectare: 5 tons.
Vinification: after a gentle crushing and de-stemming process, constant pumping-overs are performed, and the wine is macerated for 30 days at more than 30 C°.
Ageing: 24 months in French oak barrique, followed by 6 months in the bottle.
The wine: deep ruby red, almost black in colour, which turns to garnet with ageing. It has aromas of ripe fruit, spices, and the vanilla passed on from the barrique. It is soft and velvety with a slightly bitter aftertaste.
Ageing potential: 15-20 years.

Collepiano. Sagrantino di Montefalco DOCG.

Collepiano is the name of the area where the grapes are grown.
Grapes: 100% Sagrantino.
Yield per hectare: 6 tons.
Vinification: after a gentle crushing and de-stemming process, constant pumping-overs are performed in order to draw the substances from the skins; the wine is macerated for 26-28 days.
Ageing: 22 months in French oak barrique, followed by a minimum of 6 months in the bottle.
The wine: densely coloured, ruby red, almost black, which turns to garnet with ageing. It has intense aromas of ripe fruit, spices, and vanilla passed on from the barrique. It is soft and velvety with a slightly bitter aftertaste.
Ageing potential: 10-15 years.

Passito. Sagrantino di Montefalco DOCG.

Passito is an Italian word to describe a winemaking process, in which the harvested grapes are placed in a dry ventilated room,

traditionally on straw mats, to dry into raisins before being pressed. It is a tradition that dates back to the Middle Ages. The highly laborious process results in low yields and the long maturation time produces one of the best results ever obtained from Sagrantino grapes.
Grapes: 100% Sagrantino.
Yield per hectare: 5 tons.
Vinification: fermentation in stainless steel tanks for 15 days with constant pumping overs; then the wine is transferred to barrique in order to complete a slow fermentation process until it achieves a sugar level of 120/150 g/l.
Ageing: 15 months in French oak barrique, followed by a minimum of 12 months in the bottle.
The wine: deep ruby red in colour, with violet tints. It has aromas of ripe fruit, wild berries and dried fruit; and it tastes sweet, with an aftertaste of citrus fruits and liquorice.
Ageing potential: approximately 10 years.

Montefalco Rosso Riserva DOC.

Grapes: 70% Sangiovese, 15% Sagrantino, and 15% Merlot.
Yield per hectare: 8 tons.
Vinification: 26-28 days of fermentation and maceration. After racking, the wine remains in stainless steel tanks for 4 months.
Ageing: 20 months in French oak barrique, followed by a minimum of 6 months in the bottle.
The wine: ruby red in colour, with bright purple reflections; with aromas of wild berries and spices, and a hint of vanilla. It is full and well structured.
Ageing potential: 10-15 years.

Montefalco Rosso DOC.

A ruby red wine
Grapes: 70% Sangiovese, 15% Sagrantino, and 15% Merlot.
Yield per hectare: 10 tons.
Vinification: fermentation and maceration 10-15 days, with pumping over performed twice a day.

Ageing: 12 months in barrel (70%) and French oak barrique (30%), followed by a minimum of 4 months in the bottle.
The wine: rich and brilliant ruby red in colour, with aromas of ripe red fruit and delicate hints of vanilla. It tastes full-bodied, rich, and dry, with a long finish.
Ageing potential: 6-8 years.

Rosso Outsider. Umbria IGT.

Grapes: 50 % Merlot and 50% Cabernet Sauvignon.
Yield per hectare: 6 tons.
Vinification: macerated for 23-26 days at less than 30 C°.
Ageing: 18 months in French oak barrique, followed by a minimum of 8 months in the bottle.
The wine: ruby red in colour, with aromas of ripe fruit and graphite. It is potent and intense, yet soft and well rounded.
Ageing potential: 10-15 years.

Anima Umbra Rosso. Umbria IGT.

Grapes: 85 % Sangiovese and 15% Canaiolo.
Yield per hectare: 8 tons.
Vinification: fermentation on skins for 10-15 at 25 C°.
Ageing: 8 months in French oak barrique; 3 months in the bottle.
The wine: bright ruby red, its taste is mid-structured with a characteristically fruity note that allows easy pairings with traditional dishes.
Ageing potential: 3-5 years.

Anima Umbra Bianco. Umbria IGT.

Grapes: 85 % Grechetto and 15% Trebbiano Spoletino.
Yield per hectare: 9 tons.
Vinification: protected from oxidation by soft pressing in saturated nitrogen atmosphere; fermentation at 18 C°.
Ageing: 3 months in stainless steel tanks; 3 months in the bottle.
The wine: straw yellow, with green tinges; hints of floral notes and aromas of green apples. It is dry, with a slight acidity, which gives it a pleasant and fresh taste. Ageing potential: 3 years.

Grecante. Grechetto dei Colli Martani DOC.

During the Renaissance, the Grecante of Montefalco was a precious gift given by farmers to princes and cardinals.
Grapes: 100 % Grechetto.
Yield per hectare: 8-9 tons.
Vinification: gentle pressing and fermentation at controlled low temperatures.
Ageing: 3 months in stainless steel tanks; 3 months in the bottle.
The wine: straw yellow in colour, with green tinges, with floral notes and fruity aromas. It tastes soft, well balanced, and pleasantly fruity.
Ageing potential: 3-5 years.
Food matches: aperitif and goes well with fish and white meats.

Grappa di Vinacce di Sagrantino.

Distillation of the *vinacce* (the remaining skins of the fermented grapes) produces the grappa of Sagrantino. The outcome is subtly aromatic with a distinctive fruity persistence. This single variety grappa is clean and crisp with a delicate softness on the palate. The finish is reminiscent of dried fruits and chocolate.
Grapes: 100% Sagrantino.
Colour: transparent and crystalline.
Aroma: intense with a note of dried fruits.
Taste: after the burning sensation of alcohol, intense flavours of fruits develop with a smooth aftertaste of almonds and chocolate.
Alcohol content: 45 °.

Cantina Colleciocco

Agricola Spacchetti s.s.
Via B Gozzoli 1/5
06036 Montefalco PG
Tel/fax: 0742 379859
www.colleciocco.it
info@colleciocco.it

On a hillside outside the city gates of Montefalco, lies the Colle Ciocco vineyard, run by the Spacchetti family. From the vineyard there is a magnificent view of the surrounding hill-towns: Spello, Assisi and Perugia. In the valley below, flows the River Clitunno, on its banks there are medieval towers, ancient churches and earth-coloured farmhouses, set against an unspoilt green countryside.

Settimo Spacchetti established the farm in 1935, and today it is run by his sons: Lamberto and Eliseo. The estate covers 19 hectares, of which 8 are vineyards and 9 olive groves. The farm is at an altitude of 400 meters above sea level. The wine cellars are situated in the middle of the vineyards.

Sagrantino di Montefalco DOCG

Grapes: Sagrantino: 100%.
Harvest: October.
Vinification: fermentation in stainless steel. Maceration is carried out for about 3 weeks.
Ageing: 24 months in 25 hectolitre French oak barrels.
Refinement: in the bottle for 6 months. It reaches full maturity after 5 years.
Production: 1 400 bottles of 0.750 litres.
The wine: rich ruby red in colour, with grenadine shades. It has a deep and complex aroma of blackberry and black cherry, with hints of aromatic herbs and spices; strong structure and pleasantly tannic, with a persistent flavour.
Serving temperature: 16-18 C°.
Food matches: red meats, game, and mature cheeses.

Sagrantino di Montefalco Passito DOCG

Grapes: Sagrantino: 100%.
Harvest: end of September. The grapes are left to wither on the vine for three months, and lose a lot of their water content, the yield is reduced to approximately 25-30 litres for every 100 kilograms of fresh grapes.
Vinification: fermentation in stainless steel. Maceration is carried out for about 10 days. After several racking from the lees the wine is transferred to oak barrels.
Ageing: 12 months in 5 hectolitre barrels.
Refinement: in the bottle for 6 months.
Production: 3 000 bottles of 0.500 litres.
The wine: rich ruby red in colour, with grenadine shades; a deep and complex aroma of blackberry and black cherry. The flavour is a combination of sweetness and soft tannins, with good structure, consistency and balance.
Serving temperature: 16 C°.
Food matches: on its own, or with fruit and nut cakes, like the typically Umbrian *"Rocciata"* cake, also cheeses with herbs or mature pecorino cheese.

Montefalco Rosso DOC.

Grapes: Sangiovese 70%, Sagrantino 15% and Merlot 15%.
Harvest: October.
Vinification: fermentation in stainless steel vats, with 3 weeks of maceration.
Ageing: 12 months in 25 hectolitre French oak barrels.
Refinement: in the bottle for 4 months. It is a wine that may continue to develop for at least 4-5 years.
Production: 27 000 bottles of 0.750 litres.
The wine: ruby red in colour, with aromas of plum, cherry and spices. It has good structure, consistency and balance.
Serving temperature: 16 C°.
Food matches: pasta and rice, with strong sauces like truffle, goose and *porcini* mushrooms, and main course read meats.

Clarignano. Umbria Bianco IGT.

Grapes: Grechetto 50% and Viognier 50%.
Vinification: soft pressing, then fermentation in stainless steel at a controlled temperature.
Ageing: in stainless steel for 4 months.
Refinement: in the bottle for 3 months.
Production: 8 000 bottles of 0.750 litres.
The wine: yellow in colour with golden tints. The aroma is intense and fruity, with strong notes of peach and passion fruit. The flavour is fresh, soft and balanced.
Serving temperature: 12 C°.
Food matches: seafood, pasta and rice dishes with vegetable sauces, and also main course fish, or white meats.

Grappa di Sagrantino.

The grappa from the Spacchetti estate is produced using the traditional system of discontinuous distillation by steam circulation. The direct passage of the steam over the pomace allows gradual and uniform distillation that shows off the characteristics of the wine. It is a hand made grappa and its quality is due to the expertise of the master stiller. The process is a long one, but it assures a superior product, characterised by its softness and enriched by the typical aromas of Montefalco wine.
Still: Distillerie Berta, they are one of Italy's most renowned grappa manufacturers in Mombaruzzo, Asti.
Still apparatus: copper alembic, using the Bain-Marie method of discontinuous cycle.
Colour: limpid and shiny.
Aroma: strong intensity, maintaining the aromas of the wine.
Flavour: dry, soft and delicate.
Proof: 40% vol.
Format: 0.500 litres.

Còlpetrone

Via Ponte La Mandria 8/1
Loc: Marcellano
06035 Gualdo Cattaneo PG
Tel: 0742 99827
Fax: 0742 960262
www.colpetrone.it
colpetrone@saiagricola.it

Colpetrone is a subsidiary of Saiagricola, the agricultural investment company of Fordiaria-SAI Insurance Company. The same company has wine cellars in Montepulciano, Montalcino, Monterufoli, and the Barbera country of the Nizza Valley. The very fact that a major financial conglomerate considered investment in the Montefalco area is proof that there is something very special about the Sagrantino grape.

The estate in Gualdo Cattaneo is spread over 140 hectares, of which 63 are vineyards: 35 hectares in the Sagrantino di Montefalco zone, 23 in the Montefalco Rosso zone, and a further 5 in Umbria Rosso IGT. The vineyards are at an altitude of 350 metres above sea level. The territory consists of limy soil with clay deposits; exposed to the south-east, which is ideal for growing quality grapes. The density of planting is around 4 000 to 5 000 vines per hectare. The method of training is the cordoned spur.

Gòld. Montefalco Sagrantino DOCG.

The wine is from the historical vineyards of Santa Maria del Fico and San Marco.
Grapes: Sagrantino 100%.
Maturing: 12 months in French oak barrique, followed by 24 months in the bottle.
Maturing capacity: 15 years.
Available in 1.5 litre bottles.

Montefalco Sagrantino DOCG.

Grapes: Sagrantino 100%.
Maturing: 12 months in French oak barrique, followed by 18 months in the bottle.
Maturing capacity: 15 years.
The wine: ruby red in colour, with notes of red fruits, spices and vanilla. The flavour is strong with tannic concentration.
Serving temperature: 18 C° in large glasses.
Food matches: roast meats, game, and mature cheeses.
Available in 1.5 litre bottles.

Montefalco Sagrantino Passito DOCG.

Grapes: Sagrantino 100%.
Maturing: 12 months in French oak barrique, followed by 18 months in the bottle.
Maturing capacity in the bottle: 15 years.
The wine: ruby red in colour, with grenadine tints, and aromas of blackberries and cherries in alcohol. The taste is full, sweet, with a light tannic sensation and a long lasting flavour.
Serving temperature: 14-16 C° in tulip shaped wineglass.
Food match: fruit tarts, strudel, and dried fruit.

Montefalco Rosso. DOC.

Grapes: Sangiovese 70%, Sagrantino 15%, and Merlot 15%.
Maturing: 40% of the wine in wood barrels and French oak barrique for 12 months; 60% of the wine in stainless steel vats, followed by 4 months in the bottle.
Maturing capacity in the bottle: 5-6 years.
The wine: ruby red in colour, with light crimson glints. The scent is fruity with notes of raspberry, spices and vanilla. The taste is full with soft tannins.
Serving temperature: 18 C° in medium size wineglass.
Food match: grilles and roast meats, both red and white.

Grappa di Montefalco Sagrantino.

Colour: crystal clear and transparent.
Taste: an intense bouquet of the wine with notes of blackberries. It is well balanced, harmonious with a good body, and a slightly bitter aftertaste.
Serving temperature: 9-11 C° in small wineglass.

Fattoria Colsanto

Località Montarone
06031 Bevagna PG
Tel/fax: 0742 360412
www.livon.it

The Colsanto Farm is part of Livon Aziende Agricole, who are also the owners of vineyards and wine cellars in the most important wine producing regions of Toscana and Friuli. They specialise in making quality wines, and combine the most modern methods in cultivating the grapes in the vineyards with vinification in the wine cellar; whilst respecting all the traditional rules of winemaking.

The new vineyards in Bevagna are in the DCOG Montefalco production zone and cover 20 hectares. The density of planting is around 7 500 stocks per hectare. Amongst the vines, there is a farmhouse dating back to the 1700s. The wine cellar has been completely restored and furnished with the most modern wine producing equipment.

Sagrantino. Montefalco Sagrantino DOCG.

Grapes: Sagrantino 100%.
Soil: alluvial.
Density: 7 000 stocks per hectare.
Training: Guyot system.
Harvest: The grapes are handpicked and collected in small crates, followed by soft rasping.
Vinification: Fermentation at a controlled temperature of 23 C°. Malolactic fermentation is carried out 70% in barrique, and the remaining 30% in steel tanks.
Refinement: 15 months in barrels, followed by a further refinement in steel tanks for 12 months.
Maturing: a long period in the bottle.

The wine: garnet red in colour; with aromas of tobacco, red fruit and spices. It tastes of red fruits, and soft tannins.
Maturing capacity: 15-20 years.
Serving temperature: 18 C°.
Food matches: Red meats, game, and mature cheeses.
Available in 1.5 litre bottles.

Montefalco Rosso DOC.

Grapes: Sangiovese 75% and Sagrantino 25%.
Soil: alluvial.
Density: 7 000 stocks per hectare.
Training: Guyot system.
Harvest: The grapes are handpicked and collected in small crates, followed by soft rasping.
Vinification: Fermentation at a controlled temperature of 23 C° on the skins for 15 days. Malolactic fermentation and ageing for 15 months is carried out on 70% of the wine in barrique and the remaining 30% in steel tanks.
Maturing: a long period in the bottle.
The wine: intense ruby red in colour, with a bouquet of red fruits, cherries and raspberries. It is a robust, full-bodied wine with soft tannins and a long finish.
Maturing capacity: 10-12 years.
Serving temperature: 18-20 C°.
Food matches: Beef, polenta, robust stews and mature cheeses.

Ruris.

Grapes: Sangiovese 70%, Merlot 20%, and Sagrantino 10%.
Soil: alluvial.
Density: 7 000 stocks per hectare.
Training: Guyot system.
Harvest: The grapes are handpicked and collected in small crates, followed by soft rasping.
Vinification: Fermentation at a controlled temperature of 23 C° for 15 days. Malolactic fermentation and ageing is 70% in barrique and the remaining 30% in steel tanks for 10 months.
Maturing: in the bottle

The wine: intense ruby red in colour, with a fruity bouquet ranging from red berries to hints of spice. It has flavours of wild berries and spices with soft tannins and a long finish.
Maturing capacity: 6-8 years.
Serving temperature: 17-18 C°.
Food matches: Wild boar, venison, pasta dishes with meat sauces, poultry and mature cheeses.

Cantina Dionigi

Dionigi Azienda Agricola
Colli Madonna della Pia
06031 Bevagna PG
Tel: 0742 360395
Fax: 0742 369147
www.cantinadionigi.it
info@cantinadionigi.it

The Cantina Dionigi has been producing fine wines since 1896, when Gabriele Dionigi moved his family from Assisi to the beautiful hills near Bevagna, with a magical combination of altitude, climate and soil ideal for outstanding agricultural products. The family has selected the varieties of olive and vine that suited the *terroir* best, and chosen the correct techniques for making DOP Extra Virgin olive oil, and DOCG wines with unmistakable body and taste. Today, the descendants of Gabriele tend their olive groves and vineyards with the same intense care and passion, always striving to improve the quality of their products, just as much for their own satisfaction as for their customers.

Montefalco Sagrantino DOCG.

Grapes: 100% Sagrantino.
Aspect: facing south/south-east.
Age of vineyard: 10-15 years.
Altitude: 260 metres above sea level.
Soil: Limestone and clay.
Training: spurred cordon.
Vines per hectare: 5 500.
Production per hectare: 6 tons.
Vinification: On the skin maceration for about 30 days.
Ageing: 80% is aged for 24 months in large, French oak casks, the other 20% for 12 months in barrique and 12 months in large wooden casks. The wine is deliberately left unfiltered.
Bottle ageing: Minimum 12 months.

Bottles produced: About 10 000.
The wine: A ruby red wine with violet highlights. On the nose, spicy notes of black pepper and cinnamon; intense and persistent in the mouth, well structured with pleasant tannins.
Serving temperature: 18-20 C°.
Food matches: grilled red meats, game and mature cheeses.
Open at least an hour before drinking and, if possible, decant to obtain perfect oxygenation.

Montefalco Sagrantino Passito DOCG.

Grapes: 100% Sagrantino.
Aspect: facing south/south-east.
Age of vineyard: 10-15 years.
Altitude: 260 metres above sea level.
Soil: Limestone and clay.
Training: spurred cordon.
Vines per hectare: 5 500.
Production per hectare: 6 tons.
Pre-drying of grapes: About 3 months natural air drying on racks.
Vinification: On the skin maceration for about 30 days.
Ageing: 30 months in large, French oak casks.
Bottle ageing: Minimum 12 months. The wine is deliberately left unfiltered.
Bottles produced: About 3 700 of 375 ml.
The wine: intense ruby red in colour, with garnet highlights. It has concentrated flavours of mulberry, dried figs, and plum jam; it has a sweet, full and balanced taste.
Serving temperature: 15 C°.
Food matches: pastries, chocolate, *Rocciata* (a traditional Umbrian dessert), and mature cheeses. Open an hour before drinking and, if possible, decant to obtain perfect oxygenation.

Montefalco Rosso Riserva DOC.

Grapes: 70% Sangiovese, 15% Sagrantino, 7.5% Merlot and 7.5% Cabernet Sauvignon.
Aspect: facing south/south-east.
Age of vineyard: 8-10 years.

Altitude: 260 metres above sea level.
Soil: Limestone and clay.
Training: Guyot.
Vines per hectare: 5 500.
Production per hectare: 7 tons.
Pre-drying of grapes: About 3 months natural air drying on racks.
Vinification: On the skin maceration for about 15 days.
Ageing: 12 months in French barrique, then 12 months in large, wooden casks. The wine is deliberately left unfiltered.
Bottle ageing: Minimum 6 months.
Bottles produced: About 3 500.
The wine: ruby red in colour, with aromas of spices and fruits of the forest. It is well structured and with balanced tannins.
Serving temperature: 18-20 C°.
Food matches: Grilled red meats and mature cheeses. Open at least an hour before drinking and, if possible, decant to obtain perfect oxygenation.

Montefalco Rosso DOC.

Grapes: 70% Sangiovese, 15% Sagrantino, and 15% Merlot.
Aspect: facing south.
Age of vineyard: 8-10 years.
Altitude: 260 metres above sea level.
Soil: Limestone and clay.
Training: spurred cordon.
Vines per hectare: 5 500.
Production per hectare: 7 tons.
Vinification: On the skin maceration for about 15 days.
Ageing: 12 months in barrique; and 6 months in large, French oak casks. The wine is deliberately left unfiltered.
Bottle ageing: Minimum 6 months.
Bottles produced: About 13 000.
Serving temperature: 18 C°.
The wine: ruby red in colour, with aromas of redcurrants and sour cherries. The taste is harmonious with well-balanced tannins and well-structured body, with ripe red fruit flavours and a long finish.

Food matches: first courses and grilled red meats. Open an hour before drinking and decant to obtain perfect oxygenation.

Rosso della Pia. Umbria IGT.

Grapes: Montepulciano, Ciliegiolo, and Barbera.
Aspect: facing south.
Age of vineyard: 30 years.
Altitude: 260 metres above sea level.
Soil: Limestone and clay.
Training: *Palmetta* (fan).
Vines per hectare: 2 000.
Production per hectare: 10 tons.
Vinification: On the skin maceration for at least 10 days.
Ageing: 6 months in stainless steel.
Bottle ageing: 3 months.
Bottles produced: About 10 000.
The wine: intense red in colour, with violet highlights. It is a well-balanced wine with good body.
Serving temperature: 16 C°.
Food matches: suitable for every type of meal.

Gabrino. Merlot IGT Umbria.

Grapes: 100% Merlot.
Aspect: facing south-west.
Age of vineyard: 10 years.
Altitude: 260 metres above sea level.
Soil: Limestone and clay.
Training: spurred cordon.
Vines per hectare: 5 500.
Production per hectare: 8 tons.
Vinification: On the skin maceration for about 15 days at a controlled temperature of 25 C°.
Ageing: 80% of the wine is aged in large oak barrels for 24 months, the remaining 20% is aged in barrique for 12 months, and then it is blended with the rest. It is not filtered.
Bottle ageing: Minimum 6 months.
Bottles produced: About 4 000.

Serving temperature: 18 C°.
The wine: rich red in colour, with a slightly flowery bouquet and scents of ripe fruit and jam. It tastes warm and savoury.
Food pairing: Goes well with grilled and braised meats.

Civico 92. Merlot Passito IGT Umbria.

Grapes: 100% Merlot.
Aspect: facing south-west.
Age of vineyard: 10 years.
Altitude: 260 metres above sea level.
Soil: Limestone and clay.
Training: spurred cordon.
Vines per hectare: 5 500.
Production per hectare: 8 tons.
Pre-drying of grapes: About 3 months natural air-drying on racks until the sugar concentration reaches 34° Babo.
Vinification: On the skin maceration for about 20 days.
Ageing: 6 months in large wooden barrels.
Bottle ageing: Minimum 2 months.
Bottles produced: About 1 000 of 375 ml.
The wine: deep ruby red in colour, with aromas of redcurrants and fruits of the forest. It tastes of harmonious red fruits with balanced tannins and has a long finish.
Serving temperature: 15 C°.
Food matches: Easter cakes, desserts and sweet biscuits.

Colle Sorragani. Grechetto Colli Martani DOC.

Grapes: 100% Grechetto.
Aspect: facing north.
Age of vineyard: 5-10 years.
Altitude: 260 metres above sea level.
Soil: Limestone and clay.
Training: Guyot and spurred cordon.
Vines per hectare: 5 500.
Production per hectare: 6 tons.

Vinification: Cryomaceration for 36-48 hours on the skins with the must at -2 C°, then pressing and slow fermentation for a month in French barrique.
Ageing: 6 months in barrique.
Bottle ageing: minimum 3 months.
Bottles produced: about 1 500.
The wine: straw yellow in colour, with fruity and floral aromas. It tastes slightly sweet and velvety, with a mildly bitter finish.
Serving temperature: 12-14 C°.
Food matches: first courses with truffles, fish, asparagus, and mature cheeses.

Passo Greco. Grechetto Passito IGT Umbria.

Grapes: 100% Grechetto.
Aspect: facing north.
Age of vineyard: 5-15 years.
Altitude: 260 metres above sea level.
Soil: limestone and clay.
Training: Guyot and spurred cordon.
Vines per hectare: 5 500.
Production per hectare: 6 tons.
Pre-drying of the grapes: 3 months natural air-drying on racks.
Vinification: Cryomaceration for 36 months before being pressed, and fermented slowly in stainless steel for 6 months.
Ageing: 18 months in stainless steel.
Bottle ageing: minimum 6 months.
Bottles produced: About 800 of 375 ml.
The wine: intense golden yellow in colour; with a delicate scent, full and balanced, with hints of almond and honey.
Serving temperature: 14 C°.
Food matches: pastries and cakes.

Umbria Grechetto IGT.

Grapes: 100% Grechetto.
Aspect: facing south-west.
Age of vineyard: 5-10 years.
Altitude: 260 metres above sea level.

Soil: limestone and clay.
Training: Guyot and spurred cordon.
Vines per hectare: 5 500.
Production per hectare: 8 tons.
Vinification: White wine fermentation in stainless steel at 18 C°.
Ageing: 6 months in stainless steel.
Bottle ageing: minimum 2 months.
Bottles produced: About 2 500.
The wine: straw yellow in colour, with a floral aroma.
Serving temperature: 12-14 C°.
Food matches: starters, first courses, and fish.

Bianco della Pia. Bianco IGT Umbria.

Grapes: Grechetto, Trebbiano and Malvasia.
Aspect: facing south.
Age of vineyard: 20-30 years.
Altitude: 260 metres above sea level.
Soil: limestone and clay.
Training: spurred cordon.
Vines per hectare: 2 000.
Production per hectare: 12 tons.
Vinification: Controlled fermentation in stainless steel at 18 C°.
Ageing: 6 months in stainless steel.
Bottle ageing: minimum one month.
Bottles produced: About 10 000.
The wine: straw yellow with green tints, fruity, and cool
Serving temperature: 10-12 C°.
Food matches: appetisers, soups and classic fish dishes.

Scialo. Moscato Passito IGT Umbria.

Grapes: 100% Moscato.
Aspect: facing south-east.
Age of vineyard: 10-15 years.
Altitude: 260 metres above sea level.
Soil: limestone and clay.
Training: spurred cordon.
Vines per hectare: 5 500.

Production per hectare: 6 tons.
Pre-drying of the grapes: 3 months natural air-drying on racks.
Vinification: Cryomaceration for 36 months before being pressed, and fermented slowly in stainless steel for 6 months.
Ageing: 18 months in stainless steel.
Bottle ageing: minimum 6 months.
Bottles produced: About 10 000.
The wine: golden yellow in colour, with a bouquet of apricots and citrus fruit. It is balanced, full, with a long finish.
Serving temperature: 14 C°.
Food matches: blue cheeses, cakes and pastries.

Fongoli

Azienda Fongoli Soc. Agr. s.s
06036 Montefalco PG
Tel: 0742 378930
Fax: 0742 371273
www.fongoli.com
info@fongoli.com

The Fongoli family has been making wine for over eighty years. When Decio Fongoli Calvani acquired the estate, he started an enterprise that became a family tradition. The property stretches over a hundred acres, sixty-five of them vineyards; set amongst olive, oak, and walnut groves. The estate is centred on an antique farmhouse, where the wine cellars are, filled with oak barrels, *caratelli* (typical Umbrian kegs) and casks. Nearby, the grapes are turned into wine, using the latest and most modern winemaking technologies and equipment.

Vigna dei Sospiri. Montefalco Sagrantino Secco DOCG.

Grapes: 100% Sagrantino.
Harvest: the grapes are handpicked in the second half of October.
Vinification: Prolonged fermentation in wooden vats and 10 days of maceration. Membrane filtered horizontal soft pressing.
Ageing: 36 months in Slovenian oak barrels.
Refining: in the bottle for 6 months.
The wine: deep garnet in colour, with aromas of red berries and spices; a full-bodied structure, fine tannins and a long finish.
Serving temperature: 18-20 C°.
Food matches: game, stews, poultry, goat and roast lamb.
Alcohol content: 14.5% vol.

Montefalco Sagrantino Secco DOCG.

Grapes: 100% Sagrantino.
Harvest: the grapes are handpicked in the second half of October.
Vinification: Prolonged cold maceration at 10 C°, then a long temperature controlled fermentation, followed by a 10-day maceration. Membrane filtered horizontal soft pressing.
Ageing: 30 months in Slovenian oak barrels.
Refining: in the bottle for 6 months.
The wine: deep garnet in colour; with fruity and spicy notes; fine tannins and full body.
Serving temperature: 18-20 C°. Open an hour before serving.
Food matches: roast red meats and game stews.
Alcohol content: 14.5% vol.

Montefalco Sagrantino Passito DOCG.

Grapes: 100% Sagrantino.
Harvest: Late harvest; the selected grapes are handpicked and dried for approximately two months on racks.
Vinification: Prolonged cold maceration at 7 C°. Long temperature controlled fermentation followed by a 10-day maceration, then membrane filtered horizontal soft pressing.
Sugar content: 40-50 gr./lt.
Ageing: 30 months in wood barrels.
Refining: in the bottle for 6 months.
The wine: an excellent dessert and "meditation" wine.
Serving temperature: 16-18 C°. Open an hour before serving.
Food matches: *Rocciata Umbra* (dried fruit and apple strudel) or *tozzetti* (sweet biscuits with raisins and almonds).
Alcohol content: 15% vol.

Montefalco Rosso DOC.

Grapes: Sangiovese, Sagrantino, Montepulciano, and Merlot.
Harvest: handpicked in mid-October.
Vinification: Long cold maceration. Prolonged temperature controlled fermentation followed by a 10-day maceration, then membrane filtered horizontal soft pressing.

Ageing: 18 months in Slovenian oak barrels.
Refining: in the bottle for 6 months.
The wine: ruby red in colour, with a fragrance of oak, spices, cherry and blackberry.
Serving temperature: 18 C°.
Food matches: savoury red meats, beef stews, and mature cheeses.
Alcohol content: 13.5% vol.

Montefalco Rosso Riserva DOC.

Grapes: Sangiovese, Sagrantino, Barbera, and Merlot.
Harvest: handpicked in mid-October.
Vinification: Prolonged temperature controlled fermentation followed by a 10-day maceration, then membrane filtered horizontal soft pressing.
Ageing: 30 months in Slovenian oak barrels.
Refining: in the bottle for 6 months.
The wine: ruby red in colour with hints of garnet. Fruity, with a note of toasted oak; rich in tannins, with a long finish.
Serving temperature: 18 C°. Open an hour before serving.
Food matches: roast meats, stews and mature cheeses.
Alcohol content: 13.5% vol.

L'Agnoletto. Rosso IGT Umbria.

Grapes: Sangiovese, Montepulciano, and Merlot.
Harvest: handpicked at the beginning of October.
Vinification: Cold maceration for 10 days. Prolonged temperature controlled fermentation followed by a 7-day maceration, then membrane filtered horizontal soft pressing.
Ageing: 6 months in large vats.
The wine: rich ruby red in colour, with fragrances of ripe cherries and spices; and a full-bodied flavour.
Serving temperature: 18 C°.
Food matches: pasta, red meats, and medium mature cheeses.
Alcohol content: 13.5% vol.

Grechetto dei Colli Martani DOC.

Grapes: Grechetto 100%.
Harvest: handpicked in mid-September.
Vinification: Cold maceration for 5 days at 10 C°. Membrane filtered horizontal soft pressing. Followed by fermentation at 20 C° on fine lees for 15 days.
Refining: in the bottle for 3 months.
The wine: straw yellow in colour with hints of green; well balanced with a floral and fruity fragrance; full-bodied, and rich in aromas.
Serving temperature: 10-12 C°.
Food matches: pasta dishes with truffle or porcini mushrooms, white meats, soufflés and vegetarian quiches.
Alcohol content: 12% vol.

Grappa di Sagrantino

Fermented from pressed seeds and skins of Sagrantino grapes.
Distillation: Continuos system with copper distillation columns.
Refining: 4 months.
Characteristics: intense tones of white flowers and camomile, which mingle with dark chocolate and fruity notes, with the aroma of green wood and liquorice.
Serving temperature: 10-14 C°.
Alcohol content: 40% vol.

Martinelli

Cantine Martinelli, Voc. Sasso
06031 Bevagna PG
Tel: 0742 362124
Fax: 0742 369595
www.cantinemartinelli.com
info@cantinemartinelli.com

Cantine Martinelli was born from a long passion, and strong family ties to Montefalco. The first vintage was in 2002. The enthusiasm of its owners, combined with their collaborators, created a modern wine cellar. In the vineyards, pure Sagrantino grapes are cultivated with care, using traditional methods, coupled with the newest of technologies. Low yields and manual cropping help to produce top quality grapes. They are handpicked into small crates; only the healthiest and fully ripe grapes are selected for vinification. Followed by further selection in the winery and the use of modern technology allow Martinelli to produce Sagrantino di Montefalco wines of great structure, with many unique features, and extraordinary longevity.

Sagrantino di Montefalco DOCG.

Grapes: 100% Sagrantino.
Vineyard: 20 hectares.
Altitude: 350 metres above sea level.
Training: spurred cordon.
Soil: mostly sedimentary, with limestone, and clay.
Stump density: 5000/6000 vines per acre.
Production: 50 quintals per hectare. Yield in wine: 60%.
Ageing: 30 months in total, of which at least 12 months are in French oak barriques (Alliers and Tronçais), followed by 8 to 12 months in the bottle.

The wine: *Franco M Ricci – Paolo Lauciani* wrote in *Bibenda n.18, Ottobre/Novembre 2005:* "Ruby red, concentrated and dense; its fragrance is in perfect balance between ripe red fruits and oriental spices, with a hint of tobacco. Robust, with a refined tannic bite; a harmonious and well-balanced maturity".
Alcohol content: 13.5% vol.

SorAnna. Sagrantino di Montefalco DOCG.

Grapes: 100% Sagrantino.
Vineyard: about 20 hectares.
Altitude: 350 metres above sea level.
Training: spurred cordon.
Soil: mostly sedimentary, with limestone, and clay.
Stump density: 5000/6000 vines per acre.
Production: 70 quintals per hectare. Yield in wine: 60%.
Ageing: 30 months in total, of which at least 16 months are in French *sessile* oak casks, followed by 12 months in the bottle.
Alcohol content: 14% vol.

Montefalco Rosso DOC.

Grapes: Sangiovese 70%, Sagrantino 15%, and Merlot 15%.
Vineyard: about 15 hectares.
Altitude: 350 metres above sea level.
Training: spurred cordon.
Soil: mostly sedimentary, with limestone, and clay.
Stump density: 4000/5000 vines per acre.
Production: 75 quintals per hectare. Yield in wine: 65%.
Ageing: 12 months in *tons* and French *sessile* oak casks; followed by 3 months in the bottle.
Alcohol content: 13% vol.

Gaite. Umbria IGT Rosso.

Grapes: Sangiovese 70%, Sagrantino 15%, and Merlot 15%.
Vineyard: about 20 hectares.
Altitude: 350 metres above sea level.
Training: spurred cordon.

Soil: mostly sedimentary, with limestone, and clay.
Stump density: 4000/5000 vines per acre.
Production: 75 quintals per hectare. Yield in wine: 75%.
Ageing: 12 months in *tons* and French *sessile* oak casks; followed by 3 months in the bottle.
Alcohol content: 13% vol.

Gaite. Umbria IGT Bianco.

Grapes: Chardonnay, and Grechetto.
Vineyard: about 15 hectares.
Altitude: 300 metres above sea level.
Training: spurred cordon.
Soil: mostly sedimentary, with limestone, and clay.
Stump density: 4000/5000 vines per acre.
Production: 80/90 quintals per hectare. Yield in wine: 75%.
Ageing: in stainless steel vats, and approx. 3 months in the bottle.
Alcohol content: 12.5% vol.

Cantina Novelli

Località Pedrelle
06036 Montefalco PG
Tel: 0744 803301
Fax: 0744 814345
www.cantinanovelli.it
cantina@grupponovelli.it

Like most stories in the world of wine, this one began over a glass of Sagrantino being shared by Stefano Novelli and Maurilio Chiocccia, an internationally famed oenologist. It was the Trebbiano Spoletino project.

One particular grape, the Trebbiano Spoletino, had been cultivated in the vicinity of Spoleto since medieval times. The name Trebbiano has its roots in the Frank word "Traibo", which means scion of a noble family. It was the main grape grown in the Spoletino Valley since as early as 570 AD, when Spoleto became the capital of the Duchy that included Umbria and parts of Toscana, Lazio and the Marche. Sadly, this great grape has been neglected for many years.

Stefano Novelli set out to change all that. Recognising the potential of Trebbiano, he sought the collaboration of Professor Attilio Scienza of the University of Milan to resurrect this grape variety. Some of the surviving pre-Phylloxera vines were over a hundred years old and ungrafted. Their trunks had diameters of over twenty centimetres, and the vines were trained on maple trees, according to age-old practice.

The Novelli estate selected suitable clones, and new vineyards were planted on the slopes of the Colli Martani. There, the soil is loosely textured sand and gravel, which is ideal for the cultivation of quality grapes. The vineyards are at an altitude of 380 metres above sea level and exposed to the south. The climate is famous for its hot summers and very cold winters.

At full capacity the annual production target is 180 000 bottles of Trebbiano Spoletino; as well as 180 000 bottles of Montefalco

Rosso and 90 000 bottles of Montefalco Sagrantino (as the vineyards spread over to the Montefalco production zone).

Trebbiano Spoletino Bianco. IGT Umbria.

Grapes: Trebbiano Spoletino 100%.
First year of production: 2005
Average annual production: 130 000 bottles.
Training: Guyot.
Density per hectare: 4 600 vines.
Yield in grapes: 80 quintals.
Wine yield: 72%.
Harvest: handpicked during the second half of October.
Vinification: alcoholic fermentation 12 days in stainless steel vats at 18 C°. The wine remains on the lees for 5-6 months.
Stabilisation: Cold tartaric stabilisation.
The wine: straw yellow in colour with intense shades of green; with scented hints of aromatic herbs, a velvety and well-rounded taste. Long lasting with a slight citrus and almond flavour.
Available sizes: 750, 1500, and 3000 ml.
Serving temperature: 12-13 C°.
Food matches: first courses, even truffle based, and main courses of white meats, grilled fish and crustaceans.
Recommended glass: classic *Bordolese*.

Bianco Cube. IGT Umbria.

Grapes: Trebbiano Spoletino, Grechetto, and Pecorino.
First year of production: 2007
Average annual production: 16 000 bottles.
Training: spurred cordon and Guyot.
Density per hectare: 4 000 vines.
Yield in grapes: 110 quintals.
Wine yield: 70%.
Harvest: handpicked from the end of August, determined by the ripeness of the grapes in each single vineyard.
Vinification: the grapes are softly crushed and the extracted juice is fermented at low temperatures in an oxygen free environment. The most aromatic grapes are vinified with carbonic maceration

to exalt their varietal characteristics. The others are left 8 to 9 days in contact with their skins.
Stabilisation: Cold tartaric.
The wine: straw yellow in colour; the fragrance is reminiscent of yellow fruit, pineapple, peach, and apricot. Refreshing on the palate and finishes with soft tangy notes.
Available sizes: 0.75 l.
Serving temperature: 10-12 C°.
Food matches: white sauced pastas, penne with pesto, sushi, salmon salad, tuna filet and fish carpaccio.
Recommended glass: long stem wineglass.

Grechetto. IGT Umbria.

Grapes: Grechetto 100%.
First year of production: 2009
Average annual production: 20 000 bottles.
Training: spurred cordon.
Density per hectare: 4 600 vines.
Yield in grapes: 80 quintals.
Wine yield: 70%.
Harvest: handpicked during the last 10 days of September.
Vinification: the grapes are softly crushed and the extracted juice is fermented at low temperatures in an oxygen free environment in order to preserve its aromatic characteristics.
Stabilisation: Cold tartaric.
The wine: straw yellow in colour with hints of green; floral and fruity notes, particularly apples. It is full-bodied.
Available sizes: 0.75 l.
Serving temperature: 10-12 C°.
Food matches: pasta, risotto, fish, and other seafood.
Recommended glass: long stem wineglass.

Rosato. IGT Umbria.

Grapes: Sagrantino 100%.
Average annual production: 6 600 bottles.
Training: spurred cordon.
Density per hectare: 5 000 vines.

Yield in grapes: 70 quintals.
Wine yield: 50%.
Harvest: handpicked, starting from the second half of September.
Vinification: the juice is obtained by using the "Blush Wine Method". The grapes are delicately pressed, limiting colour extraction. The must is cold settled, which is followed by fermentation in stainless steel vats, then the wine is left to age in steel vats for a period of 3 months.
Stabilisation: Cold static.
The wine: cherry hued rose colour. It is an elegant, velvety wine, with subtle hints of tannins, reminiscent of its native grape.
Available sizes: 0.75 l.
Serving temperature: 10-14 C°.
Food matches: soups, cold meats, white meats and fresh cheeses.
Recommended glass: classic *Bordolese*.

Montefalco Sagrantino DOCG.

Grapes: Sagrantino 100%.
First year of production: 2003
Average annual production: 80 000 bottles.
Training: spurred cordon.
Density per hectare: 5 000 vines.
Yield in grapes: 65 quintals.
Wine yield: 65%.
Harvest: handpicked, during the first half of October.
Vinification: alcoholic fermentation for three weeks in stainless steel vats at 28 C°. Malolactic fermentation in selected French oak barrique for sixteen months.
Stabilisation: cold tartaric stabilisation.
The wine: ruby red in colour; full-bodied, with good texture, with aromas of blackberries, black currants, sour cherry, and a balsamic edge and overtones of chocolate; it is smooth with soft tannins, well balanced with the acidity.
Available sizes: 750. 1 500 and 3 000 ml.
Serving temperature: 18-20 C°.
Food matches: baked or meat sauced pastas, main courses of red meats, like roasts, game, and mature cheeses.
Recommended glass: classic *Bordolese*.

Montefalco Rosso DOC.

Grapes: Sangiovese 70%, Sagrantino 15%, Merlot and Cabernet Sauvignon 15%.
First year of production: 2005
Average annual production: 180 000 bottles.
Training: spurred cordon.
Density per hectare: 5 000 vines.
Yield in grapes: 60 quintals.
Wine yield: 70%.
Harvest: handpicked from the beginning of September, determined by the ripeness of the grapes in each single vineyard.
Vinification: alcoholic fermentation and the maceration on the skins from 10 to 12 days at 25 C°. Pump-overs and punch-dawns are frequent, and 15% of the wine is bled off. Malolactic fermentation follows, and 15% of the wine is matured in oak barrique. The final blend is then assembled, and the wine rests in stainless steel tanks until bottling.
Stabilisation: Cold tartaric stabilisation.
The wine: purplish ruby red in colour; with fragrances of ripe red fruit, dark cherry jam, and balsamic. It has a crisp acidity and judicious tannins support it through to a lingering finish.
Available sizes: 750. 1 500 and 3 000 ml.
Serving temperature: 18-20 C°.
Food matches: baked or meat sauced pastas, and main courses of red meats, and mature cheeses.
Recommended glass: classic Burgundy *ballon*.

Nero Cube. Umbria IGT.

Grapes: Sangiovese, Sagrantino, and Merlot.
First year of production: 2008.
Average annual production: 30 000 bottles.
Training: spurred cordon.
Density per hectare: 5 000 vines.
Yield in grapes: 90 quintals.
Wine yield: 65%.

Harvest: handpicked from the beginning of September, determined by the ripeness of the grapes in each single vineyard.
Vinification: alcoholic fermentation and the maceration on the skins at 28-30 C°. Malolactic fermentation and ageing in stainless steel. The final blend is assembled after fermentation.
Stabilisation: Natural.
The wine: dark ruby red in colour, with ripe dark fruit flavours, and hints of liquorice and chocolate. A wine of complexity with well balanced tannins.
Available sizes: 0.75 l.
Serving temperature: 12-15 C°.
Food matches: meat sauced pastas, red meats, and medium mature cheeses.
Recommended glass: classic *Ballon*.

Rosso Cube. Umbria IGT.

Grapes: Sangiovese, Canaiolo, and Ciliegiolo.
First year of production: 2007.
Average annual production: 16 000 bottles.
Training: spurred cordon.
Density per hectare: 5 000 vines.
Yield in grapes: 100 quintals.
Wine yield: 70%.
Harvest: handpicked at the beginning of September.
Vinification: the most aromatic grapes are fermented with carbonic maceration to exalt their varietal characteristics. The others are left 8 to 9 days in contact with their skins. Malolactic fermentation and ageing in stainless steel tanks.
Stabilisation: cold tartaric.
The wine: ruby red in colour; with fragrances of red fruits, morello cherry; refreshing and finishes on a soft note.
Available sizes: 0.75 l.
Serving temperature: 12-15 C°.
Food matches: pasta, chicken salads, fish, roast chicken and turkey, and barbecued steaks
Recommended glass: classic *Ballon*.

Sangiovese. Umbria IGT.

Grapes: Sangiovese 100%.
First year of production: 2009.
Average annual production: 20 000 bottles.
Training: spurred cordon.
Density per hectare: 5 000 vines.
Yield in grapes: 70 quintals.
Wine yield: 70%.
Harvest: handpicked during the first ten days of September.
Vinification: alcoholic fermentation 8 to 9 days with the skins.
Malolactic fermentation and ageing in stainless steel tanks.
Stabilisation: Cold tartaric.
The wine: ruby red in colour, with fragrances of small red fruits. It is a well-structured wine, and extremely drinkable.
Available sizes: 0.75 l.
Serving temperature: 12-15 C°.
Food matches: red meats and medium mature cheeses.
Recommended glass: classic *Ballon*.

Blanc de Blanc. Trebbiano Spoletino. Brut Millesimé.

Grapes: Trebbiano Spoletino 100%.
Sparkling wine made by the traditional method.
First year of production: 2007.
Yield in grapes: 70 quintals per hectare.
Wine yield: 45%.
Harvest: handpicked during the first half of September.
Production of base wine: soft crushing of the grapes in anaerobic conditions obtaining a low yield.
Decantation: cold static, with added selected yeasts.
Fermentation: around nine days in steel, then partial malolactic fermentation.
Stabilisation: cold static, followed by bottling and the addition of *liqueur de tirage* (sugar melted in sparkling wine); ageing in the bottle on the yeast lees for 10 months; then *dégorgement* (removal of the cork with the sediments), and the addition of *liqueur d'expédition* (sugar, brandy and still white wine).

The wine: creamy foam *mousse*, with a long lasting *perlage* of bubbles; straw yellow in colour, with pale green highlights; and a fragrant bouquet of citrus fruits, and subtle traces of acidity.
Available sizes: 0.75 l.
Serving temperature: 6-8 C°.
Food matches: aperitif, pasta dishes and a delicate risotto.
Alcohol: 11.12% vol. Pressure: 6 atm.
Total acidity: 6.08 g/l. Residual sugar: 11 g/l. pH: 3.15.

<u>Rosé de Noir. Sagrantino. Brut Millesimé.</u>

Grapes: Sagrantino 100%.
Sparkling wine made by the traditional method.
First year of production: 2007.
Yield in grapes: 65 quintals per hectare.
Wine yield: 45%.
Harvest: handpicked during the second half of August.
Production of base wine: soft crushing of the grapes in anaerobic conditions obtaining a low yield.
Decantation: cold static, with added selected yeasts.
Fermentation: around nine days in steel, then partial malolactic fermentation.
Stabilisation: cold static, followed by bottling and addition of *liqueur de tirage* (sugar candy melted in sparkling wine); then ageing in the bottle on the yeast lees for 10 months; then *dégorgement* (removal of the cork with the sediments), and the addition of *liqueur d'expédition* (sugar, brandy and still wine).
The wine: creamy *mousse* with good length, and a lingering cascade of tiny bubbles. The colour is an elegant shade of rose, with a fragrant bouquet of wild berries and a good body. It has a velvety flavour and subtle traces of soft tannins.
Available sizes: 0.75 l.
Alcohol: 11.88 % vol. Pressure: 6 atm.
Total acidity: 6.03 g/l. Residual sugar: 12 g/l. pH: 3.17.
Serving temperature: 6-8 C°.
Food matches: excellent as an aperitif or for drinking throughout a meal. Good with crustaceans, cured meats, and light cheeses.

Rialto Azienda Agricola

Fraz. Casale – Loc. Rialto
06036 Montefalco PG
Mobile: 392 9188672 or 329 6508323
www.casalerialto.com
info@casalerialto.com

In 1998 Eraldo Dentici took over the running of his parents' farm, which has been in existence for sixty years. It was arable land with some olive groves. During the next ten years eight hectares of vineyards were planted with the help of Dentici's parents. Five hectares were Sagrantino vines, the rest Sangiovese (several clones), Merlot, Trebbiano Toscano, and Grechetto. The density of vines planted for a sixth of the vineyards is 2.80 X 1.00 m. The training system used is spurred cordon. In 2006 an additional three hectares of vines were planted with Sangiovese (several clones), Merlot (several clones), and Chardonnay. The density of vines was increased to 2.50 X 0.90 m. The training system for these vineyards is double spurred cordon.

The wine cellars were constructed in 2001, but most of the grapes grown were sold to other winemakers. On average, a quarter of the grapes was vinified in house, but this amount increased each year, and at the latest harvest it reached 350 hectolitres. In 2001, the cellars produced only one thousand bottles of wine; this increased to eighty thousand bottles by 2010.

Montefalco Sagrantino DCOG.

Grapes: 100% Sagrantino.
Vintage year: 2005.
Yield of grapes: 60 quintals.
Yield of wine: 60 litres per 100 kg of grapes.
Age of vineyard: 8 years.
Fermentation: 15-20 days.

Ageing: in French barrique for eighteen months; in the bottle for six months.
Annual production: on average 4 000 bottles, of which 98% are sold in Italy and 2% are exported. Sale: June 2008.
The wine: ruby red in colour with violet highlights, and changing to garnet with ageing; it has a delicate fruity fragrance, with hints of oak from the barrique, and a dry and harmonious taste.
Alcohol content: 13.5% vol. Residual sugar content: 30 gr.
Minimum acidity: 5 per 1 000. Dry extracts: 26 per 1 000.

Montefalco Sagrantino Passito DCOG.

Grapes: 100% Sagrantino.
Vintage year: 2005.
Yield of grapes: 60 quintals.
Yield of wine: 35-40 litres per 100 kg of grapes.
Drying: for approximately 30 to 40 days on wooden racks.
Age of vineyard: 8 years.
Fermentation: 15-20 days.
Ageing: in French barrique for twenty-four months, followed by six months in the bottle.
Annual production: on average 3 000 bottles. Sale: June 2008.
The wine: ruby red with violet highlights, and changing to garnet with ageing. It has a fruity fragrance, with hints of oak from the barrique. It tastes medium sweet, harmonious and pleasant.
Alcohol content: 16 % vol. Residual sugar content: 30 gr.
Minimum acidity: 5 per 1 000. Dry extracts: 30 per 1 000.

Montefalco Rosso DCO.

Grapes: 70% Sangiovese, 15% Merlot, and 15% Sagrantino.
Vintage year: 2006.
Yield of grapes: 80 quintals.
Yield of wine: 70 litres per 100 kg of grapes.
Age of vineyard: 8 years.
Fermentation: 15-20 days.
Ageing: in French barrique for four to five months, then in the bottle for two to three months.

Annual production: on average 7 000 bottles, of which 98% are sold in Italy and 2% are exported, mostly to Germany.
Sale: 15th May 2008.
The wine: rich ruby red in colour; with a delicate fragrance of oak, spices, cherry and blackberry.
Alcohol content: 13 % vol.
Food matches: red meats, beef stews, and full-fat mature cheeses.

Umbria Rosso IGT.

Grapes: 80 % Merlot, 10 % Sangiovese, and 10% Sagrantino.
Vintage year: 2007.
Age of vineyard: 8 years.
Fermentation: 4-7 days.
Ageing: in French barrique for four months, then in the bottle for a further month.
Annual production: on average 4 000 bottles, of which 98% are sold in Italy and 2% are exported, mostly to Germany.
Sale: May 2008.
The wine: ruby red in colour, with garnet highlights; a fragrance of oak and spices, and tastes dry, with well-balanced tannins.
Food matches: first courses, red meats, and mature cheeses.
Alcohol content: 14 % vol.

Umbria Grechetto IGT.

Grapes: 80% Grechetto, and 20% Trebbiano.
Vintage year: 2007.
Age of vineyard: 8 years.
Fermentation: 7-10 days.
Ageing in bottle: for less than two months.
Annual production: on average 4 000 bottles, of which 98% are sold in Italy and 2% are exported, mostly to Germany.
Sale: May 2008.
The wine: golden yellow in colour, with a fragrance of floral and fruity notes; it tastes dry and fresh
Food matches: aperitif, fish and, white meats.
Alcohol content: 13.5 % vol.

Tenuta Rocca di Fabbri.

Fabbri di Montefalco
06036 PG
Tel: 0742 399379
Fax: 0742 399199
www.roccadifabbri.com
info@roccadifabbri.com

An Umbrian entrepreneur, Pietro Vitali, has established Tenuta Rocca di Fabbri in 1984. During his long experience dealing in antiques, he became aware of a strong connection between works of art and a culinary tradition, which included the appreciation of quality wines. Towns with a rich cultural history are also the focal points for excellent wines. Montefalco is the living proof, where memorable wines had been produced since the Etruscan epoch and Imperial Rome. Benedictine monks carried on the tradition of cultivating the native grapes, Sagrantino and Grechetto in particular.

The winery is located inside the walls of a XIV century fortress on the top of a hill, dominating the surrounding vineyards. A newly constructed tunnel to the custom-built vinification plant connects the wine cellars inside the castle. The estate consists of sixty hectares of vineyards. Pietro Vitali replanted all the native grape varieties using modern methods of cultivation, and older vines are continually replaced with new plantings. Only grapes grown in the estate's vineyards are used for vinification.

Pietro Vitali's wife, and his daughters, Roberta and Simona have joined him in the management of the company. Giorgio Marone and Gianfrancesco Paoletti are the wine makers and Marcello Santucci manages the vineyards. The annual production is approximately 180 000 bottles of wine. The estate also distils a Grappa di Sagrantino and produces its own Extra Virgin Olive Oil.

Sagrantino di Montefalco DOCG.

Grapes: Sagrantino 100%.
First vintage: 1985.
Average quantity per vintage: 30 000 bottles.
Exposure: south/south-east.
Altitude: 200 metres above sea level.
Soil: mainly clayey, medium alkaline, very well drained.
Planting years: 1999 – 2002 – 2004.
Training: spurred cordon.
Planting density: 5 000 vines per hectare.
Yield: 5 500 litres per hectare.
Harvest: at the end of October.
Vinification: maceration with skin contact for 20 days at a controlled temperature. Followed by fermentation in 50-hectolitre stainless steel vats at 25 C°.
Refinement: 12 months in stainless steel, then 18 months in wood (70% in oak casks and 30% in barrique).
Bottling period: 32 months after vintage.
Marketing date: end of June.
The wine: intense ruby red in colour, with a rich and intense bouquet; tastes warm, with a unique richness and depth of flavour.
This is a wine for ageing, at least 12-15 years.
Serving temperature: 18/20 C°.
Food matches: Venison, roasts, and mature cheeses.

Sagrantino Passito di Montefalco DOCG.

Grapes: Sagrantino 100%, half dried.
First vintage: 1985.
Average quantity per vintage: 8 000 bottles.
Exposure: south/south-east.
Altitude: 200 metres above sea level.
Soil: mainly clayey, medium alkaline, very well drained.
Planting years: 1997 – 2000 – 2001.
Training: spurred cordon.
Planting density: 5 000 vines per hectare.
Yield: 3 500 litres per hectare.

Marketing date: end of June.
Harvest: at the end of October. The grapes are carefully selected and dried on racks in a well-ventilated area.
Vinification: maceration with skin contact for a long period, then fermentation in 50-hectolitre stainless steel vats at 20 C°.
Refinement: in oak casks and then in the bottle.
Bottling period: 32 months after vintage.
The wine: intense ruby red in colour, with hints of ripe red fruits and a full body. The taste is well structured, balanced, with soft tannins and dried fruits.
Serving temperature: 18/20 C°.
Food matches: spicy venison, mature cheeses, and desserts with almonds. This sweet wine will enhance a conversation with friends, and this is why it is referred to as a wine for meditation.

Faroaldo. Rosso Umbria IGT.

Grapes: Sagrantino 50%, and Cabernet Sauvignon 50%.
First vintage: 1997.
Average quantity per vintage: 6 000 bottles.
Exposure: south/south-east.
Altitude: 200 metres above sea level.
Soil: mainly clayey, medium alkaline, very well drained.
Planting years: 1990.
Training: low spurred cordon.
Planting density: 5 500 vines per hectare.
Yield: 4 500 litres per hectare.
Harvest: Mid-October.
Vinification: maceration with skin contact for 14 days, then fermentation in 50-hectolitre stainless steel vats at 30 C°.
Refinement: 18 months in barrique, then 6 months in the bottle.
Bottling period: 24 months after vintage.
The wine: intense ruby red in colour; with hints of vanilla, blackberries and spices; it tastes soft, and perfectly balanced.
Serving temperature: 18/20 C°.
Food matches: red meats, and mature cheeses.

Rosso di Montefalco DOC.

Grapes: Sangiovese 65%, Sagrantino 15%, and other grapes 20%.
First vintage: 1985.
Average quantity per vintage: 80 000 bottles.
Exposure: south/south-east.
Altitude: 200 metres above sea level.
Soil: mainly clayey, medium alkaline, very well drained.
Planting years: 1999 – 2002 – 2004 – 2005.
Training: spurred cordon.
Planting density: 5 000 vines per hectare.
Yield: 6 500 litres per hectare.
Harvest: Sangiovese in the first week of October, Sagrantino the last week of October.
Vinification: maceration with skin contact for 12 days, followed by fermentation in 50-hectolitre stainless steel vats at 25 C° for around 15-18 days.
Refinement: 8 months in stainless steel, then 12 months in oak casks, then in the bottle.
Bottling period: 20 months after vintage.
Marketing date: May.
The wine: deep ruby red in colour, with hints of berries and fruits. It tastes harmonious, well structured; dry and persistent.
Serving temperature: 18/20 C°.
Food matches: any type of meat, including venison and game.

Grechetto. Colli Martani DOC.

Grapes: Grechetto 100%.
First vintage: 1985.
Average quantity per vintage: 20 000 bottles.
Exposure: east.
Altitude: 265 metres above sea level.
Soil: medium texture, alkaline, very well drained.
Planting years: 1999 – 2000.
Training: Guyot and *casarsa*.
Planting density: 5 200 vines per hectare.
Yield: 6 000 litres per hectare.

Harvest: the first week of October.
Vinification: fermentation in stainless steel vats at 20 C°.
Bottling period: March.
The wine: golden yellow in colour, with green hues; it has a fruity bouquet, with scents of golden apples; and it tastes dry, crisp, and fruity.
Serving temperature: 12/14 C°.
Food matches: seafood, fish, and white meats.

Chardonnay. Umbria IGT.

Grapes: Chardonnay 100%.
First vintage: 1985.
Average quantity per vintage: 6 000 bottles.
Exposure: east.
Altitude: 265 metres above sea level.
Soil: medium texture, alkaline, very well drained.
Planting years: 1980.
Training: *casarsa.*
Planting density: 3 200 vines per hectare.
Yield: 7 000 litres per hectare.
Harvest: the last week of September.
Vinification: fermentation in stainless steel vats, at 20 C°.
Bottling period: March.
The wine: golden yellow in colour with a fruity bouquet; it tastes dry, crisp, and clean.
Serving temperature: 10/12 C°.
Food matches: aperitif, pasta, seafood, fish, and white meats.

Grechetto. Umbria IGT.

Grapes: 100% Grechetto.
Training: Guyot and spurred cordon.
Harvest: September.
The wine: bright straw yellow in colour. It has a rich floral bouquet, with hints of green apples; tastes dry, and crisp, with a pleasant acidity.
Serving temperature: 10/12 C°.
Food matches: fish and white meats.

Trebbiano. Umbria IGT.

Grapes: 100% Trebbiano.
Training: Guyot and spurred cordon.
Harvest: September.
The wine: light straw yellow in colour. Its bouquet is flowery, fruity, with hints of green apples; and a harmonious, balanced taste, with a pleasant acidity.
Serving temperature: 10/12 C°.
Food matches: aperitif, fish and pasta dishes.

Sangiovese. Umbria IGT.

Grapes: 100% Sangiovese.
Training: spurred cordon.
Harvest: at the end of September.
Vinification: maceration with skin contact for 10-15 days.
The wine: ruby red in colour, with violet tints; and with the scents of violets. It tastes light, dry with soft balanced tannins.
Serving temperature: 14/16 C°.
Food matches: pizza and pasta with meat sauces.

Grappa di Sagrantino.

This grappa is produced in the traditional steam distillation system in copper stills. The moist, freshly pressed grapes come from the fermentation process of the Sagrantino wines. The taste is rounded, soft, delicate and gentle on the palate.

Romanelli

Azienda Agricola Romanelli
Colle San Clemente
06036 Montefalco PG
Tel/fax: 0742 371245
www.romanelli.se
info@romanelli.se

The farm and vineyards were founded in 1978, when Amedeo and Costantino Romanelli, father and son, took the decision to devote themselves full time to agriculture in the San Clemente area. They produce wine, olive oil, and grow cereals, which they use for animal fodder. Anna-Maria and Anna-Rita, the respective wives, also work in the fields and raise the livestock, grow their vegetables and cook for their family, including Devis and Fabio, their sons. Three generations live and work together; they are at one with the land, and their passion for it is expressed through the quality of their products. They understand how to grow healthy vines that produce near perfect grapes, ready to turn into wine. They use organic compost and control weeds by growing grass between the rows of vines. Close attention to pruning assures low yields and top quality grapes. They have chosen and rediscovered old varieties, like Sagrantino, which is the true soul of all Montefalco red wines. The family follows tradition and combines it with modern methods of vinification.

Montefalco Sagrantino DOCG.

Grapes: Sagrantino 100%.
Altitude: 350 metres above sea level.
Soil: silt and clay, well exposed to the sun.
System: spurred cordon.
Density: 5 000 plants per hectare.
Yield per hectare: 5 000 kilograms of grapes.
Vinification: The grapes are harvested by hand and placed into boxes, then taken to the wine cellars, where they are de-stemmed and softly pressed. The must is fermented at a controlled

temperature with frequent pumping over and punching down. Maceration on the skins follows for about 45-60 days. The wine is aged for 18 months in French oak barrels, then filtered and aged in the bottle for 10 months.

The wine: ruby red in colour, with a bouquet of blackberries and spices. It tastes warm, powerful with a long finish.

Serving temperature: 18 C°.

Food matches: Venison, roasts, and mature cheeses.

Alcohol content: 15% vol.

Montefalco Rosso DOC.

Grapes: Sangiovese 65%, Sagrantino 15%, Merlot 10%, and Cabernet Sauvignon 10%.

Altitude: 350 metres above sea level.

Soil: silt and clay, well exposed to the sun.

System: spurred cordon.

Density: 5 000 plants per hectare.

Yield per hectare: 8 090 quintals of grapes.

Vinification: The best grapes are harvested by hand and placed into boxes, then taken to the cellars, where they are de-stemmed and softly pressed. The must is fermented at a controlled temperature with frequent pumping over and punching down. Maceration on the skins follows for about 30-45 days. The wine is aged for 12 months in French oak barrels, then filtered and aged in the bottle for 2 months.

The wine: intense red in colour, with violet tints; it has a bouquet of ripe fruits, fruit jams, dried fruits, vanilla and liquorice. It tastes elegant, soft, with light tannins.

Serving temperature: 18 C°.

Food matches: red and white meats, and mature cheeses.

Alcohol content: 14% vol.

Predara. Umbria Rosso IGT.

Grapes: Sangiovese 80%, Sagrantino 12%, and Merlot 8%.

Altitude: 350 metres above sea level.

Soil: silt and clay, well-exposed hillside.

System: spurred cordon.

Density: 5 000 plants per hectare.
Yield per hectare: 9 000 kilograms of grapes.
Vinification: The best grapes are harvested by hand and placed into boxes, then taken to the cellars, where they are de-stemmed and softly pressed. The must starts fermentation on the macerated skins at a controlled temperature for about 30 days, with frequent pumping over pressing down. After racking, the wine is aged for a short period in French oak barrels.
The wine: ruby red in colour, with an elegant and fruity bouquet. It tastes dry, with light tannins.
Serving temperature: 18 C°.
Food matches: grilled meats, and cheeses.
Alcohol content: 14% vol.

Grechetto dei Colli Martani DOC.

Grapes: Grechetto 100%.
Altitude: 220 metres above sea level.
Soil: silt and clay, well-exposed hillside.
System: spurred cordon.
Density: 5 000 plants per hectare.
Yield per hectare: 5 000 kilograms of grapes.
Vinification: In the early hours of the morning, the best grapes are handpicked and placed into boxes, then taken to the cellars, de-stemmed and softly pressed. The must starts fermenting at a low temperature of 15 C° for about 15-20 days. After racking, the wine is aged in steel vats for 6 months, then filtered and bottled, followed by ageing in the bottle for 2 months.
The wine: straw yellow in colour with golden hues; with hints of fruit, apple, grapefruit, ripe pineapple, and honey. It tastes soft, full bodied and persistent.
Serving temperature: 12 C°.
Food matches: first courses, pasta, and cheeses.
Alcohol content: 14.5% vol.

Sagrantino Grappa.

Made only from Sagrantino grapes, using the discontinuous distillation method in the *bain-marie* system. The water used for the steam comes from a local stream.
It has a complex and delicate bouquet, with a smooth and persistent taste.
Alcohol content: 42% vol.

Ruggeri

Ruggeri G. Società Agricola s.s.
06036 Montefalco PG
Tel/fax: 0742 379679
Cell: 349 1781390
www.viniruggeri.it
info@viniruggeri.it

The cellar founded by Giovanni Ruggeri is the home of traditional wine production. Every aspect of production reflects the family's close attention to detail and passion for quality wines. The estate's two hectares of land were planted at the beginning of the nineteen-seventies. The density of vines is three thousand per hectare, using the spurred cordon training system. The low yield thus produced, guarantees healthy grapes, which are then turned into wines of the optimum quality. There is a unique relationship between the land and the people who work on it, which assures excellence. Constant innovation and the use of modern winemaking techniques ensure the family's success.

Sagrantino Secco DOCG.

Grapes: Sagrantino 100%.
Average annual production: 5 000 bottles.
Vinification is in the traditional method. It has an intense ruby red colour and a rich bouquet with hints of blackberries, red fruit jams, and spices. It is a full-bodied wine, with well-balanced tannins, has a long finish with aromatic hints of oak.
Serving temperature: 18 C°.
Food matches: full flavoured red meat dishes, game, pasta with rich meat sauces, and mature cheeses.
Alcoholic content: 14.5% vol.

Sagrantino Passito DOCG.

Grapes: Sagrantino 100%
Average annual production: 6 000 bottles.
The grapes dried on racks for 70 days before vinification. The wine is matured in oak barrels for 18 months. It has a ruby red colour with garnet hues; a delicate bouquet, with hints of blueberries, blackcurrants, blackberries, and fruit jams. It is a well-structured wine for "meditation"; it tastes warm, with light tannins. It is an ideal wine for ageing, anything up to 15 years.
Serving temperature: 12 C°.
Food matches: Umbrian desserts, but also mature cheeses.
Alcoholic content: 15% vol.

Montefalco Rosso DOC.

Grapes: Sangiovese 60%, Sagrantino 15%, and Merlot 25%.
Average annual production: 12 000 bottles.
The wine is matured in oak barrels for twelve months. It has a ruby red colour, and an intense bouquet, with blackcurrants, cherries and plums. It tastes dry, warm and well structured with light tannins and a long finish.
Serving temperature: 18 C°.
Food matches: first courses, like risotto and pasta, main courses of red meats, mixed grills, and mature cheeses.
Alcoholic content: 14% vol.

Grechetto. Umbria IGT.

Grapes: Grechetto and a selection of local white grapes.
Average annual production: 3 000 bottles.
Vinification is carried out in stainless steel vats under controlled temperatures. It has a straw yellow colour and an elegant bouquet with hints of fruit, apple, and honey. It tastes dry and fresh, but also soft with a persistent finish.
Serving temperature: 12 C°.
Food matches: delicate starters, cold cuts of meat, seafood, first courses, pasta, and medium mature cheeses.
Alcoholic content: 13% vol.

Scacciadiavoli

Azienda Agraria Scacciadiavoli
Loc. Cantinone, 31
06036 Montefalco PG
Tel: 0742 378272
Fax: 0742 378272
www.scacciadiavoli.it

Scacciadiavoli is one of the oldest estates in the area. The name means: "drives away devils." It derives from an ancient village located near the estate, where, once, an exorcist lived.

Built in the second half of the nineteenth century, the winery has been recently refurbished with modern equipment to facilitate up-to-date methods of wine production. In the second half of the twentieth century the grandfather of the present day owners, Amilcare Pambuffetti, acquired the estate. It covers 130 hectares; of which 35 are vineyards. The soil is composed of clay and shale, and the vineyards are exposed to east/south-east. The altitude is 400 metres above sea level. There are 5 000 vines planted per hectare, which allows the cultivation of excellent grapes, and thus the production of wines of the highest quality. The annual production is around 250 000 bottles of wine.

Sola Fides (Faith Alone) is the belief that the land will reward work with products of quality. It is the trust that Scacciadiavoli has in the territory of Montefalco. *Sola Fides* also shapes the estate's philosophy, which combines the rich potential of the territory, the microclimate, the collaboration of agronomists, oenologists, and the personal investment of the entire team.

Montefalco Sagrantino DOCG.

Grapes: Sagrantino 100%.
Yield per hectare: 60 quintals.
Harvest: from the 15th to the end of October.
Vinification: 3-4 weeks in French oak vats. The temperature is maintained below 30 C° throughout alcoholic fermentation.

Ageing: in new barrels for 16 months, and in the bottle for a minimum of 9 months.
The wine: intense ruby red in colour, with garnet hues. It has a bouquet with notes of small red fruits, ripe plums, spices, and hints of herbs and leather. It tastes slightly tannic, but balanced with fresh acidity; and a long and spicy finish. The wine lends itself to long ageing, more than 20 years.
Serving temperature: 18-19 C°.
Food pairings: roast and grilled meat, game, and mature cheeses.
Bottle sizes: 0.375 litre, 0.750 litre, 1.5 litre and 3.00 litre.

Montefalco Sagrantino Passito DOCG.

Grapes: Sagrantino 100%.
Yield per hectare: 60 quintals.
Harvest: from the 15th to the end of September.
Drying: until mid-December on *graticci* (racks) in order to concentrate the grapes' flavours and sugars.
Vinification: in stainless steel tanks.
Ageing: in new barrels for 16 months, and in the bottle for a minimum of 9 months.
The wine: intense ruby red in colour, with violet hues. The bouquet has notes of blackberry, black cherry, dried fruit, sweet spices, with a hint of minerals. It tastes soft, sweet, and velvety. The tannins are sweet, with a well balanced acidity. It has a finish with notes of fruits of the forest and intense spices. This "meditation" wine lends itself to ageing of more than 20 years.
Serving temperature: 18-19 C°.
Food pairings: dry pastries, cream or jam tarts, almond biscuits, chocolate and mature cheeses, both spicy and herbal.
Bottle sizes: 0.375 litre.

Montefalco Rosso DOC.

Grapes: Sangiovese 60%, Sagrantino 15%, and Merlot 25%.
Yield per hectare: 90-100 quintals.
Harvest: from the 15th of September to mid-October.
Ageing: in aged barrels and large tanks made from French oak for 12 months, and in the bottle for a minimum of 6 months.

The wine: deep ruby red in colour, with violet and garnet hues. It is refined, with aromas of spice, fruits of the forest and small red fruits. It has a good structure and tastes soft and voluptuous. The tannins and acidity are well balanced. It has a long fruity finish, and the wine lends itself to ageing for several years.
Serving temperature: 18-19 C°.
Food pairings: soups, pastas, rice dishes, poultry and red meat.
Bottle sizes: 0.375 litre, 0.750 litre, 1.5 litre and 3.00 litre.

Grechetto dell'Umbria IGT.

Grapes: Grechetto 100 %.
Yield per hectare: 100 quintals.
Harvest: the first ten days of September.
Vinification: in stainless steel tanks.
Ageing: in stainless steel tanks on the lees, and in the bottle for a minimum of 3 months.
The wine: canary yellow in colour, with light green hues. It has a fruity and floral bouquet, with notes of yellow and white flowers and the scent of the Mediterranean brush. It tastes soft, with fresh acidity and a long finish. Best drunk when young.
Serving temperature: 8-10 C°.
Food pairings: perfect with soups, pastas, and rice dishes, as well as fish courses.
Bottle sizes: 0.750 litre.

Spumante Brut Metodo Classico.

Not only red wines are made from the Sagrantino grape. Vinified as white, it is the base for Spumante Brut made in the traditional method. The grape reveals itself in a new form: the aromas are fresh and delicate, and the tannins typical of the Sagrantino give structure and unite the bubbles.
Grapes: Sagrantino 85%, and Chardonnay 15%.
Harvest: the first ten days of September.
Method: traditional.
Vinification: in stainless steel tanks with controlled temperature.
Ageing: in the bottle on the lees for at least 12 months.

The wine: light yellow in colour, with green hues, and fine and persistent beads. It has a fresh and floral bouquet, with notes of red apple, white peach and fresh bread; dynamic and balanced, medium structure, pleasing with a fresh acidity.
Serving temperature: 6-8 C°.
Food pairings: *hors d'oeuvres* and first courses.
Bottle sizes: 0.750 litre and 1.5 litre.

Pardi

Cantina Fratelli Pardi s.s.
Via G Pascoli, 7-9
06036 Montefalco PG
Tel/Fax: 0742 379023
www.cantinapardi.it

From 1919 to 1940 the brothers Alberto, Alfredo and Francesco Pardi used the grapes grown in the family's vineyards to produce wine in the cellars beneath the church of San Francesco in Montefalco (today it houses the Museo Civico). Their wines were marketed all over Umbria, and their most prestigious buyer was the Vatican City. Since 2002 their great-grandsons Francesco, Gianluca Rio and Alberto Mario Pardi have taken over the business of their great-grandfathers' winery.

The winery is located just outside the city walls. The cellars take up 1100 square metres. Here, the grapes are vinified, aged, bottled and marketed as DOCG and DOC wines. About 300 square metres are kept for the ageing of the wine in oak barrels.

The grapes used in the winery come from the vineyards belonging to the Pardi family. They are located around Montefalco, on the gentle hillsides of Casale, Campolungo, Lasignanao and Pietrauta. The vineyards extend for 11 hectares.

Montefalco Sagrantino Secco. DOCG.

Grapes: 100% Sagrantino.
Soil: of sedimentary origin.
Exposure: east/south-east.
Altitude: 280 metres above sea level.
Yield: 70 quintals of grapes per hectare; 1.5 kg per plant.
Harvest: beginning of October.
Vinification: fermentation on skins for 10-16 days. Alcoholic and malolactic fermentation in stainless steel tanks.

Ageing: in barrels/barrique for 18 months and in stainless steel tanks for 6-9 months.
Refining: in the bottle for 4-6 months.
Marketing: 32 months from the harvest.
Bottle sizes: 0.375 l, 0.750 l and 1.5 l.

Montefalco Sagrantino Passito. DOCG.

Grapes: 100% Sagrantino.
Soil: of sedimentary origin.
Exposure: east/south-east.
Altitude: 280 metres above sea level.
Harvest: beginning of October.
Drying: natural, on rush matting for 2 months.
Vinification: Fermentation on skins for 8 days. Alcoholic and malolactic fermentation in stainless steel tanks.
Ageing: in barrique for 12 months and in stainless steel tanks for 12 months.
Refining: in the bottle for 6 months.
Marketing: 32 months from the harvest.
Bottle sizes: 0.375 l, 0.750 l and 1.5 l.

Montefalco Rosso. DOC.

Grapes: 70% Sangiovese, 15% Sagrantino, and 15% Merlot and Cabernet.
Soil: of sedimentary origin.
Exposure: east/south-east.
Altitude: of 260 metres above sea level.
Yield: 80 quintals of grapes per hectare; 1.5-2 kg per plant.
Harvest: beginning of October.
Vinification: fermentation on skins for 10 days. Alcoholic and malolactic fermentation in stainless steel tanks.
Ageing: in barrels/barrique for 18 months and in stainless steel tanks for 6 months.
Refining: in the bottle for 4 months.
Marketing: 20-22 months from the harvest.
Bottle sizes: 0.375 l, 0.750 l and 1.5 l.

Colle di Giove. DOC.

Grapes: 60% Grechetto, 15%, Chardonnay, and 25% Trebbiano Spoletino.
Soil: of sedimentary and clayey origin.
Exposure: south-east.
Altitude of 240 metres above sea level.
Yield: 90 quintals of grapes per hectare, which produce around 55 hectolitres of wine per hectare.
Vinification: soft pressing of the whole grapes; fermentation at a constant temperature of 20 C° for 20 days in stainless steel tanks.
Bottling: April following the harvest.
Bottle size: 0.750 l.

Perticaia

Azienda Agraria Perticaia
Località Casale
06036 Montefalco PG
Tel: 0742 379014
Fax: 0742 371014
guidoguardigli@libero.it

In the archaic language of central Italy "Perticaica" means plough. The estate began making wine in 2000, when Guido Guardigli became the proprietor. For many years before he gained valuable experience as a director of winemaking estates in Tuscany and Umbria. His choice of territory could not have been any better, for the Montefalco area has been well known for the great potential and personality of the Sagrantino grape.

The farm was originally about twenty hectares, of which two and a half were olive trees and one and a half were vineyards. This has now been completely changed by the planting of fourteen hectares of vineyards and the building of modern wine cellars. The wines are aged in barrels of French oak, in barrique or *tonneaux*, in an eighteenth century cellar in the small medieval village of Gualdo Cattaneo.

The vines are all planted on a hillside with a gentle slope at the altitude of 300-350 metres above sea level, facing towards south-west. The soil has medium consistency with stones, which provide good drainage. The vineyards are divided as follows:

7 hectares 100% Sagrantino grapes.

8 hectares 60% Sangiovese, 15% Sagrantino, 25% Merlot, Cabernet Franc and Colorino grapes.

1 hectare 100% Trebbiano Spoletino grapes.

2.5 hectares of olive groves.

The vines are trained on as low spurred cordon, with a density is 5 500 plants per hectare. Production is limited to seven or eight bunches per vine, which provides ripe and well-balanced grapes. The yield is 60-70 quintals of grapes per hectare.

Products of the Perticaica Estate have been on the market since 2003, the company has been in full production since 2007 and all its products were available since 2008.

Montefalco Sagrantino DOCG.

Grapes: Sagrantino 100%.
Harvest: the second ten days of October.
Vinification: Long skin contact maceration and alcoholic fermentation for 3 weeks, with controlled temperatures between 25 C° and 28 C°; and between 20 C° and 22 C° up to the completion of malolactic fermentation. Then follows ageing: in small wood barrels of French oak, *barrique* or *tonneaux*.
Ageing: 36 months, according to the wine producers' regulations and divided as follows: 12 months in oak barrels, *barrique* or *tonneaux*; 12 months in steel vats; and 12 months in the bottle.
The wine: intense ruby red in colour, with hues of garnet; a spicy bouquet, with a scent of cinnamon that does not overpower the aroma of red fruit, cherry or black cherry. With ageing and refinement in the bottle, an aroma of dried prunes develops. It has full tannic taste, with a touch of bitterness. It is a wine that will evolve in the bottle, and it will mature for at least 10 years.
Food matches: red meat, game, and mature cheeses.

Montefalco Sagrantino Passito DOCG.

Grapes: Sagrantino 100%.
Harvest: the last two thirds of October.
Drying: the grapes are dried (*appasite*) on natural rush matting for at least forty days.
Vinification: maceration on the skins for at least ten days with a fermentation temperature between 26 C° and 28 C°; followed by refinement in French bay-oak barrels, *barrique* or *tonneaux*.
Ageing: 30 months, according to the wine producers' regulations and divided as follows: 12 months in oak barrels, *barrique* or *tonneaux*; 12 months in steel vats; and 6 months in the bottle.
The wine: intense ruby red in colour, with pomegranate hues. It has a bouquet of ripe fruit, with marmalade overtones, as well as prunes, cherries, vanilla, cinnamon, and spices. It is full-bodied,

with good structure, a tannic finish, and a touch of sweetness. It is a wine that will evolve in the bottle; it can age for many years and improve its quality.
Food matches: roast meat dishes, such as lamb, and also desserts with a dark chocolate base.

Montefalco Rosso DOC.

Grapes: Sangiovese 60%, Sagrantino 15%, Colorino 15%, Merlot and other red grapes 10%.
Harvest: varies according to grape variety.
Vinification: maceration and fermentation for one or two weeks, depending on the grape; with controlled temperatures between 25 C° and 28 C°; and between 20 C° and 22 C° up to the completion of malolactic fermentation.
Ageing: 18 months, according to the wine producers' regulations: 12 months in steel vats; and 6 months in the bottle.
The wine: ruby red in colour, with fresh aromas of wild berries, raspberries and blueberries. It is full and mildly tannic; a wine that evolves in the bottle and will mature for at least 5 years.
Food matches: salamis, cold cuts of meats, pasta and other first course dishes.

Trebbiano Spoletino. IGT.

Grapes: Trebbiano Spoletino 100%.
Harvest: the last third of October.
Vinification: soft pressing of whole grapes under inert gas.
Fermentation: cold static clarification, then the fermentation of the clear must in stainless steel vats, with controlled temperatures between 15 C° and 16 C°.
Ageing: at least 6 months on fine sediment during which time the wine is never poured.
The wine: straw yellow in colour, with greenish hues. It has a bouquet of tropical fruit, and yellow flowers. It is full-bodied, with freshness and solidity, supported by an excellent base sweetness. It can age for 4-5 years in the bottle
Food matches: aperitif, fish and seafood, and white meats.

Tabarrini

Azienda Agricola Giampaolo Tabarrini
Fraz. Turrita
06036 Montefalco PR
Tel: 0742 379351
Fax: 0742 371342
www.tabarrini.com
info@tabarrini.com

For four generations the Tabarrini family have lovingly and passionately tended their vines. Towards the end of the 1990s, thanks to the enthusiasm of the proprietor, Giampaolo, the company changed direction. They decided to bottle their own wines, and a *cantina* was built.

Half of the vineyard (11 hectares out of a total of 22) is dedicated to the Sagrantino grape, which has found its true *raison d'être* in Umbria and plays a central role in the work and the lives of everybody involved. But great wines grow only from a great love of the land, from a bunch of grapes to a bottle of wine. The whole family follows this philosophy scrupulously through every step in the production of their wines.

Montefalco Sagrantino DOCG.

Grapes: 100% Sagrantino.
Aspect: south-east/east.
Age of vines: 10-15 years.
Altitude: 420 metres above sea level.
Training: spurred cordon.
Number of vines per hectare: 5 500.
Soil: sandy, muddy, with some clay and river pebbles.
Production per hectare: 4.5 tonnes.
Vinification: soaking in the skins for over a month.
Ageing: 30 months in French oak barrels.

Ageing in the bottle: 6 months.
Annual average production: 16 000 bottles.
The wine: ruby red in colour, with intense fragrances of blackberries and spices and delicate mineral hints. It is full in the mouth, with an unending finish.
Serving temperature: 16-18 C°.
Food matches: roast and braised meats, game and cheeses.

Montefalco Sagrantino Passito DOCG.

Grapes: 100% Sagrantino.
Aspect: south-east.
Age of vines: 10-15 years.
Altitude: 420 metres above sea level.
Training: spurred cordon.
Number of vines per hectare: 5 500.
Soil: sandy, muddy, with some clay and river pebbles.
Production per hectare: 4 tonnes.
Harvest: the grapes are left to dry on racks for three months.
Vinification: soaking in the skins for over a month.
Ageing: 30 months in French oak barrels.
Ageing in the bottle: 6 months.
Annual average production: 1 800 bottles.
The wine: purplish ruby, with complex aromas of dry fruits, jams, chocolate and spices. The taste is fleshy and rich, well blended with sweetness and acidity; a wine for "meditation".
Serving temperature: 16-18 C°.
Food matches: dry biscuits, chocolate, or the traditional *rocciata* fruit rolls. It can be a bold match with game.

Montefalco Rosso DOC.

Grapes: Sangiovese, Sagrantino, Cabernet Sauvignon, and Merlot.
Aspect: south-east.
Age of vines: 10-15 years.
Altitude: 420 metres above sea level.
Training: spurred cordon.
Number of vines per hectare: 5 500.

Soil: muddy clay, with good density.
Production per hectare: 6 tonnes.
Vinification: soaking in the skins for over a month.
Ageing: 12 months in French oak barrels, and 12 months in stainless steel vats; then in the bottle for 6 months.
Annual average production: 22 000 bottles.
The wine: ruby red in colour, with intense fragrances of ripe cherries and rose petals. It is full and rounded, and retains its structure without losing its freshness in depth.
Serving temperature: 16-18 C°
Food matches: first courses with elaborate sauces, salamis and medium mature cheeses.

Bocca di Rosa. Rosato dell'Umbria IGT.

"They called her Bocca di Rosa" is the opening line of a popular Italian song by Fabrizio de André. She is a "lady of the night" and she dispenses "love all around".
Grapes: 100% Sagrantino.
Aspect: south-east.
Age of vines: 10-15 years.
Altitude: 360 metres above sea level.
Training: spurred cordon.
Number of vines per hectare: 5 000.
Soil: muddy clay, with good density.
Production per hectare: 4.5 tonnes.
Vinification: traditional white wine fermentation.
Ageing: 4 months in stainless steel; in the bottle for 3 months.
Annual average production: 3 500 bottles.
The wine: brilliant cherry in colour, with fresh fragrances and delicate tannins, juicy and sapid.
Serving temperature: 12-14 C°.
Food matches: fish and cheeses.

Il Padrone delle Vigne. Rosso dell'Umbria IGT.

This wine is dedicated to the grandfather of Giampaolo Tabarrini, in recognition of the experience he passed on.

Grapes: Sangiovese, Sagrantino, Cabernet Sauvignon, and Merlot.
Aspect: south-east.
Age of vines: 10-15 years.
Altitude: 420 metres above sea level.
Training: spurred cordon.
Number of vines per hectare: 5 500.
Soil: muddy clay, with good density.
Production per hectare: 9 tonnes.
Vinification: soaking in the skins for over a month.
Ageing: 1 month in French oak barrels; 3 months in stainless steel, then in the bottle for 3 months.
Annual average production: 10 000 bottles.
The wine: ruby red, with purple hues; a fresh bouquet of fruits of the forest; it is soft and balanced with a lasting flavour.
Serving temperature: 16-18 C°.
Food matches: first courses with elaborate sauces, salamis and medium mature cheeses.

Adarmando. Bianco dell'Umbria IGT.

Grapes: 100% Trebbiano Spoletino
Aspect: south-east.
Age of vines: 50-60 years.
Altitude: 350 metres above sea level.
Training: *Sylvoz*.
Number of vines per hectare: 3 000.
Soil: muddy clay.
Production per hectare: 8 tonnes.
Vinification: traditional white wine fermentation.
Ageing: almost 4 months in stainless steel.
Ageing in the bottle: 3 months.
Annual average production: 5 000 bottles.
The wine: straw yellow in colour with green and golden shades. The aromas are of citrus fruits and white peach, enriched by elegant mineral hints. Juicy, fresh and consistent, it is sharp on the palate with a rare complexity.
Serving temperature: 12 C°.
Food matches: starters, first courses, fish, and poultry.

THE WINE PRODUCERS
ASSISI

Assisi is normally associated with Saint Francis; however, it is also a designated area for the production of DOC wines. There are a small number of vineyards on the lower slopes of Monte Subasio, stretching along the Vale of Spoleto. Even though the area is densely populated in the vicinity of Assisi, Perugia and Spello, every suitable piece of land is planted with vines. The hillsides range anywhere from 180 to 550 metres above sea level, and as some of the vineyards are located in the Montefalco and Torgiano production zones the handful of producers located in Assisi also market Montefalco and Torgiano wines.

Sportoletti

Sportoletti Ernesto e Remo
Via Lombardia, 1
06038 Spello PG
Tel: 0742 651461
Fax: 0742 652249
Office@sportoletti.com

The Sportoletti family has been involved in agricultural activities for generations, and particularly, they have been passionately dedicated to the production of wine. During the end of the 1970s the brothers, Ernesto and Remo, decided to turn their attention exclusively to winemaking. Vittorio, their father, has passed on his experience and knowledge; and building on this, the brothers marketed their first thousand bottles of wine with their own label.

From there began the long and difficult journey in pursuit of the perfect balance between innovation and tradition. They made an effort and succeeded in realising the full potential of their twenty-two hectares of vines situated on the hillsides of Spello and Assisi. In 1998 the company engaged the highly esteemed oenologist, Riccardo Cotarella, as a consultant.

Assisi Rosso DOC.

Grapes: Sangiovese, Merlot and Cabernet.
Production area: Assisi DOC.
Production per hectare: 9 500 kg.
Harvest: second half of September.
Vinification: steeping for 10-15 days in temperature controlled stainless steel vats, followed by malolactic fermentation.
Refining: in wood for some months, then in the bottle.
It is a ruby red wine with purple tones. It is fresh, with fruity notes of cherries, raspberries, sweet spices and chocolate; with savoury tannins and a complex finish.

Assisi Grechetto DOC.

Grapes: Grechetto.
Production area: Assisi DOC.
Production per hectare: 8 500 kg.
Harvest: mid-September.
Vinification: steeping for a few hours.
Alcoholic fermentation: in stainless steel vats at a controlled temperature.
Refining: in the bottle.
It has a straw yellow colour, with aromas of jasmine, white peaches, and apples. It is smooth and warm in the mouth, with mineral notes, and a finish of a delicate taste of mint.

Villa Fidelia. Rosso IGT.

Grapes: Merlot 70%, Cabernet Sauvignon 20%, and Cabernet Franc 10%.
Production area: the hills of Assisi and Spello.
Production per hectare: 5 500 kg.
Harvest: second half of September.
Vinification: steeping for about 10-15 days in temperature controlled stainless steel vats. Malolactic fermentation is carried out in French oak casks.
Refining: for about 12 months in French oak casks, then in the bottle for another 12 months.
It has a deep, glowing, dark red colour, with aromas recalling blackberry, tobacco, spices, liquorice and chocolate. It has silky tannins, and a persistent finish.

Villa Fidelia. Bianco IGT.

Grapes: Grechetto 60%, and Chardonnay 40%.
Production area: the hills around Assisi and Spello.
Production per hectare: 5 500 kg.
Harvest: during the first days of September.
Vinification: steeping for about 8 hours at a low temperature.
Alcoholic and Malolactic fermentation: in French oak casks.

Refining: in barrels with yeast deposits for 4 months, then in the bottle for 12 months.

It has a straw yellow colour, with golden green highlights; notes of toasted hazelnuts, butter and vanilla, with faint aromas of pink grapefruit, tropical fruits, and herbs. It has a full body and aromatic persistence; and a rich balsamic finish.

NB:

The company also owns 2 500 Moraiolo olive trees, planted at an altitude of 500 metres above sea level on the slopes of Monte Subasio. These are cultivated for the production of one of the best organic extra virgin olive oils in Umbria.

Tili

Azienda Agraria Vitivinicola
Via Cannella, 2
06081 Capodacqua Assisi PG
Tel: 0758 064370
Fax: 0758 069014
www.tilivini.com
tilivini@libero.it

The Tili vineyards stretch for over 20 hectares on the hillside of Monte Subasio. The characteristic chalky soil and the mild, dry microclimate together with the constant rays of sunshine provide the perfect conditions for growing vines and olive trees. For years, the estate has been tended with love and care, respecting the wine producing and oil making traditions of the land. Yields are limited in order to improve the quality of the grapes produced, hence, selection and pruning continues all year round. Growing grass between the rows of vines controls the weeds, and eliminates the use of synthetic chemicals, pesticides and herbicides. Fungicides and fertilisers are applied to the absolute minimum. Only grapes grown on the estate are used for vinification, and the production is around 70 quintals per hectare; this low yield is balanced by the high quality of the grapes.

This enthusiastic commitment is carried through to the next stage, and the most modern oenological equipment is used for making and marketing the wines. Experimentation and innovation helped the Tili estate to reach high levels of production, which were recognised by prestigious awards over the years, both regionally and nationally. They were awarded the DOC Assisi in February 1997 for the Bianco, Rosato, Rosso and Grechetto di Assisi wines. They were first produced in 1979. Tili's creativity has been recognised in April 1996 by the Minister of Agriculture, bestowing the *l'onorificenza del Cangrande* (a prestigious honour, indeed).

Assisi Bianco DOC.

Grapes: Malvasia, Trebbiano, and Grechetto.
Vinification: free run juice fermented in stainless steel.
Serving temperature: 8-10 C°.

Assisi Grechetto DOC.

Grapes: Grechetto.
Vinification: free run juice fermented in stainless steel.
Serving temperature: 8-10 C°.

Assisi Rosso DOC.

Grapes: Sangiovese, Merlot, and Canaiolo.
Vinification: carbonic maceration in rotary fermentation tank and three years in oak casks.
Serving temperature: 18-20 C°.

Umbria Rosato IGT.

Grapes: Canaiolo.
Vinification: free run juice fermented in stainless steel.
Serving temperature: 8-10 C°.

P. Nero. Umbria Rosso IGT.

Grapes: Pinot Nero.
Vinification: on the skins in stainless steel vats.
Serving temperature: 18 C°.

Renaro. Umbria Pinot Chardonnay IGT.

Grapes: Pinot and Chardonnay.
Vinification: free run juice fermented in stainless steel.
Serving temperature: 10-12 C°.

Valditufo. Umbria Bianco IGT.

Grapes: Pinot and Chardonnay.
Vinification: free run juice fermented in stainless steel.
Serving temperature: 10-12 C°.

Sacreterre. Secco Umbria Rosso IGT.

Grapes: Sagrantino.
Vinification: carbonic maceration in rotary fermentation tank; ageing in oak casks and barrique.
Serving temperature: 18-20 C°.

Muffa Reale. Umbria Bianco IGT.

Grapes: Grechetto and Semillon.
Vinification: selected grapes with botrytis cinerea.
Serving temperature: 8-10 C°.

Gaudium. Umbria Grechetto IGT.

Grapes: Grechetto and Semillon.
Vinification: selected grapes dried before fermentation.
Ageing: for 10 years in oak barrique.
Serving temperature: 12-14 C°.

Spumante Brut

Grapes: Pinot Nero and Chardonnay.
Vinification: first fermentation free run juice, second fermentation in the bottle with yeasts added.
Serving temperature: 6-8 C°.

Antigniano and Vignabaldo

Distributo da: Brogal Vini s.r.l
Via degli Olmi, 9
06083 Bastia Umbra PG
Tel: 0758 001501 or 0758 000525
Fax: 0758 000935
www.brogalvini.com

Bastia Umbra is a town half way between Assisi and Perugia, and The Brogal winery produces wines made from grapes grown within the Torgiano, Montefalco, and Assisi DOC zones.

Antigniano and Vignabaldo are two different production lines, but all the wines are made in Bastia Umbra. The history of the winery dates back to the eighteenth century, to Father Giuseppe Brocatelli, who was a passionate wine producer and particularly fond and proud of his Vinsanto. Since then, numerous generations of the family have passed on their passion for making wines. The company has always relied on its experience to guarantee high quality products targeted at an increasingly more competent and demanding consumer.

The vineyards are located only in DOC and DOCG areas on the sun drenched hillsides of Torgiano and Montefalco, where viticulture is generous and produces excellent fruits. Careful grape selection and close attention to every step of the wine making process, using the most advanced technology, allows the company to achieve premium quality wines.

Antigniano

Antigniano. Preda del Falco. Sagrantino di Montefalco DOCG.

Grapes: Sagrantino.
The wine: ruby red in colour, with violet and garnet reflections. It has good structure and it is fruity, with blackberry and blackcurrant scents, soft tannins and a persistent finish.

Serving temperature: 14-16 C°, open an hour before consuming.
Food matches: roast meats and game dishes.
Alcohol content: 13.5%-14% vol.

Antigniano. Santa Caterina. Torgiano Rosso Riserva DOCG.

Grapes: Sangiovese, Cabernet Sauvignon, and Canaiolo.
The wine: intense ruby red in colour; with plenty of structure, a well-balanced flavour, precious, and aged in French barrique.
Serving temperature: 14-16 C°, uncork an hour before consuming.
Food matches: roast meats, game dishes, and mature cheeses.
Alcohol content: 13.5%-14% vol.

Antigniano. Re Migrante. Rosso di Montefalco Riserva DOC.

Grapes: Sangiovese and Sagrantino.
The wine: intense ruby red in colour; dry with a good body.
Serving temperature: 16-18 C°, uncork an hour before consuming.
Food matches: roast meats and game dishes.
Alcohol content: 13%-13.5% vol.

Antigniano. Bizante. Bianco Umbria IGT.

Grapes: Grechetto and Chardonnay.
Production area: Montefalco and Torgiano.
The wine: bright straw yellow in colour; full bodied, intense and fruity, with notes of apricot, and finishing with a hint of almond.
Serving temperature: 10-12 C°.
Food matches: white meats, roasts in general and mature cheeses.
Alcohol content: 13.5%-14% vol.

Antigniano. Nido del Falco. Bianco di Montefalco DOC.

Grapes: Grechetto, Chardonnay, and Trebbiano.
The wine: intense straw yellow in colour; slightly fruity, well balanced, good body.
Serving temperature: 10-12 C°.

Food matches: Grilled fish, seafood in general and white meats.
Alcohol content: 13% vol.

Antigniano. Incanto. Sagrantino di Montefalco Passito DOCG.

Grapes: Sagrantino.
The wine: ruby red with violet reflections, tending towards garnet. It is a delicate sweet wine with its unique bouquet, notes of blackberries, with a persistent finish.
Serving temperature: 12-14 C°.
Food matches: all desserts.
Alcohol content: 16% vol.

Antigniano.
Guado Alle Chiavi. Sagrantino di Montefalco DOCG.

Grapes: Sagrantino.
The wine: ruby red in colour, with violet and garnet reflections; with a slight aroma of bramble, dry flavour, full bodied, aged in French oak barrique.
Serving temperature: 14-16 C°, uncork an hour before consuming.
Food matches: Roast red meats and game.
Alcohol content: 13%-14% vol.

Antigniano. Ligajo. Rosso di Montefalco DOC.

Grapes: Sangiovese and Sagrantino.
The wine: intense ruby red in colour; with a delicate aroma, well-balanced flavour and good body. It is aged in French oak barrique.
Serving temperature: 14-16 C°, uncork an hour before consuming.
Food matches: Pasta with meat sauces, white and red roast meats, chicken and wild fowl dishes, and game.
Alcohol content: 13%-13.5% vol.

Antigniano. Arteao. Rosso di Torgiano DOC.

Grapes: Sangiovese, Cabernet Sauvignon, and Canaiolo.
The wine: ruby red in colour; dry flavour, good body; and aged in French barrique.
Serving temperature: 14-16 C°, uncork an hour before consuming.
Food matches: roast meats, and game dishes.
Alcohol content: 12.5%-13% vol.

Antigniano. Kirnao. Bianco di Torgiano DOC.

Grapes: Trebbiano, Grechetto, Chardonnay, and Malvasia.
The wine: straw yellow in colour; flowery, dry flavour, slightly fruity, and good acidity.
Serving temperature: 8-10 C°.
Food matches: aperitif, *hors d'oeuvres*, fish, white meats, and pasta dishes.
Alcohol content: 12%-12.5% vol.

Antigniano. Eko. Pinot Grigio di Torgiano DOC.

Grapes: Pinot Grigio.
The wine: pale straw yellow in colour; with a fruity and ethereal bouquet, dry, and smooth flavour.
Serving temperature: 8-10 C°.
Food matches: Creamy vegetable soups, oysters, seafood and fish in general.
Alcohol content: 12%-12.5% vol.

Antigniano. Eko Rosae. Pinot Grigio di Torgiano DOC.

Grapes: Pinot Grigio.
The wine: pale pink in colour; with a lightly fruity and ethereal bouquet, dry, and smooth flavour.
Serving temperature: 8-10 C°.
Food matches: Creamy vegetable soups, oysters, seafood and fish in general.
Alcohol content: 12%-12.5% vol.

Antigniano. Tinayo. Rosso Umbria IGT.

Grapes: Sangiovese and Sauvignon.
Production area: Torgiano and Montefalco.
The wine: bright ruby red in colour; with a persistent flavour, harmonious, fresh and elegant.
Serving temperature: 14-16 C°.
Food matches: mature cheeses, white meats, game, and roasts.
Alcohol content: 12.5%-13% vol.

Antigniano. Noi. Grechetto Umbria IGT.

Grapes: Grechetto.
Production area: Torgiano and Montefalco.
The wine: straw white in colour; with a hint of fruit, slightly sparkling, and well balanced.
Serving temperature: 8-10 C°.
Food matches: as an aperitif, fish, white meats, and pasta.
Alcohol content: 12%-12.5% vol.

Antigniano. Idillo Brut. Spumante.

Grapes: Pinot Bianco. Pinot Nero, and Riesling.
The wine: straw yellow in colour; fruity, pleasantly sparkling; made by the *charmat* method.
Serving temperature: 8-10 C°.
Food matches: as an aperitif, *hors d'oeuvres* and fish.
Alcohol content: 12%-12.5% vol.

Antigniano. Idillo Dolce. Spumante.

Grapes: Moscato.
The wine: straw yellow in colour; fruity, smooth and sweet.
Serving temperature: 8-10 C°.
Food matches: all desserts.
Alcohol content: 7%-7.5% vol.

Antigniano. Primi Sorsi. Rosso Umbria IGT.

Grapes: Sangiovese, Merlot, and Cabernet Sauvignon.
The wine: bright, lively red in colour; a wine for all occasions.
Serving temperature: 14-16 C°.
Food matches: good with seasonal dishes.
Alcohol content: 12%-12.5% vol.

Antigniano. Castalio. Vino Liquoroso.

Grapes: Malvasia and Grechetto passito.
Production area: Torgiano.
The wine: intense yellow in colour, with light purple reflections; sweet, and full-bodied.
Serving temperature: 12-14 C°.
Food matches: all desserts.
Alcohol content: 16%-16.5% vol.

Antigniano. Grappa di Sagrantino.

Grapes: Sagrantino.
Production area: Montefalco.
Colour: Bright and clear.
Characteristics: Fine, but intense bouquet, with a strong and harmonious flavour.
Serving temperature: room temperature.
Food matches: for any occasion.
Alcohol content: 40% vol.

Antigniano. Grappa di Grechetto.

Grapes: Grechetto passito.
Production area: Torgiano.
Colour: Bright and clear.
Characteristics: Mellow, smooth, and pleasantly fine.
Serving temperature: room temperature.
Food matches: for any occasion.
Alcohol content: 40% vol.

Vignabaldo

Vignabaldo. L'Orma.
Montefalco Sagrantino DOCG.

Grapes: Sagrantino.
The wine: ruby red in colour, with violet reflections; scent of blackberries, dry taste, generous and warm.
Serving temperature: 16-18 C°, open an hour before consumption.
Food matches: roast meats and game.
Alcohol content: 13%-13.5% vol.

Vignabaldo. Giamà. Montefalco Rosso DOC.

Grapes: Sagrantino and Sangiovese.
The wine: ruby red in colour; with a delicate scent, smooth flavour, and full-bodied.
Serving temperature: 14-16 C°, open an hour before consumption.
Food matches: pasta, red and white meats, game, and wild fowl.
Alcohol content: 12.5%-13% vol.

Vignabaldo. Quima. Rosso di Torgiano DOC.

Grapes: Sangiovese, Canaiolo, and Cabernet Sauvignon.
The wine: ruby red; delicate aroma, dry, smooth, with good body.
Serving temperature: 14-16 C°, open an hour before consumption.
Food matches: roast meats, and wild fowl dishes.
Alcohol content: 12.5%-13% vol.

Vignabaldo. Lunia. Bianco di Torgiano DOC.

Grapes: Trebbiano, Grechetto, Malvasia, and Chardonnay.
The wine: straw yellow in colour, with a dry flavour, slightly fruity, and with good acidity.
Serving temperature: 8-10 C°.
Food matches: aperitif, pasta, *hors d'oeuvres*, fish, white meats.
Alcohol content: 12%-12.5% vol.

Vignabaldo. Melanì. Chardonnay dell'Umbria IGT

Grapes: Chardonnay.
Production area: Torgiano.
The wine: straw white in colour; dry taste, and fruity flavour.
Serving temperature: 8-10 C°.
Food matches: Aperitif, *hors d'oeuvres,* fish, and pasta.
Alcohol content: 12%-12.5% vol.

Vignabaldo. Soleno. Pinot Grigio dell'Umbria IGT

Grapes: Pinot Grigio.
Production area: Torgiano.
The wine: pale straw yellow in colour; with a fruity and ethereal bouquet, dry, and smooth flavour.
Serving temperature: 8-10 C°.
Food matches: vegetable soups, oysters, seafood, and fish.
Alcohol content: 12%-12.5% vol.

Vignabaldo. Zìama. Assisi Rosso DOC.

Grapes: Sangiovese, Merlot, and Cabernet Sauvignon.
The wine: intense ruby red in colour, with a long lasting bouquet, and dry, smooth flavour.
Serving temperature: 16-18 C°.
Food matches: roast meat dishes, game, and wild fowl.
Alcohol content: 12%-12.5% vol.

Vignabaldo. Noella. Assisi Bianco DOC.

Grapes: Trebbiano, Grechetto, and Chardonnay.
The wine: bright straw yellow in colour, with greenish reflections; smooth, fruity, and dry.
Serving temperature: 8-10 C°.
Food matches: aperitif, *hors d'oeuvres*, white meats, and pasta.
Alcohol content: 12%-12.5% vol.

Vignabaldo. Iaco. Orvieto DOC.

Grapes: Trebbiano Toscano, Grechetto, and Malvasia.
The wine: straw yellow in colour, with greenish reflections; intense and delicate bouquet, sapid, and fresh flavour.
Serving temperature: 8-10 C°.
Food matches: aperitif, white meats, and pasta.
Alcohol content: 12%-12.5% vol.

Vignabaldo. Iaco. Orvieto Amabile DOC.

Grapes: Trebbiano, Verdello, Grechetto, and Malvasia.
The wine: straw white in colour; fresh, with a sweet flavour, subtle and delicate.
Serving temperature: 8-10 C°.
Food matches: ham and melon, strong cheeses, and fruit desserts.
Alcohol content: 12%-12.5% vol.

Vignabaldo. Soemi. Orvieto Classico DOC.

Grapes: Trebbiano, Verdello, Grechetto, and Malvasia.
The wine: bright and sparkling straw white in colour; delicate, pleasantly dry, but with a round flavour.
Serving temperature: 8-10 C°.
Food matches: *hors d'oeuvres*, first courses; fried and roast fish.
Serving temperature: 8-10 C°.
Alcohol content: 12%-12.5% vol.

Vignabaldo. Legia. Grechetto dell'Umbria IGT

Grapes: Grechetto.
Production area: Torgiano and Montefalco.
The wine: straw white in colour; delicate, fruity, clean and smooth.
Serving temperature: 8-10 C°.
Food matches: aperitif, *hors d'oeuvres*, fish, white meats, pasta.
Alcohol content: 12%-12.5% vol.

Vignabaldo. Chianti DOCG.

Grapes: Sangiovese, Canaiolo, and Ciliegiolo.
Production area: Toscana.
The wine: lively ruby red, in colour, tending towards garnet with ageing; with an intense and fruity bouquet, dry, well balanced and sapid flavour, slightly tannic and velvety.
Serving temperature: 16-18 C°.
Food matches: pasta with chilli sauces, roast and grilled meats.
Alcohol content: 12%-12.5% vol.

Vignabaldo. Tizzaio. Merlot Umbria IGT

Grapes: Merlot.
The wine: intense red, with violet reflections; fruity and long lasting bouquet, well balanced and harmonious on the palate.
Serving temperature: 14-16 C°.
Food matches: pasta with game sauce, red and grilled meats.
Alcohol content: 13%-13.5% vol.

Vignabaldo. Malù. Cabernet Sauvignon Umbria IGT

Grapes: Cabernet Sauvignon.
Production area: Torgiano.
The wine: Burgundy red in colour, with light purple reflections; with a pleasant dry taste, and fruity flavour.
Serving temperature: 16-18 C°.
Food matches: aperitif, *hors d'oeuvres,* fish, and pasta.
Alcohol content: 12.5%-13% vol.

Vignabaldo. Pagiù. Sangiovese dell'Umbria IGT

Grapes: Sangiovese.
Production area: Torgiano.
The wine: bright ruby red in colour; with an ethereal bouquet, and dry flavour.
Serving temperature: 16-18 C°.
Food matches: first courses with meat sauces, chicken dishes, fish stews, and roasts in general.
Alcohol content: 12%-12.5% vol.

Vignabaldo. Fenima. Trebbiano dell'Umbria IGT

Grapes: Trebbiano.
Production area: Torgiano.
The wine: bright straw yellow in colour; with a delicate scent, clean, lively, and fresh flavour.
Serving temperature: 10-12 C°.
Food matches: *hors d'oeuvres,* roast fish, and white meats.
Alcohol content: 12%-12.5% vol.

Vignabaldo. Calù. Rosato dell'Umbria IGT.

Grapes: Sangiovese, and Canaiolo.
Production area: Torgiano.
The wine: pale pink in colour; fresh, dry, and pleasant.
Serving temperature: 10-12 C°.
Food matches: *hors d'oeuvres,* pasta, fish, and white meats.
Alcohol content: 12%-12.5% vol.

Vignabaldo. Francesco. Rosso dell'Umbria IGT.

Grapes: Sangiovese, Canaiolo, and Montepulciano.
Production area: Torgiano and Montefalco.
The wine: ruby red; with a delicate scent and dry flavour.
Serving temperature: 16-18 C°.
Food matches: roasts in general, chicken in sauce, and fish stews.
Alcohol content: 12%-12.5% vol.

Vignabaldo. Chiara. Bianco dell'Umbria IGT.

Grapes: Grechetto, Chardonnay, and Malvasia.
Production area: Torgiano and Montefalco.
The wine: straw yellow; delicate scent, and fruity flavour.
Serving temperature: 8-10 C°.
Food matches: *hors d'oeuvres*, first courses, roast fish and meat.
Alcohol content: 12%-12.5% vol.

Vignabaldo. Est Est Est di Montefiascone DOC.

Grapes: Trebbiano Toscano, and Malvasia.
Production area: Montefiascone, Lazio.
The wine: bright straw yellow in colour; sapid, with a good body and dry flavour.
Serving temperature: 8-10 C°.
Food matches: aperitif, pasta, and white meats.
Alcohol content: 12%-12.5% vol.

Vignabaldo. Briò. Vino Frizzante.

Grapes: Pinot, Chardonnay, and Riesling.
Production area: Umbria.
The wine: white in colour; fresh, pleasantly sparkling, dry taste with delicate perlage, clean and with a hint of fruit.
Serving temperature: 7-8 C°.
Food matches: aperitif, delicate and light dishes.
Alcohol content: 10.5%-11% vol.

Vignabaldo. Solare. Vino da Tavola Rosso.

Grapes: Sangiovese, and Canaiolo.
Production area: Umbria.
The wine: ruby red; with a delicate scent and dry flavour.
Serving temperature: 16-18 C°.
Food matches: white meats and roasts.
Alcohol content: 11.5%-12% vol.

Vignabaldo. Solare. Vino da Tavola Bianco.

Grapes: Trebbiano and Grechetto.
Production area: Umbria.
The wine: straw yellow in colour; delicate with a fruity aroma.
Serving temperature: 8-10 C°.
Food matches: *hors d'oeuvres*, first courses, and white meats.
Alcohol content: 11.5%-12% vol.

Vignabaldo. Il Canonico. Vino Liquoroso.

Grapes: Malvasia, and Grechetto passito.
Production area: Umbria.
The wine: intense yellow in colour, with purplish reflections; sweet and full-bodied.
Serving temperature: 12-14 C°.
Food matches: all desserts.
Alcohol content: 16% vol.

Vignabaldo. Dono d'Autunno. Novello IGT

Grapes: Sangiovese, and Merlot.
Production area: Umbria.
The wine: lively, sparkling red in colour; fresh with a round flavour.
Serving temperature: 14-16 C°.
Food matches: for all occasions, particularly seasonal dishes.
Alcohol content: 12%-12.5% vol.

THE WINE PRODUCERS
COLLI PERUGINI

Perugia is the capital of Umbria, a bustling city with two universities. One is for foreigners, established in Mussolini's time, the other is about 700 years old. There are early references to winemaking on the stone carvings of the *Fontana Maggiore* in the city centre, which was completed in 1278 AD. It depicts the work cycle in the vineyards month by month. The city is three thousand years old. It was founded by the Umbrii, then later developed by the Etrusci, and eventually conquered by the Romans. During the Middle Ages, it was a dark and murderous place, sick with political plots and bloody vendettas.

Today, Perugia is a modern metropolis with a population of 150 000, which is a considerable number for Umbria with less than a million inhabitants. It has a modern booming economy to compliment its rich history. The Umbria Jazz Festival draws famous musicians to the city, and a host of tourists. And there are students from every corner of the world, and affordable restaurants: some serving typical Umbrian meals, as well as the fast food so much beloved by the younger generation.

The vineyards of the Colli Perugini are some distance away from the centre, though still in sight of the Medieval City. They are located in the *communi* of Deruta, Marsciano, Fratta Todina, Monte Castello di Vibio, Piegaro and Perugia itself, plus a little further away, San Venanzo in the province of Terni.

This area, which extends south of Perugia on the right side of the river Tiber, has a climate particularly favourable for viticulture. The soil is generally clayey and chalky. There is archaeological evidence of wine producing activity all over the countryside, going back to Etruscan and Roman times. Cultivating vines in this zone just carries on the tradition.

Busti

Azienda Agraria Flavio Busti
Loc. Sant'Elena
06052 Marsciano PG
Tel/Fax: 0758 79458
www.cantinebusti.it

The winery is located in Sant'Elena, near Marsciano. The vineyards are extended over 10 hectares. Both the vineyards and the winery date back to the 1950s, when mostly white wines were produced from Trebbiano, Malvasia and Grechetto grapes.

The old winery was near the family house, built around 1800. Since then a lot has changed, the old vines were replaced with new ones, mostly red varieties, like Merlot, Cabernet Sauvignon and Sangiovese, but the same passion for cultivating the grapes has remained. The new winery uses the most modern techniques, combined with the old traditions of winemaking.

Sangiovese. Umbria IGT.

Grapes: Sangiovese.
Altitude: 300-400 metres above sea level.
Soil: rocky, mixed with clay.
Training: spurred cordon.
Production per hectare: 70 quintals.
Yield per hectare: 4000 litres.
Harvest: mid-September.
Annual production: 12 000 bottles.
The wine: ruby red in colour; clean and sharp, with soft tannins, and fragrance of raspberries, strawberries, with floral hints.
Serving temperature: 14-16 C°.
Alcohol content: 13.5% vol.

Merlot. Umbria IGT.

Grapes: Merlot.
Altitude: 300-400 metres above sea level.
Soil: rocky, mixed with clay.
Training: spurred cordon.
Production per hectare: 60 quintals.
Yield per hectare: 4000 litres.
Harvest: the beginning of September.
Ageing: in oak barrique.
Refining: in the bottle.
Annual production: 12 000 bottles.
The wine: intense ruby red in colour; full, intense, with soft tannins, harmonious, with a persistent finish.
Alcohol content: 14% vol.

Grechetto. Umbria IGT.

Grapes: Grechetto.
Altitude: 300-400 metres above sea level.
Terrain: rocky, mixed with clay.
Training: spurred cordon.
Production per hectare: 70 quintals.
Yield per hectare: 4000 litres.
Harvest: the second half of September.
Ageing and refining: In stainless steel vats.
Annual production: 6 000 bottles.
The wine: straw yellow in colour, with golden reflections; clean and sharp, with a pleasant softness and the delicate fragrance of pears, peaches, and white fruits, with floral hints.
Alcohol content: 13.5% vol.

Chiorri

Cantina Chiorri.
Azienda Vitivinicoli Chiorri.
Via Todi, 100
06070 Sant 'Enea PG
Tel/Fax: 0756 07141
www.chiorri.it
info@chiorri.it

The Azienda Vitivinicoli Chiorri came into being at the end of the 1800s on the holding at Sant 'Enea. The vineyards cover a gentle sun-lit hill overlooking the towns of Assisi and Todi, where grapes have been grown since Etruscan times. A variety of vines are planted on the 20 hectares of land: Grechetto, Trebbiano, and Malvasia for producing white wines; and Sangiovese, Cabernet Sauvignon, and Merlot for reds. The cultivation of the grapes combines ancient traditions with the most modern technologies, without ever losing sight of the final objective: the pleasure of enjoying a glass of good wine with a unique and genuine flavour. The vineyards are managed using biological treatments with low environmental impact, including shoot pruning and hand picking the grapes during harvest into traditional woven baskets. No additives or extra yeasts are used during vinification, or any forced stabilising methods. Thus, the wine is a living entity, and the presence of some slight sediment indicates a natural refinement.

Bianco DOC Colli Perugini.

Grapes: Trebbiano Procanico 65%, and Grechetto 35%.
Vintage year: 2004; mild winter, high rainfall until mid-June, hot summer, though not particularly sunny.
Exposure: east and west.
Training: spurred cordon.
Density: 3 000 plants per hectare.
Yield: 95 quintals of grapes.

Production: 8 000 bottles (0.75 l)
Harvest: second week of October.
Vinification: the white wine method with natural fermentation using must bloom at a controlled temperature less than 16 C°.
Ageing: for 5 months in stainless steel barrels.
Bottling: March 2005.
The wine: straw yellow in colour, with golden highlights; with fresh floral scents and aromas of ripe fruit, peaches in particular. It is full-bodied, well balanced with a warm aftertaste.
Serving temperature: 8-10 C°.
Food matches: starters, cold cured meats, chicken-liver patè, bean soup, onion soup, fish, and cheeses.
Alcohol: 12% vol.

Rosato DOC Colli Perugini.

Grapes: Sangiovese 50%, and Cabernet Sauvignon 50%.
Vintage year: 2004; mild winter, high rainfall until mid-June, hot summer, though not particularly sunny.
Exposure: east and west.
Training: spurred cordon.
Density: 2 000 plants per hectare.
Yield: 35 quintals of grapes.
Production: 2 500 bottles (0.75 l)
Harvest: the last week of October.
Vinification: the white wine method; the red grapes are steeped with their skins, but with the stalks removed, for 16-20 hours. Fermentation of the must bloom at 20 C°.
Ageing: for 5 months in stainless steel barrels.
Bottling: March 2005.
The wine: bright cherry red in colour; notes of dark fruits of the forest, and a fresh flavour, with pleasing acidity, and a savoury almond aftertaste.
Serving temperature: 8-10 C°.
Food matches: starters, rice dishes, pasta, white meats, and fish, cured Norcia meats, and stuffed Lake Trasimeno perch.
Alcohol: 13% vol.

Rosso DOC Colli Perugini.

Grapes: Sangiovese 50%, Merlot 30%, and Cabernet Sauvignon 20%.
Vintage year: 2003; cold winter, hot summer with high temperatures and low rainfall.
Exposure: east and west.
Training: spurred cordon.
Density: 3 000 plants per hectare.
Yield: 80 quintals of grapes; 70% of must yield.
Production: 13 000 bottles (0.75 l)
Harvest: the first ten days of September.
Vinification: the grapes are separated from the stalks and steeped in the skins for 15 days, whilst frequently re-mixed and aerated; then followed by fermentation at less than 27 C°.
Ageing: 10 months in stainless steel barrels, then a further 18 months in the bottle.
Bottling: August 2004.
The wine: very intense ruby red in colour; with aromas of ripe cherries, and a hint of mint, and a good structure.
Serving temperature: 18 C°.
Food matches: pasta dishes with meat sauce (*ragu*), roast meats, and cheeses. Also with *pappardelle* and wild hare sauce, and chicken cooked on the spit, with pieces of seasoned lard.
Alcohol: 13.7% vol.

Saliato. Rosso DOC Colli Perugini.

Grapes: Sangiovese 50%, Merlot 30%, and Cabernet Sauvignon 20%.
Vintage year: 2002; heavy rain from July until harvest.
Exposure: east and west.
Training: spurred cordon.
Density: 3 000 plants per hectare.
Yield: 40 quintals of grapes.
Production: 6 000 bottles (0.75 l)
Harvest: at the end of August the fruit damaged by the unkind weather were removed, then in the second half of September the healthy grapes were handpicked.

Vinification: the grapes are separated from the stalks and steeped in the skins for 15 days, aerobic re-mixing; and then followed by fermentation at a controlled temperature less than 27 C°.
Ageing: both in stainless steel vats and small Spanish barrels made of American oak, then in the bottle for 18 months.
Bottling: August 2003.
The wine: ruby in colour, almost garnet red; with chocolate and oak overtones. It is smooth, dry, with a clean aftertaste.
Serving temperature: 18 C°.
Food matches: pasta with meat sauces, roast meats, game, wild boar, roast lamb and mature cheeses.
Alcohol: 13% vol.

Grechetto Chiorri. IGT Umbria.

Grapes: Grechetto 100%.
Vintage year: 2004; mild winter, high rainfall until mid-June, hot summer, though not particularly sunny.
Vineyard: 3 hectares of Sterpeto vines planted in 1998.
Exposure: east and west.
Training: spurred cordon.
Density: 3 000 plants per hectare.
Yield: 90 quintals of grapes.
Production: 25 000 bottles (0.75 l)
Harvest: the week between September and October.
Vinification: the white wine method with natural fermentation using must bloom at a controlled temperature less than 16 C°.
Ageing: for 5 months in stainless steel barrels.
Bottling: March 2005.
The wine: straw yellow, with golden highlights; aromas of ripe tropical fruits, well controlled acidity, and a savoury finish.
Serving temperature: 8-10 C°.
Food matches: cheeses, cured meat starters, fish, perch fillets, pasta, boiled meats, and chocolate.
Alcohol: 13.5% vol.

Zeffiro. IGT Bianco Umbria.

Grapes: Trebbiano, Grechetto, and Malvasia in equal amounts.
Vintage year: 2004; mild winter, high rainfall until mid-June, hot summer, though not particularly sunny.
Exposure: east and west.
Training: spurred cordon.
Density: 3 000 plants per hectare.
Yield: 110 quintals of grapes.
Production: 20 000 bottles (0.75 l)
Harvest: second week of October.
Vinification: the white wine method with natural fermentation using must bloom at a controlled temperature less than 16 C°.
Ageing: for 6 months in stainless steel barrels.
Bottling: April 2005.
The wine: straw yellow in colour, with golden highlights; a scent of yellow flowers. It is fresh, fruity, with a savoury aftertaste.
Serving temperature: 8-10 C°.
Food matches: starters; bean soup, onion soup, *tortellini* in broth, lentils, savoury vegetables, trout, young and mature cheeses.
Alcohol: 12% vol.

Sangiovese Chiorri IGT Umbria.

Grapes: Sangiovese 100%.
Vintage year: 2004; mild winter, high rainfall until mid-June, hot summer, though not particularly sunny.
Exposure: east and west.
Training: spurred cordon.
Density: 3 000 plants per hectare.
Yield: 95 quintals of grapes.
Production: 20 000 bottles (0.75 l)
Harvest: at the end of October.
Vinification: the grapes are separated from the stalks and steeped in the skins for 12 days, with frequent re-mixing of the must; then fermentation at less than 27 C°.
Ageing: for 5 months in stainless steel barrels.
Bottling: March 2005.

The wine: bright ruby red in colour; with intense floral and fruity fragrances – violet, blackberry, rose, and cherries; well balanced, with a pleasant tannic taste.
Serving temperature: 18 C°.
Food matches: cured meats, aged sheep cheese *di fossa*, also *tagliatelle* with duck sauce, and grilled meats.
Alcohol: 13% vol.

Garbino. IGT Rosso Umbria.

Grapes: Sangiovese, Cabernet Sauvignon, and Merlot in equal proportions.
Vintage year: 2004; mild winter, high rainfall until mid-June, hot summer, though not particularly sunny.
Exposure: east and west.
Training: spurred cordon.
Density: 3 000 plants per hectare.
Yield: 110 quintals of grapes.
Production: 20 000 bottles (0.75 l)
Harvest: at the end of October.
Vinification: the grapes are separated from the stalks and steeped in the skins for 8-10 days, with frequent re-mixing to aerate the must; followed by fermentation at less than 27 C°.
Ageing: for 6 months in stainless steel barrels.
Bottling: April 2005.
The wine: intense ruby red, in colour with purple highlights, floral and red fruit fragrances, and a smooth aftertaste.
Serving temperature: 18 C°.
Food matches: cured meats, *umbrichelli* with duck sauce, sausages, jugged wild boar, grilled meats, and sheep cheese
Alcohol: 13% vol.

Selezione Antonio Chiorri – Cabernet Sauvignon IGT Umbria.

Grapes: Cabernet Sauvignon 100%.
Vintage year: 2004; mild winter, high rainfall until mid-June. The summer was not too hot, with average temperatures of 28 C° and a medium to high humidity.
Exposure: east and west.

Training: spurred cordon.
Density: 2 000 plants per hectare.
Yield: 90 quintals of grapes; with a must yield of less than 80%.
Production: 780 bottles of 0.75 l., and 168 bottles of 1.00 l.
Harvest: at the end of September.
Vinification: the grapes are separated from the stalks and steeped in the skins for 15 days, with frequent re-mixing to aerate the must; followed by fermentation at less than 27 C°.
Ageing: for 10 months in stainless steel, followed by some months in wooden barrels, then a further 5 months in the bottle.
Bottling: June 2005.
The wine: intense red in colour, with liquorice black highlights; fruity, well structured, full bodied and tannic.
Serving temperature: 18 C°.
Food matches: pasta with game sauces, *gnocchi* with duck sauce, roasts and grilled meats, and mature cheeses.
Alcohol: 13% vol.

Gabri. IGT Rosso Umbria.

Grapes: Sangiovese, Cabernet Sauvignon, and Merlot.
Vintage year: 2005; very cold winter with several snowfalls and abundant rain. The hot season started early, in May, and the season boasted high temperatures and many summer storms.
Exposure: east and west.
Training: spurred cordon.
Density: 3 000 plants per hectare.
Yield: 85 quintals of grapes.
Production: 1000 bottles (0.75 l).
Harvest: at the end of September.
Vinification: the grapes are separated from the stalks and steeped in the skins for 5-6 days, with frequent re-mixing to aerate the must; followed by fermentation at less than 27 C°. The wine is drawn off from the vat when the reducing sugars reach 5 g/l.
Bottling: at the beginning of November 2005.
The wine is marketed soon after the harvest, during November and December, on account of it being a *novello* (new) wine.

The wine: intense red in colour, with violet highlights; fresh, fruity, with a light grassy hint, well balanced with the evident sweetness of the sugar residue, and naturally lively.
Serving temperature: 18 C°.
Food matches: cured meats, tripe and beans, pork stuffed with chestnuts, grilled red meats, and roasted chestnuts.
Alcohol: 13% vol.

Goretti

Cantina Goretti.
Strada del Pino, 4
06132 Pila, Perugia PG
Tel: 0756 07316
Fax: 0756 079187
www.vinigoretti.com
goretti@vinigoretti.com

The Goretti Gisberto company and the Goretti winery began in the 1960s. In 1992 the agricultural company divided and became Goretti Gisberto farming and Goretti wine production: the first being responsible for the cultivation of the grapes, and the second involved in the winemaking process. The vineyards stretch over the gently rolling hillsides on the outskirts of Perugia in the centre of the area classified as DOC Colli Perugini. They have been run by generations of the Goretti family, who combine the ancient traditions with the most recent methods of wine making. Mostly typical Umbrian vines are cultivated, like Grechetto, Sagrantino di Montefalco, and Sangiovese, but other international vine varieties have also been introduced, for example Chardonnay.

The estate is dominated by the fourteenth century tower, which is today used for wine tasting. Illustrations and stylised graphics of the tower are used as a logo on the labels produced for Goretti's wines. More recently, the family invested in Montefalco with the creation of a new and modern winery, the "Fattoria le Mura Saracene", and launched their production of two significant red wines: the Montefalco Sagrantino DOCG and the Rosso of Montefalco DOC. The family's involvement continues with the fourth generation: Stefano, Gianluca and Sara Goretti, who are committed to the production of quality wines. Their efforts are recognised by many prestigious awards.

L'Arringatore. DOC Colli Perugini.

The name Arringatore comes from the first century BC. It is the famous bronze statue of Aulo Metello, which was discovered in 1566 in the village of Pila, near Perugia. It symbolises the end of the Etruscan era and Aulo Metello's death in Rome.
Grapes: 60% Sangiovese, 30% Merlot and 10% Ciliegiolo.
Vineyard: Trebbio.
Training: spurred cordon.
Exposure: east and west.
Age of vines: around 15 years.
Density: 4 000 vines per hectare
Soil: a medium textured mix of limestone and clay.
Altitude: 300 metres above sea level.
Yield: 80 quintals.
Harvest: the beginning of September. The grapes are handpicked and carried to the winery in baskets.
Vinification: in red, for obtaining red wines from red grapes.
Ageing: 12 months in wooden barrels.
Refining: 6 months in the bottle.
The wine: ruby red in colour, with purple reflections; full bodied, with aromas of fruits, particularly cherries. It is slightly tannic.
Ageing potential: 10 years.
Serving temperature: 20-22 C°.
Food matches: red meats, cheeses, and dark chocolate.
Alcohol: 14% vol.

Il Moggio. Grechetto IGT Umbria Bianco.

Grapes: Grechetto 100%.
Vineyard: Trebbio and Fontanella.
Training: spurred cordon.
Exposure: east and west.
Age of vines: around 15 years.
Density: 4 000 vines per hectare.
Soil: a medium textured mix of limestone and clay.
Altitude: 330 metres above sea level.
Yield: 70 quintals.

Harvest: the first half of October. The grapes are handpicked and carried to the winery in baskets.
Vinification: the grapes are soft pressed, and the must is fermented in new wood barrels (barrique) under controlled temperature, where it remains for 6 months.
Ageing: 4 months in the wood.
Refining: 6 months in the bottle.
The wine: straw yellow in colour, with greenish hues; aromas of honey and exotic fruit, with a long harmonious finish.
Serving temperature: 12-13 C°.
Food matches: white meat, fish, and pasta dishes; also mature and semi-mature cheeses served with jam or honey.
Alcohol: 13.5% vol.

Grechetto DOC Colli Perugini.

Grapes: Grechetto 100%.
Vineyard: Trebbio.
Training: spurred cordon.
Exposure: east and west.
Age of vines: around 15 years.
Density: 4 000 vines per hectare.
Soil: a medium textured mix of limestone and clay.
Altitude: 330 metres above sea level.
Yield: 75 quintals.
Harvest: the beginning of September. The grapes are handpicked and carried to the winery in baskets.
Vinification: in white, the fermentation takes place in stainless steel vats and a controlled temperature of 18-20 C° for 10 days.
Refining: 3 months in the bottle.
The wine: bright yellow in colour; fruity and delicate with hints of exotic fruit, broom flowers and almonds. It is dry, velvety, with a slightly bitter aftertaste.
Serving temperature: 8-10 C°.
Food matches: aperitif, starters, white meat, and fish.
Alcohol: 13% vol.

Torre del Pino DOC Colli Perugini Bianco.

Grapes: 50% Trebbiano Toscano, 30% Grechetto, and 20% Chardonnay.
Vineyard: Trebbio e Pino.
Training: spurred cordon.
Exposure: east and west.
Age of vines: around 15 years.
Density: 3 500 vines per hectare.
Soil: a medium textured mix of limestone and clay.
Altitude: 330 metres above sea level.
Yield: 75 quintals.
Harvest: at the end of September.
Vinification: in white, the fermentation takes place in stainless steel vats and a controlled temperature of 18-20 C° for 10 days.
Refining: 3-4 months in the bottle.
Colour: pale straw yellow, with green tints.
Taste: delicate aroma of flowers, with hints of fruit, a deep and elegant wine; the taste is dry, fresh and fruity.
Serving temperature: 8-10 C°.
Food matches: aperitif, shellfish and fish dishes, and poultry.
Alcohol: 12.5% vol.

Chardonnay DOC Colli Perugini.

Grapes: Chardonnay 100%.
Vineyard: Localita Fontanella.
Training: spurred cordon.
Exposure: east and west.
Age of vines: around 15 years.
Density: 3 500 vines per hectare.
Soil: a medium textured mix of limestone and clay.
Altitude: 330 metres above sea level.
Yield: 70 quintals.
Harvest: the end of August. The grapes are handpicked and taken to the winery in baskets.
Vinification: in white, the fermentation takes place in stainless steel vats and a controlled temperature of 18-20 C° for 10 days.
Refining: 3-4 months in the bottle.

The wine: straw yellow in colour, with green tints; a fresh bouquet, and fruity and balanced taste. It is dry, velvety, and it leaves a delicate aftertaste.
Serving temperature: 8-10 C°.
Food matches: aperitif, soups, pasta dishes, and fish.
Alcohol: 13% vol.

Sagrantino di Montefalco DOCG. La Mura Saracene.

Grapes: Sagrantino 100%.
Vineyard: Pietrauta, Montefalco.
Training: spurred cordon.
Exposure: east and west.
Age of vines: around 8 years.
Density: 4 000 vines per hectare.
Soil: a medium textured mix of limestone, clay, and gravel.
Altitude: 400 metres above sea level.
Yield: 60 quintals.
Harvest: during the first half of October.
Vinification: in red, for obtaining red wines from red grapes.
Ageing: 12-18 months in the wood.
Refining: 6 months in the bottle.
The wine: ruby red in colour, with purple tints, turning to garnet with ageing; spicy, and well balanced, with pleasing tannins.
Ageing potential: 15 years.
Serving temperature: 20-22 C°
Food matches: sausages, red meat, game, and mature cheeses.
Alcohol: 14% vol.

Rosso di Montefalco DOCG. La Mura Saracene.

Grapes: Sangiovese 60%, Merlot 20%, and Sagrantino 20%.
Vineyard: Pietrauta, Montefalco.
Training: spurred cordon.
Exposure: east and west.
Age of vines: around 8 years.
Density: 4 000 vines per hectare.
Soil: a medium textured mix of limestone, clay, and gravel.
Altitude: 400 metres above sea level.

Yield: 75 quintals.
Harvest: at the end of September, and the beginning of October. The grapes are handpicked and taken to the winery in baskets.
Vinification: in red, the fermentation is carried out in barrique.
Ageing: 12 months in the wood.
Refining: 6 months in the bottle.
The wine: ruby red in colour, with purple tints; clean aromas of blackberries and violets, with a delicate fragrance. Warm, austere and harmonious, with sharp, but pleasing tannins.
Ageing potential: 8-10 years.
Serving temperature: 20-22 C°.
Food matches: sausages, red meat, game, and mature cheeses.
Alcohol: 13.5% vol.

Fontanella Rosso dell'Umbria IGT.

Grapes: Sangiovese 50%, and Merlot 50%.
Vineyard: Trebbio.
Training: spurred cordon.
Exposure: east and west.
Age of vines: around 15 years.
Density: 4 000 vines per hectare
Soil: a medium textured mix of limestone and clay.
Altitude: 330 metres above sea level.
Yield: 80 quintals.
Harvest: at the end of September and the beginning of October.
Vinification: in red, fermentation is carried out in stainless steel vats and a controlled temperature of 28-30 C° for 7 days.
Refining: 5 months in the bottle.
The wine: intense ruby red in colour, with purplish reflections; a fruity aroma, dry and delicate flavour, and slightly tannic.
Serving temperature: 8-10 C°.
Food matches: salamis, roasted red meats, game, and cheeses.
Alcohol: 13% vol.

Fontanella Rosato dell'Umbria IGT.

Grapes: Sangiovese 50%, and Merlot 50%.
Vineyard: Trebbio.

Training: spurred cordon.
Exposure: east and west.
Age of vines: around 15 years.
Density: 4 000 vines per hectare
Soil: a medium textured mix of limestone and clay.
Altitude: 330 metres above sea level.
Yield: 80 quintals.
Harvest: at the end of September and the beginning of October.
Vinification: maceration on the skins for 20 hours at a low temperature. The fermentation is carried out in stainless steel vats and a controlled temperature of 18-20 C° for 10 days.
Refining: 3-4 months in the bottle.
The wine: bright pink in colour, with a hint of purple; fruity, lively, soft and velvety.
Ageing potential: 3 years.
Serving temperature: 16-18 C°.
Food matches: aperitif, soups, eggs, red and white meat.
Alcohol: 13% vol.

Fontanella Bianco dell'Umbria IGT.

Grapes: Trebbiano Toscano 55%, and Grechetto 45%.
Vineyard: Fontanella and Pino.
Training: spurred cordon.
Exposure: east and west.
Age of vines: around 15 years.
Density: 4 000 vines per hectare.
Soil: a medium textured mix of limestone and clay.
Altitude: 330 metres above sea level.
Yield: 80 quintals.
Harvest: at the end of September and the beginning of October.
Vinification: in white, fermentation is carried out in stainless steel vats and a controlled temperature of 18-20 C° for 10 days.
Refining: around 3-4 months in the bottle.
The wine: yellow in colour; floral, dry, but with a fresh aftertaste.
Serving temperature: 8-10 C°.
Food matches: first courses, soups, pasta, shellfish, and fish.
Alcohol: 12% vol.

Chardonnay Vino Spumante.

Grapes: Chardonnay 100%.
Vineyard: Pila.
Training: spurred cordon.
Exposure: east and west.
Age of vines: around 15 years.
Soil: a medium textured mix of limestone and clay.
Altitude: 330 metres above sea level.
Harvest: beginning of September.
Vinification: traditional method.
The wine: pale yellow in colour; with a soft and lively flavour.
Serving temperature: 8-10 C°.
Food matches: aperitif, *horse d'oeuvres*, and a fish based menu.
Alcohol: 11% vol.

Vin Santo.

Grapes: Grechetto.
Vineyard: Pila.
Training: spurred cordon.
Exposure: east and west.
Age of vines: around 15 years.
Density: 4 000 per hectare.
Soil: a medium textured mix of limestone and clay.
Altitude: 330 metres above sea level.
Harvest: late November.
Vinification: in white, the fermentation takes place in stainless steel vats and a controlled temperature of 18-20 C° for 10 days.
The wine: golden, almost amber yellow in colour; it has a sweet, flavour, but full bodied and light.
Serving temperature: slightly cool.
Food matches: the ideal dessert wine for fruit and pastries.
Alcohol: 16% vol.

Grappa di Grechetto.

Distilled from the pomace of Grechetto grapes in a discontinuous steam alembic system. It is clear, colourless; and fragrant.

Grappa di Sagrantino.

Distilled from the pomace of Sagrantino grapes in a discontinuous steam alembic system. It is clear, colourless; the taste is fragrant.

Grappa de L'Arringatore Riserva.

Distilled from the marc of red grapes, then aged for 18 months in Livonia oak barrels. The colour is amber yellow and the flavour is fruity, with notes of vanilla, spices, and burnt oak.

Brandy la Torre.

Distilled from wine, then aged in oak casks for 20 years. It has a golden amber colour, which becomes intensely dark with ageing. It is elegant, pronounced, but especially ethereal.

Sasso dei Lupi

Sasso dei Lupi. Soc. Coop. Agr.
Viale Carlo Faina 18
06055 Marsciano PG
Tel: 0758 749523
Fax: 0758 749510
www.sassodeilupi.it
info@sassodeilupi.it

Sasso dei Lupi is the largest co-operative winery in Umbria. Dating back to 1967, the society inherits a tradition of working with big and small vine growers for over forty years. More than eight hundred active members cultivate at least a thousand hectares of vineyards. They demonstrate the values of the co-operative model, capable of combining reasonable prices with excellent wines. High quality grapes enable the society to take on ambitious projects. The society bottles only the best of its vast output, giving Umbrian wine a good reputation the world over. The families working in the co-operative are the society's greatest strength and inspiration.

Secondoatto. Colli Perugini Rosso DOC.

Grapes: Sangiovese, Merlot, and other autochthonous varieties.
Production area: Marsciano.
Training: spurred cordon.
Soil: a medium textured mix of limestone and clay.
The wine: full ruby red in colour; aromas of red fruits, with hints of liquorice and balsamic. It is soft to the palate, with a pleasantly refreshing and slightly tannic finish.
Food matches: first courses, roast meats, and cheeses.

Sagrantino di Montefalco DOCG.

Grapes: 100% Sagrantino.
Production area: Montefalco. Training: spurred cordon.
Soil: a medium textured mix of limestone and clay.
The wine: deep ruby red colour with purplish highlights that turn to garnet with ageing. The scents vary from red fruits, like blackberries, to aromas of cacao and cinnamon. It is rich in tannins, which make it suitable for a long period of ageing.
Food matches: roast red meat, game, and mature cheeses.

Sangiovese Umbria IGT.

Grapes: 100% Sangiovese.
Production area: Marsciano. Training: spurred cordon.
Soil: a medium textured mix of limestone and clay.
The wine: ruby red, with violet hues; floral scents and aromas of red fruits. It has a tannic flavour, with a pleasant finish.
Food matches: it is perfect with all red meats, and cheeses.

Quintotema. Merlot Umbria IGT.

Grapes: 100% Merlot.
Production area: Marsciano. Training: spurred cordon.
Soil: a medium textured mix of limestone and clay.
The wine: intense ruby red in colour; it displays fruity and floral hints with herbaceous notes. It is soft, with unobtrusive tannins and a rich, well-balanced style.
Serving temperature: 18 C°.
Food matches: red meats, game, and moderately mature cheeses.

Regio. Rosso Umbria IGT.

Grapes: Sangiovese, Cabernet Sauvignon, and other autochthonous varieties.
Production area: Marsciano. Training: spurred cordon.
Soil: a medium textured mix of limestone and clay.
The wine: deep ruby red; with aromas of cherry and black fruit, hints of spices and balsamic; well structured and a fruity finish.

Serving temperature: 18 C°.
Food matches: perfect with roasted meats, and mature cheeses.

L'Intruso. Cabernet Sauvignon Umbria IGT.

Grapes: 100% Cabernet Sauvignon.
Production area: Marsciano. Training: spurred cordon.
Soil: a medium textured mix of limestone and clay.
The wine: ruby red in colour with purplish highlights; aromas of red fruits with spices; good structure with well-balanced tannins.
Serving temperature: 18 C°.
Food matches: meat dishes, and mature cheeses.

Primotempo. Colli Perugini Bianco DOC.

Grapes: Trebbiano, Grechetto, and Chardonnay.
Production area: Marsciano. Training: spurred cordon.
Soil: a medium textured mix of limestone and clay.
The wine: straw yellow in colour; floral bouquet with notes of yellow fruit; soft, with a fresh finish.
Serving temperature: 12-14 C°.
Food matches: light first courses, and fresh cheeses.

Montali. Bianco Umbria IGT.

Grapes: Viognier, and Chardonnay.
Production area: Marsciano. Training: spurred cordon.
Soil: a medium textured mix of limestone and clay.
The wine: straw yellow in colour; with aromas of white fruits and citrus, with hints of herbs. It is well structured and fresh.
Serving temperature: 12-14 C°.
Food matches: first courses, fish, and raw seafood.

Trebbiano. Umbria IGT.

Grapes: Trebbiano Toscano.
Production area: Marsciano. Training: spurred cordon.
Soil: a medium textured mix of limestone and clay.

The wine: straw yellow in colour, with green hues; floral aromas and notes of white fruits; medium structure and pleasantly fresh.
Serving temperature: 12-14 C°.
Food matches: light first courses, perfect with fish dishes.

Chardonnay. Umbria IGT.

Grapes: 100% Chardonnay.
Production area: Marsciano. Training: spurred cordon.
Soil: a medium textured mix of limestone and clay.
The wine: straw yellow in colour, with golden tones; a bouquet of yellow fruits, with tropical notes; smooth and a good structure.
Serving temperature: 12-14 C°.
Food matches: first courses, white meat, and cheeses.

Terzastrada. Grechetto Umbria IGT.

Grapes: 100% Grechetto.
Production area: Marsciano. Training: spurred cordon.
Soil: a medium textured mix of limestone and clay.
The wine: yellow in colour; with floral notes, and a sensation of yellow fruits with tropical overtones; well structured, balanced and sapid, with freshness and an almond finish.
Serving temperature: 12-14 C°.
Food matches: oven cooked fish and grilled white meats.

Quartanota. Pinot Grigio Umbria IGT.

Grapes: 100% Pinot Grigio.
Production area: Marsciano. Training: spurred cordon.
Soil: a medium textured mix of limestone and clay.
The wine: straw yellow in colour, with scents of pears and bananas, and a delicate floral note; fruity with pleasing acidity.
Serving temperature: 8-10 C°.
Food matches: aperitif, and fish dishes and soups.

Cantina La Spina

Cantina La Spina – di Moreno Peccia
Via E. Alessandrini, 1
06072 Spina, Marsciano PG
Tel/Fax: 0758 738120
www.cantinaspina.it
cantinaspina@tiscali.it

Cantina La Spina combines the old traditions in growing vines with modern winemaking methods. The vineyard is located around the village of Spina. The exposure is east and west, at an altitude of 300 meters above sea level, with good soil, rich in lime. The winery has a charming tasting room, open throughout the year, with a large terrace overlooking the vineyards, where guests can enjoy the wines made on the premises in the company of the winemaker himself.

Rosso Spina. Umbria IGT Rosso.

Grapes: mostly Montepulciano, with other local red grapes.
Training: Low Guyot method, allowing for growing taller rows of vines with a larger leaf area to obtain better quality grapes.
Harvest: the grapes are harvested by hand, then carefully placed into small baskets and immediately taken to the winery to ensure that they remain perfectly intact.
Vinification: the grapes are de-stemmed and lightly crushed, then fermented in stainless steel vats at 28-30 C°. Racking is performed once the alcoholic fermentation is completed.
Ageing: in December, when the malolactic fermentation is completed, the wine is transferred into medium toasted, small oak barrels of various ages, where it is left for one year. After bottling, the wine is allowed to mature in the bottle.

Polimante della Spina. Umbria IGT Rosso.

Grapes: mostly Merlot, with other local red grapes.
Training: Low Guyot
Harvest: handpicked, then carefully placed into small baskets and immediately taken to the winery.
Vinification: the grapes are de-stemmed and lightly crushed, then fermented in stainless steel vats at 28-30 C°. Racking is performed once the alcoholic fermentation is completed.
Ageing: in December, when the malolactic fermentation is completed, the wine is transferred into medium toasted, small oak barrels of various ages, where it is left for one year. After bottling, the wine is allowed to mature for in the bottle.

Merlato. Umbria IGT Merlot.

Grapes: 100% Merlot grapes.
Training: Low Guyot.
Harvest: the grapes are harvested by hand, then placed into small baskets and immediately taken to the winery.
Vinification: the grapes are de-stemmed and lightly crushed, then fermented in stainless steel vats at 28-30 C°. After a few days of maceration, the must and wine are separated from the residue and the fermentation process is allowed to finish at a low temperature in order to enhance the fragrance of the fruit. The malolactic fermentation is performed in November.
Ageing: The wine is bottled in the spring and made available for sale after a brief ageing period. The fruity and aromatic flavour of Merlato is at its height during the first few years after it has been produced.

Eburneo. Umbria IGT Bianco.

Grapes: Grechetto, both the classic variety and Grechetto di Todi, plus Trebbiano Spoletino and Malvasia Bianca di Candia.
Training: Low Guyot.
Harvest: each variety of the grapes is harvested separately, according to their ripening cycle; then placed into small baskets

and immediately taken to the winery to ensure that they remain perfectly intact.

Vinification: the grapes are lightly crushed. The must is separated from the skins and left to ferment in stainless steel vats at 20 C°.

Ageing: Eburneo is bottled the following spring and made available for sale after a brief ageing period.

THE WINE PRODUCERS
COLLI MARTANI

The gentle rolling Martani Hills stretch from north to south, roughly following the course of the River Tiber. The old road from Perugia to Todi runs along a ridge in more or less a straight line, parallel with the river, overlooking the Vale of Spoleto towards the east. Most of the vineyards and wineries are located along this ancient road with a colourful past.

In 212 BC Caio Flaminio constructed the Flaminia Vetus that connected Rome with Ariminum (Rimini). Along the road, every fifteen to eighteen miles *mansiones* were built, offering hospitality to civilian dignitaries: they were in Narnia (Narni), Carsuale, Martana (Massa Martana), and Mevania (Bevagna). The military built *castrum* (camps) for their officers, and ordinary business travellers were catered for in *cauponae* (inns, barely more than huts). One of them became notorious. Between Martana and Mevania, where many roads cross each other, as they do today, connecting Todi with Massa Martana, Foligno, Spoleto and Perugia, and eventually linking with the Flaminia; the *Cappanna del Bastardo* (the bastard's inn) was built. It soon became the meeting place for people of ill repute, who enjoyed good food, good drink, and the good life. The innkeeper served scented wine, amongst the other comforts offered to the weary traveller. Today the town is known as Bastardo, although many of its inhabitants have no idea how the name came about. Going south, Bastardo is the last town of any size before reaching Todi.

Todi is reputed to have the best *piazza* in Italy, and it is also considered to be the "world's most liveable town." Discerning tourists flock to the mediaeval hilltop-city to pay their respects to the living past. Set in a high position and approached by winding roads, Todi is yet another town founded by the Umbrii, enlarged by Etruscans and Romans, and untouched since the Middle Ages. It has an excellent museum housed in the *Palazzo del Capitano,* overlooking the *piazza* and facing the elegant *duomo.*

The surrounding countryside has an air of biblical beauty about it. No wonder it has become home to an ever-expanding community of ex-patriot artists from every corner of the world. The vineyards are not easy to spot, as they are dotted amongst some very impressive villas and estates, but they are there, and produce excellent wines. Wine has been produced in the area since Etruscan times, and was noted for its quality, especially for its suitability for long ageing, as testified by Martial and Pliny the Elder. Within the Colli Martani DOC area a subdivision was created, Todi DOC. It recognises the importance of Todi as a wine-producing centre, and since its introduction the planting of Grechetto grapes has greatly increased.

Throughout the Colli Martani production zone the main bases for red wines are Sangiovese grapes, but also Canaiolo, Barbera, Montepulciano, Ciliegiolo and Merlot; and for white wines Trebbiano, Grechetto, Malvasia bianca di Candia, Malvasia bianca del Chianti, Garganeca and Verdicchio.

The designated Colli Martani DOC zone includes the towns of Perugia, Gualdo Catteneo, Giano dell'Umbria, Todi, Massa Martana, Monte Castello di Vibio, Montefalco, Castel Ritaldi, Spoleto, Bevagna, Cannara, Bettona, Deruta and Collazzone. The same area overlaps with Colli Perugini and Montefalco vineyards, and most of the wineries produce all the relevant wines. For anyone wishing to visit the wineries, they are signposted along the *Strada dei Vini Cantico*" (the wine road of the canticle, songs with a biblical text). It is the modern road that connects these towns and villages, and follows, more or less, the course of the old Roman road from Perugia to Todi. The Association of the *Strada dei Vini Cantico* was instituted in 2002 in order to promote tourism and all aspects of farm, wine, and food production. It is a road intended to help visitors discover ancient villages, cities, castles, churches, and the vineyards where noble wines were, and are, born.

Baldassari

Cantina Baldassari
Loc. Pianelli,
Collazzone PG
Tel: 0758 707299
www.cantinabaldassari.it
info@cantianbaldassari.it

The L'Azienda Agricola Baldassari was born from the passion and entrepreneurial skills of Luciano Baldassari and his sons. The vineyards stretch over 10 hectares, planted mostly with Grechetto, Merlot, Sangiovese and Sagrantino grapes. In 2005 a new winery was built with a capacity of 2 000 hectolitres in order to process the grapes grown on the estate. Then another 5 hectares were planted with international grape varietals.

The basic principle of cultivation consists of low yields and high density planting, in order to produce quality grapes. Green pruning and thinning out grape clusters, further helps the production of first grade grapes. Harvest is carried out precisely at the right time, when the grapes reach optimum ripeness.

The winery is furnished with modern enological equipment. Red grapes are vinified in stainless steel tanks and clarified by gravity, which produces the minimum level of lees. Racking is carried out by belt elevators. Using this method, the fermented wine marc receives a gentler treatment and also reduces the amount of lees.

In the vinification of white wine, the must produced by a pneumatic press clarifies naturally by being kept static in temperature controlled stainless steel vats. This allows for the minimum amount of oxygenation. The wine is decanted at a low temperature, avoiding any undesired fermentation. A constant temperature is maintained all year round throughout the winery during the ageing and bottling processes.

Lucardo. Rosso dell'Umbria IGT.

It is a highly aromatic wine, reminiscent of blackcurrants, blackberries, and raspberries. A subtle hint of wood, vanilla, coconut and spices further enhance its flavour. Lucardo has a smooth finish, and it is rich and full on the palate. It can be drunk when young, but it can also age in the bottle for some time.

Cabernet Sauvignon. Umbria IGT.

This mellow red wine is characterised by a depth of complexity, balance, finesse and richness of flavour. The primary taste is cut grass, with overtones of pepper, mint, and sage. Its high tannin content provides a good structure, and it is full on the palate, with a long aftertaste.

Verzaro. Merlot dell'Umbria IGT.

Merlot is a grape variety that has been cultivated in Umbria for some years, and it adapts well to the terrain. The grapes are harvested at the peak of their ripeness and are subjected to a long period of maceration, which helps to obtain a good colour, and intense bouquet, and an extremely soft flavour.

Archetto Dorato. Grechetto dell'Umbria IGT.

Grechetto is Umbria's foremost native grape. It produces rich, full-bodied white wines, with a unique and distinctive flavour. It is bright yellow in colour, with a nose reminiscent of the Umbrian hills, and it has a bouquet of pears, apples, and a hint of musk.

Chardonnay. Umbria IGT.

The Chardonnay grape is well suited to the Mediterranean climate and produces full-bodied and well-structured white wines. The low yields in the vineyards, coupled with state-of-the-art winemaking techniques create a wine of remarkable complexity and style.

Pinot Grigio. Umbria IGT.

The wine has a soft structure, but it is superbly balanced and intensely aromatic. Its fresh, refined style is ideal for a modern cuisine. It has a full flavour and aromatic profile, which is remarkable, because Pinot Grigio is a notoriously heat sensitive grape variety, and it is mostly grown in the north of Italy.

Custodia

Terre de la Custodia Azienda Agraria
Loc. Palombara
06035 Gualdo Catteneo PG
Tel: 0742 92951
Fax: 0742 929595
www.terredelacustodia.it

The Farchioni family owns *Terre de la Custodia*. They have been farmers since the enterprise was started in 1780, growing cereals and producing olive oil and wine. Today, Pompeo and Roberto Farchioni are the managers, and work closely with their parents, Lanfranco and Domenico, who developed Farchioni into the successful company it is. Pompeo's children, Giampaolo and Marco, also work in the family business.

In recent years the Farchioni Group has invested in the construction of new headquarters, which was inaugurated in 2004. They also set up of the new winery, *Terre de la Custodia*, and planted new vineyards. They wanted to achieve the same success in producing wine, as they have done in olive oil. Farchioni is one of the leading brands in Umbria, with a reputation for offering quality olive oil within every consumer's budget. In the past they had taken olive oil and flour to the shelves of Italy and the world; now, they aim to do the same with *Terre de la Custodia* wines.

The family set about the task with enthusiasm knowing that good wine comes from a land with intrinsic *terroir*, and where nothing is left to chance. The vineyards are lovingly tended with respect to the local traditions, but it is also equipped with the best that technology can offer. Riccardo Cotarella, a winemaker of international renown, is their consultant. The agronomist is Tiziano Maschio, and the winemaker is Marco Miniciarelli.

Desiata. Bianco dell'Umbria IGT. Duca Odorato.

Grapes: Grechetto, and Trebbiano.
Production zone: Torrececcona di Todi.
Production per hectare: 10 000 kg.
Area cultivated: 4.5 hectares.
Soil: medium consistency, sloping slightly towards the east.
Altitude: 250 metres above sea level.
Training: specialised runner system.
Vineyard density: 3 300 plants per hectare.
Harvest: late September.
Vinification: classic white fermentation on the skins, with soft pressing and settling of the must; at a controlled temperature and a long time on the lees.
The wine: straw white in colour, with fresh and intense aromas of white flowers reminiscent of elder. It has a full, round, and persistent flavour.
Food matches: soup, fish, and cheese. Alcohol: 12 % vol.

Vocante. Rosso dell'Umbria IGT. Duca Odorato.

Grapes: Sangiovese, Merlot, and Sagrantino.
Production zone: Torrececcona di Todi.
Production per hectare: 10 000 kg.
Area cultivated: 22 hectares.
Soil: medium consistency, sloping steeply towards the south.
Altitude: 350 metres above sea level.
Training: specialised runner system.
Vineyard density: 3 250 plants per hectare.
Harvest: 20-30 September.
Vinification: medium maceration with frequent pumping over and *delestage* (separation of part of the must for oxygenation); then alcoholic fermentation at a controlled temperature.
Ageing: a brief period in wood.
The wine: ruby red in colour; with aromas of fresh red fruits and ripe plums. It has a smooth and medium bodied flavour.
Serving temperature: 8-10 C°.
Food matches: red meats, but also with fish.
Alcohol content: 12.5 % vol.

Sagrantino Montefalco DOCG. Duca Odorato.

Grapes: Sagrantino.
Production zone: La Palombara, Gualdo Cattaneo.
Production per hectare: 6 000 kg. Area cultivated: 18 hectares.
Soil: compact and clayey, rich in lignite; on gentle hills with a southern exposure.
Training: specialised runner system.
Vineyard density: 3 300 plants per hectare.
Harvest: 7-15 October.
Vinification: cold pre-maceration, temperature controlled fermentation, with frequent pumping over, punching down the cap, and *delestage*, followed by post-fermentation maceration, and a long time on the lees.
Ageing: barrique for 12-15 months, in the bottle for 6-8 months.
The wine: ruby red in colour, with purple overtones; and notes of blackberries, raspberries and spices. It is full-bodied, well-structured, warm and soft.
Ageing potential: 15-20 years.
Serving temperature: 18 C°.
Food matches: roast red meats, game, lamb or mutton on the spit, and sharp mature cheeses.
Alcohol content: 13.5 % vol.

Grechetto. Colli Martani DOC. Duca Odorato.

Grapes: Grechetto.
Production zone: Torrececcona di Todi.
Production per hectare: 10 000 kg.
Area cultivated: 4.5 hectares.
Soil: medium consistency, clayey, on south-facing hills.
Altitude: 250 metres above sea level.
Training: specialised runner system.
Vineyard density: 3 300 plants per hectare.
Harvest: mid-September.
Vinification: soft pressing on the skins; alcoholic fermentation at a controlled temperature and a long time on the lees.
Ageing: in stainless steel, followed by 2 months in the bottle.

The wine: brilliant straw white in colour, with rich aromas of white flowers, ethereal, very persistent. It has mineral flavours, saline, with a round and structured body.
Serving temperature: 10-11 C°.
Food matches: aperitif, *hors d'oeuvres*, pasta and rice dishes, fish, white meats, and fresh cheeses.
Alcohol content: 12.5 % vol.

Montefalco Rosso DOC. Duca Odorato.

Grapes: Sangiovese, Sagrantino, Merlot, and Montepulciano.
Production zone: Giano dell'Umbria, and Gualdo Cattaneo.
Production per hectare: 10 000 kg.
Area cultivated: 5 hectares.
Soil: slightly calcareous, on south-facing and gently sloping hills.
Training: specialised runner system.
Vineyard density: 5 000 plants per hectare.
Harvest: early October.
Vinification: temperature controlled alcoholic fermentation, medium length maceration with frequent pumping over, and *delestage;* followed by a long time on the lees.
Ageing: in barrique for 8-10 months, in the bottle for 6 months.
The wine: intense, brilliant ruby red in colour; with hints of ripe red fruits and plums. It has a good body, velvety, and soft.
Ageing potential: 4-5 years.
Serving temperature: 16-18 C°.
Food matches: pasta dishes with spicy tomato sauces, cold cuts, grilled meats, and mature cheeses.
Alcohol content: 13 % vol.

Novello Rosso dell'Umbria IGT. Duca Odorato.

Grapes: Ciliegiolo and Merlot.
Production zone: Torrececcona di Todi.
Production per hectare: 10 000 kg.
Area cultivated: 15 hectares.
Soil: medium consistency, clayey; on hills with southern exposure. Altitude: 500 metres above sea level.
Training: specialised runner system.

Vineyard density: 3 200 plants per hectare.
Harvest: early September.
Vinification: carbonic maceration at a temperature of 18 C°.
The wine: ruby red in colour; fresh, velvety, fruity and lively.
Serving temperature: room temperature.
Food matches: winter meals that require a light wine with a good bouquet; ideal with roasted chestnuts, pizza and pasta dishes.
Alcohol content: 12.5 % vol.

Di Filippo

Di Filippo Azienda Agraria
Vocabolo Conversino, 153
06033 Cannara PG
Te: 0742 731242
Fax: 0742 72310
www.vinidifilippo.com
intfo@vinidifilippo.com

The agricultural concern of the Di Filippo family was established in 1971 between Torgiano and Montefalco. Cannara, where the winery is situated is near Pian d'Arca, the place where Saint Francis spoke to the birds in 1212. The birds are still there (similar ones perhaps), for the eco system of the countryside has changed little since the Middle Ages.

Since 1994, the Di Filippo family has cultivated 30 hectares of vineyards according to EU norms for organic farming, which means that diseases are controlled using traditional Bordeaux mixture and sulphur. The estate does not apply chemical weed killers, and only organic fertilisers are used. "Our philosophy begins in the vineyard," explains Roberto Di Filippo. "Only by working closely with natural principles, and by having a passion for our plants and our land, can quality grapes be produced – without these, every wine loses significance. This is why we have embraced organic cultivation: natural products, which fertilise nature. We also believe that a low yield, correct management of the earth's resources and harvesting when the grapes are perfectly ripe, help the land to give of its very best."

Although the cellars are equipped with modern machinery, traditional methods of winemaking are preferred where possible. The winery welcomes visitors, where a warm, family atmosphere meets them. A great attraction to visitors is the Vernaccia di Cannara, a sweet wine of the area, which has been re-discovered recently, thanks to the enthusiasm of the Di Filippo family. They keep the main stems of this special grape variety. In 2010, with a change to the regulations of the Disciplinary Commission, the Di Filippo estate was appointed as tester, then later as guardian of Vernaccia di Cannara DOC.

Vernaccia di Cannara Colli Martani DOC.

Grapes: Cornetta, also known as Vernaccia Nera.
Soil: clayey-calcareous hills.
Training: spurred cordon.
Plants per hectare: 4000-5000.
Yield per hectare: 6000 kg of grapes.
Annual production: 4000 bottles.
Vinification: with prolonged maceration.
Ageing: *appasito* for two months.
The wine: ruby red in colour; fruity and sweet, slightly tannic with a dry aftertaste.
Food matches: sweet biscuits, hams, salamis, and cheese bread.

Montefalco Sagrantino DOCG.

Grapes: Sagrantino 100%.
Soil: clayey-calcareous hills.
Training: spurred cordon.
Plants per hectare: 5000.
Yield per hectare: 6000kg of grapes.
Annual production: 18 000 bottles.
Vinification: with prolonged traditional maceration.
Ageing: in barrique and tonneaux for 18-24 months.
The wine: ruby red, turns to garnet with ageing; scents of red berries, with a hint of flint, velvety and a strong tannic flavour.
Food matches: game and mature cheeses.

Sallustio. Montefalco Rosso DOC.

Grapes: Sangiovese 60%, Barbera 25%, and Sagrantino 15%.
Soil: clayey-calcareous hills.
Training: spurred cordon.
Plants per hectare: 5000.

Yield per hectare: 10 000 kg of grapes.
Annual production: 20 000 bottles.
Vinification: red, with 10 days of fermentation.
Ageing: in large casks for 12 months.
The wine: ruby red in colour, turns to garnet with ageing; spicy with hints of tobacco, slightly tannic, smooth with ageing.
Food matches: red meats, hams, salamis, and mature cheeses.

Montefalco Rosso DOC.

Grapes: Sangiovese 60%, Barbera 30%, and Sagrantino 10%.
Soil: clayey-calcareous hills.
Training: spurred cordon.
Plants per hectare: 5000.
Yield per hectare: 10 000 kg of grapes.
Annual production: 15-20 000 bottles.
Vinification: traditional red.
Ageing: in large stainless steel tanks.
The wine: ruby red, tending to garnet with ageing; spicy with woody tones, and a hint of red berries; medium bodied.
Food matches: red meats, hams, salamis, and cheeses.

Properzio. Sangiovese Colli Martani DOC Riserva.

Grapes: Sangiovese 100%.
Soil: clayey-calcareous hills.
Training: spurred cordon.
Plants per hectare: 4-5000.
Yield per hectare: 7 000 kg of grapes.
Annual production: 7 000 bottles.
Vinification: traditional red.
Ageing: in barrique for 12 months.
The wine: ruby red in colour, tending to garnet with ageing; strong tobacco scent, fruity, velvety with pleasant tobacco undertones.
Food matches: red meats, hams, salamis, and mature cheeses.

Sangiovese Colli Martani DOC.

Grapes: Sangiovese 100%.
Soil: clayey-calcareous hills.
Training: spurred cordon.
Plants per hectare: 4-5000.
Yield per hectare: 10 000 kg of grapes.
Annual production: 20 000 bottles.
Vinification: traditional red.
Ageing: in stainless steel.
The wine: ruby red, tending to garnet with ageing; scents of morello cherries and fruits of the forest; smooth and velvety.
Food matches: red meats, hams, salamis, and mature cheeses.

Poggio Madrigale. Rosso dell'Umbria IGT.

Grapes: Sagrantino, and Merlot.
Soil: clayey-calcareous hills.
Training: spurred cordon.
Plants per hectare: 4000.
Yield per hectare: 5000 kg of grapes.
Annual production: 3500 bottles.
Vinification: with prolonged maceration.
Ageing: in French oak and in Slovenian oak.
The wine: ruby red, tending to garnet; with scents of red berries; full bodied, robust, with soft tannins, and a long finish.
Food matches: game, and mature cheeses.

Villa Conversino. Rosso dell'Umbria IGT.

Grapes: Sangiovese, and Cabernet.
Soil: clayey-calcareous, partly hilly and flat land.
Training: spurred cordon.
Plants per hectare: 4000.
Yield per hectare: 10 000 kg of grapes.
Annual production: 30 000 bottles.
Vinification: traditional red; with 30% carbon maceration in stainless steel vats.

The wine: bright ruby red in colour; fine, fruity, and velvety with pleasant tobacco undertones.
Food matches: pasta dishes, boiled meats, and fresh cheeses.

Terre di San Nicola. Rosso dell'Umbria IGT.

Grapes: Sangiovese, Merlot, and Sagrantino.
Soil: clayey-calcareous hills.
Training: spurred cordon.
Plants per hectare: 4000.
Yield per hectare: 7000 kg of grapes.
Annual production: 10 000 bottles.
Vinification: traditional red.
Ageing: 50% in tonneaux, 50% in large casks for 12 months.
The wine: ruby red, tending to garnet with ageing; intense bouquet with red berries, robust texture, tannic, and full-bodied.
Food matches: red meats, hams, salamis, and mature cheeses.

Villa Conversino. Rosato dell'Umbria IGT.

Grapes: Sangiovese, and Cabernet.
Soil: clayey-calcareous, partly hilly and flat land.
Training: spurred cordon.
Plants per hectare: 4000.
Yield per hectare: 10 000 kg of grapes.
Annual production: 3500 bottles.
Vinification: maceration for one day, with fermentation at a controlled temperature.
Ageing: in stainless steel tanks.
The wine: clear cherry in colour; fruity, with hints of strawberries and cherries; with a strong fruity aftertaste.
Food matches: first courses with vegetables, and white meats.

Sassi d'Arenaria. Grechetto Colli Martani DOC.

Grapes: Grechetto 100%.
Soil: clayey-calcareous hills.
Training: spurred cordon.
Plants per hectare: 5000.

Yield per hectare: 6000 kg of grapes.
Annual production: 3500 bottles.
Vinification: white vinification fermentation off skins at a low temperature, then maturation on yeast lees for 6 months.
Ageing: in stainless steel tanks.
The wine: straw in colour; spicy, full bodied and soft tannins.
Food matches: cheese, white meats, and rich aromatic dishes.

Grechetto Colli Martani DOC.

Grapes: Grechetto 100%.
Soil: clayey-calcareous hills.
Training: spurred cordon/Guyot.
Plants per hectare: 4-5000.
Yield per hectare: 10 000 kg of grapes.
Annual production: 40 000 bottles.
Vinification: white vinification fermentation at 18 C°.
Ageing: in stainless steel tanks.
The wine: bright straw in colour, brightness varies from year to year; fruity, rounded, tangy, with a pleasant bitter aftertaste.
Food matches: fish, white meats, and fresh cheeses.

Villa Conversino. Bianco dell'Umbria IGT.

Grapes: Trebbiano, and Grechetto.
Soil: clayey-calcareous, partly hilly and flat land.
Training: spurred cordon.
Plants per hectare: 1500-4000.
Yield per hectare: 12 000 kg of grapes.
Annual production: 25 000 bottles.
Vinification: white, with fermentation at 16 C°.
Ageing: in stainless steel tanks.
The wine: straw in colour, with greenish tones; fruity, fragrant, young, with the taste of grapes, slightly tangy, and well balanced.
Food matches: starters, fish, and white meats.

Cantina Peppucci

Società Agricola S. Antimo s.s.
Località S. Antimo 4
Frazione Petrorio, Todi PG
Tel/Fax: 0758 947253
www.cantinapeppucci.com
info@cantinapeppucci.com

The Monastery of San Antimo sits on top of a hill 422 metres above sea level. Todi stands out in the distance dominating the valley. The castle of Petroro is nearby, guarding the old Roman road leading from Todi to the Flaminia. Benedictine monks built the monastery in 1275 AD. The chapel still exists and services are held there each week for a small congregation, but the rest of the buildings had been altered throughout the centuries to make way for a magnificent private residence.

Today, the abbey complex belongs to the Peppucci family, and it is a part of their winery. The brother and sister team of Filippo and Elisabetta manage the winery. Their mother, Luisa, is responsible for the agricultural aspects of the business.

The estate planted thirteen hectares of vines on the land renowned for its favourable position and exposure, and a rocky soil perfectly suited for the cultivation of quality grapes. The high density of rows allows five thousand and fifty plants per hectare, and the spurred cordon training system is especially suitable for growing grapes. Judicious pruning throughout the growing cycle reduces yields, and at harvest time the grapes are picked by hand separately, selecting only the perfectly ripe bunches. Forests surround the vineyards, and the high elevation produces a breeze that never ceases to blow. The favourable exposure to constant sunshine and the rocky soil all contribute to the production of wines of a superior class.

Lorenzo Landi, one of Italy's most appreciated winemakers, is the enological advisor to the estate. Cantina Peppucci produces three wines: Montorsolo, a white DOC wine made from the grapes of Grechetto di Todi, as well as two red IGT wines: Alter Ego and Petroro 4, for which Sagrantino, Sangiovese, Merlot, and Cabernet Sauvignon grapes are used.

Montorsolo. Grechetto di Todi DOC.

Grapes: Grechetto di Todi 100%.
The vineyards: the hills of Montorsolo.
Soil: rocky, rich in clay and limestone.
Harvest: mid-September.
Vinification: the grapes are de-stemmed and soft pressed, and the must is clarified by *debourbage* (racking of the must), then fermented in stainless steel tanks at 15-18 C°.
Ageing: in stainless steel tanks with periodic *batonnages* (stirring up of the must from the lees), a procedure that allows the wine to develop all its aromas and flavours.
The wine: pale yellow with greenish reflections; fruity, full and smooth taste, with a tart and refreshing finish. The wine fully develops its characteristics during the year following the harvest.
Serving temperature: 10-12 C°.
Food matches: appetisers, pastas, fish, and meat courses.
Alcoholic content: 13.5% vol.

Alter Ego. Rosso Umbria IGT.

Grapes: Sagrantino 100%.
The vineyards: the hills around the Abbey San Antimo
Soil: rocky, rich in clay and limestone.
Cultivation: the grapes are subjected to a rigorous selection for the best bunches by the means of "green" harvesting. Only the best quality grapes are allowed to ripen and to be picked for vinification.
Harvest: during the first 10 days of October.
Vinification: the grapes are de-stemmed, then fermentation in stainless steel tanks at 25-28 C°, which helps the best extraction from the skins, with periodical pumping over and punching down the cap. The maceration on the skins takes 18-21 days.
Ageing: in French oak *barriques* for 12 months, and an additional 12 months in the bottle. The wine fully develops its

characteristics over a long period and acquires its beautiful, aromatic taste.
The wine: deep ruby in colour; full bodied, with aromas of red berries, tobacco, oak, and dense tannins; full and structured.
Serving temperature: 18 C°.
Food matches: main courses, and game.
Alcoholic content: 14.5% vol.

Petroro 4. Rosso Umbria IGT.

Grapes: Sangiovese, Merlot and Cabernet Sauvignon.
The vineyards: the hills around the Abbey San Antimo.
Soil: rocky, rich in clay and limestone.
Harvest: during the last 10 days of September.
Vinification: the grapes undergo a gentle crushing, followed by fermentation in stainless steel tanks at 25-28 C°, with periodical pumping over. The maceration on the skins takes 10-15 days.
Ageing: in stainless steel tanks, with regular decanting until the wine is ready. A further two months follows in the bottle.
The wine: brilliant ruby in colour, with aromas of red berries and floral hints; soft tannins, and a good structure. The wine fully develops its characteristics during the year following the harvest.
Serving temperature: 18-20 C°.
Food matches: mature salamis and cheeses, and well-seasoned main courses.
Alcoholic content: 13.5% vol.

San Rocco

Azienda Agrituristica e Vitivinicola
Località Due Santi,
06059 Todi PG
Tel: 0758 989102
Fax: 0758 980971
www.agriturismo-sanrocco.com
info@agriturismo-sanrocco.com

Villa San Rocco rises up above the hills facing Todi. The estate was named after an old site called San Rocco, which belonged to the Order of the Knights of Malta. In the 16th century the knights were replaced by the Confraternity of St John the Baptist and the Roman Arch-confraternity of San Rocco. In 1599 the Bishop Angelo Cesi donated the estate to a religious order, The Servants of Mary. They built an Oratory and dedicated it to San Rocco. The monks soon recognised the favourable climate and the fertility of the land, and planted vineyards and olive trees.

In 1860 the noble Marquis Massei-Bargagli family of Todi purchased the estate. They built the present day villa in the eclectic style of the age. It was used for holidays. Since then, the Villa San Rocco continued to be the country residence and farm of the aristocratic family up to the early 20th century, when it became the property of Luigi Gianni, a notary and a native of Todi. He was renowned for hosting grand parties during the hunting season.

In 1934 Professor Nello Morghetti of Todi purchased the estate. His descendants are the current owners, and they adhere faithfully to the age-old vocation of San Rocco with regards to wine production and country hospitality. Their aim is to produce and obtain excellence in both the wines and the food served to the guests at the inn. The focus is on vine cultivating techniques and subsequently the winemaking process. The estate stretches over 57 hectares of rolling hills 350 metres above sea level. The vineyards cover 12 hectares, sloping downwards to south and south-west. The cellars are equipped with temperature controlled stainless steel fermentation tanks, a grape processing area, a selection table, de-stemmer/crusher, and a hydraulic press. The basement of the Villa houses the centuries old cellars where the wines are aged in oak barrels (Tonneaux) and egg shaped cement barrels. The grapes are harvested by hand, and placed into small crates and only the best are selected. Modern winemaking techniques, plus the added professionalism and passion of the oenologist, Dottoressa Graziana Grassini, ensure the production of prestigious wines

Palombaccio.
Vino Rosso DOC Colli Martani Sangiovese Riserva.

Grapes: 85% Sangiovese, and 15% Merlot.
Soil: loamy, sandy, and rich in lime.
Altitude: 350 metres above sea level.
Exposure: south-south/west.
Number of plants per hectare: 4000.
Training: spurred cordon
Year of planting: 2000/2003.
Average production per plant: 1200 grams.
Harvest: first ten days of September for Merlot, end of September beginning of October for Sangiovese.
Vinification: the grapes are de-stemmed, then fermented at a controlled temperature in stainless steel tanks for 20-25 days, then malolactic fermentation follows partly in stainless steel and partly in oak barrels.
Ageing: 14 months, partly in oak tonneaux of 500 litre, and partly in 600 litre cement barrels.
The wine: ruby red in colour, with violet reflections; blackberry and blackcurrant notes, balsamic and spicy fragrances; full-bodied, round, with good structure and velvety tannins.
Food matches: red meats, game, and mature cheeses.
Analytical data:
Alcohol: 13.5 % vol.

Moretto. Vino Rosso DOC Colli Martani Sangiovese.

Grapes: 100% Sangiovese.
Soil: loamy, sandy, and rich in lime.
Altitude: 350 metres above sea level.
Exposure: south.
Number of plants per hectare: 3350.
Training: spurred cordon.
Year of planting: 2000.
Average production per plant: 1200 grams.
Harvest: the second ten days of September.
Vinification: the grapes are de-stemmed, followed by maceration, and then fermentation at a controlled temperature in stainless steel tanks for 15-20 days, followed by malolactic fermentation also in stainless steel.
Stabilisation and clarification: natural settling of the sediments.
Ageing: two months in the bottle minimum.
The wine: ruby red in colour, with violet reflections; fruity and floral, full-bodied, round, and well structured.
Food matches: red meats, game, and mature cheeses.
Analytical data:
Alcohol: 13.29 % vol.

Poggio Marcigliano.
Vino Bianco DOC Colli Martani Grechetto di Todi.

Grapes: 100% Grechetto di Todi.
Soil: loamy, sandy, and rich in lime.
Altitude: 350 metres above sea level.
Exposure: south-south/west.
Number of plants per hectare: 3350.
Training: hanging cordon.
Year of planting: 1990.
Average production per plant: 1500 grams.
Harvest: the second ten days of September.
Vinification: the grapes are de-stemmed and soft crushed, followed by maceration at a low temperature; then fermentation at a controlled temperature in stainless steel for 20-30 days.
Stabilisation and clarification: natural settling of the sediments.

Ageing: 3 months partly in barriques and partly in stainless steel.
The wine: straw yellow in colour, with green reflections; a fruity bouquet, delicate and a good structure.
Food matches: aperitif, fish dishes, white meats, and cheeses.
Analytical data:
Alcohol: 13.5 % vol.

Cesarini Sartori

Loc. Purgatorio
06035 Gualdo Cattaneo PG
Tel: 0742 99590
Fax: 0742 969462
www.rossobastardo.it
info@rossobastardo.it

The Cesarini Sartori winery is built on a hilltop between Bastardo and Todi. The postal address is Purgatory, *Purgatorio;* it could easily be assumed that wine production goes back to biblical times, but the first mention goes only as far as 79 BC, when Pliny the Elder writes about the place. There is archaeological evidence of vineyards from the Longobard epoch. The Land Register of 1340, kept in the Historical Archives of Todi, and the Gregorian Land register of 1800 describe the *Vignone Marchetti*, near *Cappana del Bastardo*, the very place of the present day winery.

The cultivation of the land started with ploughing metre-deep furrows. Cattle manure was used for fertiliser, and five thousand vines were planted per hectare. They are trained to single wooden poles exposed towards the south. During the cultivation cycle the vines are pruned rigorously, leaving only the best bunches to ripen. At harvest the grapes are handpicked, then carried to the winery in small boxes. The winery is built on the top of a hill and it is constructed to make maximum use of gravity, thus eliminating the use of pumps for transferring must and wine (a modern version of the three-level Etruscan system used in Orvieto). The grapes are received at ground level, where the selection of grapes continues by hand through three vibrating tables. After rasping, the residues are separated and the grapes make their way down to a lower level. There are no storage tanks to be seen anywhere, all the vinification takes place underground, totally isolated from electromagnetic fields.

Instead of stainless steel, the winery uses Slovenian oak casks of various sizes, holding 10, 20 or 30 hectolitres of wine.

As the vineyards are spread over both the Montefalco and Colli Martani designated production zones, the Cesarini Sartori winery makes both types of wines.

Montefalco Sagrantino DOCG.

Grapes: Sagrantino 100%.
Production: 10-15 000 bottles.
Harvest: handpicked during 2nd and 3rd weeks of October.
Vinification: pre-fermentation cold maceration, followed by fermentation at a controlled temperature.
Clarification: natural, without filtering.
Ageing: 24 months in the barrel, 12 months in the bottle.
Ageing potential: 10-15 years.
The wine: deep ruby red in colour, with reflections turning to garnet; rich and intense aromas of blackberry, spiced with pepper, vanilla, coffee, cocoa, and a hint of balsamic. It is full-bodied, warm, with good tannins.
Serving temperature: 18 C°.
Food matches: grilled and roasted meats, and game.
Alcohol content: 14% vol.

Seméle. Montefalco Sagrantino Passito DOCG.

Grapes: Sagrantino 100%.
Production: 6 000 bottles.
Harvest: handpicked during 3rd and 4th weeks of October.
Drying process: trellis and crates.
Vinification: pre-fermentation cold maceration, followed by fermentation at a controlled temperature.
Clarification: natural, without filtering.
Ageing: 24 months in the barrel, 12 months in the bottle.
Ageing potential: 10 years.
The wine: intense ruby red in colour, with purple nuances; a rich, persistent fruity flavour, reminiscent of dried fruits, hint of balsamic, spiced with pepper, vanilla, coffee, and cocoa. It is

full-bodied, very rich, warm with good tannins; and long finish; the contrast is unique between the tannins and sweetness.
Serving temperature: 16 C°.
Food matches: lamb, mature cheeses, chocolate and fruits tarts.
Alcohol content: 15% vol.

Montefalco Rosso DOC.

Grapes: Sangiovese, Merlot, Cabernet Sauvignon, and Sagrantino.
Production: 18-20 000 bottles.
Harvest: handpicked during 3rd and 4th weeks of September.
Vinification: pre-fermentation cold maceration, then fermentation at a controlled temperature.
Clarification: natural, without filtering.
Ageing: 12 months in the barrel, 8 months in the bottle.
Ageing potential: 5-10 years.
The wine: intense ruby red in colour, with purple reflections; fruity aromas, with hints of wild cherries, wild berries, blackberries, vanilla, and black pepper. It is well balanced, and rich with smooth tannins and a sweet finish.
Serving temperature: 16-18 C°.
Food matches: red meats, game, cold cuts, and mature cheeses.
Alcohol content: 13.5% vol.

Rossobastardo. Rosso IGT Umbria.

Grapes: Sangiovese, Merlot, and Cabernet.
Production: 70 000 bottles.
Harvest: handpicked during 2nd and 3rd weeks of September.
Vinification: pre-fermentation cold maceration, followed by fermentation at a controlled temperature.
Clarification: natural, without filtering.
Ageing: 75% in INOX steel and 25% in the barrel.
Ageing potential: 5 years.
The wine: intense ruby; fragrances of red wild berries, mostly blackberries. It is soft, well rounded, with a long finish.

Serving temperature: 16-18 C°.
Food matches: perfect throughout a meal.
Alcohol content: 14.5% vol.

Peperosa. Rosato IGT Umbria.

Grapes: Sagrantino 100%.
Production: 6 600 bottles.
Harvest: handpicked during the 1st week of October.
Vinification: at a controlled temperature of about 16-18 C°.
Ageing: on the lees for 2 months at 18 C°.
The wine: vivid pink, with tones of crimson; elegant aroma; delicately mineral, full-bodied, with sweet tannins.
Serving temperature: 10-12 C°.
Food matches: appetisers, first courses, and fish soup.
Alcohol content: 13% vol.

Grechetto. DOC Colli Martani.

Grapes: Grechetto 100%.
Production: 6 600 bottles.
Harvest: handpicked during the 1st week of September.
Vinification: at a controlled temperature of 16-18 C°.
Ageing: on the lees for about 2 months.
The wine: brilliant straw yellow in colour, with green reflections; aromas of white peaches, medlar, broom, and camomile. It is well balanced, fresh, with a mineral aftertaste.
Serving temperature: 10-12 C°.
Food matches: aperitif, fish, white meats and soups.
Alcohol content: 13% vol.

Aliara Bianco. IGT Umbria.

Grapes: Trebbiano, and Pecorino.
Production: 18-20 000 bottles.
Harvest: handpicked in the 1st and 2nd weeks of September.
Vinification: at a controlled temperature of about 16-18 C°.
Ageing: on the lees for about 2 months.

The wine: brilliant straw yellow in colour, with a golden hue; floral and fruity; reminiscent of almond blossoms, broom and hawthorn; fresh and tasty, with a long finish and almond aftertaste.
Serving temperature: 10-12 C°.
Food matches: starters, first courses, white meats and fish.
Alcohol content: 12.5% vol.

<u>Grappa di Sagrantino. Monovitigno.</u>

Grapes: Sagrantino 100%.
Production: 1 500 bottles.
Marc press: 0.3 atmosphere.
Transport to distillery: vacuum packed containers.
Colour: transparent and crystalline.
Aroma: bursting, intense, stark fragrance, the perfume is reminiscent of the Sagrantino's vine shoot.
Taste: persistent and wide, smooth and enjoyable.
Alcohol content: 42% vol.

Terre de Trinci

Cantina Terre de' Trinci s.c.a.
Via Fiamenga, 57
06034 Foligno PG
Tel: 0742 320165/320243
Fax: 0742 20386
www.terredetrinci.com
cantina@terredetrinci.com

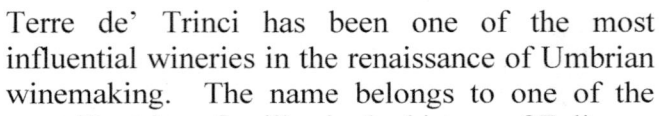

Terre de' Trinci has been one of the most influential wineries in the renaissance of Umbrian winemaking. The name belongs to one of the most illustrious families in the history of Foligno. They were the lords of Foligno in the XIV and XV centuries, and the Trinci family guided the area through a particularly magnificent period.

The winery invested extensively in the production of native local Sagrantino grapes in order to promote a wine inextricably entwined with its *terroir*. The vineyards are cultivated with the consultancy of an agronomist who ensures grapes of outstanding quality. The cellars are furnished with modern vinification equipment and special stock barrels, barriques and tonneaux; and there is a desire to discover new ways and an ongoing search for the perfect blend of tradition and innovation.

Ugolino. Montefalco Sagrantino DOCG.

Grapes: Sagrantino 100%.
First vintage: 2000.
Production area: Montefalco.
Production: 10 000 bottles.
Maximum production per plant: 1.5 kg.
Vinification: controlled temperature fermentation, maceration for 15-20 days.
Ageing: minimum 12 months in barriques.

Bottle ageing: about 6 months.
Ageing potential: 10-15 years.

Montefalco Sagrantino DOCG.

Grapes: Sagrantino 100%.
First vintage: 1972.
Production area: Montefalco, Bevagna, and Gualdo Cattaneo.
Production: 140 000 bottles.
Maximum production per plant: 1.7 kg.
Vinification: controlled temperature fermentation, maceration for 15-20 days.
Ageing: minimum 12 months in barriques.
Bottle ageing: about 6 months.
Ageing potential: 10-15 years.

Montefalco Sagrantino Passito DOCG.

Grapes: Sagrantino 100%.
First vintage: 1992.
Production area: Montefalco.
Production: 5 000 bottles.
Maximum production per plant: 1.7 kg.
Harvest: as late as possible, allowing the grapes to dry by a natural process in the vineyards.
Vinification: controlled temperature fermentation, maceration for 15-20 days.
Ageing: minimum 12 months in barriques.
Bottle ageing: about 6 months.
Ageing potential: 10-15 years.
Sagrantino passito is a wine born from ancient traditions. Thanks to its low sugar content it is perfect for the end of the meal with mature cheeses served with preserves or honey.

Montefalco Rosso Riserva DOC.

Grapes: Sangiovese 65%, Merlot 20%, and Sagrantino 15%.
First vintage: 1997.
Production area: Montefalco, Bevagna, and Gualdo Cattaneo.

Production: 20 000 bottles.
Maximum production per plant: 1.7 kg.
Vinification: controlled temperature fermentation, maceration for 15-20 days.
Ageing: minimum 12 months in barriques and barrels.
Bottle ageing: about 6 months.
Ageing potential: 5-10 years.

Montefalco Rosso DOC.

Grapes: Sangiovese 65%, Merlot 20%, and Sagrantino 15%.
Production area: Montefalco, Bevagna, and Gualdo Cattaneo.
Production: 160 000 bottles.
Maximum production per plant: 1.7 kg.
Vinification: controlled temperature fermentation, maceration for fifteen days.
Ageing: in large barrels and barriques.
Bottle ageing: about 3 months.
Ageing potential: 5-7 years.

Cajo. Umbria IGT.

Grapes: Merlot, Cabernet Sauvignon, and Sagrantino.
First vintage: 1998.
Production area: Montefalco, Bevagna, and Foligno.
Production: 150 000 bottles.
Maximum production per plant: 1.7 kg.
Vinification: controlled temperature fermentation, maceration for 15-20 days.
Ageing: in barriques.
Bottle ageing: about 3 months.
Ageing potential: 5-7 years.

Grechetto Colli Martani DOC.

Grapes: Grechetto 100%.
First vintage: 1992.
Production area: Colli Martani.
Production: 50 000 bottles.

Maximum production per plant: 2 kg.
Vinification: controlled temperature fermentation.
Bottle ageing: about 2 months.
Ageing potential: 2 years.

Grechetto dell'Umbria IGT.

Grapes: Grechetto 100%.
First vintage: 1992.
Production area: Montefalco, Bevagna, and Foligno.
Production: 70 000 bottles.
Maximum production per plant: 2 kg.
Vinification: controlled temperature fermentation.
Bottle ageing: about 2 months.
Ageing potential: 2 years.

Luna. Umbria IGT.

Grapes: Grechetto and Chardonnay.
First vintage: 2001.
Production area: Montefalco, Bevagna, and Foligno.
Production: 10 000 bottles.
Maximum production per plant: 2 kg.
Vinification: controlled temperature fermentation.
Ageing: a short period in barriques.
Bottle ageing: about 3 months.
Ageing potential: 2-4 years.

Trebbiano dell'Umbria IGT.

Grapes: Trebbiano 100%.
Production area: Spello, Cannara, Montefalco, Bevagna, and Foligno.
Production: 150 000 bottles.
Vinification: controlled temperature fermentation in stainless steel.
Bottle ageing: about 3 months.
Ageing potential: 1 year.

Grappa di Sagrantino.

Grapes: Sagrantino 100%.
Production area: Spello, Cannara, Montefalco, Bevagna, and Foligno.
Production: 3 000 bottles.
Ageing: at least 3 months in stainless steel vats.
Ageing potential: 10 years.

Grappa di Grechetto.

Grapes: Grechetto 100%.
Production area: Spello, Cannara, Montefalco, Bevagna, and Foligno.
Production: 3 000 bottles.
Ageing: at least 3 months in stainless steel vats.
Ageing potential: 10 years.

Spumante Brut and Demi Sec.

Grapes: based on Grechetto.
Production area: Spello, Cannara, Montefalco, Bevagna, and Foligno.
Production: 5 000 bottles.
Vinification and ageing: temperature controlled in stainless steel.
Ageing potential: 2 years.

Franco Todini

Cantina Todini s.r.l.
Frazione Rosceto,
Voc Collina, 29/1
06059 Todi PG
Tel: 075887122/222
Fax: 075887231
www.cantinafrancotodini.com
agricola@agricolatodini.com

Agricola Todini is in the locality of Collevalenza di Todi, situated amongst the hills overlooking the city. The estate is spread over 300 hectares, 25 of which are vineyards. Recently, new vines have been added to the existing classical grape varieties. The microclimate and the composition of the soil are ideal for growing grapes. The company practices modern cultivation techniques with a low impact on the environment, at the same time they produce quality grapes, which are essential for making good wines.

Nero della Cervara. Umbria IGT.

Grapes: Merlot 50%, and Cabernet Sauvignon 50%.
Vineyards: 3 hectares of hillsides surrounding Cervara castle, built by the Earl of Monaldeschi in 1334 AD.
Soil: volcanic, sedimentary, and partly stony.
Altitude: 340 metres above sea level.
Exposure: north/east.
Age of vines: 7 years on average.
Density of plants: 2.20 x 0.80 metres.
Training: spurred cordon.
Yield of grapes: 60 quintals per hectare.
Yield of wine: 50 hectolitre per hectare.
Harvest: handpicked during the first ten days of October.
Vinification: maceration on the skins for 18-24 days, with periodical pumping over. 20-25% of the must is drawn off and separated. Alcoholic fermentation in stainless steel vats at a

controlled temperature of 27 C° max. Malolactic fermentation is carried out entirely in barriques.
Ageing: 12 months in French oak barriques of 225 litres (Fontainbleau, Allier, Tronçais, and Gran Riserva) followed by 6 months in the bottle.
Production per annum: 3 500 bottles.
The wine: deep ruby red in colour; aromas of ripe red fruits, wilted flowers, spices, black pepper, and tobacco; soft and slightly tannic.
Serving temperature: 18-20 C°.
Food matches: grilled, roast, and braised meats, and game.

Rubro. Umbria IGT.

Grapes: Sangiovese 85%, and Merlot 15%.
Vineyards: spread over 9 hectares of mostly hilly terrain.
Soil: clayey, sedimentary, with gravel.
Altitude: 340 metres above sea level.
Exposure: north/east.
Density of plants: traditional 3.00 x 1.00 metres; newly planted vines 2.80 x 0.80 metres.
Age of vines: 20-25, years on average; newly planted 4 years.
Training: spurred cordon and fan.
Yield of grapes: 70 quintals per hectare.
Yield of wine: 50 hectolitre per hectare.
Harvest: handpicked during the first ten days of October.
Vinification: maceration on the skins for 15-18 days, with frequent pumping over and punching down. 20-25% of the must is drawn off and separated. Alcoholic fermentation in stainless steel vats at a controlled temperature of 27 C° max. Selected varietal and aromatic yeasts are added. Malolactic fermentation is carried out entirely in barriques.
Ageing: 12 months in French oak barriques of 225 litres (of which 50% are new) followed by 6 months in the bottle.
Production per annum: 16 000 bottles.
The wine: ruby red in colour; warm and full, with fragrances of ripe fruits of the forest and undertones of oak; dense tannins.
Serving temperature: 18 C°.
Food matches: grilled, roast, and braised meats, and game.

Rosso Sobrano. Umbria IGT.

Grapes: Sangiovese 70%, Cabernet Sauvignon 10%, Merlot 10%, and other red grapes 10%.
Vineyards: hilly and well exposed to the sun.
Soil: clayey and sedimentary.
Altitude: 300 metres above sea level.
Density of plants: traditional 3.00 x 1.50 metres, new plantings 3.00 x 0.80 metres.
Age of vines: 20-25, years on average, new plants 3 years.
Training: spurred cordon and fan.
Yield of grapes: 90 quintals per hectare.
Yield of wine: 70 hectolitre per hectare.
Harvest: at the end of September and the beginning of October.
Vinification: maceration on the skins for 7-8 days, with frequent pumping over and punching down. 20% of the must is drawn off and separated. Alcoholic fermentation is carried out at 27 C°, with selected varietal and aromatic yeasts added.
Bottling: at the beginning of March following the harvest.
Ageing: about 40 days in the bottle.
Production per annum: 30 000 bottles.
The wine: ruby red in colour; light hints of spices, full-bodied and dry, with aromas of fruits of the forest.
Serving temperature: 15 C°.
Food matches: red and white meats, substantial first courses even when truffle based.

Bianco della Cervara. Grechetto di Todi Colli Martani DOC.

Grapes: Grechetto 100%.
Vineyards: situated in the best Colli Martani production zones.
Soil: clayey and sedimentary.
Altitude: 300 metres above sea level.
Density of plants: traditional 3.00 x 1.50 metres, new plantings 3.00 x 0.80 metres.
Age of vines: 20-25, years on average, new plants 3 years.
Training: fan, cordon trained and spur pruned.
Yield of grapes: 90 quintals per hectare.

Yield of wine: 65 hectolitre per hectare.
Harvest: from 10th of September until 25th of September.
Vinification: pressing with pneumatic presses, then immediate separation from the skins, followed by settling and the removal of the must from lees. Alcoholic fermentation at a controlled temperature of 18 C° for 15 days in stainless steel; selected varietal and aromatic yeasts are added.
Blending: 10-15 % obtained from cold maceration, and 5% obtained from carbonic maceration.
Bottling: at the beginning of March following the harvest.
Ageing: at least 60 days in the bottle.
Production per annum: 25 000 bottles.
The wine: pale yellow in colour; complex but sharp and fresh.
Serving temperature: 13 C°.
Food matches: *hors d'oeuvres,* fish, seafood, and pasta.

Bianco S Isidiro. Umbria IGT.

Grapes: Grechetto 85%, other local white grape varieties 15%.
Soil: clayey and sedimentary.
Altitude: 300 metres above sea level.
Age of vines: 5 years on average, new plants 2 years.
Density of plants: traditional 2.80 x 0.80 metres.
Training: double cordons.
Yield of grapes: 110 quintals per hectare.
Yield of wine: 90 hectolitre per hectare.
Harvest: from the end of August to the beginning of September.
Vinification: pressing with pneumatic presses, then separation from the solid parts, then cold static decanting for clearing the must. Alcoholic fermentation at 18 C° for 15 days in stainless steel vats. Selected varietal and aromatic yeasts are added.
Bottling: at the beginning of February following the harvest.
Ageing: 30 days in the bottle.
Production per annum: 30 000 bottles.
The wine: yellow in colour, with shades of green; delicate, fruity, smooth, with a slightly bitter aftertaste.
Serving temperature: 10-12 C°.
Food matches: oysters, shellfish, delicate *hors d'oeuvres,* fish and vegetable dishes.

Spoletoducale Casale Triocco

Cantina Spoletoducale Casale Triocco
Località Petrognano, 54
06049 Spoleto PG
Tel: 0743 56224
Fax: 0743 56065
www.casaletriocco.it
info@casaletriocco.it

The Spoletoducale Casale Triocco is located amongst the hills surrounding Spoleto. The winery was established in 1969, and it also produces extra virgin olive oil. The *terroir* is ideal for the cultivation of vines and olive trees. The estate respects the vine growing and wine producing traditions of the land, and combines it with avant-garde technology. The wines are marketed as Casale Triocco and Spoletoducale separately. As the vineyards are spread over both the Montefalco and Colli Martani designated production zones, the winery makes both types of wines. The vineyards are located in the communes of Montefalco, Giano dell'Umbria, Trevi, Spoleto, Campello sul Clitunno, Castel Ritaldi, Cannara, Bevagna, Gualdo Cattaneo, Foligno, and Spello.

Casale Triocco. Montefalco Rosso DOC.

Grapes: 60-70% Sangiovese, 10-15% Sagrantino, and the rest is made up of other local red grapes.
Altitude: mostly hills around 250 and 450 metres above sea level.
Vinification: steeped on the skins for 8-10 days.
Ageing: 9 months in wooden casks, and 6 in the bottle.
The wine: ruby red in colour, tending to garnet; it is dry, well balanced and velvety.
Serving temperature: 18-20 C°.
Alcohol content: minimum 12% vol.

Casale Triocco. Sagrantino di Montefalco DOCG.

Grapes: Sagrantino 100%.
Altitude: mostly hills around 250 and 450 metres above sea level.
Vinification: steeped on the skins for 15 days.
Ageing: 12 months in wooden casks, and 6 in the bottle.
The wine: ruby red in colour, tending to garnet; with scents of blackberries; it is dry, well balanced, and velvety.
Serving temperature: 18-20 C°.
Alcohol content: minimum 13% vol.

Casale Triocco. Sagrantino di Montefalco Passito DOCG.

Grapes: Sagrantino 100%.
Altitude: mostly hills around 250 and 450 metres above sea level.
Vinification: after the drying, the grapes are steeped on the skins.
Ageing: 30 months.
The wine: vivid ruby red in colour, with violet reflections; scents of blackberries, a medium sweet and well balanced dessert wine.
Serving temperature: 18-20 C°.
Alcohol content: minimum 14% vol.

Casale Triocco. Pagina. Sagrantino di Montefalco DOCG.

Grapes: Sagrantino 100%.
Altitude: mostly hills around 250 and 450 metres above sea level.
Vinification: steeped on the skins for 15 days.
Ageing: 12 months in wooden casks, and 6 in the bottle.
The wine: ruby red in colour, tending to garnet; with scents of blackberries; dry, well balanced and velvety.
Serving temperature: 18-20 C°.
Alcohol content: minimum 13% vol.

Casale Triocco. Arcato. Colli Martani Sangiovese DOC.

Grapes: Sangiovese for at least 85%, the rest is made up of other local red grapes.
Altitude: mostly hills around 250 and 450 metres above sea level.

Vinification: steeped on the skins.
Ageing: in wooden casks, and in the bottle.
The wine: ruby red in colour, tending to garnet with ageing; dry, well balanced, slightly tannic when young, and pleasantly bitter.
Serving temperature: 18-20 C°.
Alcohol content: minimum 12% vol.

Casale Triocco. Arcato. Colli Martani Grechetto DOC.

Grapes: Grechetto 100%.
Altitude: mostly hills around 250 and 450 metres above sea level.
Vinification: soft pressing, then cold clarification of the must, followed by fermentation under controlled temperature.
The wine: straw yellow in colour; dry, or slightly sweet, velvety, fruity, and well balanced, with a slightly bitter aftertaste.
Serving temperature: 8-10 C°.
Alcohol content: minimum 12% vol.

Casale Triocco. Grappa di Sagrantino.

Grapes: pomace of Sagrantino di Montefalco.
Altitude: mostly hills around 250 and 450 metres above sea level.
Distillation: distilled with the traditional alembic technique.
Colour: transparent white.
Bouquet: delicate, fruity, with the scents of Sagrantino grapes.
Taste: intense, velvety, and smooth.
Serving temperature: serve at room temperature.
Alcohol content: 42% vol.

Spoletoducale. Montefalco Rosso DOC.

Grapes: 60-70% Sangiovese, 10-15% Sagrantino, and the rest is made up of other local red grapes.
Altitude: mostly hills around 250 and 450 metres above sea level.
Vinification: steeped on the skins for 8-10 days.
Ageing: 9 months in wooden casks, and 6 in the bottle.
The wine: ruby red, tending to garnet; dry, well balanced.
Serving temperature: 18-20 C°.
Alcohol content: minimum 13% vol.

Spoletoducale. Sagrantino di Montefalco DOCG.

Grapes: Sagrantino 100%.
Altitude: mostly hills around 250 and 450 metres above sea level.
Vinification: steeped on the skins for 15 days.
Ageing: 12 months in wooden casks, and 6 in the bottle.
The wine: ruby red in colour, tending to garnet; with scents of blackberries; dry, well balanced, and velvety.
Serving temperature: 18-20 C°.
Alcohol content: minimum 13.5% vol.

Spoletoducale. Sagrantino di Montefalco Passito DOCG.

Grapes: Sagrantino 100%.
Altitude: mostly hills around 250 and 450 metres above sea level.
Vinification: after the drying, the grapes are steeped on the skins.
Ageing: 30 months.
The wine: ruby red in colour, sometimes with violet reflections tending to garnet with ageing; with scents of blackberries; medium sweet, a well balanced and pleasant dessert wine.
Serving temperature: 18-20 C°.
Alcohol content: minimum 14.5% vol.

Spoletoducale. Pievano. Colli Martani Sangiovese DOC.

Grapes: Sangiovese for at least 85%, the rest is made up of other local red grapes.
Altitude: mostly hills around 250 and 450 metres above sea level.
Vinification: steeped on the skins.
Ageing: in wooden casks, and in the bottle.
The wine: ruby red in colour, tending to garnet with ageing; dry, well balanced, slightly tannic when young, and pleasantly bitter.
Serving temperature: 18-20 C°.
Alcohol content: minimum 12.5% vol.

Spoletoducale. Colli Martani Grechetto DOC.

Grapes: Grechetto 100%.
Altitude: mostly hills around 250 and 450 metres above sea level.
Vinification: soft pressing, then cold clarification of the must, followed by fermentation under controlled temperature.
The wine: straw yellow in colour; dry, or slightly sweet, velvety, fruity, and well balanced.
Serving temperature: 8-10 C°.
Alcohol content: minimum 12.5% vol.

Spoletoducale. Umbria Trebbiano Spoletino IGT.

Grapes: Trebbiano Spoletino 100%.
Altitude: mostly hills around 250 and 450 metres above sea level.
Vinification: soft pressing, then cold clarification of the must, followed by fermentation under controlled temperature.
The wine: straw yellow in colour, with greenish reflections; dry, with a slightly bitter aftertaste.
Serving temperature: 8-10 C°.
Alcohol content: minimum 12% vol.

Spoletoducale. Ducato del Sole. Umbria Rosso IGT.

Grapes: Sangiovese for at least 50%, the rest is made up of other local red grapes.
Altitude: mostly hills around 250 and 450 metres above sea level.
Vinification: steeped on the skins.
Ageing: in wooden casks, and in the bottle.
The wine: bright ruby red in colour, more or less intense; vinous, dry, savoury, and slightly astringent.
Serving temperature: 8-10 C°.
Alcohol content: minimum 12% vol.

Cantina Tudernum

Pian di Porto, 146
06059 Todi PG
Tel: 0758 989403
Fax: 0758 989189
www.tudernum.it
info@tudernum.it

Cantina Tudernum was founded in 1958 by 57 vineyard owners who joined together to produce and market wine as a co-operative. Initially, the estate consisted only of a few hectares of cultivated land, but grew steadily to reach 650 hectares of vineyards between 1975 and 1995.

In 1995 the vineyards were reduced to the current 400 hectares as part of a company-wide development plan. Over 320 hectares were planted with reduced spacing between the vines, and for this, grape varieties of higher quality were selected. New pruning technologies were introduced, which reduced production costs, yet at the same time, produced higher quality grapes.

These changes were matched by changes in the winery. Stainless steel tanks with 50, 80, and 100-hectolitre capacity were introduced. Ageing was carried out in wooden barrels and barriques. Soft pressing technologies were adapted, and processing equipment for red grapes was introduced to allow working with small quantities of selected grapes for the production of superior quality wines. In addition, bottling and packaging were brought back in-house.

The last ten years have also been defined by constant research. In collaboration with the University of Milan, studies were made on identifying the original Grechetto di Todi grape, much admired for its superior quality and unique characteristics. A new study is underway to identify the Grechetto Nero, a red grape, in order to bring this long lost variety back on the market.

In 2006 Cantina Tudernum has begun distribution in the European Union, and the United States of America.

Sagrantino di Montefalco DOCG.

Grapes: Sagrantino 100%.
Production zone: Montefalco.
Altitude: 400 metres above sea level.
Density of vines: 2.5 x 0.90 metres.
Density of cultivation: 4500 vines per hectare.
Training: spurred cordon.
Yield of grapes: 70-80 quintals per hectare.
Harvest: 10th to 15th October.
Vinification: long steeping.
Ageing: for 30 months total; 12 months in oak barrels and 6 months in the bottle.
The wine: ruby red in colour, with garnet reflections; scents of ripe fruits and spices; dry, tannic, and a good structure.
Serving temperature: 18 C°.
Food matches: red meat, game, and mature cheeses.
Alcoholic content: 14-14.5% vol.

Collenobile. Grechetto di Todi. Colli Martani DOC.

Grapes: Grechetto 100%.
Production zone: Colli Martani.
Altitude: 300-400 metres above sea level.
Density of vines: 3.00 x 1.00 metres.
Density of cultivation: 3300 vines per hectare.
Training: spurred cordon.
Yield of grapes: 90-100 quintals per hectare.
Harvest: 25th September to 15th October.
Vinification: soft pressing, cryomaceration at 7 C°, followed by fermentation in barriques.
Ageing: in stainless steel vats.
The wine: straw yellow in colour, with golden reflections; fruity, with the scent of apples and caramel; soft, with balanced acidity and a light almond aftertaste.
Serving temperature: 10-12 C°.
Food matches: starters, fish, shellfish, and spicy cheeses.
Alcoholic content: 13-13.5% vol.

Rojano. Rosso dell'Umbria IGT.

Grapes: Sangiovese, Merlot, and Sagrantino.
Production zone: Umbria.
Altitude: 300-400 metres above sea level.
Density of vines: 3.00 x 1.00 metres.
Density of cultivation: 3300 vines per hectare.
Training: spurred cordon.
Yield of grapes: 80 quintals per hectare.
Harvest: 1st to 15th October.
Vinification: long steeping.
Ageing: 12 months in barrels then refined in the bottle.
The wine: red in colour with violet reflections; scents of ripe fruits and spices; a gentle structure, with a tannic aftertaste.
Serving temperature: 18 C°.
Food matches: red meat, game, mature cheeses, and soups.
Alcoholic content: 13-13.5% vol.

Grechetto di Todi. Colli Martani DOC.

Grapes: Grechetto 100%.
Production zone: Colli Martani.
Altitude: 300-400 metres above sea level.
Density of vines: 3.00 x 1.00 metres.
Density of cultivation: 3300 vines per hectare.
Training: spurred cordon.
Yield of grapes: 100 quintals per hectare.
Harvest: 15th September to 5th October.
Vinification: soft pressing followed by fermentation at 15-16 C°.
Ageing: in stainless steel vats.
The wine: intense straw yellow in colour, with golden reflections; fruity, with scents of honey and caramel; soft, with balanced acidity and a light almond aftertaste.
Serving temperature: 10-12 C°.
Food matches: soups, white meat, cheeses, fish, and shellfish.
Alcoholic content: 12.5-13% vol.

Sangiovese. Colli Martani DOC.

Grapes: Sangiovese, and Merlot.
Production zone: Colli Martani.
Altitude: 300 metres above sea level.
Density of vines: 3.00 x 1.00 metres.
Density of cultivation: 3300 vines per hectare.
Training: spurred cordon.
Yield of grapes: 100-120 quintals per hectare.
Harvest: 1st to 10th October.
Vinification: medium steeping.
Ageing: 6 months in oak barrels, refined in the bottle.
The wine: ruby red, with violet reflections; scents of ripe red fruits and vanilla; with a gentle structure and tannic aftertaste.
Serving temperature: 18 C°.
Food matches: red meats, game, mature cheeses, and soups.
Alcoholic content: 12.5-13% vol.

Bianco. Colli Martani DOC.

Grapes: Grechetto, and Chardonnay.
Production zone: Colli Martani.
Altitude: 200-300 metres above sea level.
Density of vines: 3.00 x 1.00 metres.
Density of cultivation: 3300 vines per hectare.
Training: spurred cordon.
Yield of grapes: 120 quintals per hectare.
Harvest: 20th September to 10th October.
Vinification: soft pressing followed by fermentation at 15-16 C°.
Ageing: in stainless steel vats.
The wine: soft yellow in colour, with greenish reflections; fruity, with the scent of white thorn; fresh with a balanced acidity and pleasant aftertaste of nuts.
Food matches: soups, white meat, fish, shellfish, and mussels.
Serving temperature: 8-10 C°.
Alcoholic content: 12-12.5% vol.

Zàzzera

Zàzzera Vigne e Vini
Via Tiberina, 159
06059 Todi PG
Tel: 0758 948557
Fax: 0758 944970
www.zazzeravini.it
info@zazzeravini.it

The *Azienda Agraria "Il Vallone"* is situated in a small valley amongst the Martani Hills, some 5 kilometres from Todi. It is a little oasis of unspoilt beauty, spread over 50 hectares of rich and fertile land. The hillsides are constantly exposed to the sun, and the terrain is particularly well suited for the cultivation of vines. The Zàzzera winery is located in an old fashioned farmhouse at the foot of a gently sloping hill amongst the vineyards and olive groves. A closely-knit family runs the estate: they cultivate the vines, handpick the grapes, and carry out the vinification of the grapes. They are constantly looking for new ways to make the best use of the land. Their hard work and professional dedication to winemaking results in top quality wines.

Biccicocco. Colli Martani Rosso IGT.

Grapes: Merlot 100%.
The wine: deep red in colour, with purple reflections; an intense fragrance of fruits of the forest, with spicy hints acquired from having been aged and refined in barriques. It is a dry, well-structured and fully balanced wine.
Alcohol content: 14% vol.

Rubaconte. Colli Martani Rosso IGT.

Grapes: Sangiovese 100%.
The wine: deep ruby red in colour; with floral notes; dry taste and medium structure.
Alcohol content: 13.5% vol.

Barbadoro. Grechetto di Todi. Colli Martani DOC.

Grapes: Grechetto di Todi 100%.
The wine: straw yellow in colour, with golden reflections; the fragrance of fresh fruits with floral notes; soft, fruity and dry.
Alcohol content: 14% vol.

THE WINE PRODUCERS
LAGO DI CORBARA

In 1998 an executive Decree recognised the DOC appellation for the Lago di Corbara red wines, for which the IGT had already been conferred in 1995. The designated production area is spread around the hills surrounding Lake Corbara, including the municipality of Baschi, and the outlying territory of Orvieto: i.e. Corbara, Fossatello, Colonetta di Prodo, and Titignano.

The principal grapes used are Cabernet Sauvignon, Merlot, Pinot Nero and Sangiovese, and they should either be used alone or blended for at least 70%. The additional grapes are Aleatico, Barbera, Cabernet Franc, Canaiolo, Cesanese, Ciliegiolo, Colorino, Dolcetto and Montepulciano. The Lago di Corbara DOC wines containing the specific name of one of the grapes, such as Cabernet Sauvignon, Merlot, or Pinot Nero, have to be made of at least 85% from the designated variety. The remaining 15% can be composed of red wine grapes recommended and/or authorised by the Province of Terni.

The lake is the dominant geographical feature of the area. It was created in the 1960s, when a 641-metre long dam was erected across the River Tiber. The lake is between 30-40 metres deep and extends for some 13 square kilometres from Todi towards Orvieto. The road that runs around the lake is particularly spectacular as it winds in and out a number of gorges amongst steep hills covered with dense woods. The lake is named after the village of Corbara, dating back to the 12th century, when it was situated on the right-bank of the Tiber.

The river had been navigable since Etruscan times. During 1889 the remains of the Roman port of Pagliano were discovered at the confluence of the rivers Paglia and Tevere, just downstream from the present-day lake. This archaeological site gained great importance in the study of commercial and economic relations between Imperial Rome and the hinterland. Wine from Orvieto was sent to Rome amongst many other things. Later, stones from the Travertino quarries were rowed down on huge rafts to Rome, and used for building churches and palaces. The Tiber was a major thoroughfare in the past, and important enough to be safely guarded, hence, the Counts of Montemarte constructed a fortified castle overlooking the Tiber at Corbara. Today only its ruins remain. Farolfo di Montemarte built another castle further up a hill at Titignano. Stones from the Travertino quarries were used for its construction.

During the 1300s the inhabitants of Todi imprisoned Andrea di Montemarte for some misdemeanour. He was set free eventually, but obliged to retire to the castles of Titignano and Corbara. Over the following centuries the Montemarte family extended their lands increasingly towards Orvieto, and became active in the political life of the city. The family seat was at Corbara, although the Montemarte name was listed amongst the Orvieto city gentry at least up to the 17th century.

There is archaeological evidence that the cultivation of vines and the production of wine continued without interruption from the Etruscan period right up to today.

Castello di Corbara

Azienda Agricola Castello di Corbara s.r.l.
Località Corbara n° 7,
05018 Orvieto TR
Tel: 0763 304035
Fax: 0763 304055
www.castellodicorbara.it
info@castellodicorbara.it

In the land register of 1292 Corbara was listed as a *Castrum* (Castle) in the rural parish of Santa Maria da Stiolo, the same area covered by the present day Castello di Corbara estate. The castle was the home of the Montemarte family, then, at the end of the 19th century it became the property of the Banca Romana.

In 1997 the estate changed hands again, and the new proprietors are dedicated to carry on the tradition, with respect for the land and a desire to reflect the unique qualities of the *terroir* in every single bottle of wine produced.

The estate covers more than 1000 hectares of vineyards of different grape varieties grown in a wide variety of soils located between 100 and 350 metres above sea level. The red wines are produced as Lago di Corbara DOC. However, some of the vineyards are in the DOC Orvieto and Orvieto Classico DOC production area. Each new planting is carried out after analysing the microclimate and studying the soil profile. The great extent of the land allows experimentation in cultivation, which leads to producing quality grapes reflecting the character of the land.

The estate is equipped with a modern wine cellar designed for precision vinification. Only grapes grown in the estate's vineyards are harvested. They are carefully selected for the best bunches and handpicked only when they are completely ripe. The harvest takes place during the coolest hours of the day, in order to avoid any sort of undesired form of fermentation. The numerous clones of the different grape varieties are picked separately. The selection continues at the winery as the grapes are placed on a conveyor belt, before being processed. The different grapes are also vinified separately, and only after the fermentation process is completed, are they blended. For ageing the wine in the wood, a separate area is provided, where humidity and temperature is meticulously controlled. The barriques are made of French oak (Alliers, Jupille, and Nevers). Larger barrels are made of Slovenian oak.

Castello di Corbara. Lago di Corbara DOC.

Grapes: predominance of Sangiovese, Merlot, and Cabernet Sauvignon; some presence of Montepulciano.
Vineyards: Poggio, Nocetto, Ponticello, Corone, Calistri, and Viavalle.
Altitude: hilly slopes at 200-300 metres above sea level with south-south/west exposure.
Soil: from medium to loosely packed clayey and sandy soil.
Training: spurred cordon, pruned with 6-8 buds.
Yield: not more than 70 quintals per hectare.
Harvest: during the last ten days of September and early October; selected and handpicked grapes.
Vinification: alcoholic fermentation in stainless steel vats at a controlled temperature of 25-28 C°, maceration for around 12-15 days with frequent punching down the head, then followed by malolactic fermentation in the wood.
Ageing: 80% in French oak barriques and 20% in Slovenian oak casks for 12 months. Followed by bottle ageing for 5-6 months in the cellars at a temperature of 15-16 C°.
Bottle: Bordolese Storica 75 cl.
The wine: ruby red in colour; scents of ripe fruit with hints of spices, coffee, vanilla, prunes, violets, chestnut, and tobacco. It tastes full and round, with soft tannins and a lingering aftertaste.
Alcohol content: 13.5% vol.

Castello di Corbara. Lago di Corbara DOC Cabernet Sauvignon.

Grapes: Cabernet Sauvignon 100%.
Vineyards: Ponticello.
Altitude: hilly slopes at 200-300 metres above sea level with a south-south/west exposure.

Soil: alluvial, with the presence of pebbles.
Training: spurred cordon, pruned with 6-8 buds.
Yield: not more than 70 quintals per hectare.
Harvest: during the last ten days of September and early October; selected and handpicked grapes.
Vinification: alcoholic fermentation in stainless steel vats at a controlled temperature of 25-28 C°, maceration for around 12-15 days with frequent punching down the head, then followed by malolactic fermentation in the wood.
Ageing: in French oak casks for 12 months. Followed by bottle ageing for 5-6 months in the cellars at a temperature of 15-16 C°.
Bottle: Bordolese Storica 75 cl.
The wine: intense ruby red in colour; with fragrances of wild red berries and ripe prunes, herbaceous nuances, tobacco and vanilla overtones. It tastes full and round, with soft tannins and a lingering aftertaste.
Alcohol content: 13.5% vol.

Castello di Corbara. Lago di Corbara DOC Merlot Riserva.

Grapes: Merlot 100%.
Production zone: hilly slopes at 300 metres above sea level with a south-south/west exposure.
Vineyards: De Coronis (Corone).
Soil: medium consistency, alluvial substrata.
Training: spurred cordon, pruned with 6-8 buds.
Yield: not more than 40 quintals per hectare.
Harvest: during the first half of September; selected and handpicked grapes.
Vinification: alcoholic fermentation at 25-28 C°, maceration for around 15-18 days with punching down the head, then followed by malolactic fermentation in the wood.
Ageing: in 500 litre French oak casks (Tonneaux) for 16 months, then in the bottle from 7-9 months at 15-16 C°.
Bottle: Bordolese Ducale 75 cl.
The wine: intense ruby red in colour; with aromas of ripe fruit, blackberries, cherries, vanilla and black pepper. It has soft tannins and a lingering aftertaste.
Alcohol content: 13.5% vol.

Calistri. Sangiovese Riserva IGT Umbria.

Grapes: Sangiovese 100%.
Production zone: hilly slopes at 250 metres above sea level with a south-south/west exposure.
Vineyards: Calistri.
Soil: loosely packed soil, alluvial.
Training: Guyot, pruned with 6-8 buds.
Yield: not more than 50 quintals per hectare.
Harvest: during the second half of September; selected and handpicked grapes.
Vinification: alcoholic fermentation at 25-28 C°, maceration for around 15-18 days with punching down the head.
Ageing: in small French oak casks for 16 months, then bottle ageing from 7-9 months at 15-16 C°.
Bottle: Bordolese Ducale 75 cl.
The wine: intense ruby red in colour; with aromas of violets, tobacco and liquorice; soft tannins, with a long aftertaste.
Alcohol content: 13.5% vol.

Podere il Caio. Rosso IGT Umbria.

Grapes: Sangiovese, Merlot, Cabernet Sauvignon, and Montepulciano.
Production zone: hilly slopes at 150-300 metres above sea level with a south-south/west exposure.
Vineyards: Poggio, Noceto, Il Caio, and Ponticello.
Soil: from medium to loosely packed clayey and sandy soil.
Training: spurred cordon, pruned with 6-8 buds.
Yield: not more than 70 quintals per hectare.
Harvest: during the last third of September to early October.
Vinification: alcoholic fermentation in stainless steel vats at a controlled temperature of 25-28 C°, maceration for around 12-15 days with punching down the head.
Ageing: 80% in French oak barriques and 20% in Slovenian oak casks for 3-5 months, then bottle ageing from 2-3 months in a temperature controlled wine cellar at 15-16 C°.
Bottle: Bordolese Vip 75 cl.

The wine: ruby red in colour; with aromas of ripe fruit, spices, prunes, chestnut, and tobacco; soft tannins and a long aftertaste.
Alcohol content: 13% vol.

Campo della Fiera. Rosso Sangiovese IGT Umbria.

Grapes: Sangiovese 80%, Cabernet Sauvignon 10%, and Merlot 10%.
Production zone: hilly slopes at 150-300 metres above sea level with a south-south/west exposure.
Vineyards: Poggio Noceto, Ponticello, and Viavalle.
Soil: from medium to loosely packed clayey and sandy soil.
Training: spurred cordon, pruned with 6-8 buds.
Yield: not more than 80 quintals per hectare.
Harvest: during the last third of September to early October.
Vinification: alcoholic fermentation in stainless steel vats at a controlled temperature of 25-28 C°, maceration for around 12-15 days with punching down the head. Malolactic fermentation in stainless steel vats.
Ageing: in the bottle from 2-3 months at 15-16 C°.
Bottle: Bordolese standard 75 cl.
The wine: ruby red in colour; delicate scents, with violet and liquorice hints; soft tannins and a long aftertaste.
Alcohol content: 13% vol.

Podere il Caio. Orvieto Classico Superiore DOC.

Grapes: Grechetto, Malvasia, and Sauvignon.
Production zone: hilly slopes at 200 metres above sea level with a South/Southwest exposure.
Vineyards: Terzano, Il Caio, and Il Poggio.
Soil: clayey, with good loam deposits.
Training: spurred cordon, pruned with 8-10 buds.
Yield: not more than 80 quintals per hectare.
Harvest: during the second half of September; selected and handpicked separately, according to the grape variety.
Vinification: separately vinified according to grape variety in stainless steel vats at a controlled temperature of 15-18 C°, using

The Wines of Umbria

selected yeasts; alcoholic fermentation continues for 20-25 days, leaving the wine on the lees for around 2 months.
Ageing: once the wine is racked, it is decanted and bottled.
Bottle: Bordolese Vip 75 cl.
The wine: straw gold in colour; with scents of ripe fruit, pears and apricots; aromatic, with the right degree of tartness.
Alcohol content: 13% vol.

Podere il Caio. Grechetto IGT Umbria.

Grapes: Grechetto 100%.
Production zone: hilly slopes at 200 metres above sea level with a south-south/west exposure.
Vineyards: Il Caio, and Il Poggio.
Soil: clayey, with good loam deposits.
Training: spurred cordon, pruned with 8-10 buds.
Yield: not more than 80 quintals per hectare.
Harvest: during the second half of September.
Vinification: in stainless steel vats at a controlled temperature of 15-18 C°, using selected yeasts; alcoholic fermentation continues for 20-25 days, leaving the wine on the lees for around 2 months.
Ageing: once the wine is racked, it is decanted and bottled.
Bottle: Bordolese Vip 75 cl.
The wine: pale yellow in colour, with greenish reflections; with a delicate aroma of fruit, pears in particular. It is moderately tart, with a fruity aftertaste.
Alcohol content: 13% vol.

Orzalume. Bianco IGT Umbria.

Grapes: Grechetto, Sauvignon, Falanghina, and Greco di Tufo.
Production zone: hilly slopes at 350 metres above sea level with a south-south/west exposure.
Vineyards: Orzalume.
Soil: medium consistency, alluvial substrata, clayey, with good loam deposits.
Training: spurred cordon, pruned with 8-10 buds.
Yield: not more than 60 quintals per hectare.

Harvest: during the first half of September; selected and handpicked, according to the grape variety.

Vinification: separately vinified according to grape variety, fermentation takes place in small (225 litres) French barriques, using selected yeasts; then leaving the wine on the lees for 5 months in order to impart full aroma and bouquet to the wine.

Ageing: once the wine is racked the wines are blended, decanted and prepared for bottling.

Bottle: Bordolese Vip 75 cl.

The wine: straw gold in colour; with aromas of ripe fruits, mainly pears and apricots, with overtones of vanilla. It is complex, well structured, with some mineral notes; and a ripe fruit aftertaste enriched by hints of oak.

Alcohol content: 13% vol.

Salviano

Tenuta di Salviano
Loc. Titignano
05018 Orvieto TR
Tel: 0763 308000 and 0763 308002
www.titignano.com
info@titignano.com

Titignano castle was an important supporting fort to the Castle of Corbara, home to the Counts of Montemarte. During the 16th and 17th centuries the Guelphs of Orvieto and the Ghibellines of Todi contested it. With hostilities over, the fort was transformed into a palace and a small village. In 1800 an auction was held at which the estate fell into the hands of Prince Don Tommaso di Filippo Corsini, and today, it is a flourishing farm, and still a castle. It has been restructured into an "Agriturismo" without losing its charm. It welcomes visitors to enjoy their stay in the romantic setting inside the walls of Titignano Castle, and to sample the traditional cuisine and the wines produced on the estate. From the side of the swimming pool there is a wonderful view of the lake and the mountains all around, and naturally, it is an ideal venue for a weekend break from city life, or for a wedding reception accommodating hundreds of guests.

Facing Titignano on the opposite side of Lake Corbara, there is another castle, Salviano. It also belongs to the Corsini family. The winery of the estate is located at Salviano. The vineyards cover 70 hectares amongst the hills surrounding the lake, ranging from 150 to 500 meters above sea level, with a south-south/west exposure. The clayey, sandy soil is rich in limestone, and it is ideal for the cultivation of vines.

The winery is equipped with modern equipment for the vinification of the grapes. Ageing is carried out in small oak barrels inside the caves dug into the tufa under the castle, which guarantees even temperatures and humidity all year round.

Solideo. Lago di Corbara DOC.

Grapes: Cabernet Sauvignon 80%, and Merlot 20%.
Annual production: 15 000 bottles.
Vineyards: hilly slopes at 150-380 metres above sea level, and the density of 5000 vines per hectare.
Vinification: the grape varieties are handpicked, and harvested separately. Alcoholic fermentation takes place on the skins for 15-20 days at a controlled temperature. After racking the wine, malolactic fermentation is carried out in French barriques (new, and some used once before), still keeping the varietals separately.
Ageing: 18-20 months, followed by stabilisation of the wines, blending and bottling, then a period of refinement in the bottle.
The wine: intense ruby red in colour, verging on garnet with ageing. It has a fruity and spicy fragrance, with hints of vanilla; well-balanced, soft tannins, and a good ageing potential.
Alcoholic content: 13.5-14% vol.

Turlo. Lago di Corbara DOC.

Grapes: Sangiovese 50%, Cabernet Sauvignon 30%, and Merlot 20%.
Annual production: 80 000 bottles.
Vineyards: at 150-380 metres above sea level; south-south/west exposure, with clayey, sandy soil, and rich in limestone.
Vinification: alcoholic fermentation takes place in small stainless steel vats at a controlled temperature. Steeping lasts for 12 days, with frequent pumping over. Malolactic fermentation is carried out for 20 –25 days at 20-22 C°. The wine is refined partly in vitrified cement vats, and partly in oak barriques.
The wine: intense ruby red in colour. It has a fruity fragrance, with well-balanced, soft tannins, and a good ageing potential.
Alcoholic content: 13-13.5% vol.

Salviano. Orvieto Classico Superiore DOC.

Grapes: Trebbiano Toscano (Procanico) 30%, Grechetto 30%, Chardonnay and Sauvignon Blanc 40%.
Annual production: 80 000 bottles.

Vineyards: hilly slopes at 150-380 metres above sea level, above the North bank of Lake Corbara. The exposure varies from south/west-south to east-south/east.
Vinification: The grapes are harvested separately according to their variety and their musts are also kept separately. They are chilled for static clarification, then fermented at a controlled temperature in stainless steel. When fermentation is completed, the wine is drawn off, and refined in vitrified cement vats.
The wine: straw yellow in colour. It has an aromatic and tasty intensity, thanks to the mature Chardonnay, Sauvignon and Grechetto. The acidic freshness is guaranteed by the Procanico.
Alcoholic content: 12.5-13.5% vol.

Salviano di Salviano. Bianco IGT Umbria.

Grapes: Sauvignon 50%, and Chardonnay 50%.
Annual production: 6 000 bottles.
Vineyards: hilly slopes at 350-500 metres above sea level. The exposure varies from south-west/south to east-south/east. The soil contains old fossils and sedimentary rocks.
Vinification: The grapes are harvested separately according to their variety and their musts are also kept separately. They are chilled for static clarification of the must, then fermented in barriques, where the wine remains for 4-5 months. When the wine is drawn off, it is refined in vitrified cement vats until it is ready to be bottled, which happens at the end of March.
The wine: golden yellow in colour. It has a fresh fragrance of grapes and soft aromatic notes and tannins. It is fruity and floral; savoury and rounded to the palate, but persistent and elegant.
Alcoholic content: 12.5% vol.

Vendemmia Tardiva.

Grapes: Procanico, Grechetto, and Sauvignon.
Annual production: 5 000 bottles.
Vineyards: hilly slopes at 150-500 metres above sea level. The exposure varies from south-west/south to east-south/east.
Vinification: Late harvest. The grapes are handpicked and carried in cases to the cellars. They are then soft pressed and

chilled for static clarification, then fermented in barriques used before for the vinification of white wines. Selected yeasts are added. The fermentation takes place at room temperature until the wine reaches 14.5% vol. After decanting the wine it is filtered and cool sterile bottled during April and May.

The wine: pale gold in colour. It is concentrated and elegant, with subtle aromas of the grapes, and a complex bouquet due to the development of noble rot before harvesting. It has an aromatic and acidic freshness, which makes it pleasant and inviting.

Alcoholic content: 14.5% vol.

Barbi

Azienda Agricola Decugnano dei Barbi
Loc. Fossatello, 50
05019 Orvieto TR
Tel: 0763 308255
Fax: 0763 308118
www.decognanodeibarbi.com
info@decognanodeibarbi.com

IL ROSSO
DECUGNANO
2008

The estate of is perched on a hill overlooking Orvieto. The vineyards are within the old zone of production of Orvieto Classico wines. The name "Decugnano" has been used for at least eight centuries to indicate the land of the estate, and vine growing dates back to ancient times: Decugnano wine appears in old documents going back to the 13th century when the clergy owned the estate, known as "Santa Maria di Decugnano".

Claudio Barbi bought the property in 1973, and turned it into a modern and innovative estate. Decugnano dei Barbi introduced the first sparkling wine from Umbria to the market in 1978, and also the first Italian *muffa nobile, "Pourriture Noble"* in 1981.

The soil is of marine origin, marly, clayey, and rich in fossilised oysters and shells of the Pliocene age. The climate, the microclimate, the constant breeze, and a wide temperature range make it particularly suitable for growing vines. In addition to a modern and technologically advanced wine cellar, Decugnano dei Barbi uses large and impressive caves excavated in the lava rock, in order to produce the sparkling wine and to age certain wines in barrels. The temperature is always around 14 C° and the relative humidity is close to 100%. These conditions are essential factors for producing top quality wines.

<u>Il Bianco di Decugnano. Orvieto DOC Classico Superiore.</u>

Grapes: typical of Orvieto Classico.
First year of production: 1978.
The best grapes from eight different vineyards are picked to produce this wine. They are separately fermented, then blended.

It is a wine of great elegance, good balance, very mineral: the best expression of Decugnano's terroir.

Maris. Umbria IGT.

Grapes: Chardonnay.
First year of production: 2008.
Maris comes from Chardonnay grapes grown on soil rich in fossils and oyster shells. The harmonious balance between the grapes and the soil, originated from Pliocene seas, produces a sophisticated wine, fine on the palate, refreshing and mineral.

Il Rosso di Decugnano. Umbria IGT.

Grapes: Sangiovese, Montepulciano, and Syrah.
First year of production: 1979.
The best vineyards of the estate contribute to the creation of this wine. A meticulous vinification, a partial ageing in French oak barrels and a precise blending of the grape varieties, contribute to make an aristocratic wine, harmonious and elegant.

Decugnano Pinot Nero. IGT Umbria.

Grapes: 100% Pinot Nero.
Vintage: 2007.
The wine is ruby red in colour. The bouquet is intense, and typical of Pinot Nero. The taste is rich, full-bodied, and intensely sapid.
Ageing: in barriques for six months in natural caves, at ideal temperature and humidity, then in the bottle for six months.
Ageing: it is excellent when four years old
Serving temperature: 16°-18 ° C, (61°-64° F).
Food matches: strong, savoury dishes such as roasts and game, red meat, and hard cheeses.
Alcohol content: 13.5% vol.
Total acidity: 4.50 g/l.
Residual sugar: 3.5 g/l.
Available in 750 ml bottles.

Pourriture Noble (Muffa Nobile). Umbria IGT.

Grapes: Grechetto, Sauvignon Blanc, and Semillon.
First year of production: 1981.
Pourriture Noble is a sweet wine, originating from grapes that, due to natural microclimatic conditions have been affected by the noble rot. Harvesting is performed in different stages. The immediate pressing and a long fermentation, produces this rarity: a precious wine, which is the result of a natural phenomenon.

Decugnano Brut Metodo Classico.

Grapes: Chardonnay, Verdello, and Procanico.
First year of production: 1978
This Brut vintage is born from the selection of the best grapes and intelligent vinification. Refined in bottles for four years, with selected yeasts, it is kept in natural caves with a constant temperature of 13° C. It is fresh on the palate, with a fine and persistent perlage.

Villa Barbi Bianco. Orvieto DOC Classico.

Grapes: Grechetto, Procanico, Vermentino, and Sauvignon Blanc.
It is a fresh wine, fine on the palate, harmonious, and it is ideal for serving with everyday dishes.

Villa Barbi Rosso. Umbria IGT.

Grapes: Sangiovese, Montepulciano, and Merlot.
It is an intense wine, soft, with a well-balanced body. It is the perfect match for traditional dishes.

Barberani

Azienda Agricola Barberani,
Loc. Cerreto – Baschi TR
Tel: 0763 341820
Fax: 0763 340773
www.barberani.com
barberani@barberani.it

There is an additional point of sale at the Barberani Wine Shop on the corner of Piazza del Duomo and Via Maitani in Orvieto.

The Barberani Wine Company is situated just south of Orvieto, amongst the hills above Lake Corbara, along the River Tiber. The estate covers more than 100 hectares, of which 55 are specialised vineyards, each unique for its *terroir*. Every single vineyard has been planted to harmonise the different grape varieties, the micro-climatic conditions, and the soil. The vines are mostly indigenous grape varieties that have grown on the hillsides for thousands of years. The estate believes in the opportunities offered from such a long tradition, combined with a modern and innovative approach. The high density of the vines per hectare and the Guyot training system raises the level of the varietal taste of every single grape grown. The cellars are equipped with the best that modern technology can offer in controlling vinification, using natural procedures instead of chemical treatments. Visitors are invited to taste and purchase the wines in the shop attached to the winery. The estate also produces grappa, and Extra Virgin Olive Oil.

Castagnolo Secco. Orvieto DOC Classico Superiore.

Grapes: the five traditional varieties, mostly Grechetto, but also including Chardonnay and Riesling.
The wine: light and brilliant straw yellow in colour; fruity, with an intense bouquet, good structure and a lingering finish.
Serving temperature: 10-12 C°.

Food matches: aperitif, seafood appetisers, delicate first courses, boiled and grilled fish, and white meats.

Pulicchio Amabile. Orvieto DOC Classico Superiore.

Grapes: Grechetto, Trebbiano Procanico, Verdello, Malvasia, and Drupeggio.
The wine: light and brilliant straw yellow in colour; fruity, medium sweet, with a good structure and a lingering finish.
Serving temperature: 8-10 C°.
Food matches: appetisers, *pâté de foie gras*, sharp cheeses, desserts and sweet biscuits.

Calcaia Dolce "Muffa Nobile". Orvieto DOC Classico Superiore.

Grapes: the five traditional varieties used for Orvieto wine, with Sauvignon in addition.
First vintage: 1986.
On autumn mornings, a thick fog surrounds the Calcaia vineyards that helps the development of *Botrytis Cinera* (Noble Rot), and followed by sunny evenings, the grapes dehydrate, which concentrates the sugar content and the level of acidity. This is why the wines are so aromatically complex compared to other late harvest wines, or wines made from dried grapes. The *Botrytis Cinera* attacks every different bunch of grapes at different times. The harvesters only pick the grapes affected by the Noble Rot. For this reason, there are five or six different separate harvests during November in order to gather all the grapes. The musts are rich and concentrated. The fermentation process takes a long time, until it stops naturally.
The wine: golden yellow in colour; rich, mellow, and a buttery taste, a sweet dessert wine, with a lingering finish.
Serving temperature: 8-12 C°.
Food matches: *pâté de foie gras*, appetisers, goat and sharp cheeses, and sweet biscuits. Truly a "meditation wine".

Orvieto DOC Classico. Secco e Amabile.

Grapes: Grechetto, Trebbiano, Procanico, Verdello, Malvasia, and Drupeggio.
The wine: light straw yellow in colour; fresh, and fruity, with a good structure; dry or medium sweet.
Serving temperature: 8-10 C°.
Food matches: the dry for aperitifs, appetisers, fish, and white meat dishes. The medium sweet is best at the end of a meal.

Grechetto. Umbria IGT Bianco.

Grapes: Grechetto.
The wine: brilliant straw yellow in colour; aromas of pears; dry, full-bodied, with a complex structure.
Serving temperature: 10-12 C°.
Food matches: first courses, fish, and white meat dishes.

Grechetto. Villa Monticelli. Umbria IGT Bianco.

Grapes: Grechetto.
The wine: brilliant straw yellow in colour; dry, full-bodied, with a slightly mineral aftertaste.
Food matches: first courses, fish, and white meat dishes.
Serving temperature: 14-15 C°.

Moscato Passito. Villa Monticelli. Umbria IGT Bianco.

Grapes: Moscato.
The grapes are allowed to ripen and mature on the vine. The sun dries the grapes, and concentrates their sugar content.
The wine: amber yellow in colour; fruity, fragrant, with scents of tropical fruits, peaches, and apricots; a good "meditation wine".
Serving temperature: 12-14 C°.
Food matches: fruit cakes, almond tarts, nuts, and sweet biscuits.

Rosato Vallesanta. Umbria IGT.

Grapes: Sangiovese, and Montepulciano.
White winemaking methods are used to produce this rosé wine.
The wine: brilliant and intense pink in colour; fruity scents, with floral hints; lively and fresh.
Ageing: in the bottle.
Serving temperature: 10-12 C°.
Food matches: a very versatile wine; makes an ideal aperitif.

Rosso Villa Monticelli. Lago di Corbara DOC.

Grapes: Sangiovese, Cabernet Sauvignon, and Merlot.
The wine: ruby red in colour; ethereal scents, and a smooth body.
Ageing: 18 months in French oak barrels.
Serving temperature: 16-18 C°.
Food matches: grilled and roast red meats, game, and cheeses.

Foresco. Umbria IGT Rosso.

Grapes: Sangiovese, Cabernet Sauvignon, and Merlot.
The wine: ruby red; pleasantly tannic, with a good body.
Ageing: 12 months in French oak barrels.
Serving temperature: 16-18 C°.
Food matches: first courses, game, grilled and roast red meats.

Polago. Umbria IGT Rosso.

Grapes: Sangiovese, and Montepulciano.
The wine: ruby red in colour; fruity and slightly herbaceous, a good body, and a lively, lingering aroma.
Ageing: in the bottle.
Serving temperature: 16-18 C°.
Food matches: roast red meats, game, and sharp cheeses.

Sangiovese. Umbria IGT Rosso.

Grapes: Sangiovese.
The wine: ruby red in colour; fruity and spicy, with floral hints.

Ageing: in the bottle.
Serving temperature: 16-18 C°.
Food matches: chicken, pork, game, and sharp cheeses.

Grappa di Orvieto Classico. Castagnolo and Calcaia Riserva.

Distilled with traditional methods, using a "charente" steam still, with low degree columns and a discontinuous system.
Ageing: Calcaia grappa only, eighteen months in 225-litre French oak barriques.
Colour: Castagnolo is white, the Calcaia is intense straw yellow.
Bouquet: Castagnolo has a fresh, delicate, but highly pronounced bouquet, and Calcaia has a rounded, fragrant and intense nose.
Taste: Castagnolo is dry, elegant and pleasant. Calcaia is smooth, and harmonious.

Vagile

Podere Vagile srl
Via del Filatoio, 12
05023 Baschi TR
Tel: 0758 741570
Fax: 0758 748958
cantina.vagile@libero.it
Point of sale: Hotel Orvieto,
Via A Constanzi, Orvieto Scalo.

Azienda Agricola Vagile is a small company, with 70 hectares of vineyards spread around the hills near the town of Baschi. The vineyards are located in the production zones both for Orvieto DOC and Lago di Corbara DOC wines. The soil is mostly marly, clayey, and rich in fossils from the Pliocene age on the higher grounds. Lower down, on the floodplains of the rivers Paglia and Tevere, sand and silt are the main types. The climate is characterised by warm temperatures, and almost constant sunshine, yet there is sufficient supply of rainwater: the best conditions for the correct ripening of grapes. The yield of production is kept low by "green" harvesting in July; only the best bunches are left to ripen. The winery is equipped with a thoroughly modern vinification system.

Masseo. Umbria IGT.

Grapes: 60% Cabernet Sauvignon, and 40% Merlot.
The wine: deep ruby red in colour; spicy, with a good structure.
Food matches: red meats, game, and mature cheeses.
Alcoholic content: 13% vol.

Confidenza. Umbria IGT.

Grapes: 60% Sangiovese, and 40% Merlot.
The wine: intense ruby red in colour; notes of ripe red fruits, dry, and a good structure.
Food matches: red meats, game, and mature cheeses.
Alcoholic content: 12.5% vol.

Momenti. Umbria IGT.

Grapes: 40% Sangiovese, and 60% Merlot.
Colour: deep ruby red in colour, with violet reflections; clean, with notes of ripe red fruits and cherries, and a good structure.
Food matches: red meats, game, and mature cheeses.
Alcoholic content: 13% vol.

L'Origine. Orvieto DOC Classico.

Grapes: Trebbiano, Grechetto, Malvasia, Verdello, and Drupeggio.
The wine: straw yellow in colour; dry, fruity, with floral notes.
Food matches: *hors d'oeuvres*, fish, white meats, and cheeses.
Alcoholic content: 12% vol.

Marticale. Orvieto DOC Classico Secco.

Grapes: Chardonnay, Grechetto, Malvasia, Verdello, Drupeggio.
The wine: straw yellow in colour; dry, fruity with floral notes, and a good structure.
Food matches: *hors d'oeuvres*, fish, white meats, and cheeses.
Alcoholic content: 12.5% vol.

L'Alba. Umbria IGT Passito.

Grapes: Moscato 85%, and Chardonnay 15%.
The wine: golden yellow in colour; fruity, with notes of coffee and chocolate; dessert wine with a good structure.
Food matches: cakes, tarts, and some mature cheeses.
Alcoholic content: 13% vol.

Spumante Brut.

Grapes: Chardonnay 60%, and Pinot Grigio 40%.
The wine: pale straw yellow in colour, dry, lively, and fruity.
Food matches: as an aperitif, *hors d'oeuvres,* and fish.
Alcoholic content: 12% vol.

Spumante Dolce.

Grapes: Chardonnay 60%, and Moscato 40%.
The wine: straw yellow in colour, lively, fruity, with sweet tones.
Food matches: aperitif, or a dessert wine.
Alcoholic content: 7% vol.

WINE PRODUCERS
COLLI AMERINI

A decree was granted for Colli Amerini DOC wines in 1990. The area is over the middle reaches of the rivers Tiber and Nera; and includes the towns of Amelia, Narni, Calvi, Otricoli, Alviano, Lugano, Penna in Teverina, Giove, and a part of Terni.

The red wines are made from: Sangiovese, Aleatico, Barbera, Sagrantino, Canaiolo, Merlot, Ciliegiolo, Cabernet Sauvignon, Syrah, Barbera, and Montepulciano grapes.

The white wines from: Trebbiano, Trebbiano Toscano, Riesling, Pinot Grigio, Grechetto, Malvasia, Verdello, Drupeggio, Garganega, Chardonnay, and Moscato.

The *Strada dei Vini Etrusco-Romana* winds its way along the ridge over the river Tevere from Orvieto to Narni. Most of the wineries are situated alongside this road, following the course of an older Roman road. From Narni to Terni the *Strada dei Vini Etrusco-Romana* coincides with the *Via Flaminia* on the banks of the river Nera. The towns and villages of the area are steeped in history; each has something to offer to the inquiring visitor.

Amelia is renowned for its city walls, constructed by Cyclopes, according to local legend. The vast polygonal blocks of stones are up to seven meters across and they reach the height of twenty meters in places. The ancient settlement dates back to eleventh century BC, yet the walls are still standing today.

Narni is set on top of a cliff overlooking the River Nera. At the very top, *Rocca Albornoz*, there is a magnificent old castle, guarding the otherwise undefended road to Rome. Narni was the gateway into Umbria, and there is an old Roman bridge just outside the town, still in use today.

Terni is better known for its steelworks than its vineyards; however, the city houses the remains of St Valentine, the patron saint of lovers. The new city may have little to offer to a visitor, but the surrounding countryside is staggeringly beautiful, especially along the River Nera. The Valnerina is considered to be one of the most beautiful valleys in Umbria. The *Cascata delle Marmore* is a popular attraction, being the highest waterfall in Europe at 165 metres. It was created by the Romans in 271 BC, when they diverted the river Velino into the River Nera, during the drainage of some marshlands to the south.

But there is more to the Colli Amerini than historical relics. Not unlike the rest of Umbria, vine growing and wine making have a tradition going back thousands of years; and this tradition lives on, in the wonderful wines produced today.

Le Crete

Le Crete. Località Piscicoli snc
05024 Giove TR
Cell: 328 7011808 or 340 9675163
Fax: 0744 992443
www.cantinalecrete.it
az.agr.lecrete@virgilio.it

"My winery belongs to all those who work here and put their best efforts into making it a success. The business turns on three essentials: Passion, Vineyard, and Wines," says Giuliano Stellari, the owner of the Le Crete. He remembers his father talking about winemaking. The family had wine cellars dug out of the rock in the medieval town of Giove. The grapes were picked by using ladders and taken to the cellars by mule, often at some distance from the town. A number of decades have come and gone since then, but the passion for making wines has remained with the family.

Located amidst rolling hills stretching down to the Tiber Valley, the vineyard is called after the ancient name given to the area: Le Crete. The vineyard is exposed to the south, and it is protected from cold north winds by the gentle hill of Giove at 300 metres above sea level. The land is fertile, sandy clay, interspersed with alluvial limestone, silt and tufa. The humidity level is ideal even during hot summers. The conditions create a unique microclimate for growing grapes with exceptional ripeness, even in the driest of years. The vines are trained using the low spurred cordon system; 4000 plants per hectare, with a yield of 60/70 hectolitres of wine.

The family carries out all the work in the vineyard. "We attend to our garden on a daily basis," they say. Roses stand guard over the rows of vines, flanked by apple trees, and gazed upon by the wild animals that the family hold in high regard (three of them are featured on their wine labels). The family cultivates the land with respect. Despite the hard work involved, they follow traditional methods. No weed killers are used, their chosen method relies on ladybirds. However, they allow the use of copper and sulphur treatments, just as it was accepted practice in times past.

The harvest is carried out during the months of September and October. The grapes are picked by hand, allowing the careful selection of only the ripe and wholesome bunches. The degree of ripeness can vary from one plant to the next, given the different conditions even within a few metres. The work carried out in the vineyard is continued in the winery. The grapes are carefully selected, then vinified. Five wines are produced: two reds: Petra Nera and Spira Bruna, one rosé: Costa Volpara, and two whites: Cima del Giglio and Spira Clara.

Petra Nera. Umbria IGT Rosso.

Grapes: Sangiovese 70%, Barbera 20%, and Merlot 10%.
Vineyard: exposed to south-south/east.
Yield and density per hectare: 65 hectolitres; 4500 vines.
Training: spurred cordon.
Harvest: handpicked.
Vinification: the grapes are crushed and allowed to stabilise for 12 hours. The alcoholic fermentation takes place on the skins in stainless steel vats for 12/15 days at 25-27° C. There are periodic *delestages* (the separation of part of the must for oxygenation), and repeated pumping over in order to achieve a well-balanced extraction of polyphenols, tannins, and colour.
Ageing: the wine is drawn off the skins and left to mature for 2/3 months. Later the sediments are removed and the wine is transferred to French oak barrels (Alliers). It is here that micro oxygenation takes place, which gives red wines their characteristic smoothness, and refinement of taste. Further refinement takes place in the bottle for 6 months.
Bottles produced: 10 000.
The wine: ruby red in colour, fruity with vegetal notes; smooth and well balanced.
Food matches: roast suckling pig with herbs (*porchetta*), roast quail, and red meats.
Alcoholic content: 14% vol.

Spira Bruna. Umbria IGT Rosso. (Until 2009).
Poggio Jago. Umbria IGT Rosso. (Since 2010).

Grapes: Sangiovese 70%, Barbera 20%, and Merlot 10%.
Vineyard: exposed to south-south/east.
Yield and density per hectare: 70 hectolitres; 4500 vines.
Training: spurred cordon. Harvest: handpicked.
Vinification: fermentation in stainless steel vats on the skins at a controlled temperature of 25-27° C.
Ageing: 6 months in steel vats, then 6 months in the bottle.
Bottles produced: 8000.
The wine: ruby red, fruity with vegetal notes; pleasantly smooth and well balanced.
Food matches: roast suckling pig with herbs (*porchetta*), roast quail, and red meats.
Alcoholic content: 13.5% vol.

Costa Volpara. Umbria IGT Rosato.

Grapes: Sangiovese 70%, Barbera 20%, and Merlot 10%.
Vineyard: exposed to south-south/east.
Yield and density per hectare: 70 hectolitres; 4500 vines.
Training: spurred cordon. Harvest: handpicked.
Vinification: the wine is created from the must of the red grapes, which gives it a strong body. After having been left in contact with the skins for several hours, the wine is drawn off and left to ferment in stainless steel vats on the skins at 15° C.
Ageing: 3 months in steel vats resting on the lees, then a further 3 months in the bottle.
Bottles produced: 4000.
The wine: salmon pink in colour, with fresh floral notes reminiscent of ripe red fruits. The wine is an excellent marriage between robust red grape body and the earthy exuberance obtained from white wine vinification.
Food matches: trout with sage and butter, or rabbit with herbs.

Cima del Giglio. Umbria IGT Bianco.

Grapes: Malvasia 85%, Trebbiano and Verdello 15%.
Vineyard: exposed to south-south/east.
Yield and density per hectare: 70 hectolitres; 4500 vines.
Training: spurred cordon. Harvest: handpicked.
Vinification: cold maceration in order to maximise the extraction of the skins' aromatic content. The grapes are then crushed; the must ferments at 15° C. Some of the grapes are separated and dried on racks, and crushed later, then added to the wine.
Ageing: 5/6 months in stainless steel vats on the lees, where the wine undergoes *remouage* (stirring up) of its yeast content once every 15/20 days. Further fermentation and ageing takes place in the bottle for 2/3 months.
Bottles produced: 5000.
The wine: straw yellow in colour, with green reflections; aromas of white fruit pulp, acacia and wisteria, smooth and full-bodied.
Food matches: Sicilian *a beccafico* style sardines with oranges, or turkey with aromatic herbs.

Spira Clara. Umbria IGT Bianco. (Until 2011).
Ripa Bianca. Umbria IGT Bianco (Since 2012)

Grapes: Trebbiano 70%, Verdello, Malvasia and Garganega 30%.
Vineyard: exposed to south-south/east.
Yield and density per hectare: 70 hectolitres; 4500 vines.
Training: spurred cordon. Harvest: handpicked.
Vinification: the grapes undergo cold maceration in order to maximise the extraction of the grape skins' aromatic content. Then the grapes are crushed and the must ferments at 15° C.
Ageing: 4/5 months in stainless steel vats on the lees, then continued in the bottle for 2/3 months.
Bottles produced: 5000.
The wine: straw yellow in colour, with green reflections; smooth, full-bodied and well balanced.
Food matches: *tagliolini* pasta with shrimps and courgettes, or *risotto alla Milanese.* .

Cantina dei Colli Amerini

Fornole di Amelia TR
Tel: 0744 989721/2
Fax: 0744 989 695
www.colliamerini.it
info@colliamerirni.it

The Cantina dei Colli Amerini was established in 1975, as a co-operative with 278 members. The vineyards are spread over seven hundred hectares amongst the rolling hills and ridges surrounding the old town of Amelia. The combination of altitude, soil, and microclimate are ideal for the cultivation of vines. In addition, there is an extraordinary wealth of grape varieties, which have evolved since time immemorial. The area has a wine producing tradition going back centuries. The estate carries on this tradition, while introducing innovation and a sense of continuous renewal. The improved agronomic practices has achieved a gradual and balanced reduction of the yield of grapes produced. This led to obtaining grapes of high quality, character and personality. The selection of clones best suited to the vineyards with optimum exposure to the sun was a part of this process. Improved winemaking techniques and efficient, state-of-the-art equipment helped the winery to produce high quality wines, sold at reasonable prices, for the past thirty years.

The grape varieties include Trebbiano, Merlot, Sangiovese, Ciliegiolo, and Montepulciano. The wines made from them are invariably pleasant, with fruity notes in the whites, and soft and involving tannins in the reds. The Ciliegiolo of Narni is just one example, and the 2007 vintage Ciliegiolo di Narni 30 Anni celebrates thirty years of the wine's production. Other great vintage years include both the Grechetto and Orvieto Classico of 2008. The same year also produced the Merlot Umbria Olmeto, and the Ameroe, with its intense sour black cherry fragrance. All the wines receive high marks from wine experts; particularly for their quality and affordable prices. Value and quality are the key words in the philosophy of the winery.

Carbio. Colli Amerini DOC Rosso Superiore.

Grapes: Merlot, Sangiovese, Ciliegiolo, and Cabernet.
Production area: Amelia, Narni, and Sangemini.
Area of the vineyard: 15 hectares.
Altitude: 350 metres above sea level.
Training: double spurred cordon.
Density of vines: 4100 per hectare.
Production per hectare: 7000 kg.
Yield in wine: 65%.
Average age of the vines: 15/20 years.
Harvest: October.
Vinification: alcoholic fermentation with skin contact for fifteen days in steel tanks. Malolactic fermentation: in barriques.
Ageing: in barriques for 12 months, then in the bottle.
Alcohol content: 13% vol.
Total acidity: 5.35 g/l.
pH: 3.55 g/l.

Ciliegiolo di Narni 30 Anni. Umbria IGT Rosso.

Grapes: Ciliegiolo.
Production area: Narni.
Area of the vineyard: 4 hectares.
Altitude: 350 metres above sea level.
Training: double spurred cordon.
Density of vines: 4100 per hectare.
Production per hectare: 7000 kg.
Yield in wine: 65%.
Average age of the vines: 10 years.
Harvest: September.
Vinification: alcoholic fermentation with skin contact for 15 days in steel tanks, then malolactic fermentation also in steel tanks.
Ageing: in barriques for 6 months, then in the bottle.
Alcohol content: 13.5% vol.
Total acidity: 5.35 g/l.
pH: 3.55 g/l.

Rocca Nerina. Umbria IGT Malvasia Chardonnay.

Grapes: 80% Malvasia, and 20% Chardonnay.
Production area: Amelia.
Area of the vineyard: 20 hectares.
Altitude: 300 metres above sea level.
Training: double spurred cordon.
Density of vines: 4000 per hectare.
Production per hectare: 6500 kg.
Yield in wine: 60%.
Average age of the vines: 15 years.
Harvest: the first days of September.
Vinification: cold maceration on the skins for 10 hours at 3° C then followed by malolactic fermentation in steel tanks.
Ageing: in the bottle.
Alcohol content: 13.5% vol.
Total acidity: 5.60 g/l.
pH: 3.45 g/l.

Olmeto. Umbria IGT Merlot.

Grapes: 100% Merlot.
Production area: Amelia, and Narni.
Area of the vineyard: 40 hectares.
Altitude: 350 metres above sea level.
Training: double spurred cordon.
Density of vines: 4000 per hectare.
Production per hectare: 7000 kg.
Yield in wine: 65%.
Average age of the vines: 10 years.
Harvest: October.
Vinification: alcoholic fermentation on the skins for 15 days in steel tanks, then malolactic fermentation also in steel tanks.
Ageing: in the bottle.
Alcohol content: 13% vol.
Total acidity: 5.10 g/l.
pH: 3.50 g/l.

Sagrantino di Montefalco DOCG.

Grapes: 100% Sagrantino.
Production area: Montefalco, Bevagna, Gualdo Cattaneo, Castel Ritaldi, and Giano dell'Umbria.
Area of the vineyard: 10 hectares.
Altitude: 320 metres above sea level.
Training: double spurred cordon.
Density of vines: 4000 per hectare.
Production per hectare: 8000 kg.
Yield in wine: 60%.
Average age of the vines: 7 years.
Harvest: October.
Vinification: alcoholic fermentation on the skins for 15 days in steel tanks, then malolactic fermentation in barriques.
Ageing: in barriques for 12 months; in the bottle for 18 months.
Alcohol content: 14% vol.
Total acidity: 5.50 g/l.
pH: 3.50 g/l.

Rosso di Montefalco DOC.

Grapes: Sangiovese 60%, Sagrantino 15%, and Merlot 25%.
Production area: Montefalco, Bevagna, Gualdo Cattaneo, Castel Ritaldi, and Giano dell'Umbria.
Area of the vineyard: 12 hectares.
Altitude: 320 metres above sea level.
Training: double spurred cordon.
Density of vines: 4100 per hectare.
Production per hectare: 110 quintals.
Yield in wine: 70%.
Average age of the vines: 7 years.
Harvest: October.
Vinification: alcoholic fermentation on the skins for 15 days in steel tanks, then malolactic fermentation in barriques.
Ageing: in barriques for 12 months; in the bottle for 6 months.
Alcohol content: 12.5% vol.
Total acidity: 5.40 g/l.
pH: 3.35 g/l.

Ameroe. Collin Amerini DOC Rosso.

Grapes: Sangiovese, Merlot, Ciliegiolo, and Montepulciano.
Production area: Amelia, Narni, and Sangemini.
Area of the vineyard: 20 hectares.
Altitude: 350 metres above sea level.
Training: double spurred cordon.
Density of vines: 3500 per hectare.
Production per hectare: 7000 kg.
Yield in wine: 70%.
Average age of the vines: 25 years.
Harvest: October.
Vinification: alcoholic fermentation with skin contact for 10 days in steel tanks, followed by malolactic fermentation also in steel tanks.
Ageing: in the bottle.
Alcohol content: 12.5% vol.
Total acidity: 5.00 g/l.
pH: 3.40 g/l.

Ciliegiolo di Narni. Umbria IGT Rosso.

Grapes: Ciliegiolo 100%.
Production area: Narni.
Area of the vineyard: 45 hectares.
Altitude: 350 metres above sea level.
Training: double spurred cordon.
Density of vines: 3500 per hectare.
Production per hectare: 9000 kg.
Yield in wine: 70%.
Average age of the vines: 20 years.
Harvest: September.
Vinification: alcoholic fermentation with skin contact for 10 days in steel tanks, then malolactic fermentation also in steel tanks.
Ageing: in the bottle.
Alcohol content: 12.5% vol.
Total acidity: 5.00 g/l.
pH: 3.35 g/l.

Grecolevante. Collin Amerini DOC Bianco.

Grapes: Trebbiano, Grechetto, and Malvasia.
Production area: Amelia, Narni, Guardea, Sangemini, and Alviano.
Area of the vineyard: 20 hectares.
Altitude: 320 metres above sea level.
Training: double spurred cordon.
Density of vines: 3500 per hectare.
Production per hectare: 9000 kg.
Yield in wine: 70%.
Average age of the vines: 25 years.
Harvest: at the end of September.
Vinification: alcoholic fermentation off the skins at a controlled temperature. There is no malolactic fermentation.
Ageing: in the bottle.
Alcohol content: 12% vol.
Total acidity: 5.70 g/l.
pH: 3.30 g/l.

Grechetto. Umbria IGT.

Grapes: Grechetto 100%.
Production area: Amelia, Narni, Sangemini, Alviano, and Baschi.
Area of the vineyard: 20 hectares.
Altitude: 340 metres above sea level.
Training: double spurred cordon.
Density of vines: 4000 per hectare.
Production per hectare: 7000 kg.
Yield in wine: 68%.
Average age of the vines: 15 years.
Harvest: in the middle of September.
Vinification: alcoholic fermentation with skin contact for 12 hours at 7 C°, then in steel tanks at a controlled temperature.
Ageing: in the bottle.
Alcohol content: 13% vol.
Total acidity: 5.50 g/l.
pH: 3.35 g/l.

Orvieto Classico DOC.

Grapes: Grechetto, Verdello, Drupeggio, Malvasia, and Trebbiano.
Production area: Baschi, and Montecchio.
Area of the vineyard: 33 hectares.
Altitude: 350 metres above sea level.
Training: double spurred cordon.
Density of vines: 3500 per hectare.
Production per hectare: 6800 kg.
Yield in wine: 60%.
Average age of the vines: 15 years.
Harvest: during the first days of October.
Vinification: alcoholic fermentation with skin contact for 12 hours at 7 C°, then in steel tanks at a controlled temperature.
Ageing: in the bottle.
Alcohol content: 12% vol.
Total acidity: 5.70 g/l.
pH: 3.30 g/l.

Poggio dei Salici. Umbria IGT Trebbiano.

Grapes: 100% Trebbiano.
Production area: Alviano.
Area of the vineyard: 40 hectares.
Altitude: 320 metres above sea level.
Training: double spurred cordon.
Density of vines: 4000 per hectare.
Production per hectare: 9000 kg.
Yield in wine: 70%.
Average age of the vines: 20 years.
Harvest: September.
Vinification: alcoholic fermentation off the skins at a controlled temperature.
Ageing: in the bottle.
Alcohol content: 12% vol.
Total acidity: 5.40 g/l.
pH: 3.25 g/l.

Poggio dei Salici. Umbria IGT Sangiovese.

Grapes: 100% Sangiovese.
Production area: Amelia, and Narni.
Area of the vineyard: 40 hectares.
Altitude: 320 metres above sea level.
Training: double spurred cordon.
Density of vines: 4000 per hectare.
Production per hectare: 9000 kg.
Yield in wine: 70%.
Average age of the vines: 20 years.
Harvest: September.
Vinification: alcoholic fermentation with skin contact for 10 days in steel tanks, then malolactic fermentation also in steel tanks.
Ageing: in the bottle.
Alcohol content: 12.5% vol.
Total acidity: 5.00 g/l.
pH: 3.40 g/l.

Terre Auree. Umbria IGT Bianco.

Grapes: 100% Trebbiano.
Production area: Alviano.
Area of the vineyard: 40 hectares.
Altitude: 320 metres above sea level.
Training: double spurred cordon.
Density of vines: 4000 per hectare.
Production per hectare: 9000 kg.
Yield in wine: 70%.
Average age of the vines: 20 years.
Harvest: September.
Vinification: alcoholic fermentation off the skins at a controlled temperature.
Ageing: in the bottle.
Alcohol content: 12% vol.
Total acidity: 5.40 g/l.
pH: 3.25 g/l.

Terre Auree. Umbria IGT Rosso.

Grapes: 100% Sangiovese.
Production area: Amelia, and Narni.
Area of the vineyard: 40 hectares.
Altitude: 320 metres above sea level.
Training: double spurred cordon.
Density of vines: 4000 per hectare.
Production per hectare: 9000 kg.
Yield in wine: 70%.
Average age of the vines: 20 years.
Harvest: September.
Vinification: alcoholic fermentation with skin contact for 10 days in steel tanks, followed by malolactic fermentation also in steel tanks.
Ageing: in the bottle.
Alcohol content: 12.5% vol.
Total acidity: 5.00 g/l.
pH: 3.40 g/l.

Aleatico. Umbria IGT.

Grapes: 100% Aleatico.
Production area: Amelia.
Area of the vineyard: 1 hectare.
Altitude: 320 metres above sea level.
Training: double spurred cordon.
Density of vines: 3000 per hectare.
Production per hectare: 70 quintals.
Yield in wine: 60%.
Average age of the vines: 15 years.
Harvest: October.
Vinification: alcoholic fermentation with skin contact for 15 days in steel tanks, then malolactic fermentation also in steel tanks.
Ageing: in the bottle.
Alcohol content: 13% vol.
Total acidity: 5.40 g/l.
pH: 3.30 g/l.

Castello Albornoz. Vino Spumante Brut.

Grapes: Chardonnay.
Production area: Amelia.
Area of the vineyard: 5 hectares.
Altitude: 350 metres above sea level.
Training: double spurred cordon.
Density of vines: 4000 per hectare.
Production per hectare: 65 quintals.
Yield in wine: 60%.
Average age of the vines: 10 years.
Harvest: in the middle of August.
Vinification: alcoholic fermentation in steel tanks at 17 C°.
Sparkling process: 2 to 3 months in autoclave.
Alcohol content: 12% vol.
Total acidity: 6.00 g/l.   pH: 3.30 g/l.

Grappa di Ciliegiolo.

Distilled in a Charente still from the pomace of Ciliegiolo grapes. It is aged briefly in oak; pale straw in colour, transparent, with fruity notes and delicate hints of vanilla. Serving temperature 15 C°.

Grappa Riserva.

Steam distilled in a continuous still. It is aged in oak for at least 18 months; straw in colour and transparent. It is a grappa of great balance, with floral and fruity fragrances, with delicate hints of vanilla and wood. Serving temperature 17 C°.

Montoro

Marchesi Patrizi Montoro
Piazza Baronale 1
05035 Montoro TR
Tel/Fax: 0744 735 128
www.patrizimontoro.com
montoro@alice.it

Montoro is an ancient hilltop town overlooking the River Nera on its lower reaches, before it merges with the Tevere. A castle, perched on the edge of a ridge, dominates the town. Although the settlement dates back to Etruscan times, the town is medieval, with some more recent buildings on its outskirts.

The tradition of winemaking in Montoro goes back to time immemorial. For centuries, vines were cultivated on the estate of the Montoro Family. A Papal bull in 1020 AD sanctioned the production of wines, and the wines of the *Castello di Montoro* have been famous ever since. During the second half of the XVI century some caves were excavated under the castle. Their constant temperature and excellent levels of humidity were ideal for ageing and refining wines. They are still used to this day.

In 1770 AD the estate passed on to the present owners and the name of the castle changed to Patrizi Montoro.

The estate covers 800 hectares, of which 90 are vineyards. The *terroir* is ideal for the cultivation of vines and growing grapes of high quality. The winery is furnished with modern winemaking equipment and uses the best up-to-date technology.

Castello di Montoro. Umbria IGT Rosso.

Grapes: 85% Merlot, and 15% Sangiovese.
Yield per hectare: 55 quintals.
Harvest: in the middle of September. Handpicked in boxes.
Vinification: the grapes are de-stemmed and soft pressed; alcoholic fermentation in stainless steel tanks at 28 C° for 15-20

days. Malolactic fermentation is carried out partly in stainless steel tanks and partly in barriques.
Ageing: 12 months in 225-litre lightly toasted Alliers oak barriques; followed by 3 months in the bottle.
The wine: intense ruby red in colour, with violet reflections. It has an intense fragrance of freshly picked fruits of the forest. It is well balanced, with a good structure and rich in tannins.
Annual production: 20 000 bottles.
Alcohol content: 13.5% vol.

Donna Porzia. Umbria IGT Bianco.

Grapes: 85% Grechetto, and 15% Chardonnay.
Yield per hectare: 50 quintals.
Harvest: in the beginning of September. Handpicked in boxes.
Vinification: the grapes are de-stemmed and subjected to cold cryomaceration under an atmospheric pressure of 0.1 to 0.2 atm; followed by alcoholic fermentation in stainless steel tanks at a controlled temperature of 16 C° for 15-20 days.
Ageing: 3 months on the lees.
The wine: pale straw yellow in colour, with green reflections. It has an intense fragrance with floral and fruity notes; a well-balanced and fresh wine.
Annual production: 14 000 bottles.
Alcohol content: 13% vol.

Grechetto. Umbria IGT Bianco.

Grapes: 100% Grechetto.
Yield per hectare: 80 quintals.
Harvest: during the middle of September. Handpicked in boxes.
Vinification: the grapes are de-stemmed and soft pressed under a pressure of 0.1 to 0.4 atm; followed by alcoholic fermentation in steel tanks at a controlled temperature for 15-20 days.
Ageing: 3 months on the lees.
The wine: intense golden yellow, with green reflections. It is a fresh and soft wine, ready to be drunk when young.
Annual production: 10 000 bottles.
Alcohol content: 13% vol.

Sangiovese. Umbria IGT Rosso.

Grapes: 100% Sangiovese.
Yield per hectare: 80 quintals.
Harvest: in the beginning of October. Handpicked in boxes.
Vinification: the grapes are de-stemmed and crushed; followed by alcoholic fermentation in stainless steel tanks at a controlled temperature for 15-20 days, then malolactic fermentation also in stainless steel tanks.
Ageing: six months in stainless steel tanks; followed by one month in the bottle.
The wine: intense ruby red in colour; fragrances of freshly picked fruits; well balanced and ready to be drunk when young.
Annual production: 25 000 bottles.
Alcohol content: 13% vol.

Sola Fides. Umbria IGT Rosso.

Grapes: 100% Sangiovese.
Yield per hectare: 60 quintals.
Harvest: in the beginning of October. Handpicked in boxes.
Vinification: the grapes are de-stemmed and soft pressed; alcoholic fermentation in stainless steel tanks at 28 C° for 15-20 days, then 3 to 4 days of warm maceration follows. Malolactic fermentation is carried out partly in stainless steel tanks and partly in barriques.
Ageing: 15 months in 225-litre lightly toasted Alliers oak barriques; followed by 3 months in the bottle.
The wine: intense ruby red in colour, with bold violet reflections. It has a rich fruity fragrance of blackberries and blueberries. It is pleasingly spicy, well balanced; rounded and rich in tannins.
Annual production: 6 000 bottles.
Alcohol content: 13.5% vol.

Palazzola

Agricola La Palazzola
Cantina di Vasciligliano di Stroncone, 05100 TR
Tel: 0744 609091
Fax: 0744 609092
www.lapalazzola.it
info@lapalazzola.it

The Agricola La Palazzola is located six kilometres south of Terni, in a valley below the town of Stroncone. The vineyards and the winery are amongst the surrounding hills. It is an ancient location; the estate's old name was *Castel di Laja,* which meant a castle paid for. It was just one of the many fortifications between Stroncone and Amelia. The road was guarded by towers and surrounded by walls similar to the one outside Amelia; built to repel invaders.

The Farfense land register records a gift of the estate by Tomasso di Narni to a certain Mavo, a person reputed to have been completely mad. Eventually, the estate became the property of the Abbazia di Farfa (Monastery of Farfa). Water from thermal springs in the hills were brought to the monastery through lead pipes, but apart from hot water, the place was also noted for its excellent wines – *ac eccellentissimas vineas.*

Polano Manassei, the agricultural historian and agrarian economist described them as *franciose ed il biancone,* probably the local name for the red grapes. The same grapes were grown throughout France during the eighth century. A similar vine can still be found growing in the wild in the area. In Manassei's time the vines were grown inside walled gardens, and trained up the trunks of elm trees or wooden poles.

La Palazzola's new owner is Stefano Grilli, who carries on the ancient tradition. However, the estate is a benchmark winery for innovative and top quality red wines; partly due to the efforts of

Riccardo Cotarella. He was La Palazzola's winemaker during the 1990s, and he recognised the vast potential of the area's grapes, the soil, and its exposure. He encouraged the estate to produce their own wines, whereas in the past the grapes were sold to other winemakers. Today, all the wines La Palazzola produces are made from grapes grown in their own vineyards. Dottore Stefano Ronconi is the new viticulturist.

Red wines: Rubino 2001 - IGT Umbria Rosso, Rubino 2003 – IGT Umbria Rosso, Pinot Nero 1999 – IGT Umbria, Merlot 2004 – IGT Umbria, Sangiovese 2001. – IGT, Le Petrare 2006 – IGT Umbria Rosso Syrah, Costa dell'Aja 2004 – IGT Umbria Rosso.

Passito Wines: Vendemmia Tardiva 2007 – IGT Umbria Bianco, Vinsanto Passito 2003 – IGT Umbria, Trebbiano and Malvasia, Vinsanto Passito 2005 "Bacca Rossa" – IGT Umbria, Sangiovese.

Sparkling wines made in the classical traditional method: Riesling 2003 Brut, Moscato 2004 Demi-Sec, Rosé 2003 Demi Sec (Pinot Nero 85% and Chardonnay 15%), Rosé 2006 Brut (Pinot Nero 85% and Chardonnay 15%), Sangiovese Rosé 2005 (Sangiovese 100%).

Pizzogallo

Pizzogallo Vigneti & Agriturismo
Località Pizzogallo,
S P Amelia-Orte, Amelia TR
Tel/Fax: 0744 970018
www.pizzogallo.it
info@pizzogallo.it

The Pizzogallo estate is located alongside the provincial road from Amelia leading to Orte. The vineyards, set amongst rolling hills facing south, surround the guesthouse and the winery. On the distant horizon the peaks of the nearby mountains dominate the scenery. The view is magnificent over the valley below, and the *terroir* is ideal for growing grapes. Pizzogallo is a small, family run estate, and produces only two types of wines, one red, one white.

Pizzogallo. Umbria IGT Rosso.

Grapes: Sangiovese 40%, Montepulciano 40%, and Ciliegiolo 20%.

Pizzogallo. Umbria IGT Bianco.

Grapes: Malvasia 80%, and other white grapes 20%.

Fattoria Le Poggette

Fattoria Le Poggette
Località Le Poggette, 141
05026 Montecastrilli TR
Tel/Fax: 0744 940338
Cell: 333 6165315
www.fattorialepoggette.it
info@fattorialepoggetteit.191.it

Colli Amerini
DENOMINAZIONE DI ORIGINE CONTROLLATA
ROSSO SUPERIORE
Umbria
2006
ITALIA

The estate extends over 1120 acres in the neighbourhood of Montecastrilli and Sangemini, of which 46 acres are vineyards. The area is blessed with intense sunshine, and a rich soil of chalky clay and sand. The microclimate is influenced by the topography; the estate is like a large amphitheatre, totally encircled by hills, which protect the vineyards from wind and cold.

The property was acquired by Giorgio Lanzetta in 1960. He dedicated part of the land to viticulture, bringing with him the Montepulciano grape from his native Abruzzo. This grape has shown itself to be one of real quality and character in its newly found setting.

New vineyards were planted between 1975 and 1980 with Sangiovese, Canaiolo, and Montepulciano grapes. Initially, they were harvested and sold in bulk before the Colli Amerini DOC production zone was designated. Another 12 acres of vineyards were planted more recently, and in 1995, the estate started to produce its red wines in house. Ever since then, cultivation techniques in the vineyards changed with the aim of producing superior grapes. The good results achieved, led to the estate's Trebbiano vineyards being grafted over to Montepulciano grapes. Training systems have also been modified to lower the yield, and to favour quality over quantity.

Grechetto IGT Umbria.

The grapes are harvested at maximum ripeness towards the end of September. The wine is noted for its complexity. It is bottled during February following the harvest.
Serving temperature: 54-56° Fahrenheit (12-13° C)

Rosato IGT Umbria.

Grapes: Montepulciano grapes.
Vinification: soft pressing and early must extraction is followed by a temperature-controlled fermentation.
The wine: pink in colour; slightly sweet, but with a strong body.
Serving temperature: 58-60° Fahrenheit (15° C), in crystal glasses for white wines with a good body.

Colli Amerini DOC Rosso Superiore.

Grapes: Sangiovese, Canaiolo, and Montepulciano.
Harvest: during the first ten days of October. The grapes are selected and only the best bunches are used for vinification.
Vinification: after de-stemming and soft pressing, the must is fermented for 25 days, with pumping over the cap twice every day. Several racking over and malolactic fermentation follows, then a period of ageing before the wine is bottled.
The wine: ruby red in colour; good body and pleasantly fruity.
Food matches: red meats, game, and most main meals.
Serving temperature: 61-63° Fahrenheit (16-17° C).

Canaiolo IGT Umbria.

Grapes: Canaiolo 100%.
Vinification: fermentation and maceration for 25 days. After the malolactic fermentation, the wine ages for a year in 135 gallon oak barrels. That is followed by refinement in the bottle, and marketed two years after the harvest.
The wine: brilliant red in colour; with a good body and a silky texture, with hints of liquorice.
Serving temperature: 61-63° Fahrenheit (16-17° C).

Torre Maggiore Rosso IGT Umbria Montepulciano.

Grapes: Montepulciano 100%.
Harvest: during the last ten days of October
Vinification: the grapes de-stemmed and soft pressed, followed by fermentation for 30-40 days, with pumping over the cap twice every day. The wine is racked off, and transferred to 135 gallon oak barrels, where the malolactic fermentation takes place.
Ageing: at least twenty months in the wood, followed by refinement in the bottle.
The wine: deep ruby red in colour; with fruity fragrances and soft tannins, and a long ageing potential.
Serving temperature: 65° Fahrenheit (18° C).

Agraria Ponteggia

Agraria Ponteggia
Loc Belvedere, 223
05029 San Gemini TR
Tel/Fax: 0744 630531

Agraria Ponteggia was established in the mid 1960s, and bottled its first wine in 1968. The grape varieties for red wines are Barbera, Ciliegiolo, Sangiovese, Merlot, Cabernet, and Montepulciano. The white grapes are Malvasia di Candia, Malvasia Toscana, Pinot Bianco, Grechetto, and Trebbiano. Today, the estate is planting new vines, which is combined with constant improvement of production methods in the winery. New machinery and working methods allow an increasingly more delicate treatment of the grapes. However, local tradition is strictly adhered to, and an environmentally friendly approach is the philosophy of the estate.

Anita. IGT Umbria Malvasia.

Grapes: Malvasia, Trebbiano, and Grechetto.
Altitude: 280 metres above sea level.
Density: 3600 vines per hectare.
Yield: 80 quintals per hectare.
Ageing: in stainless steel vats.
Annual production: 15 000 bottles.
The wine: light straw yellow in colour; floral and fruity, with delicate notes of citrus fruits and green apples. The taste is dry and fresh, it is a wine with a fine structure.
Food matches: aperitif, fish and chicken dishes.
Alcoholic content: 13% vol.

Milicchio. IGT Umbria Bianco.

Grapes: Malvasia, and Trebbiano.
Altitude: 280 metres above sea level.
Density: 3600 vines per hectare.
Yield: 90 quintals per hectare.
Ageing: in stainless steel vats.
The wine: straw yellow in colour; with notes of ripe yellow fruits and delicate floral and aromatic hints; dry, warm, but also fresh.
Food matches: pasta, fish and chicken dishes.
Alcoholic content: 11% vol.

Eva. IGT Umbria Rosato.

Grapes: Sangiovese, Montepulciano, and Ciliegiolo.
Altitude: 280 metres above sea level.
Density: 4200 vines per hectare.
Yield: 90 quintals per hectare.
Ageing: in stainless steel vats.
Annual production: 15 000 bottles.
The wine: light red in colour; fruity, herbaceous and spicy; soft, well balanced, with a pleasant acidity.
Food matches: fish, salamis and cheeses.
Alcoholic content: 13% vol.

Petalo di Rose. Colli Amerini DOC Rosato.

Grapes: Sangiovese, Merlot, and Montepulciano.
Altitude: 280 metres above sea level.
Density: 4200 vines per hectare.
Yield: 90 quintals per hectare.
Ageing: in stainless steel vats.
The wine: light red in colour; fruity, herbaceous and spicy; soft, well balanced, with a pleasant acidity.
Food matches: fish, salamis and cheeses.
Alcoholic content: 12.5% vol.

Floridiana. IGT Umbria Rosso.

Grapes: Sangiovese, Merlot, and Cabernet.
Altitude: 280 metres above sea level.
Density: 4200 vines per hectare.
Yield: 80 quintals per hectare.
Ageing: first in stainless steel vats, then later in barriques.
Annual production: 30 000 bottles.
The wine: ruby red in colour, with violet reflections; fruity, flowery, slightly herbaceous and spicy, full-bodied, and suitably tannic.
Food matches: pasta, red meats and cheeses.
Alcoholic content: 13.5% vol.

Goliath. IGT Umbria Merlot.

Grapes: Merlot 100%.
Altitude: 280 metres above sea level.
Density: 4200 vines per hectare.
Yield: 65 quintals per hectare.
Ageing: first in stainless steel vats, then later in barriques.
Annual production: 25 000 bottles.
The wine: deep ruby red in colour, with violet reflections; intense, fruity and spicy, with hints of fruits of the forest and tobacco; full-bodied, soft with sweet tannins.
Food matches: pasta, red meats and cheeses.
Alcoholic content: 14% vol.

Lorenzo. IGT Umbria Merlot.

Grapes: Cabernet 100%.
Altitude: 280 metres above sea level.
Density: 4200 vines per hectare.
Yield: 65 quintals per hectare.
Ageing: first in stainless steel vats, then later in barriques.
Annual production: 20 000 bottles.

The wine: deep ruby red, with garnet reflections; with hints of blackberries and blackcurrants, sweet spices, vanilla, cinnamon, and black pepper; dry and warm, soft, with balanced tannins.
Food matches: red meats, chicken, and cheeses.
Alcoholic content: 14% vol.

Beatrice. IGT Umbria Sangiovese.

Grapes: Sangiovese 100%.
Altitude: 280 metres above sea level.
Density: 4200 vines per hectare.
Yield: 65 quintals per hectare.
Ageing: first in stainless steel vats.
Annual production: 40 000 bottles.
The wine: ruby red in colour, with purple reflections; with hints of blackberries and blackcurrants, vanilla, black pepper, and floral notes of violets; dry and warm, soft, with balanced tannins.
Food matches: salamis, chicken, and cheeses.
Alcoholic content: 13.5% vol.

Lori Lori. IGT Umbria Rosso.

Grapes: Sangiovese 65%, Montepulciano 20%, and Merlot 15%.
Altitude: 280 metres above sea level.
Density: 4200 vines per hectare.
Yield: 65 quintals per hectare.
Ageing: first in stainless steel vats.
Annual production: 60 000 bottles.
The wine: ruby red in colour, with purple reflections; floral and fruity, and slightly spicy; well structured, with soft tannins.
Food matches: pasta, fish and chicken dishes.
Alcoholic content: 12.5% vol.

Novello dell'Umbria. IGT Umbria Rosso.

Grapes: Sangiovese, Ciliegiolo, and Montepulciano.
Altitude: 280 metres above sea level.
Density: 4200 vines per hectare.
Vinification: carbonic maceration

Ageing: first in stainless steel vats.
Annual production: 15 000 bottles.
The wine: purple red in colour; floral and fruity, and slightly spicy; well structured, with soft tannins.
Food matches: pasta, fish and chicken dishes.
Alcoholic content: 12% vol.

Castello delle Regine

Castello delle Regine,
Strada di Castelluccio Amerino
Loc. Le Regine
05022 Amelia TR
Tel: 0744 702005
Fax: 0744 702006
www.castellodelleregine.com
castellodelleregine@virgilio.it

Castello delle Regine is the property of Paolo Nodari, a lawyer from Milan. Livia Colantonio runs the day to day business. The estate extends over 400 hectares surrounding the old fort, Castelluccio Amerino, which dominates the valley known as *le Regine* (the Queens) between Narni and Amelia. From the 1600s onwards the ownership of the land has been hotly disputed by a number of powerful families in the area. Consequently, in 1998 the estate had to be reconstituted and extended to ensure the continued existence of the traditional vineyards. According to Paolo Nodari: "When you own 398 hectares of land, with a hunting estate, olive groves, a luxury *agriturismo*, a herd of *Chianina* cattle, and more than 80 hectares of vineyards; it is not easy to be a lawyer in Milan, and a wine producer in Umbria".

Castello delle Regine has 10 hectares of vineyards over 40 years old, 70 hectares newly planted, and 10 hectares being developed. The terrain is sandy clay, and exposed mostly to the south, which provides the ideal conditions for the cultivation of vines. They include the indigenous Sangiovese, and Merlot, which has been grown in the area for over a hundred years, and is considered to be a native variety. Other varieties were also planted: Cabernet Sauvignon, Syrah, and Montepulciano; as the result of a study carried out by the oenologist, Franco Bernabei in the beginning of the 1990s. The grapes used for white wines include Chardonnay, Sauvignon Blanc, and Rhine Riesling. The density of planting is somewhere around 5000 vines per hectare, with a low yield of grapes, 50 quintals per hectare. The grapes are picked by hand and they are subject to a rigorous selection.

The wines produced are an authentic expression of the *terroir*. They are well structured, which requires long ageing in the bottle in order to develop their elegant taste.

Selezione del Fondatore. Sangiovese Grosso Umbria IGT.

Grapes: Sangiovese Grosso, from 40-45 year old vines.
Altitude: 280 metres above sea level, exposed to south-south/west.
Soil: mostly sand and clay.
Harvest: handpicked from the last week of September and throughout October.
Vinification: fermentation in 50 and 110 hectolitre stainless steel INOX tanks at a controlled temperature for 14 to 18 days. The malolactic fermentation takes place in French oak barriques (Alliers) from 12 to 14 months.
Ageing: 36 months in the bottle.
The wine: ruby red, garnet reflections; fragrances of blackberries and cherries, with balsamic notes; soft and well balanced.
Serving temperature: 18° C.
Alcohol content: 14% vol.

Merlot. Umbria IGT Rosso.

Grapes: Merlot 100%.
Altitude: 280 metres above sea level; exposed to south-south/west.
Soil: sandy and clayey.
Harvest: Hand picked from the first week of September.
Vinification: fermentation in 50 and 110 hectolitre stainless steel INOX tanks at a controlled temperature for 14 to 18 days, followed by malolactic fermentation.
Ageing: in barriques (Alliers) for 12 months, and refined in the bottle for an additional 24 months.
The wine: intense ruby red in colour; fragrances of ripe sour cherries, wild cherries, black cherries, with notes of coffee and chocolate; good structure and well balanced.
Serving temperature: 18° C.
Alcohol content: 14% vol.

Princeps. Umbria IGT Rosso.

Grapes: Cabernet Sauvignon 60%, Sangiovese 20%, and Merlot 20%.
Altitude: 280 metres above sea level; exposed to the south/west.
Soil: mostly sandy and clayey.
Age of vines: 12 to 15 years.
Yield per hectare: 40 to 50 quintals.
Harvest: handpicked according to the ripeness of each varietal from the last week of September and throughout October.
Vinification: alcoholic fermentation is carried out separately for each variety at a slow, controlled temperature for 14 to 20 days; followed by malolactic fermentation.
Ageing: in oak barriques (Alliers), then refined in the bottle for a minimum of two years.
The wine: intense ruby red in colour; fragrances of sour cherries, cherries, with notes of liquorice and tobacco; warm and soft, with a good structure and well balanced.
Serving temperature: 18° C.
Alcohol content: 13.5% vol.

Rosso di Podernovo. Umbria IGT Rosso.

Grapes: Sangiovese 80%, Montepulciano 10%, and Syrah 10%.
Altitude: 280 metres above sea level, with a south/west exposure.
Soil: well-structured sand and clay, with good drainage.
Age of vines: 30 years.
Harvest: from the last week of September to the end of October.
Vinification: fermentation takes place in 50 and 110 hectolitre stainless steel INOX tanks at a controlled temperature for 14 to 18 days; then malolactic fermentation follows.
Ageing: in Alliers Tonneaux and oak barrels, then refined in the bottle for a minimum of 8 months.
The wine: ruby red in colour, with violet reflections; fragrances of sour and wild cherries; well balanced, with soft tannins.
Serving temperature: 16-18° C.
Alcohol content: 13.5% vol.

Rose delle Regine. Umbria IGT Rosato.

Grapes: 100% Montepulciano.
Altitude: 150-180 metres above sea level, with south/West exposure.
Soil: a good balance of sand and clay.
Harvest: from the middle of September to the middle of October.
Vinification: cold maceration for 36 hours, the must is separated from the skins and transferred to 75 to 110 hectolitre stainless steel tanks, where alcoholic fermentation takes place for 25 days, then refined in stainless steel tanks at a controlled temperature.
The wine: intense rose, with transparent ruby reflections; with floral scents of violet and lilac and fragrances of black cherries and pomegranate; fresh, well balanced, with pleasant aromas.
Serving temperature: 10-12° C.
Food matches: light summer dishes, ideal with shellfish and fish.
Alcohol content: 12.5% vol.

Bianco delle Regine. Umbria IGT Bianco.

Grapes: Chardonnay 30%, Sauvignon Blanc 30%, Riesling 30%, and Pinot Grigio 10%.
Altitude: various, with woods surrounding the vineyards.
Soil: mostly sand and clay.
Harvest: Handpicked from the middle of August.
Vinification: the musts are crushed separately, according to grape variety, and kept in 50 to 75 hectolitre stainless steel INOX tanks, with cold temperature skin maceration and controlled temperature fermentation. The wines are blended just before bottling, without malolactic fermentation, or ageing in wood.
The wine: pale straw yellow in colour; floral notes and citrus flavours; fresh, with a pleasant acidity.
Serving temperature: 10-12° C.
Alcohol content: 13% vol.

Poggio delle Regine. Umbria IGT Rosso.

Grapes: Sangiovese 85%, Syrah and Merlot 15%.
Altitude: from 80 to 280 metres above sea level.

Soil: mostly sand and clay.
Density of vines per hectare: 5600.
Harvest: from the middle of September to the middle of October.
Vinification: in 75 to 115 hectolitre stainless steel INOX tanks, at a controlled temperature for 10 to 15 days.
Ageing: partly in stainless steel INOX tanks, and partly in medium size oak barriques for a minimum of 10 months.
The wine: ruby red in colour; well balanced, and slightly spicy.
Serving temperature: 12-14° C.
Alcohol content: 13% vol.

Poggio delle Regine. Umbria IGT Bianco.

Grapes: Trebbiano, Grechetto, and Malvasia.
Altitude: 200/300 metres above sea level; south/west exposure.
Soil: a mixture of sand and clay.
Harvest: from the end of August to the middle of September.
Vinification: cold maceration in 50/75 hectolitre stainless steel INOX tanks, then fermented at a controlled temperature, and refined in stainless steel INOX tanks until bottled.
It is a fresh white wine suitable to drink on any occasion.
Serving temperature: 8-10° C.
Alcohol content: 12% vol.

Le Vigne di Castelluccio

Two grappas made from Merlot grapes. Distilled by using a manually controlled discontinuous system with copper distillation columns. *La grappa di Merlot* is refined in oak barriques for four years, which gives it an extraordinary softness.

Ruffo

Marchesi Ruffo delle Scaletta Azienda Agricola
Via della Luna, 6
05035 Narni TR
Tel: 0744 715227
Fax: 0744 760686
ruruffo@tin.it

The Marchesi Ruffo delle Scaletta Azienda Agricola has its winery in Narni. The wine cellars are below the ancient castle of *Rocca Albornoz*. The estate is a large and profitable farm, growing plants of great variety, including bio-diesel crops. Cultivating grapes and producing wine is only a small part of the business, however, the estate retains the winery because it is part of the family tradition. The vineyards, surrounding the town of Narni, grow top quality grapes and the cellars produce wines of distinction, very much in the traditional way.

Collemarco. Umbria IGT Rosso.

Grapes: Merlot and Sangiovese.
Vinification: in oak barrels. Ageing: in small oak barrels.
Alcoholic content: 14% vol.

Camminata. Umbria IGT Rosso.

Grapes: Merlot and Sangiovese.
Vinification: in oak barrels. Ageing: in small oak barrels.
Alcoholic content: 13.5% vol.

San Giovenale. Umbria IGT Bianco.

Grapes: Chardonnay and Grechetto.
Alcoholic content: 12% vol.

Zanchi

Azienda Agricola Zanchi
Via Ortana, 122
05022 Amelia TR
Tel/Fax: 0744 970011
www.cantinezanchi.it
info@cantinezanchi.it

The origins of Azienda Agricola Zanchi go back to 1970, when the family purchased a century-old farm on the hills outside Amelia. There were ancient olive trees, a few rows of vines and uncultivated fields. They were brought back to a fruitful life, and over the following years the estate was given over to vineyards and olive groves. New vines were planted, particularly the native grape varieties.

The estate is a leader in producing premium quality wines, and it was one of the main forces behind gaining DOC recognition for Colli Amerini wines. Today, the hard work continues with the same passion by members of the family, generation after generation. They watch over every aspect of the cultivation of the grapes, vinification and the ageing of the wines.

Sciurio. Colli Amerini Rosso Superiore DOC.

Grapes: Sangiovese, Canaiolo, and Merlot.
Traditional vinification and controlled temperature alcoholic fermentation. Followed by malolactic fermentation and maturation for 36 months, 18 of which are in oak barrels, and 6 in the bottle.
The wine has a deep ruby red colour, showing notes of spice and nuances of wild berries, blackcurrant in particular. It is velvety on the palate, displaying dense, but soft tannins.

Armané. Colli Amerini Rosso Superiore DOC.

Grapes: Sangiovese, and Ciliegiolo.
Traditional vinification and controlled temperature alcoholic fermentation. Followed by malolactic fermentation and a maturation period of 16 months, with a period in oak barrels.
The wine has a ruby red colour, nose with fragrances of wild red berries. It is velvety, well balanced and judiciously tannic.

Carmìno. Ciliegiolo Umbria IGT.

Grapes: 100% Ciliegiolo.
Traditional vinification and controlled temperature alcoholic fermentation. Followed by malolactic fermentation and a maturation period of 6 months.
The wine has a brilliant red colour; crisp and heady nose, fruity, complex and dry on the palate.

Floresìo. Novello Umbria IGT.

Grapes: Sangiovese.
Obtained from carbonic maceration of the whole grapes.
The wine has a brilliant red colour; deep nose of recent fermentation. It has a fresh and fruity palate.

Lu. Aleatico Umbria IGT.

Grapes: 100% Aleatico.
Traditional vinification and controlled temperature alcoholic fermentation, which is arrested at the desired residual sugar level.
The wine has a ruby red colour, with purple reflections; and ripe red berries on the nose. It is appealingly sweet on the palate.

Tomeo. Colli Amerini Rosato DOC.

Grapes: Sangiovese, and Ciliegiolo.
Vinification of the red grapes is carried out with soft pressing. The must is separated from the skins, and controlled temperature fermentation follows. There is a maturation period of 6 months.

The wine has a distinctive salmon pink colour, a rich and fruity nose, elegantly rounded, crisp and young on the palate, with a good body and structure.

Majolo. Bianco Umbria IGT.

Grapes: Malvasia Toscana.
Vinification is carried out by soft pressing of the whole clusters of grapes, followed by controlled temperature fermentation, and a maturation period of 20 months, 12 of which are in oak tonneaux and 4 in the bottle.
The wine has a golden yellow colour. It is soft, rounded and crisp, with a high alcohol content and a rich palate.

Pizzale. Colli Amerini Bianco DOC.

Grapes: Trebbiano Toscano, Grechetto, and Malvasia.
Vinification is carried out by soft pressing of the whole clusters of grapes, followed by controlled temperature fermentation, and a maturation period of 5 months.
The wine has a straw yellow colour; rich fruit on the nose, dry and well balanced on the palate.

Flavo. Colli Amerini Malvasia DOC.

Grapes: Malvasia Toscana.
Vinification is carried out by soft pressing of the whole clusters of grapes, followed by controlled temperature fermentation, and a maturation period of 5 months.
The wine has a sparkling golden yellow colour; fruity and lingering, well balanced and velvety on the palate, with a judicious body.

Areia. Chardonnay Umbria IGT

Grapes: 100% Chardonnay.
Vinification is carried out by soft pressing of the whole clusters of grapes, followed by controlled temperature fermentation, and a maturation period of 5 months.

The wine has a straw yellow colour; delicate and floral on the nose; dry, full-bodied and well balanced on the palate.

Arvore. Grechetto Umbria IGT

Grapes: 100% Grechetto.
Vinification is carried out by soft pressing of the whole clusters of grapes, followed by controlled temperature fermentation, and a maturation period of 5 months.
The wine has a straw yellow colour with green tinges; fruity and velvety; dry and rounded on the palate.

Ciliegiolo Grappa.

This grappa is made from the pomace of Ciliegiolo. It is distilled using the alembic Charantais system. It has an elegantly fragrant nose, with hints of fruits and vanilla; and it is harmonious on the palate.
Alcohol Content: 45% vol.

THE WINE PRODUCERS
COLLI DEL TRASIMENO

In 1972 a Decree designated the production zone for Colli del Trasimeno or Trasimeno DOC wines. It includes the hills surrounding Lake Trasimeno, the districts of Perugia, Castiglione del Lago, Cittá della Pieve, Paciano, Panicale, Corciano, Magione, Passignano sul Trasimeno, and Tuoro sul Trasimeno.

The red, white and rosé wines produced are Bianco, Bianco Scelto, Cabernet Sauvignon, Gamay, Grechetto, Merlot, Rosato, Rosso, Rosso Scelto, Spumante Classico and Vino Santo or Vinsanto. The main basis for red wine is Sangiovese grapes, but also used are Gamay, Cabernet Sauvignon, Ciliegiolo and Merlot. For white wines the basis is Trebbiano, and Grechetto grapes, but also Chardonnay, Pinot Bianco and Pinot Grigio.

Lago Trasimeno is the fourth largest lake in Italy. Its waters are clean, its depth does not exceed seven metres, hence, it is an unusually warm lake, and a great tourist attraction. The lake is ringed with wooded hills, lush green valleys, and an unspoilt rolling countryside. There are ancient hilltop towns and villages dotted all over the horizon. They are all deeply steeped in history. The lakeside towns of Sanguineto (place of blood) or Ossia (place of bones) are where the Imperial Roman army was defeated by Hannibal in 217 BC. A more recent figure of interest is Giovanni da Pian di Carpine, a 12th century Franciscan monk, who preceded Marco Polo on the road to the Orient.

Like everywhere else in Umbria, the tradition of winemaking goes back to Etruscan times, and perhaps even earlier. The land surrounding Lake Trasimeno is ideal for the cultivation of vines, and the classical native varieties were grown on the hillsides since time immemorial. There is one international grape that found a new home here, Gamay, which is normally associated with Beaujolais in France. It thrives around the lake, and it has been grown for so long that it is considered to be a native variety.

Bertaio

Società Agricola Poggio Bertaio
Loc. Frattavecchia, 29
Casamaggiore
06061 Castiglione del Lago PR
Tel/Fax: 0759 56921
www.poggiobertaio.it
info@poggiobertaio.it

The Ciufoli family has owned the Poggio Bertaio winery since 1972. The estate began when Fabio, the father of the present owners, left the Castelli Romani (home of the famous Frascati wines), and moved to Castiglione del Lago. He bought a suitable piece of land, and planted some vineyards and continued his passion for winemaking, but in small quantities, just for the family and friends. Today, the estate spreads over 20 hectares.

11 hectares of Sangiovese, planted in 1972.
   1.5 hectares of Cabernet Sauvignon, planted in 1998.
   1.5 hectares of Merlot, planted in 1998.
   1.5 hectares of Cabernet Sauvignon, planted in 2000.
   1.5 hectares of Merlot, planted in 2000.
   3 hectares of Sangiovese, planted in 2004.

In the meantime, his two sons grew up. While Ugo spent more and more time with the management of the family estate, Fabrizio began his career as a winemaker, working for a number of important wineries. Having succeeded in making great wines for others, he wanted to test his skills further on the family's vineyards. He experimented with new techniques for producing the ideal wine, and to verify the theories he formulated during the preceding years whilst he was widening his experience.

Cimbolo. Umbria IGT Rosso.

Cimbolo was the first wine the two brothers made in 1998. "Cimbolo" means a bunch of grapes, and as they say: everything begins with the grape. Ugo Ciufoli was in charge of producing the grapes, and it was for Fabrizio to make an outstanding wine

from them. Presently, it is an IGT wine, but with some changes it could qualify for a DOC or even DOCG wine.
Grapes: 100% Sangiovese.
Age of vineyard: 25 years on average.
Density: 1600 vines per hectare.
Yield: 3 kg per plant.
Ageing: 24 months in French oak barriques, of which 20% are new, 40% used once before, and 40% used twice before, then in the bottle for another 12 months.
Ageing potential: 10 years in the bottle.
The wine: ruby red, with violet reflections; fragrances of cherries, cinnamon and liquorice; good tannins, and a long finish.

Crovello. Umbria IGT Rosso.

It is the second wine produced by the estate. "Crovello" refers to a must obtained for fermentation without pressing, or another way of saying: the pick of the wines of the highest quality.
Grapes: 50% Cabernet, and 50% Merlot.
Ageing: 24 months in new French oak barriques, then 18 months in the bottle.
Ageing potential: 15 years in the bottle.
The wine: deep and impenetrable ruby red in colour; fragrances of ripe fruits of the forest, with hints of chocolate; warm and well balanced, with soft tannins, and a long and lingering finish.

Stucchio. Umbria IGT Rosso.

Stucchio in the local dialect means field maple. In times past, grapevines were sometimes trained by winding them around the trunks and branches of field maple trees.
Grapes: 100% Sangiovese.
Ageing: 18 months in French oak barriques used three and four times before, then 4 to 5 months in the bottle.
Ageing potential: 5 to 6 years in the bottle.
The wine: ruby red in colour; fragrances of cherries, wild berries, and violets, and liquorice; full in the mouth, and a long finish.

Rosso 2008. Rosso dell'Umbria IGT.

Grapes: 70% Sangiovese, 20% Merlot, and 10% Cabernet.
Ageing: 12 months in stainless steel tanks.
Ageing potential: 2 to 3 years in the bottle.
2008 vintage production: 20 000 bottles.

Carpine

Terre del Carpine
Via Forma Nuova, 87
06063 Magione PR
Tel: 0758 402298
Fax: 0758 43744
www.trasinet.com/cit
cit@trasinet.com

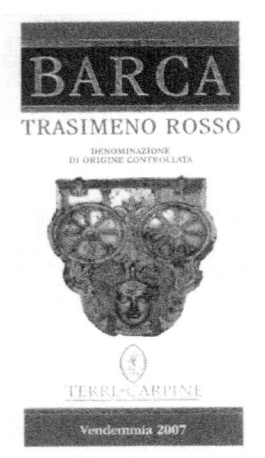

The winery is located in Magione by the lakeside. Small valleys, low wooded hills, surround the nearby localities of Corciano and Montersperello with an abundance of Mediterranean scrub, olive groves and vines. The countryside is staggeringly beautiful, and the land is ideal for the cultivation of vines. Not unexpectedly, the winemaking tradition goes back to Etruscan times.

The winery was founded in 1966. Since, it has developed and expanded with the arrival of new partners, the planting of new vineyards, and the construction of new premises. Today, the Terra del Carpine Cantina has 400 contributing winegrowers, and vineyards covering 420 hectares of land, with an average annual production of twenty thousand hectolitres of wine.

Since 1998 the winery replanted 200 hectares, in line with the most up-to-date vine growing methods, still mindful of the area's centuries old traditions. The new vineyards are located on slightly alkaline soil that also contains limestone and sandstone. The density of vine stocks is from three to six thousand per hectare. The use of the low cordon training, early thinning out the bunches of grapes, and harvesting by hand all contribute to producing top quality grapes. Attentive winemaking ensures that all the qualities of the original grapes are expressed to the full.

A tasting room welcomes customers and tourists for a visit, after they have travelled the Colli Trasimeno Wine Road.

Antìo. Colli del Trasimeno DOC.

Grapes: Trebbiano 40% minimum, Grechetto, Chardonnay, Pinot Bianco and Pinot Grigio, alone or mixed, at least 30%.
Yield: maximum 12 500 kg of grapes per hectare.
Yield in wine: not more than 70%.
The wine: straw in colour; lively, with a medium body.
Serving temperature: 10° C.
Food matches: aperitif, first courses, fish, vegetables and soups.
Alcohol content: 11.5% vol.
Minimum total acidity: 5 g/l.
Minimum net dry extract: 15 g/l.

Grìeco. Umbria IGT Bianco.

Grapes: 100% Grechetto.
Yield: maximum 8-9000 kg of grapes per hectare.
Yield in wine: not more than 70%.
The wine: intense straw yellow in colour, possibly golden; dry or slightly sweet, smooth, fruity with a bitter almond aftertaste.
Serving temperature: 10° C.
Food matches: aperitif, fish first courses, white meats, cooked vegetables and soups.

Chardonnay. Umbria IGT Bianco.

Grapes: 100% Chardonnay.
Yield: maximum 10 000 kg of grapes per hectare.
Yield in wine: not more than 70%.
The wine: straw yellow in colour; dry or slightly sweet, smooth, fruity with a slight bitter almond aftertaste.
Serving temperature: 8-10° C.
Food matches: aperitif, *hors d'oeuvres*, first courses, fish dishes, cooked vegetables and soups.
Alcohol content: 12% vol.
Minimum total acidity: 5 g/l.
Minimum net dry extract: 16 g/l.

Erceo. Colli del Trasimeno DOC Rosso.

Grapes: Sangiovese 40% minimum, Ciliegiolo, Gamay, Merlot, and Cabernet, alone or mixed 70%.
Yield: maximum 12 500 kg of grapes per hectare.
Yield in wine: not more than 70%.
The wine: intense garnet in colour; aromas of violets; dry, slightly tannic, with a medium body.
Serving temperature: 17° C.
Food matches: meat based second courses, game, and beans *all'uccelletto* (cooked with tomatoes).
Alcohol content: 11.5% vol.
Minimum total acidity: 5 g/l.
Minimum net dry extract: 19 g/l.

Barca. Colli del Trasimeno DOC Rosso.

Grapes: Sangiovese 50% minimum, Gamay 20%, Merlot 20%, and Cabernet 10%.
Yield: maximum 9 000 kg of grapes per hectare.
Yield in wine: 65 hectolitre per hectare.
Ageing: 3 months in the bottle.
The wine: intense garnet in colour; aromas of violets, dry, slightly tannic, with a full body.
Serving temperature: 18-20° C.
Food matches: country style soups, meat based second courses, roasts, game, and mature cheeses.
Alcohol content: 12.5% vol.
Minimum total acidity: 5 g/l.
Minimum net dry extract: 19 g/l.

Merlot. Umbria IGT Rosso.

Grapes: Merlot 100%.
Yield: maximum 9 500 kg of grapes per hectare.
Yield in wine: 65 hectolitre per hectare.
Ageing: medium term in barriques, then in the bottle.
The wine: ruby red in colour, turning to garnet with ageing; aromas of plums, dry, slightly tannic, with a full body.

Serving temperature: 18° C.
Food matches: meat based second courses, roasts, game, and mature cheeses.
Alcohol content: 13-14% vol.
Minimum total acidity: 5 g/l.

Tuori. Umbria IGT Rosso.

Grapes: Merlot, and Cabernet Sauvignon.
Yield: maximum 9 000 kg of grapes per hectare.
Yield in wine: 70 hectolitre per hectare.
Vinification: on the skins for 22 days in stainless steel tanks.
Ageing: 6 months in the bottle.
The wine: ruby red in colour; aromas of plums and undertones of red berries; dry, slightly tannic, with a full body.
Serving temperature: 18° C.
Food matches: first courses, roasts, game, and mature cheeses.
Alcohol content: 13-14% vol.
Minimum total acidity: 5 g/l.
Dry extract: 22 g/l.

Vinsanto.

Made from white grapes from Colli del Trasimeno vines. Colour ranges from straw yellow to amber, with golden reflections. The aroma is intense and characteristic; the flavour is harmonious and persistent. It is a dessert wine, excellent with dry patisserie.

Guizzo del Lago.

White sparkling wine made with 60% Grechetto, 20% Trebbiano, and 20% Malvasia grapes. For aperitif, *hors oeuvres*, and also with patisserie. It has fine bubbles and a fruity taste.

Agilla.

Made from the marc from Colli del Trasimeno DOC vines. It is a noble grappa, obtained by double distillation, using the steam method in a copper distilling plant. It is transparent with a sophisticated aroma.

Duca Della Corgna

Via Roma, 236
06061 Castiglione del Lago PG
Vine cellars: Via Pò di Mezzo
06062 Città della Pieve PG
Tel: 0759 652493
and 0759 9653210
Fax: 0759 9525303
www.ducadellecorgna.it
ducacorgna@libero.i

Castiglione del Lago sits on top of a limestone hill overlooking Lake Trasimeno. It is the land of the Della Corgna Dukes. The view from the 13th century fortress is marvellous: the spurs of the promontory fade into the lake, surrounded by gentle hills dotted with vineyards and olive groves. During the Renaissance the duke ruled the land and castle. He was a soldier of fortune, architect, and military engineer; and respected throughout Europe for his heroic achievements.

The Cantina del Trasimeno sells its products under a brand that takes its name from the great nobleman, Duca Della Corgna. With an eye on tradition, the company continues to improve the quality of its wines. Adopting modern growing techniques results in lower yields and better quality grapes. Investment in the winery and technical assistance from highly qualified professionals contributes to the making of exceptionally good wines. The Duca Della Corgna co-operative is one of the leading enterprises of the area and it is becoming more and more prominent on the national and international wine scene.

Divina Villa. Trasimeno Gamay DOC.

Grapes: 100% Gamay.
Vineyard: the hills of Castiglione del Lago, Paciano, and Panicale.
Density of vines: traditional 3.00 x 1.50 m. - new 2.20 x 0.90 m.
Training: low spurred cordon.

Average age of vines: 10-30 years.
Soil: sedimentary, sandy, and clayey, with some outcrops of clay.
Altitude: 300-350 metres above sea level.
Harvest: starts 15th October; the grapes are picked slightly over ripe in order to extract the most of the aromas and flavours.
Yield of grapes: 4000-4500 kg per hectare.
Yield of wine: 25-30 hectolitres per hectare.
Vinification: the grapes are de-stemmed, pressed and fermented on the skins for 20 days. Alcoholic fermentation is carried out at a controlled temperature of not higher than 30° C. After the wine is drawn off the skins, it is kept in temperature controlled stainless steel vats for malolactic fermentation.
Ageing: 12 months in French oak barriques, followed by 7 months in the bottle.
Bottling: in February, two years after the harvest.
Average annual production: 20-30 000 bottles.
The wine: dark, intense ruby red in colour; with aromas of wild berries, fruits of the forest; dry and elegant, with notes of cherries, strawberries, plums, and delicate spices.
Serving temperature: 18° C.
Food matches: grilled meats and roast game.

Baccio Del Rosso. Colli del Trasimeno DOC Rosso.

Grapes: 70% Sangiovese, 30% Gamay.
Vineyard: the hills of Petrignano del Lago, Vaiano, and Agello.
Density of vines: traditional 3.00 x 1.50 m. - new 2.20 x 0.90 m.
Training: spurred cordon; ground covered with grass.
Average age of vines: 10-20 years.
Soil: sedimentary, firm medium structure, with some fossils.
Altitude: 300-350 metres above sea level.
Harvest: from 5th to 10th October, when the grapes are ripe.
Yield of grapes: 60 quintals per hectares.
Yield of wine: 35-40 hectolitres per hectare.
Vinification: the grapes are de-stemmed, pressed and fermented on the skins for 7-10 days. Alcoholic fermentation is carried out at a controlled temperature of not higher than 25° C. After the wine is drawn off the skins, it is kept in temperature controlled stainless steel vats for malolactic fermentation.

Ageing: 4-5 months in the bottle.
Bottling: from July following the harvest.
Average annual production: 100 000 bottles.
The wine: ruby red in colour; with notes of red fruits, herbal scents and spices; dry and soft, with notes of cherries, strawberries, and plums; it has well-balanced tannins.
Serving temperature: 16° C.
Food matches: starters, salamis, first courses, grilled red meats and roast game.

Corniolo. Colli del Trasimeno DOC Rosso.

Grapes: Sangiovese, Gamay Perugino, and Cabernet Sauvignon.
Vinification: the grapes are de-stemmed, pressed and fermented on the skins for 20-25 days. Alcoholic fermentation is carried out at a controlled temperature.
Ageing: in French oak barriques, then in the bottle for twenty months.
Bottle ageing: 7 months.
The wine: intense ruby red in colour; dry, full, with complex fruit flavours and notes of sweet spices.
Serving temperature: 18° C.
Food matches: grilled red meats, roasts, and braised dishes.

Corio. Umbria IGT Rosso.

Grapes: 60% Sangiovese, 20% other red grape varieties.
Vineyard: on the hills of Castiglione del Lago, and Magione.
Density of vines: traditional 3.00 x 1.50 m. - new 2.20 x 0.90 m.
Training: double Guyot; ground covered with grass.
Average age of vines: 10-30 years.
Soil: sedimentary, mostly limestone, but poor in fossils.
Altitude: 250-300 metres above sea level.
Harvest: the grapes are picked when ripe.
Vinification: the grapes are de-stemmed, pressed and fermented at not higher than 25° C. Contact with the skins is reduced to the minimum in order to produce a fresh wine, ready to be consumed when young.
Average annual production: 300 000 bottles.

The wine: ruby red; fresh, soft, with notes of almond flowers.
Food matches: starters, delicate first courses, and white meats.

Martavello. Umbria IGT Rosato.

Grapes: 100% Gamay Perugino.
Vinification: after harvesting the grapes are immediately subjected to cold maceration for 10-12 hours to get the typical colour and to extract all the varietal aromas. Alcoholic fermentation takes place in stainless steel tanks at a controlled temperature of 14-18° C.
The wine: bright pink in colour, with purple reflections; aromas of rose, red berries, and spices; fresh, with mineral notes.

Nuricante. Colli del Trasimeno DOC Grechetto.

Grapes: 100% Grechetto dell'Umbria.
Vineyard: on the hills of the best DOC production zone.
Density of vines: traditional 3.00 x 1.50 m. - new 2.20 x 0.90 m.
Training: spurred cordon.
Average age of vines: 10-30 years.
Soil: sedimentary, with yellow sands and some fossils.
Altitude: 300-350 metres above sea level.
Harvest: from 10th to 25th September.
Yield of grapes: 65 quintals per hectare.
Yield of wine: 45 hectolitres per hectare.
Vinification: the grapes are de-stemmed and soft pressed; and the skins are immediately removed. Alcoholic fermentation takes place at a controlled temperature of not more than 18° C. Part of the must is fermented in oak barriques in order to enhance its varietal characteristics.
Bottling: starting end of March, early April after the harvest.
Ageing: 2 months in the bottle.
Average annual production: 20 000 bottles.
The wine: pale straw yellow in colour; with fruity and floral notes; dry, full and fragrant.
Serving temperature: 12° C.
Food matches: fish based *hors d'oeuvres*, pasta with seafood, baked fish dishes and white meats.

Baccio del Bianco. Colli del Trasimeno DOC Bianco.

Grapes: 60% Trebbiano, 40% Malvasia del Chianti and Grechetto.
Vineyard: Castiglione del Lago, Piana, and Petrignano del Lago.
Density of vines: traditional 3.00 x 1.50 m. - new 2.20 x 0.90 m.
Training: double Guyot; tilled land.
Average age of vines: 10-30 years.
Soil: sedimentary, sandy, and clayey, with some fossils.
Altitude: 200-250 metres above sea level.
Harvest: from 15th to 30th September.
Yield of grapes: 80 quintals per hectare.
Yield of wine: 40-55 hectolitres per hectare.
Vinification: the grapes are de-stemmed and soft pressed; followed by static clarification. Alcoholic fermentation takes place at a controlled temperature of not more than 18° C.
Bottling: starting in February after the harvest.
Ageing: 2 months in the bottle.
Average annual production: 100 000 bottles.
The wine: pale straw yellow in colour; with fruity and floral notes; dry and soft.
Serving temperature: 12° C.
Food matches: aperitif, delicate *hors d'oeuvres*, steamed shellfish, and baked fish dishes.

Corio. Umbria IGT Bianco.

Grapes: 80% Trebbiano, 20% or other white wine grapes.
Vineyard: on the hills of Castiglione del Lago, and Piana.
Density of vines: traditional 3.00 x 1.50 m. - new 2.20 x 0.90 m.
Training: double Guyot; grassed land.
Average age of vines: 10-30 years.
Soil: sedimentary, mostly sandy, with limestone and clay, poor in fossils and chalk.
Altitude: 200-250 metres above sea level.
Vinification: the grapes are de-stemmed and soft pressed; followed by static clarification. Alcoholic fermentation takes place at a controlled temperature of not more than 18° C.

Average annual production: 200 000 bottles.
The wine: pale straw yellow in colour, with green reflections; fresh, with floral notes; soft and lively.
Food matches: light starters, and delicate fish dishes.

Ascanio. Umbria IGT Bianco.

Grapes: 100% Grechetto dell'Umbria.
Vineyard: on the hills of Castiglione del Lago, and Piana.
Density of vines: 4 000 vines per hectare.
Training: low spurred cordon.
Average age of vines: 10 years.
Soil: sedimentary, with yellow sands, clay, and small fossils.
Altitude: 300 metres above sea level.
Harvest: during the first ten days of September.
Vinification: the grapes are de-stemmed and soft pressed and the skins are immediately removed. Alcoholic fermentation takes place at a controlled temperature of not more than 18° C.
Ageing: 2 months in the bottle.
Average annual production: 40 000 bottles.
The wine: pale straw yellow in colour; aromas of white flowers and apples; dry, fresh, with pleasant notes of white fruits.
Serving temperature: 12° C.
Food matches: aperitifs, *hors d'oeuvres*, light first courses, fish dishes, and white meats.

Grappa Gamè.

Distilled exclusively from Gamay Perugino grapes. It is completely transparent; the taste is dry, and delicate.
Serving temperature: 15-18° C.
Alcohol content: 40% vol.

Fanini

Cantina Fanini
Petrignano del Lago PG
Tel: 075 9528116
Fax: 075 500303
www.cantinafanini.it
info@cantinafanini.it

The Italian countryside changed drastically due to the upheavals of World War II and the following rapid industrial development. The farmers gave up their traditional way of life of cultivating the fields and raising cattle. They left their old family farmsteads and sought work in the big cities. The countryside changed into a desolate landscape, with its population reduced and the land left to ruin.

However, it was a two-way traffic, because a new breed of landowners moved in, townsfolk who left their frenetic city existence behind. They were lovers of nature, open air, and life in the country. They took over the old farms and revitalised the countryside with new methods of farming and wine growing.

Cantina Fanini is a good example of this movement. Starting from scratch, the family combined modern grape cultivation with their newly found knowledge of the territory and its traditions. It was a challenge that led to the production of outstanding wines.

Morello del Lago. Trasimeno Rosso DOC.

Grapes: Sangiovese, Canaiolo, Gamay, and other red grapes.
Density of vines: 4 500 vines per hectare.
Vinification: maceration and fermentation in 60 hectolitre stainless steel INOX vats.
Ageing: in 50 hectolitre oak barrels for at least 13 months, then in the bottle for at least 6 months.
Annual production: 120-150 hectolitres, or 15-20 000 bottles.

The wine: ruby red in colour, with the fragrance of ripe red fruits; the taste of soft tannins and a persistent finish.
Food matches: red meats, roasts, and mature cheeses.
Alcohol content: 12-12.5 % vol.
Total acidity: 5.4 g/l.

Vigna la Pieve. Sangiovese dell'Umbria IGT.

Grapes: Sangiovese 80%, and other red grapes.
Vinification: maceration and fermentation in 60 hectolitre stainless steel INOX vats.
Ageing: for 12 months in French oak barriques, already used once and twice before, then in the bottle for at least 6-8 months.
Annual production: 200 hectolitres, or 20-25 000 bottles.
The wine: ruby red in colour, with a good structure; and a rich fragrance of unique aromas.
Food matches: red meats, roasts, grills, and mature cheeses.
Alcohol content: 13.5-14 % vol.
Total acidity: 5.4 g/l.

Merlo+T. Merlot dell'Umbria IGT.

Grapes: Merlot 75%, and 15% Cabernet Sauvignon.
Vinification: maceration and fermentation in 60 hectolitre stainless steel INOX vats.
Ageing: at least for 12 months in new French oak barriques, then in the bottle for at least 6-8 months.
Annual production: 200 hectolitres, or 20-25 000 bottles.
The wine: ruby red in colour; good structure and unique aromas.
Food matches: red meats, roasts, grills, and mature cheeses.
Alcohol content: 14-14.5 % vol.
Total acidity: 5.5 g/l.

Balestrino. Rosato dell'Umbria IGT.

Grapes: Sangiovese and Merlot.
Vinification: maceration in INOX vats for 12-18 hours, followed by temperature controlled fermentation.
Ageing: in the bottle for 1-2 months.

Annual production: 30 hectolitres, or 4 000 bottles.
The wine: brilliant pink in colour, well rounded, with rich fragrances of ripe fruits.
Food matches: starters, seafood, roast and grilled fish, white meats, and young cheeses.
Alcohol content: 12.5 % vol.
Total acidity: 5.5 g/l.

<u>Robbiano. Chardonnay dell'Umbria IGT.</u>

Grapes: 100% Chardonnay.
Vinification: the grapes are de-stemmed and soft pressed, followed by fermentation in new French oak barriques from *Massiccio Centrale*, lightly toasted under control.
Ageing: in the bottle for at least 4 months.
Annual production: 100 hectolitres, or 10-12 000 bottles.
The wine: intense yellow in colour, well rounded and powerful, with rich fragrances of ripe fruits.
Food matches: starters, seafood, roast and grilled fish, white meats, and young cheeses.
Alcohol content: 13-13.5 % vol.
Total acidity: 5.5 g/l.

<u>Albello del Lago. Bianco dell'Umbria IGT.</u>

The latest wine produced by Cantina Fanini with the first harvest in 2008. It is a truly a great gamble! The best white grapes of Umbria were combined to produce a young and fresh white wine: made from Pinot Blanc, Sauvignon Blanc, and Tocai Friulano grapes; designed to produce a well rounded and powerful wine to accompany the best of dishes.

Lamborghini

Tenuta Patrizia Lamborghini S.r.l.
Loc. Soderi di Panicarola
06064 Panicale PR
Tel: 075 8350029
Fax: 075 9680280
www.lamborghinionline.it
info@lamborghinionline.it

2007

CAMPOLEONE
UMBRIA
INDICAZIONE
GEOGRAFICA
TIPICA

1997
★
2007

The Lamborghini estate is situated south of Trasimeno Lake, near the medieval village of Panicale. Travelling in the area, Ferruccio Lamborghini fell in love with the soft rolling hills of the landscape, and purchased the property in the 1970s. After retiring from manufacturing his world famous racing cars, he returned to his roots: that of being a farmer. He soon started to plant new grape varieties beyond the traditional Sangiovese and Ciliegiolo, like Merlot and Cabernet Sauvignon, which were unusual at that time. The estate covers a hundred hectares. It is divided between a nine-hole golf course, an agriturismo hotel, and thirty-two hectares of vineyards.

In 1997, Patrizia Lamborghini took over the management of the estate, pursuing, and even strengthening the ambition of making quality wines that her father has started. The majority of the vineyards have been replanted, removing the white grape varieties, and replacing them with Sangiovese and Merlot. At present, the new vineyards extend for a total area of 20 hectares. Dramatic improvements were achieved, due to the constant search for quality and the will to succeed. The most up-to-date methods are used for cultivating top grade grapes, and a modern winery is fully equipped to realise the potential of the *terroir*.

Campoleone. IGT Umbria Rosso.

Grapes: 50% Sangiovese, and 50% Merlot.
Vineyard: partly planted in the 1970s, and partly in the 1990s.
Density of vines: 5 500 vines per hectare.
Yield of grapes: not more than 1 kg per plant.
Vinification: maceration on the skins for 22 days, followed by malolactic fermentation.
Ageing: separately for each variety in new French oak barriques for 12 months, followed by blending, then in the bottle for 6 months.
Annual production: around 40 000 bottles.
Alcohol content: 13.5 % vol.
Total acidity: 5.0 g/l.
pH: 3.7 g/l.
Dry extract: 34.5 g/l.

Trescone. IGT Umbria Rosso.

Trescone is the name of a ball held for celebrating the harvest.
Grapes: Sangiovese, Ciliegiolo, and Merlot.
Vineyard: Sangiovese and Ciliegiolo were planted in the 1970s. The Merlot was planted in 1997.
Vinification: maceration on the skins for 20 days. Alcoholic fermentation in stainless steel INOX vats, also for 20 days.
Ageing: in 50 hectolitre barrels for 4 months.
Annual production: around 110 000 bottles.
Alcohol content: 13 % vol.
Total acidity: 5.1 g/l.
pH: 3.7 g/l.
Dry extract: 31.5 g/l.

Torami. IGT Umbria Rosso.

Grapes: Cabernet Sauvignon, Sangiovese, and Montepulciano.
Vineyard: partly planted in the 1970s, and partly in the 1990s.
Vinification: maceration on the skins for 22 days. Alcoholic fermentation in stainless steel INOX tanks for another 22 days.

Ageing: in new French oak barriques for 10 months, then for 6 months in the bottle.
Annual production: around 4 000 bottles.
Alcohol content: 13 % vol.
Total acidity: 5.15 g/l.
pH: 3.73 g/l.
Dry extract: 33.5 g/l.

<u>Era. IGT Umbria Sangiovese.</u>

Era was the wife of Zeus, patron of marriages and fertility.
Grapes: Sangiovese.
Vineyard: partly planted in the 1970s, and partly in the 1990s.
Density of vines: 5 500 vines per hectare.
Yield of grapes: not more than 1.5 kg per plant.
Vinification: maceration on the skins for 15 days, including alcoholic fermentation.
Ageing: malolactic fermentation and ageing is carried out in tonneaux barrels for 5 months, then for 6 months in the bottle.
Alcohol content: 13.5 % vol.
Total acidity: 5.1 g/l.
pH: 3.5 g/l.
Dry extract: 30 g/l.

Mezzetti

Azienda Agricola Stefania Mezzetti
Loc. Casella
06069 Tuoro sul Trasimeno PG
Tel: 0575 678528
Fax: 0575 679395
www.vinimezzetti.it
info@vinimezzetti.it

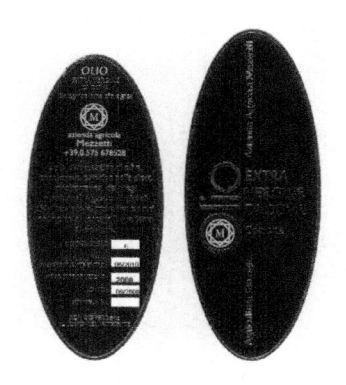

The Azienda Agricola Stefania Mezzetti is a small family farm. It grows grapes and olives organically, and produces wines and extra virgin olive oil in the cellars of La Casa Colonica. In addition, there is an agriturismo guesthouse with nine apartments, and a luxurious private villa, Villa Giulia. The fertile land, which surrounds the farmhouse, is the key to their success. The small-scale business is based on local farming traditions handed down from father to son over generations. The Mezzetti family maintains the love and respect for nature and the environment, which means that the organic farm requires daily attention, both to the vineyards and the olive groves.

It begins in the spring when the vines are tied and pruned with care, as it is at this stage that the final product is determined. The harvesting of the grapes is a festive occasion, where work is mixed with friendly local gossip. The handpicked grapes are taken to the cellars, where the stalks are removed and the grapes are pressed. The must is placed into vats to ferment for about a week, then the juice is separated from the skins, and transferred into oak barrels, where it stays until the spring.

The vineyards are spread over the border to Tuscany and wines are produced according to the regulations of both regions. The following list includes only the wines produced in Umbria.

Annibale. IGT Umbria Rosso.

Grapes: Sangiovese 80%, Merlot 10%, Cabernet Sauvignon 10%.
Ageing: 6 months in stainless steel.
The wine: ruby red; fragrances of ripe red fruits and spices.
Serving temperature: 16-18° C.
Food matches: a wine for all meals.

Annibale 217. IGT Umbria Rosso.

Grapes: Sangiovese 33%, Merlot 33%, Cabernet Sauvignon 34%.
Ageing: 12 months in oak barrels.
The wine: deep ruby red in colour, with garnet reflections; fragrances of spices, cocoa, vanilla, and toasted bread; full bodied, warm, soft and velvety, with soft tannins.
Serving temperature: 18-20° C.
Food matches: roast red meats, game, and mature cheeses.

Didone. IGT Umbria Bianco.

Grapes: Trebbiano Toscano, and Grechetto.
Ageing: 6 months in stainless steel vats.
The wine: straw yellow in colour; fresh, with floral notes; full bodied, warm, soft and velvety, with soft tannins.
Serving temperature: 18-20° C.
Food matches: roast red meats, game, and mature cheeses.

Elissa. IGT Umbria Rosato.

Grapes: Sangiovese 33%, Merlot 33%, and Cabernet Sauvignon 34%.
Ageing: 6 months in stainless steel vats.
The wine: pale pink in colour: delicate, fresh, and fruity; full bodied, with hints of red fruits and flowers in the finish.
Serving temperature: 10-11° C.
Food matches: soup, fish soup, seafood appetisers, lake fish, and soft cheeses.

La Querciolana

Azienda Agricola Agrituristica La Querciolana
Via Vieniche, 4
06064 Panicale PG
Tel/Fax: 075 837477
Cell: 334 1066686
www.laquerciolana.it
info@laquerciolana.it

La Querciolana is located near the ancient hilltop village of Panicale. A Benedictine monastery built during the 12th century has been completely refurbished to provide apartments for the agriturismo side of the business. It is a family-run enterprise; it makes wines and olive oil of high quality. All the members of the Carrà family are involved. Tullio and Maria Luisa have established the farm; and run the business assisted by their sons, Alessio and Guelfo. Alessio is the winemaker, and Guelfo manages the catering and hospitality services.

The vineyards cover approximately 20 hectares at an altitude of 350-400 metres above sea level, with an east/west exposure. They produce around 90 quintals of grapes per acre. The system of training is the Guyot and the spurred cordon. Organic fertilisers are used in order to give the soil a greater physiological balance. The harvest is carried out by hand; the grapes are selected and handpicked and taken to the winery in boxes.

The cellars are in the monastery building, a hundred square metres divided into three sections: vinification, ageing, and bottling. Slovenian oak barrels and vats are used for ageing. The wines are named Boldrino in honour of the famous mercenary captain, Boldrino Paneri of Panicale. For a short period he lived at La Querciolana, which was a Benedictine monastery at the time.

Grifo di Boldrino. Rosso Riserva, Colli del Trasimeno DOC.

Grapes: Sangiovese, Cabernet Sauvignon, and Gamay.
Ageing: 24 months in oak barrels.
The wine: ruby red in colour, with garnet reflections; delicate, fruity and floral; dry, warm, soft, rather tannic, and full-bodied.
Food matches: roast meats, and mature cheeses.

Rosso di Boldrino. Colli del Trasimeno DOC.

Grapes: Sangiovese, and Gamay.
The wine: ruby red in colour; delicate, fruity and floral; dry, warm, soft, rather tannic and full-bodied.
Food matches: starters, pasta, meats, and cheeses.

Gamay di Boldrino. Rosso dell'Umbria IGT.

Grapes: 100% Gamay.
The wine: ruby red in colour; with delicate scents and a dry taste.
Food matches: starters, pasta, and cheeses.

Rosato di Boldrino. Umbria IGT.

Grapes: Sangiovese, Gamay, and Merlot.
The wine: pink in colour; fruity, light and dry.
Food matches: aperitif, starters, white meats, and cheeses.

Bianco di Boldrino. Sauvignon dell'Umbria IGT.

Grapes: 100% Sauvignon.
The wine: straw yellow in colour; aromas of nettles and black currants, with a fresh taste.
Food matches: aperitif, starters, white meats, and cheeses.

NB: The estate also produces Grappa di Boldrino, and Extra Virgin olive oil.

Il Poggio

Azienda Vitivinicola Il Poggio
Via Petrarca 60
06060 Macchie,
Castiglione del Lago PG
Tel/Fax: 075 9680381
www.vitivinicolailpoggio.com
info@vitivinicolailpoggio.com

The Il Poggio is a family run business, which has been making wines for over forty years. They combine modern technology with ancient traditions and produce quality wines. Enthusiasm and the love of work is the key to their success.

The vineyards are set amongst the hills surrounding Lake Trasimeno, in the commune of Castiglione del Lago; an area recognised as particularly suitable for the production of full-bodied wines with complex structures.

The wine cellar was designed to provide close control over all the phases of production: winemaking and bottling. It also allows experiments on a small scale in order to produce special wines of ever increasing quality. Visitors are welcome to taste the wines, but please book in advance.

Trasimeno Merlot 04, 05, and 07 DOC.

Grapes: Merlot 100%.
Vintages: 2004, 2005, and 2007.
Yield: 90 quintals of grapes per hectare.
Ageing: partly in cement vats, partly in stainless steel INOX tanks, then 6 months in the bottle.
The wine: intense garnet in colour, turning to brick red with ageing; aromas of ripe cherries and violets; dry, with soft tannins and a spicy aftertaste, with a hint of black pepper.
Serving temperature: 18-20° C.
Food matches: all kinds of meats, game, and mature cheeses.
Alcoholic content: 13 to 14% vol.

Trasimeno Rosso Scelto 06 DOC.

Grapes: 80% Merlot, and 20% Sangiovese.
Vintage: 2006.
Yield: 90 quintals of grapes per hectare.
Ageing: partly in cement vats, partly in stainless steel INOX tanks, then 6 months in the bottle.
The wine: intense garnet, turning to brick red with ageing; aromas of ripe red berries; dry, with soft tannins and a slightly spicy aftertaste, with a hint of black pepper.
Serving temperature: 18° C.
Food matches: all kinds of meats; grilled or roast.
Alcoholic content: 13.5% vol.

Umbria Rosso IGT.

Grapes: 100% Sangiovese.
Yield: 90 quintals of grapes per hectare.
Ageing: partly in stainless steel INOX tanks, then in the bottle.
The wine: intense garnet, turning to brick red with ageing; aromas of cherries and violets; dry, velvety, with soft tannins and a slightly spicy aftertaste, with a hint of black pepper.
Serving temperature: 18° C.
Food matches: country style soups, and most main courses.
Alcoholic content: 13% vol.

Umbria Rosato IGT.

Grapes: Sangiovese 60%, and Ciliegiolo 40%.
Yield: 90 quintals of grapes per hectare.
Vinification: 24 hours of maceration on the skins, then fermentation under a controlled temperature.
Ageing: in cement vats and in stainless steel INOX tanks.
The wine: pink in colour, with garnet reflections; aromas of tropical fruits, full-bodied, with just the right amount of acidity for freshness; fruity, slightly spicy, with an aftertaste of cherries.
Serving temperature: 10-14° C.
Food matches: with all kinds of pastas.
Alcoholic content: 12.5% vol.

Umbria Bianco IGT.

Grapes: Grechetto 100%.
Yield: 60 quintals of grapes per hectare.
Vinification: fermentation under a controlled temperature.
Ageing: in cement vats and in stainless steel INOX tanks.
The wine: straw yellow in colour, with green reflections; aromas of ripe pears, fresh, fruity slightly bitter, with a pleasant acidity.
Serving temperature: 10-12° C.
Food matches: starters, fish, and typical Italian first courses.
Alcoholic content: 12.5% vol.

Umbria Vermentino IGT.

Grapes: Vermentino 100%.
Yield: 80 quintals of grapes per hectare.
Vinification: fermentation under a controlled temperature.
Ageing: in cement vats and in stainless steel INOX tanks.
The wine: straw yellow in colour, with lemon reflections; spicy, with aromas of tropical fruits; slightly sharp, fruity, with a pleasant acidity and an aftertaste of cinnamon.
Serving temperature: 10-12° C.
Food matches: aperitif, all pastas, but best with fish.
Alcoholic content: 13% vol.

Umbria Pinot Bianco IGT.

Grapes: Pinot Bianco 100%.
Yield: 60 quintals of grapes per hectare.
Vinification: fermentation under a controlled temperature.
Ageing: in cement vats and in stainless steel INOX tanks.
The wine: straw yellow in colour, with green reflections; aromas of peaches, sharp, slightly bitter and an aftertaste of citrus fruits.
Serving temperature: 8-10° C.
Food matches: aperitif, ideal with fried fish.
Alcoholic content: 13% vol.

Pucciarella

Azienda Agricola Pucciarella S.r.l.
Via Case Sparse, 37
Località Villa
06063 Magione PG
Tel: 075 8409147
Fax: 075 8409440
www.pucciarella.it
info@pucciarella.it

The Azienda Agricola Pucciarella is situated amongst the hills around Lake Trasimeno. Its vineyards cover 58 hectares at an average height of 300 metres above sea level. The combination of altitude, exposure, soil characteristics, and the climate, with soft breezes blowing in from the lake, make the area suitable for producing wine. The low yields in the vineyards ensure top quality grapes, which in turn produces wines of distinction that fully express the *terroir*.

Riccardo Cotarella wrote: "I have been collaborating with Pucciarella Farm for over four years. I can proudly affirm the high level of quality achieved by all products, thanks to the work of diversification of the different wines, which have acquired their own personality."

Berlingero. Colli del Trasimeno Rosso DOC.

It is a wine with a balanced round taste, the result of careful winemaking, aimed to enhance the fruity and spicy notes of Sangiovese, Merlot, and Cabernet. It is best consumed when young, and it also adapts to discrete ageing.
Food matches: pasta dishes, white meat, semi-mature cheeses.

Agnolo. Colli del Trasimeno Bianco Scelto DOC.

A wine made at a low temperature vinification and a careful blend of indigenous and international varietals – Chardonnay, Grechetto, Sauvignon, and Pinot Bianco. It highlights the potential of Pucciarella's *terroir*, and it is intense, delicate, and fruity, with floral scents. It tastes fresh and well rounded.
Food matches: appetisers, light pasta dishes, and fish.

Vin Santo. Colli del Trasimeno, Vin Santo DOC.

It is made with Trebbiano, Malvasia and Grechetto, handpicked and left to dry for over three months. The fermentation and refinement is carried out in traditional kegs for over three years, which give the wine a coppery colour and a distinctively intense aroma of dried fruit and honey. The flavour is sweet, intense, very long, and mellow.
Food matches: cakes and biscuits, and mature cheeses.

Arsiccio. Chardonnay dell'Umbria IGT.

It is a full bodied and warm white wine made of Chardonnay grapes. It is harvested manually at the end of August. The vinification is carried out in steel and oak barrels, which gives the wine complex fruity aromas, supported by delicate hints of wood. It is soft, but it has a firm texture.
Food matches: light appetisers and first courses, also baked fish.

Empireo. Rosso dell'Umbria IGT.

It is made from Cabernet and Merlot, grown on soil rich in fossils ideal for producing quality grapes. The wine is deep red in colour, with a full structure, firm, yet soft and enveloping. It is aged in oak barrels for 14 months and in the bottle for 12 months.
Food matches: red meat, game, and mature cheeses.

Sant' Anna. Colli del Trasimeno Rosso Riserva DOC.

It is made from Sangiovese, Merlot, and Cabernet grapes, and aged in oak barriques and barrels for 12 months. Ruby red in colour, with intense aromas of violets, wild berries, plum, tobacco, and leather. It has firm tannins and a good structure, and is ideal for ageing in the bottle.
Food matches: red meat, game, and mature cheeses.

Ca' de Sass. Colli del Trasimeno DOC.
Spumante Metodo Classico. Brut.

It is made with Chardonnay grapes, harvested by hand in boxes, and crushed whole to enhance the flavours. The slow second fermentation and extended ageing on the lees imparts a characteristic and unmistakable aroma to this sparkling wine.
Food matches: shellfish, fish, an ideal accompaniment to any meal.

Vino Spumante Rosé.
Metodo Classico. Brut.

It is made of Pinot Nero grapes, harvested by hand in boxes, and taken directly to the press in order to obtain a light pink coloured must. The slow second fermentation and ageing on the lees for 12 months, enhances the floral and fruity notes that make this sparkling wine particularly enjoyable.
Food matches: appetisers, shellfish, fish, an ideal accompaniment to any meal.

Grappa di Uve di Vin Santo.

This grappa is made from the grapes of Vin Santo, distilled using a traditional batch system. It is produced in limited quantities, solely from the heart of the distillation.
Available in 350 ml bottles.

THE WINE PRODUCERS
COLLI ALTOTIBERINI

In 1980, a Decree designated the production zone for Colli Altotiberini DOC wines. It covers the hills by the Upper Tiber including the districts of Citerna, Cittá di Castello, Gubbio, Monte Santa Maria Tiberina, Perugia, San Giustino and Umbertide.

The whites are Bianco with Trebbiano Toscano, Malvasia del Chianti, and an addition of three other whites from the local area. The wines are straw yellow in colour, with a dry aromatic bouquet and a minimum alcoholic content of 10.5% vol.

The red and rosé wines are Rosso and Rosato, made from Sangiovese, Merlot, Trebbiano Toscano and Malvasia del Chianti grapes. Other red vines from the area can also be used. The wines produced are intense ruby-red in colour, with a dry and rounded note, and a minimum alcoholic content of 11.5%.

The River Tiber enters Umbria from the north near the town of San Giustino as it winds its way down south; passing by Cittá di Castello, Umbertide and Perugia. This is the section that includes the Colli Altotiberini DOC production zone. The countryside on either side of the river is impressively desolate; not the Umbrian pastoral idyll of the lower reaches of the Tiber. There are only a few roads leading to small villages set amongst thousands of hectares of natural woodland and abandoned pasture. The place teems with wildlife: exotic birds, deer, wild boar, and even wolves. Apart from sheep farming, the main agricultural activity seems to be growing tobacco. However, there is also a tradition of winemaking going back to Etruscan times, just like anywhere else in Umbria.

I Girasoli di Sant'Andrea

Azienda Agricola I Girasoli di Sant'Andrea S.p.a.
Loc. Molino Vitelli
06019 Umbertide PG
Tel: 075 9410798/837
Fax: 075 9427114
www.grittivini.eu
info@vitiarium.it

In 1994 Carlo and Ursula Gritti bought an old country house in the Niccone Valley with 120 hectares of farmland and vineyards known as La Fattoria I Girasoli di Sant'Andrea (The Farm of the Sunflowers of Saint Andrew). Their passion for winemaking led to the production of the first bottles of wine in 2000. Today the farm is almost self-sufficient and includes a restaurant. A diverse variety of agricultural production includes vines, olives, arable crops, and the raising of livestock. However, wine production is the principal activity, and the aim is to make quality wine that reflects the *terroir* of Umbria, and in particular, the Niccone Valley.

La Fattoria I Girasoli di Sant'Andrea is situated in the Niccone Valley, (The River Niccone joins the Tiber just north of Umbertide), near Umbria's border with Tuscany. The climate is mild and the land is fertile. Clouds do not linger in the fresh air over the hills and the humidity is low throughout the year. The soil is alluvial, workable clay with a moderate lime content. The vineyards are situated on south facing hills at altitudes of 280 to 400 metres above sea level.

The vines are carefully looked after all year round to obtain the perfect balance between quality and quantity. The grapes are harvested between early September and mid-October, and are immediately transferred either to stainless steel or large (400-litre) oak fermenting vats. The winery is equipped with the latest modern equipment and a new bottling plant. There is a large, temperature controlled barrel room with barriques of different capacities and level of toasting to allow the wines to age.

Filare 78. IGT Umbria Rosso.

Filare 78 (Row 78) is named after the first row of Montepulciano grapes planted in the vineyard.
Grapes: Montepulciano 95%, and other varieties 5%.
First year of production: 2007.
Yield: 6500 kg per hectare.
Age of vines: 10 years.
Density of vines: 6600 per hectare.
Harvest: mid-October.
Vinification: fermentation on the skins for around 16-18 days in stainless steel temperature controlled vats.
Ageing: 20 months in French oak barriques from the Alliers Forest.
Bottles produced: 3000-4000.
The wine: Deep ruby red in colour, with purple tones; aromas of vanilla, violets, morello cherry, blackberry, coffee, and liquorice; warm, with smooth tannins and flavours of ripe fruit and spices.
Ageing potential: medium to long, and continues to evolve over time. Keep in a cool dry place, and store at 15° C.
Serving temperature: 16-18° C.
Food matches: red meat, game, and very mature cheeses. Also Umbrian jugged wild boar.

Sant'Andrea. IGT Umbria Rosso.

Grapes: Sangiovese 100%.
First year of production: 2006.
Yield: 6500 kg per hectare.
Age of vines: 10 years.
Density of vines: 6600 per hectare.
Harvest: mid-October.
Vinification: fermentation on the skins for around 18 days in stainless steel temperature controlled vats.
Ageing: 18 months in French oak barriques and large barrels from the Alliers Forest.
Bottles produced: 4000-5000.

The wine: clear ruby red in colour; aromas of fruits of the forest, violets, cherries, leather, liquorice, tobacco, sweet spices, and herbs and a good level of tannins.
Keep away from light in a cool dry place, and store at 15° C.
Serving temperature: 16-18° C.
Food matches: red meat, grilled steak, and mature cheeses.

Mazzaforte. IGT Umbria Rosso.

Grapes: Sangiovese 70%, and Merlot 30%.
First year of production: 2007.
Yield: 7500 kg per hectare for Sangiovese; 6000 kg for Merlot.
Age of vines: 10 years.
Density of vine: 5000 per hectare for Sangiovese; and 6600 vines per hectare for Merlot.
Harvest: for Sangiovese during the first two weeks in October; for Merlot in mid-September.
Vinification: fermentation on the skins for around 15-18 days in stainless steel temperature controlled vats.
Ageing: in large capacity oak vats (4000-litre) for 12 months.
Bottles produced: 4000-5000.
The wine: ruby red in colour; aromas of fruits of the forest, with notes of violet, rose, fern, aromatic herbs and spices. It is full, well rounded and soft with balanced and persistent tannins.
Keep in a dark, cool, and dry place; store at 15° C.
Serving temperature: 16-18° C.
Food matches: red meats, pasta, tagliatelle with ragù of wild boar.

Syrah. IGT Umbria Rosso.

Grapes: Syrah 100%.
First year of production: 2007.
Yield: 6500 kg per hectare.
Age of vines: 10 years.
Density of vines: 5000 per hectare.
Harvest: during the second two weeks in September.
Vinification: fermentation on the skins for around 16-18 days in stainless steel temperature controlled vats.

Ageing: in large capacity oak vats (4000-litre) for 12 months.
Bottles produced: 5000-8000.
The wine: deep ruby red in colour, with violet reflections; aromas of blackberries, prunes, pepper and vanilla; rich fruity flavour, with delicate and soft tannins.
Keep away from the light, in a cool and dry place; store at 15° C.
Serving temperature: 16-18° C.
Food matches: cold meats, mature cheeses; and stuffed pigeon.

Malvasia Nera. IGT Umbria Rosso.

Grapes: Malvasia Nera 100%.
First year of production: 2007.
Yield: 8000 kg per hectare.
Age of vines: 10 years.
Density of vines: 5000 per hectare.
Harvest: during the second two weeks in September.
Vinification: fermentation on the skins for around 12-15 days in stainless steel temperature controlled vats.
Ageing: in stainless steel tanks for several months.
Bottles produced: 5000-7000.
The wine: ruby red in colour, with floral aromas; red roses and fruity notes of cherry jam; a tangy flavour is supported by a fresh spiciness. Malvasia Nera is a young wine to be drunk preferably within 2-3 years of bottling.
Keep away from the light, in a cool and dry place; store at 15° C.
Serving temperature: 16-18° C.
Food matches: cold meats, cheeses, and baked guinea fowl.

Sangiovese Merlot. IGT Umbria Rosso.

Grapes: Sangiovese 60%, and Merlot 40%.
First year of production: 2008.
Yield: 8000 kg per hectare for Sangiovese, and 8000 kg for Merlot.
Age of vines: 10 years.
Density of vines: 5000 per hectare.
Harvest: for Sangiovese during the first two weeks in October; for Merlot in mid-September.

Vinification: fermentation on the skins for around 12-15 days in stainless steel temperature controlled vats.
Ageing: in stainless steel tanks for several months.
Bottles produced: 2000-2500.
The wine: ruby red in colour; aromas of blackberries, and redcurrant jam, plums, and background notes of spices and mint; fresh and lively, with delicate tannins and a hint of minerals.
Keep away from the light, in a cool and dry place; store at 15° C.
Serving temperature: 16-18° C.
Food matches: cold meats, cheeses, and pasta dishes.

Trian. IGT Umbria Bianco.

Grapes: Friulano 80%, and Sauvignon 20%.
First year of production: 2007.
Yield: 9000 kg per hectare both for Friulano and for Sauvignon.
Age of vines: 10 years.
Density of vines: 5000 per hectare.
Harvest: for Friulano in mid-September, for Sauvignon at the start of September.
Vinification: the grapes are macerated on the skins for 8 hours in a horizontal press; afterwards the must is cleared by natural settling; then fermented in temperature controlled stainless steel vats at a low temperature of 16-18° C.
Bottles produced: 5000-8000.
The wine: pale yellow in colour; aromas of lime flowers, sage, green apples and white peaches; dry, warming, with good acidity and a hint of minerals. It has an aftertaste of almonds and herb.
Keep away from the light, in a cool and dry place; store at 15° C.
Serving temperature: 8-10° C.
Food matches: vegetable soups, risotto, fish, and Umbrian chickpea and black cabbage soup.

Rhea. IGT Umbria Passito.

Grapes: Grechetto 33%, Malvasia Bianco 33%, and Trebbiano Toscano 34%.
First year of production: 2000.

Yield: 7000 kg per hectare for Grechetto, 8000 kg for Malvasia Bianca, and 10 000 kg for Trebbiano Toscano.
Age of vines: 10 years.
Density of vines: 5000 per hectare.
Harvest: for Grechetto last two weeks in September, for the other varieties during the first two weeks in October.
Vinification: the grapes are dried on racks for more than two months, then soft pressed and the must is transferred to small oak barrels (80-100 litres) and left to ferment for five years, while the wine slowly clears through natural settling. The beautiful amber colour of this wine is obtained without filtration, and there may be some natural sediment.
Bottles produced: 1000-2000.
The wine: copper yellow in colour, with tones of amber; aromas of dried figs, dates, sultanas, walnuts, with notes of coffee and chestnut honey. It is an unusually concentrated wine that envelopes the mouth with its sweetness and noticeable acidity.
Keep away from the light, in a cool and dry place; store at 15° C.
Serve at 8-10° C.
Food matches: desserts and mature cheeses.

Blasi

Cantine Blasi Bertanzi e Agriturismo Vigne di Pace
Via Case Sparse, 64
Loc. S Benedetto
06019 Umbertide PG
Tel: 339 8697891
Fax: 075 9413451
www.cantineblasi.it
blasibertanzi@libero.it

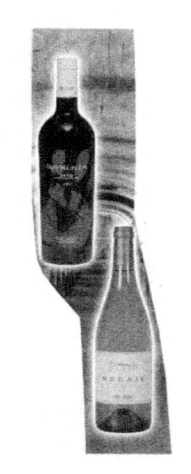

Members of the Blasi family have lived and worked in Umbertide for years and were successful in a number of commercial activities. In the late 1990s they bought part of the Conti Bertanzi Mochi Onori mansion, including a wine cellar that dates back to 1742. They completely restored and refurbished the cellar and made it a place where modernity meets tradition; where elegance mingles with practicality, and winemaking is felt like a moral duty. In the old parts of the cellar they found ancient casks and barriques of French oak, and they are still used for ageing the wines. The annual production is around 20 000 bottles. Honouring tradition, the Blasi family added the name Bertanzi to the logo of the winery's products. The vineyards cover 20 hectares of land where autochthonous and international grape varieties are cultivated side by side, like geometric gardens surrounding the buildings of the old mansion.

The Agriturismo Vigne di Pace is part of the estate. The ancient buildings have been completely restored and divided into elegant self-catering apartments. There are also three adjoining cottages, a luxurious swimming pool, and a traditional inn specialising in authentic Umbrian cuisine.

Impronta. Umbria Rosso IGT. 2008.

Grapes: Sangiovese 30%, Merlot 30%, and Sagrantino 40%.
Vinification: in stainless steel vats.

Ageing: in French oak barriques for 18 months, then for 6 months in the bottle.
The wine: deep violet in colour, with blackcurrant, cherry and blackberry aromas, and with hints of tobacco. It is full bodied, with soft tannins and a long finish with balanced acidity.
Alcoholic content: 14% vol.

Rogaie. Umbria Bianco IGT. 2007.

Grapes: Chardonnay 50%, Riesling 30%, and Trebbiano 20%.
Vinification: in stainless steel vats.
Ageing: in French oak barriques for twelve months, followed by four months in stainless steel.
The wine: straw yellow in colour, with aromas of herbs, green apples, sage, vanilla and minerals. It has soft, light tannins well balanced with the wine's acidity, and a long finish.
Alcoholic content: 12.5% vol.

Blasi Bertanzi. Umbria Rosso IGT. 2005.

Grapes: Merlot, and Cabernet Sauvignon.
Vinification: in stainless steel vats.
Ageing: in French oak barriques and barrel for 12-13 months, then for 3 months in the bottle.
The wine: deep red in colour, with violet reflections; blackcurrant, and blackberry aromas. It is full bodied, with soft tannins and a long finish with a balanced acidity.
Alcoholic content: 13.5% vol.

Regghia. Umbria Rosso IGT. 2005.

Grapes: Sangiovese, Syrah, and Aleatico.
Vinification: in stainless steel vats.
Ageing: in French oak barrels for 12-13 months, then for 3 months in the bottle.
The wine: deep ruby red in colour, with cherry and blackberry aromas; full bodied, and a long finish with a balanced acidity.
Alcoholic content: 13.5% vol.

Rosato. Umbria Rosato IGT.

Grapes: Sangiovese, Merlot, and Gamay.
Vinification: maceration on the skins for 10-12 hours, then fermentation in stainless steel vats at less then 18° C.
Ageing: in French oak barrels, then for 3 months in the bottle.
The wine: bright pink in colour, with fresh, fruity aromas.
Alcoholic content: 13% vol.

Mam Mam Ia. Umbria Bianco Passito IGT. 2006.

Grapes: Trebbiano Toscano and Semillon.
The grapes are dried for 3-4 months on mats, followed by vinification in stainless steel vats.
Ageing: in French oak barriques for five years.
The wine: golden yellow in colour, with amber reflections and a long and lingering finish.
Alcoholic content: 16% vol.

Donini

Donini s.n.c. di Donini Diego Alvaro & Co.
Via Nestoro 59
Fraz. Verna
06019 Umbertide PG
Tel: 075 9410330
Fax: 075 9410411
www.vinidonini.it
info@vinidonini.it

The winery started producing and selling wines in 1921, when Donini Domenico (born in 1899), and his brother, Donini Ruggero (born in 1895) returned from World War I and decided to open a shop in Verna to sell their home made wines. With the help of their sons, Dino and Mario, they increased the production of wine, even though it was aimed towards the local market. In the early 1980s they widened their marketing effort in the Upper Tiber Valley, and began to produce wines with selected local grapes and varieties traditionally cultivated in the Valtiberino.

Even though the Upper Tiber Valley represents a small part of Umbria's wine production, it is an important oenological area. The place has a favourable climate for wine production, influenced by the Apennine Mountains and the River Tiber. The *terroir* defines the characteristics of the wines produced: they have well balanced acidity, are always fresh, young, fragrant, but full bodied with a high alcoholic content.

Nero Fratta. Colli Altotiberini DOC.

Grapes: Sangiovese 100%.
Vinification: the grapes are steeped for 10-14 days on the skins, then fermented in stainless steel tanks on the lees for 6-7 months.
Ageing: in Slovenian oak barrels for 12 months.
The wine: red in colour; fresh, with a good structure.

Paliotto. Colli Altotiberini DOC.

Grapes: Merlot 85%, Sangiovese and Cabernet 15%.
Ageing: partly in stainless steel tanks and partly in Slovenian oak barrels for 24 months.
The wine: ruby red in colour; elegant, with noble tannins and a long ageing potential.

Tarragoni Riserva. Colli Altotiberini DOC.

Grapes: Sangiovese 85%, and Cabernet 15%.
Each year only the best grapes are used, thus the percentage of Sangiovese grapes can increase accordingly.
Vinification: macerated on the skins for 15 days; then malolactic fermentation follows in stainless steel tanks for at least 6 months.
Ageing: in oak barrels for 18 months, then 6 months in the bottle.
The wine: a versatile red wine suitable for meat dishes and game.

Merlot. Rosso Umbria IGT.

Grapes: Merlot 100%.
It is a good wine to drink when young. Deep ruby red in colour, with herbal hints. Dry, fruity, with an intense aftertaste, yet it is less strong in alcoholic content than other full-bodied red wines.

Spina di Rosa. Colli Altotiberini Rosato DOC.

Grapes: Sangiovese 100%.
Vinification: the grapes are steeped for 12 hours, and then the must is drawn off the skins and fermented at 18-20° C.
The wine: ruby red in colour; fresh, with a good structure and aromatic consistency.

Spina di Rosa. Rosso Umbria IGT.

Grapes: Sangiovese, Ciliegiolo, and Malvasia Nero.
Vinification: the must is fermented at low temperatures.

The wine: light ruby in colour, almost pink; fruity taste, with hints of rose scents; clear, sprightly, and naturally sweet.

La Fonte. Cuvèe di Grechetto Umbria IGT.

Grapes: Grechetto.
Harvest: after careful selection, the ripe grapes are picked during a short and late harvest.
Vinification: a low-temperature fermentation in stainless steel tanks and left on the lees for ageing.
Bottling: at the beginning of the autumn
The wine: pale yellow in colour; soft, well structured, and some years it is medium dry.

Elma. Grechetto e Malvasia Umbria IGT.

Grapes: Grechetto, and Malvasia.
Harvest: the sugar rich grapes are picked during a late harvest.
Ageing: in Slovenian oak barrels throughout the winter. After a short spring re-fermentation it becomes drier and more austere.
Bottling: 18-20 months after the harvest, and refined for another six months in the bottle.
The wine: pale yellow in colour; with a subtle variety or aromas.

Grechetto Bianco Umbria IGT.

Grapes: Grechetto 100%.
The grapes produce a wine with good alcoholic content, (never under 12% vol.) with a characteristic bitter aftertaste. It has an unmistakable pale yellow colour.

Brigante.

Grapes: Grechetto, Trebbiano and Chardonnay.
Made from early harvested grapes, a natural sparkling wine is obtained by natural fermentation of *Vermino* wine, without adding carbon dioxide. It has a dry fruity taste; very strong, but sprightly and not very fizzy; best served fresh.

Fra Santo.

Grapes: Trebbiano, Malvasia and Canaiolo.
Vinification: a sweet must is obtained from dried grapes pressed between January and March following the harvest. The must is placed into small casks (kegs) to ferment for three years, when it reaches a particular and sweet taste. This production technique is the ancient traditional method of making Vinsanto.
The wine: a liqueur wine.

Dono di Dio.

The name means God's Gift. It is a sweet wine aged for three years in *caratelli* (small chestnut barrels holding 40 litres), then it is transferred to glass containers (54 litres) for one year. After such a long fermentation and ageing period the wine is bottled without any other form of production. The time of maturation is subject to changes and it is only bottled when it reaches its optimum taste and aromatic complexity.

Polidori

Azienda Bio Vitivinicola Colle del Sole di L. Polidori
06015 – Pierantonio Colle, 41 PG
Tel: 075 9414390 and 975 9414415
Fax: 075 9414390
www.vinipolidori.it
info@vinipolidori.it

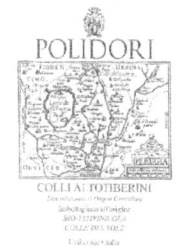

The Polidori family's winery is just south of Umbertide. The vineyards are in an ideal position with regard to altitude and exposure to the sun. The estate grows grapes according to strict ecological regulations; without weed killers and pesticides. Only organic-mineral fertilisers are used, with periodic green manure from Leguminosae. Thus the land retains its natural fertility, and produces healthy plants. L'Agriturismo Casale Polidori is part of the estate, and caters for visitors interested in organic farming. There are large apartments and a swimming pool

Rosso DOC Colli Altotiberini.

Grapes: Sangiovese and Merlot.
The wine: deep ruby red in colour; delicate aromas and a dry and slightly tannic flavour. It is good young, but improves with age.
Serving temperature: 18-20° C.
Food matches: roast meats and mature cheeses.

Rosso Rubino.

Grapes: Sangiovese and Merlot.
The wine: deep and intense ruby red in colour; full bodied and strong, with soft tannins and the fragrance of blackberries. It is produced only from great harvests.
Serving temperature: 20-22° C.
Food matches: roast meats, game dishes, and mature cheeses.

Rosso Fincio.

Grapes: Sangiovese, Merlot, and Ciliegiolo,
The wine: ruby red in colour, with purple reflections; fragrances of ripe red fruits; full and warm, with soft tannins.
Serving temperature: 18-20° C.
Food matches: roast meats, and mature cheeses.

Bianco DOC Colli Altotiberini.

Grapes: Trebbiano Toscano, Malvasia del Chianti, and Verdicchio.
The wine: straw yellow in colour, with green reflections; complex aromas; dry wine, with a pleasantly bitter aftertaste.
Serving temperature: 10-12° C.
Food matches: *hors d'oeuvres* and fish dishes.

Bioverdello.

Grapes: Verdello.
The wine: pale straw yellow in colour, with a delicate and fruity fragrance; dry, but delicately round, full and savoury.
Serving temperature: 10-12° C.
Food matches: *hors d'oeuvres*, meats, and fish dishes.

Casibaldo.

Grapes: Chardonnay and Trebbiano.
The wine: pale straw yellow, and a soft but lively flavour.
Serving temperature: 8-10° C.
Food matches: aperitif, *hors d'oeuvres,* and fish dishes.

Rosato DOC Colli Altotiberini.

Grapes: Sangiovese and Merlot.
Vinification: the grapes fermented off the skins.
The wine: light pink colour and a fruity fragrance.
Serving temperature: 10-12° C.
Food matches: *hors d'oeuvres*, first courses, or fish soup.

Passito.

Grapes: Trebbiano Toscano and Malvasia.
Vinification: the grapes are dried on mats before fermentation.
The wine: golden yellow, almost amber in colour; with a full and penetrating aroma. It is sweet and full-bodied.
Food matches: a dessert wine; fruits, pastry and cheeses.

Grappa.

It is a grappa distilled from the pomace of red grapes. The distillation is carried out in a series of independent steam boilers, which were especially designed in the 19th century for distilling small amounts of spirits. The grappa has a soft, smooth flavour and a deep and intense fragrance.

THE END

AUTHOR'S NOTE

I spent four months visiting most of the wineries of Umbria during 2011, and in this guide I only include the places that I have seen. There were some I missed for one reason or another. Needless to say, I had not sampled the full product range of every winery.

All the technical details are taken from the producers' brochures and handouts; most of which were written in Italian. The English versions required some editing and I performed that task to the best of my ability without altering anything.

As far the quality of the wines goes, I have no preferences; my aim was simply to pass on the information I was provided with.

References - Publications:

The Rough Guide to Italy – Rough Guides
ISBN 978-1-84353-855-4

Wine Grapes and Wines by Jancis Robinson – Mitchell Beazley
1986 ISBN 0-85533-581-5

The Wine Museum Guidebook.
Published by the Fondazione Lungarotti, Torgiano, Italy

Miracolo è Fatto – History and culture of wine in Orvieto.
Published by Associazone Gust'Arte
Email: info@gustarte.com

Il Saporetto. Wine and food almanac of Orvieto and its environs.
Published by Associazone Gust'Arte
Email: info@gustarte.com

Cantine dell'Umbria – The Wineries of Umbria.
Published by Il Palazzo del Gusto. Enoteca Regionale dell'Umbria.

Eccellenze in Tavola – guida all'esplorazione enogastronamia dell'Orvieto
Published by Il Palazzo del Gusto. Enoteca Regionale dell'Umbria.

Strada dei Vini Etrusco Romana in Umbria
Published by Enti e Assocciazioni Adrenti, Piazza Duomo, 24
05018 - Orvieto, (TR) Italia
www.stradedeivinietruscoromana.it

Andar per Vigne – Guide to the Orvieto wine producers.
Published by Consorzio per la Tutela dei Vini DOC
Orvieto e Rosso Orvietano
Email: consvino@tiscali.it

Useful web-sites:

thewinedoctor.com/.../technicaltrainin...
http://www.stradadeivinidelcantico.it/en/chi_siamo.asp
http://www.aboutperugia.com
http://www.mysteriousetruscans.com
http://history-world.org/etruscans.htm
http://www.umbriaitaly.net/umbria-history.asp
http://gram.eng.uci.edu/~alberto/orvieto/en_history.html
http://en.wikipedia.org/wiki/Umbria
http://en.wikipedia.org/wiki/Orvieto
http://en.wikipedia.org/wiki/Italian_wine

Printed in Great Britain
by Amazon